MW00807384

PONIES WEST
A TRUE AMERICAN ADVENTURE
★

JEFF PAPPAS

WITH MURPHY HOOKER

SUNBURY
P R E S S
Mechanicsburg, PA USA

Published by Sunbury Press, Inc.
Mechanicsburg, Pennsylvania

www.sunburypress.com

Copyright © 2020 by Jeff Pappas and Murphy Hooker.
Cover Copyright © 2020 by Sunbury Press, Inc.

Sunbury Press supports copyright. Copyright fuels creativity, encourages diverse voices, promotes free speech, and creates a vibrant culture. Thank you for buying an authorized edition of this book and for complying with copyright laws by not reproducing, scanning, or distributing any part of it in any form without permission. You are supporting writers and allowing Sunbury Press to continue to publish books for every reader. For information contact Sunbury Press, Inc., Subsidiary Rights Dept., PO Box 548, Boiling Springs, PA 17007 USA or legal@sunburypress.com.

For information about special discounts for bulk purchases, please contact Sunbury Press Orders Dept. at (855) 338-8359 or orders@sunburypress.com.

To request one of our authors for speaking engagements or book signings, please contact Sunbury Press Publicity Dept. at publicity@sunburypress.com.

FIRST SUNBURY PRESS EDITION: March 2020

Set in Adobe Garamond. Interior design by Crystal Devine | Cover by Lawrence Knorr.
Edited by Lawrence Knorr.

Publisher's Cataloging-in-Publication Data
Names: Pappas, Jeff, author | Hooker, Murphy, author.
Title: Ponies west : a true american adventure / Jeff Pappas with Murphy Hooker.
Description: First trade paperback edition. | Mechanicsburg, PA : Sunbury Press, 2020.
Summary: In 1986 jeff pappas and his buddy chet rode their horses across the usa, from connecticut to washington, to raise money for charity, achieving national attention.
Identifiers: ISBN 978-1-620067-13-0 (softcover).
Subjects: BISAC: SPORTS & RECREATION / Equestrian. | TRAVEL / Special Interest / Adventure. | PETS / Horses. | BIOGRAPHY & AUTOBIOGRAPHY / Adventurers & Explorers. | BIOGRAPHY & AUTOBIOGRAPHY / Personal Memoirs.

Product of the United States of America
0 1 1 2 3 5 8 13 21 34 55

Continue the Enlightenment!

CONTENTS

INTRODUCTION

★ ★ ★

SOMETIMES WHEN YOU'RE looking for more out of life, you just have to "get on your horse and ride." For people nowadays, that may mean taking a long drive down the coast in a convertible, but back in 1986, for my best friend Chet and me, it meant saddling up our horses on the East Coast and riding west until we hit the Pacific. *Ponies West* is the amazing true story of what happened to two modern-day cowboys on our four-and-a-half-month adventure across the United States on behalf of charity. The following pages will take you inside our incredible journey, called Cross America '86 (CA86), while reliving the many perilous situations we overcame as well as the heart-warming and strange encounters we experienced on our way across this beautiful land.

All these years later, people still ask me the age-old question, "why did we do it?" During CA86 when people inquired, we often just smiled, gave a quick squeeze to the flanks of our faithful companions, and moved on with a tip of our hats to the friendly stranger in search of answers that we kept locked inside. When we had to put it into words, Chet and I said we "wanted to give something back and get to the heart of America by realizing a dream that few had ever dared." But the burning truth was, all my life, I wanted to do something that would make a difference in other people's lives and a difference in my own. In the end, we achieved all our goals. The $100,000 CA86 raised was vital to Connecticut's Governor's State Shelter Program that sponsored us. I have to thank all of the good people who were inspired by our actions and got involved in some way. Everyone connected with this project can truly say, "I made a difference."

As for how the whole crazy idea got started, Chet and I had talked about our CA86 dream for a couple of years until one fateful night when, after a few beers, we challenged each other to finally do it. Sometimes that's how life-changing decisions are made. Thank God for cocktail napkins and cold drafts! When we decided to just do it, we trained hard for nearly two years. We ran every day, practiced in the martial arts, and worked our ponies (Thunder, Rebel, Sonny, and Big Red) hard, particularly in the last three months. We prepared for all elements: rain, snow, ice storms, extreme heat, and wind. We would encounter them all.

Next, we recruited our team, enlisting two locals, one to drive my rig and pull my trailer, and the other to ride shotgun. Chet and I planned to ride two horses (Thunder and Rebel) for fourteen to fifteen miles each day then switch to our other two four-legged brothers (Sonny and Big Red) to finish the day's work. We estimated we had to make 25 to 30 miles per day until we hit the Rockies, or we'd miss the summer weather window. And the thought of being holed up for the winter somewhere in the Rockies was unthinkable. So we studied maps and planned a route that followed America's back roads (called "grey roads" in map terminology). If and when we ran out of roads, we would pave our own.

On May 5th, 1986, we set off from Long Island Sound in Connecticut, determined to travel west across the United States to the Pacific shores. We were thrilled to be following in the same footsteps as the great explorers and cowboys on America's grey roads. Thunder was our fearless four-legged leader that would carry us to hell and back. A two-year-old "green-broke" thoroughbred-draft mix; he was packed with dynamite and a heart of gold. Although most equine experts say you can't take a two-year-old on a cross-country trip, we were out to show them Thunder had what it took to make it to the Pacific. His posse of Rebel, Big Red, and Sonny were willing to follow him over the cliff if need be. We were a tight team.

As our journey progressed, we learned that some of the best parts of life happen when you meet new people. All the good folks we encountered along the way gave us the strength to dig deep within ourselves to overcome all the physical and mental challenges we faced. And we needed all the inspiration we could get. Traversing the country on the back of a horse sure wasn't easy. There were many times on the trail when Chet waxed philosophic about the true meaning and purpose of our trip, usually in good weather conditions, mind you. There were other times when I had to remind him (at the top of my lungs) why we were risking our lives as softball-sized hail pelted us, high winds whipped us, and lightning struck so close to us it blew chunks of earthy dust our way. But now that I've had nearly thirty years to reflect on the events of CA86, I've come to truly understand the "why?" of it all. We did it to discover what too many folks forget these days: There are good people everywhere from all walks of life. Despite life's hardships, we found people are optimistic about their future and the future of America. Can you believe, those with the least offered the most?

Every day on the trail, we were amazed by the generosity of the human spirit. We met countless people who were willing to give the shirt off their backs to help a couple of strangers like us. But I'm getting ahead of myself.

I can still remember how I felt that first day riding off into the unknown. I was full of anticipation and fear, but there was no looking back. I knew this would be a life-changer for me, and that was an understatement. On our fantastic journey west, we would sleep under the stars every night, in fields and shacks, by railroad tracks, and if we were lucky, in a hayloft of a kind farmer's barn. We would camp with the Amish in Pennsylvania, travel through real ghost towns in the Midwest, and party with Hell's Angels in Montana. We would be attacked by Dobermans, chased by buffalo and protected by police escorts. We straddled the Continental Divide, avoiding grizzlies, and rode like the wind through the forests of Yellowstone National Park, doing our best *Butch Cassidy and the Sundance Kid* impersonation as we played hide-and-seek from a posse of Park Rangers (and police helicopters) who were trying to arrest us.

Yes, Chet and I almost got thrown in the pokey a few times. But if you ask me, some of the best parts of our ride were all the historical connections we could feel to the old American West. We were lucky enough to ride in the old pioneer wagon ruts of the famed Oregon Trail, and carve our names in the same rocks next to pioneer families who had scrawled messages of hope and despair back in the 1860s. We even got to meet one of the toughest cowboys of our time, Mark White, while crossing Togwotee Pass just outside Jackson Hole, where we camped together and exchanged stories. Mark and his family remain friends to this day. Then on the final glorious stretch, we followed the Lewis and Clark trail all the way to the promised land of the Pacific, where we capped the trip with a gallop into the ocean waves. Truly exhilarating! As I've said to many people who have asked about it in the years since, "Wouldn't you want to take an adventure of a lifetime?"

Looking back, I realize I had prepared my entire life for our trip. Ever since I could remember, I had a great love for horses and adventure. When I was a boy, my parents often took me riding, and my heroes were larger-than-life pioneers, explorers, and cowboys who blazed the trail we now call the West. Maybe I was born a century too late. All these years later, my soul still relates to the spirit of the great "American Cowboy" who held a strong belief in rugged individualism and personal freedom that came to define what it is to be American. This book is dedicated to the spirit of the old cowboy and the American West. We hope our journey of perseverance and grit, hope and dreams, daring and danger, and laughter and friendship will help keep alive the icon of the American Cowboy and all it represents.

—Jeff Pappas

A CALLING IN CONNECTICUT

"We are people born to the frontier.
It has been a part of our thinking,
walking and sleeping since man first landed
on this continent. The frontier is the line that
separates the known from the unknown,
wherever it may be, and we have a
driving need to see what lies beyond."
—*Louis L'Amour*

I CAN'T RECALL exactly when my dream of riding my trusty steed across the United States first dawned on this cowboy, but it must've been during one of my ritual rides into the vast wilderness that bordered my property back in 1984. I've found my best ideas come when I'm riding alone in the great outdoors. Whenever I get stuck on something, I get on my horse and ride. I call it going to my "idea spring." It's my sanctuary for free-thinking and creative problem-solving. Maybe it's the solitude or the absence of white noise, but it gives me a great sense of peace and calm. I feel a certain oneness with the earth.

In the mid-1980s, I was living in the country outside of Hartford, Connecticut, on four acres next to a vast protected area that was made up of several pieces of land, the largest being Enders State Park and the McLean Game Refuge. My ritual was to come home from work and head straight to my barn where I'd saddle up one of my horses (Thunder, Rebel, or Big Red) and ride out the back gate into the thicket.

I made a habit of riding alone every chance I got. I love the freedom a horse lends you when he takes you on a gallop away from the troubles of the workaday world. It's the closest a man can get to flying without leaving the ground.

Once I'm lost in the forest, away from the sights and sounds of the modern world, I become transported back to a place where time doesn't exist. On my horse, I feel a profound connection with everyone who rode before me.

On more than one occasion, my tired eyes nearly convinced me I'd caught a glimpse of one of the pioneer spirits who rode before me across this beautiful land. I knew it was the exhaustion of the day playing tricks on me, but I do believe there are spirits out there in the trees. Native Americans call it the "Great Spirit" or the "Great Mystery." The Choctaws call it, "the one who dwells in the woods." Now, I'm not a god-fearing man, but I do know one thing: Just because you can't see it with your eyes, doesn't mean it isn't there.

Once the sun set on one of my rides, I'd let go of my spiritual connection with nature and head home to my loving wife, Sue. I would get back to the business of life with my "idea spring" perking again, and my soul recharged.

A few years before the trip, I moved to Hartford to start a franchise company with my brother Brian. We started it from scratch with just $15,000, and it took all my energy to make it a multi-million-dollar success. I was, for all intents and purposes, the chief visionary officer. I was giving it my all, working ungodly hours and traveling three to five days per week. After putting in several years to get the business off the ground, I started to feel this aching in my soul. My friends told me it was the first sign of burnout. I couldn't believe it. I was just 32. I wasn't an unhappy man by any means; I loved my wife Sue dearly. I kept telling myself I was just a restless spirit searching for something more. But I knew with all the hours I was working, I'd eventually need to take some time off to reflect on my life, my business, and my purpose. But there was always work to do. So I kept doing it. But as more days passed, even though I was a "successful" businessman with a happy marriage, I began to have this thought that I suspect many Americans have: Is there anything left to dream that doesn't involve currency?

Maybe that notion is what got me thinking about doing something outside of the norm; something no one has ever done. I began to ask myself, was there something I could do in life that only I could accomplish?

Something with meaning that also touched my soul?

That question stuck in my craw for weeks. Day after day, I'd go to work, then come home and ride through the woods trying to crack that nut. Until one day, my "idea spring" produced a gusher. I remember I was thinking about Joseph Campbell's key to happiness, which (he says) are three simple words: "Follow your bliss," when I came up with one phrase that spelled happiness to me. "Get on your horse and ride."

My key to happiness had been staring me in the face the whole time.

It was the motto by which my heroes, the old cowboys of the West, lived. When they needed a change of scenery, they changed it. When they didn't "find their bliss" in the east, they got on their horse and rode west until they found a place that fit their soul. It was a simple concept that led to a fundamental realization: I wanted more simplicity in my life. I looked around the modern world and yearned to live in a simpler time.

On those solitary rides into the wild, I was slowly discovering what I needed to be a "fulfilled person"—I didn't just want a simpler life; I wanted more adventure and discovery in my day-to-day. I also wanted to be closer to nature full-time, not just as a weekend warrior out for an early evening ride. Could a man accomplish all these things without setting fire to his entire life?

I had to live the question.

One day in 1984, I heard about a guy named Joe Kittinger who had become the first person to cross the Atlantic in a hot air balloon. "Now that's a man with a vision," I said to my best friend Chet while we were playing softball on a team my company sponsored.

"Wonder how far a man could get on his horse?"

"Not far, unless the Atlantic froze over!" Chet shot back as he warmed up in the on-deck circle. I looked up into the sky and watched a small plane fly by; I remember wondering where it was headed.

"You couldn't cross an ocean. But could you make it to one?"

"What are you talking about, boss?"

"Could an expert horseman start on the East Coast and make it to the Mississippi? Could he make it past the snowstorms of the Rockies without freezing to death?"

"Not in winter, he couldn't."

"But if he timed it right, could he make it all the way to the Pacific?"

Chet looked at me with a quizzical smirk, "How many drafts you had? And why aren't you sharing?"

"None yet. Think you'd have the cojones?

"To do what; ride across country?"

"Wanna do it with me?"

"On ponies? Shit man, you'd need more than one horse, and a pair the size of Jeremiah Johnson—or Davy Crockett!"

"How hard can it be? Those fellas did it with no safety net. Hell, all the pioneer families did. That's why they're called pioneers!"

"C'mon boss, get your mind in the game, let's play ball!" Chet yelled as he went up to bat. Two pitches later, Chet belted a home run.

That night, I started to wonder if there was a record of anyone riding across the country in modern times. I couldn't "Google it" since the Internet didn't exist yet, so I tracked down a copy of the *Guinness Book of World Records*. It turns out old Guinness didn't have a record of anyone riding a horse across America. But he did have a record of people doing it on foot, motorcycles, and bicycles. I went to bed, wondering why anyone hadn't tried it before. Then my thoughts turned to the brave pioneer families who risked their lives to venture west into the unknown to find a better life. I drifted off to sleep asking myself,

"If they could do it without any modern amenities, why couldn't I?"

The next morning, I stopped dreaming and went back to the grind. But the whole crazy idea, which began as a fleeting thought, became a slowly building pipedream that gained steam and kept coming back for more. I wanted to keep spit-balling my idea with someone who wouldn't look at me like I'm crazy; I had the perfect accomplice in my crazy best friend Chet, a fellow horseman.

I met Chet in 1982. I got to know him through my company sponsored softball team that was full of misfits. We finished last three years in a row, so I invited Chet to play with us, and boy was I glad I did. We still finished last, but Chet was a great athlete and became our star clean-up hitter. I never saw anyone hit a ball as far as Chet. We bonded through softball and became fast friends. When I discovered Chet loved horses, I liked him even more. I asked him if he wanted to help me work some of my horses in his spare time. He accepted my offer, and we became best friends. Soon, my solitary rides turned into rides with

Chet. We explored the many miles of hidden spaces in the preserve behind my property, camping as often as possible on weekends with the ponies.

We often talked about taking a long trip on horseback over the campfire. Every time I mentioned my "crazy" idea of going cross-country, Chet would just laugh and say,

"You must've worked for the Pony Express in a past life, boss."

During our long talks, we both revealed being confined to office jobs left us both unfulfilled. We were fellow outdoorsman who had a restlessness about us that we couldn't quell with a larger paycheck or a bigger house.

Would we ever do anything about it?

After talking about it for months, one Friday after work, I finally got a wild hair and threw down the gauntlet. Maybe it was the full moon or the cold drafts, or maybe it was just time to make a change in my life. Chet and I had ridden Thunder and Rebel up to one of our hangouts called "The Coach and Four." I don't know if it's around anymore, but back in 1984, we could get there by riding through the woods behind my house. On that fateful night, we decided to stop in for a few since we didn't have to work the next day. Lucky for us, the Inn had iron hitching posts in the back. They were purely decorative, but we used them to tie up the Boys. We were probably the only ones who ever did.

We entered the old Inn in our cowboy boots and hats. The place was dimly lit and covered in dark wood. We walked toward the big fireplace that was burning a few fresh logs by the bar. I noticed only a few diners were in the dining room. We grabbed a few stools at the empty bar and ordered two drafts.

"This looks like a good spot to have a clandestine meeting."

"What do you have cookin' boss?" Chet asked. I didn't answer him immediately, but I knew with just the bartender around, we would be free to discuss "the topic" passionately. After knocking back a few cold ones, Chet broke the news that he'd just been laid off from his job as a sales rep for Sysco Foods. He said he was now a "free agent" with a girlfriend (Diane) he wasn't sure he loved. He confided he didn't know where his life was headed.

"Sounds like we both need a change of scenery," I said, sipping my beer.

We proceeded to have one of those long talks that only best friends have. It was clear to any eavesdropper we were both struggling with our purpose in life. After listening to Chet bare his soul, I suggested we "take bold action."

"What kind of bold action?" Chet said, devouring a handful of bar peanuts.

"You remember that idea I had?"

"Oh, no."

"I propose we finally do it. No more talking. Throw down, man!"

"You're crazy."

"Do you ever ask yourself, what are we waiting for?"

"Are you getting all philosophical on me?"

"Maybe. As Pancho said to the Cisco Kid, 'soon we'll be hanging from the end of a rope, with no music.' We need to shake things up; am I right?"

"Well yeah. But is this the right way to do it?"

"We don't have any kids, and we still got our health."

"True."

"But if we're gonna do it, I say we do it right. I say we go all the way!"

"Pony Express?"

"Coast-to-coast."

Chet busted out laughing, "Well, I'll be damned, you got some cojones; I'll give you that!"

"That's not a 'yes' partner."

He thought for a while, "That's bitin' off a lot of land boss. How long you planning on being gone?"

"A few months. four, maybe."

"I need to get a j.o.b. now!"

"Go ahead. We need time to prepare."

"As you know, my coffer isn't exactly full."

"I know, don't worry, buddy. I got you covered."

"Just answer me one question, why in the hell are we doing this?"

"It's hard to put into words. Haven't you ever wanted to commit to something larger than yourself?"

"I guess so. Yeah."

"Haven't you ever wanted to make a difference? I just wanna prove I can do something that's never been done. That we can do something great together—Know what I mean?"

"I do. Can't leave your mark pushing papers around a desk."

"It would be one helluva test of our horseman skills."

"And our stamina. We'll have to train our asses off, the ponies too."

"And one helluva spiritual journey."

"If we don't die on some godforsaken mountain. Think the boys would make it?"

"We gotta be smart. And plan it right, so we aren't risking anyone's life."

"Ok, then. I guess you sold me."

"That's what I like to hear!"

"But. You realize, sellin' me ain't the hard part."

"Oh. Right.kinda forgot about her for a second there."

We agreed to take the trip that night if Sue would okay it. We shook hands, and I wrote our agreement on a bar napkin, which we both signed. I wish I still had that bar napkin. I'd have framed that sucker.

I remember our ride home; it was getting late and cold out. I was worried Thunder might have one of his freak-outs in the woods. He tended to get spooked at night, but he didn't, and we made it home, hooting and hollering the whole way. I felt alive again. Several days later, when we were sober, I reminded Chet of our pact by presenting him with Exhibit A. "You remember this thing?" I asked while slipping the napkin in front of his morning cup of coffee.

"What is that? Our bar tab?"

"This here is a signed contract."

Chet laughed, "That night got a little blurry. What damn fool thing did you talk me into again?" It took a few more passionate discussions at the bar for us to solidify our plans. But once it was settled, Chet and I started to meet regularly to divide up responsibilities and plan the logistics.

I never exactly asked for Sue's permission; it kind of happened organically. Once Chet and I started talking turkey, Sue overheard some Chet and my conversations about the trip. At first, she thought we were just blowing smoke. She'd pop into the kitchen or living room or wherever we were gabbing and give me several looks like she didn't think we were going through with the plan. But she wasn't ready to make an official comment just yet.

Then, after a month or so of planning, Sue finally had enough. She sat me down one evening after Chet went home to talk about the trip. When I sat down at the kitchen table, she just looked at me and said, "You're really going to do this, aren't you?"

"Yes, honey. I believe I am. This may sound nuts, but I think this is my destiny."

"It wouldn't matter if I said 'no,' would it?"

"Well, yes, it would. You're the most important thing in the world to me."

Sue didn't say a word for a long time. She just stared into my eyes, then she sighed. "I see how much you want this. I'm not going to stand in the way of your dream."

"So."

"So. So what? Go ahead on with it."

"Are you the best wife in the history of the world, or what?"

"I don't know. But you can treat me as such if you know what's good for you. Let's just say you owe me one."

"I owe you big time."

"Just don't get yourself killed out there."

"Trust me," I smiled and sidled up to her. I gave her a big hug and a kiss and eventually got her to crack a smile too. We had a long embrace there in the kitchen that I'll never forget. It felt great to know she had my back. Sue was still unsure if I was just talking—but in time, she came to realize this was no pipe dream and fully embraced how deeply I believed in the purpose of the trip. To say I couldn't have done it without her would be an understatement.

Chet and I spent the next two years planning every aspect of our trip. It was almost as taxing as the trip itself. You have to remember that the world was a different place back in the 1980s. We didn't have the luxury of technology like we do today. There was no MapQuest or Google Earth. No one had computers or Smartphones. We plotted our course the old-fashioned way, by studying the World Atlas (state-by-state) and all the topographical maps (called "Topo Maps") we could get our hands on. We wanted to find a way to avoid the big cities by plotting a route that would take us through small towns via the "back roads" (called "grey roads" on a map). Nothing against big cities, but we wanted to experience what the real "rural" America was like, and we thought this was our best chance at getting a glimpse into their walk of life.

We methodically mapped a route that would take us through ten states: Connecticut, New York, Pennsylvania, Indiana, Illinois, Iowa, Nebraska, Wyoming, Montana, and Washington (State) on the "roads-less-traveled."

In order not to wear out our "Boys," we decided to ride four horses in two shifts: Thunder and Rebel in the morning for fourteen to fifteen miles, then we'd switch to our other four-legged brothers (Sonny and Big Red) to finish the day's work. We figured it would take us four to five months to accomplish if we stayed on schedule.

After we were satisfied we had plotted a reasonable course, we turned our attention to how we could avoid any bad weather that could endanger the trip or our lives. We went to the Hartford Public Library on Main Street and checked out all the almanacs we could find: *The Old Farmer's Almanac*, the *Encyclopedia Britannica Almanac*, and *The New York Times Almanac*—to name a few. Then we laid them out on my kitchen table and just stared at them. "This is a little intimidating boss," Chet said.

"Psshaw, we got it easy. The old pioneers had nothing but the sun to guide them," I said as I dug into the books like I was cramming for finals. We started doing our homework and had to confront the "big unknown" looming over the entire trip. It was the one question we had no way of truly answering even if we did have computers.

"Think Winter's gonna come early this year?" Chet asked, pouring us both some more coffee.

"That's the sixty-four-thousand-dollar question, isn't it," I said. "If snow comes early to the Rockies, we could be ambushed by Mother Nature, with no way out."

"How early is early, do you think?" Chet asked.

"August, maybe. We'll be threading the needle if we start any later than Spring."

"I don't wanna deal with any Donner Party type situation. Besides, you're too skinny to eat," Chet said. We knew it would be a disaster if we got stuck where bad weather could bear down on us. It wasn't just snow we were worried about; we were also headed straight into tornado country. Any false step could prove fatal to the ponies (and us), so we took our time and were methodical about our research.

After much deliberation, we decided an early May departure would give us the best chance of avoiding any major snowfall. We estimated we had to log 25 to thirty miles per day until we hit the Rockies, or we'd miss the summer weather window. There was no way to predict when a tornado would hit, so we had to trust our gut and put any fear of the unknown out of our minds. We returned the Almanacs to the library. I looked at Chet and said, "You're Catholic, right?"

"According to my mother."

"Pray nature will cooperate."

"I got us, covered boss," he said as he pulled out his keychain. I saw it had a St. Christopher dangling from it.

The dream was starting to take shape.

Chet and I even came up with a name for the trip—Cross America '86 (CA86 for short.) We marked May 1986 on the calendar hanging in my barn and started counting down the days. Now that we had a departure date, I decided it was time to let my business partner (and brother) Brian know about my plans. I broke it to him one day at lunch. When I finished my pitch, he just sat there dumbfounded and said, "You want to do what now? And when?"

"Ride across the country. On a horse. Next year. I need to take a sabbatical."

"You're shittin' me. What on earth would compel you to do such a thing?"

When I tried to explain it to him; Brian said he thought I was "crazier than hell" and "didn't understand why any sane human would throw his life away for this."

"You've been hearing me say I need a vacation for over a year now. This is the perfect way for me not to waste my time laying on some beach somewhere and do something productive."

"Productive? What are you gonna produce out there other than horse paddies?"

"Experience. Wisdom. And we're gonna raise money for charity."

"Good for you."

"Look. I'm giving us plenty of time to plan for my leave of absence. I don't expect you to understand my motives, but I hope you will support me, brother to brother."

"What if I don't?"

"Are you declining my vacation request?"

"No, not at all. I can appreciate you havin' a dream. All I'm saying is you're gonna be putting us in a helluva bind here."

"I know it sounds crazy, but I really need a break."

"We both need a break, Jeff."

"I know. Take one; I'll cover you. I'm not leaving for another year."

"Thanks for the approval."

"That's all I want from you. I'm giving you plenty of fair warning."

"It's a warning, but I'm not sure how fair it is."

Brian stared silently out the window.

I got up to leave, "I hope you'll get it one day."

"Well, I don't. Not now. Not ever."

Brian didn't get it for a long time. He loved horses from a distance, but he's not an outdoors person, just the opposite of me in that regard. It took many conversations to get him to accept I would be gone for nearly five months. After the shock wore off, I explained to Brian that I had a plan to cover my absence. I was not going to abandon the business and leave him in the lurch. Fortunately for both of us, Sue volunteered to take up much of the business slack while I was gone. You see Sue is not only my amazing wife; back then, she was also one of my top managers at work.

Brian eventually agreed to let me take a sabbatical, but it took him a few years to be ok with it. In time, he was proud of my accomplishment. I remember many years later, he even bragged about my trip to a few business associates, which made me feel good.

Once I got Sue's blessing and Brian's begrudging approval, I started to brainstorm how I could turn the trip into a fundraising event. I blurted out the charity angle to Brian without really thinking it through, but once I did, it felt like the right thing to do. Sue and I had a history of helping others. Before we moved to Connecticut, I went to Denison University in Ohio. After graduation, I drove west and landed in West Yellowstone, Montana, where I got my first guide job at Lionshead Outfitters running horseback trips into the Gallatin National Forrest. After one season, I decided to head back to Ohio before winter came and look for more permanent work.

I got a job at a shelter for mentally challenged adults where I worked my way up to the director's position. That was where I met Sue. I hired her to work with me at the shelter. Together we received a grant to develop a program where we placed mentally challenged adults into jobs in the community. The project was a success. We developed such a close friendship working together that, almost two years later, I asked her to marry me. Thankfully, she said yes.

Fast-forward to Connecticut and the opportunity to turn CA86 into a charity event began when I tried to recruit a woman named Kathy Wyler to work for my company. I met her when she was part of a popular morning drive radio team at WDRC in Hartford. Kathy politely declined my initial offer, but we became friends. She had a very impressive resume and was talented in Public Relations and Marketing, so I didn't give up trying to recruit her.

When CA86 was coming together, Kathy and I met again for lunch. I updated her on our progress, and she told me she was finally thinking about leaving her job. "I love what I do, but getting up at 3 A.M. every day wears you out. Sometimes I think I'd like to try something new."

"I know exactly how you feel, Kathy, that's why I'm taking the trip. You know, if you really want to try something new, maybe you'd reconsider coming to work for me. Not just for the business, but as PR director for Cross America '86."

"That would be a change. Let me think about it, ok?" is all she said at first. Kathy was a strong supporter of the trip, but it took some convincing to get her to come aboard. When she finally agreed, I helped negotiate Kathy's severance package with WDRC, and she came to work for me as our PR director for CA86, among other things. Kathy worked closely with Sue.

One day, Kathy, Sue, Chet, and I were discussing fundraising opportunities. Kathy had an idea, "What if I got WDRC to support the trip?" She thought her friend Brad Davis, who was the other half of WDRC's popular morning drive team, could help us garner support at the station. "Having Brad on board would be a big PR coup," she said. We all knew Brad; he was very well known in Hartford and was always in the news. Kathy got on the phone and spoke to Brad about our trip. Something about our idea must have clicked with him because Brad jumped at the chance to meet with us.

Chet and I hit it off with Brad immediately. After we explained our trip to him, I saw a light bulb go on in his head. He snapped his fingers and said, "Let's get this thing going!" Brad offered to promote CA86 on his morning radio show.

"You guys can call in from the road. We'll be with you every step of the way!"

"OK, but we may have trouble finding a payphone," I said.

"Giddyup!" Brad yelped; his enthusiasm was infectious.

"Well, that went well," I said to Chet as we left our first meeting with him. "Brad was really into it; I think he can help us."

"Pretty sure Brad thinks he's a cowboy too," Chet said.

I laughed, "Just like you and me, partner."

Our CA86 team was growing larger by the day. With Kathy and Brad on-board, we were still looking for a charity to partner with in which we believed. During one of our brainstorming sessions, Brad mentioned he was supporting a new program to help feed underprivileged families that was started by the Governor of Connecticut, Bill O'Neill, and his wife, Nikki. The program was (and still is) called the "Connecticut Governor's Care and Share Program." I saw how passionate Brad was about the cause, so I said, "That sounds great. I'd like to learn more about the program."

"I'll try to set up a meeting with the Governor," he said. And so, he did.

The next thing we knew, Brad was driving us to the Governor's Mansion to meet with Governor Bill and Nikki. We were a little overwhelmed walking into the Governor's Mansion, but Bill and Nikki made us feel right at home. We all sat down and talked turkey and Bill laid out his program for us, "As you know, times are tough for a lot of people, Jeff. The high cost of gas, coupled with inflation and the rising price of essential foods like bread, meat, and eggs, have put a lot of pressure on people all over Connecticut," Governor Bill said.

Nikki jumped in, "Families that were already struggling are simply overwhelmed, and our most vulnerable residents need help more than ever."

Chet and I were moved by what Bill and Nikki were trying to do with the "Care and Share Program." When Bill and Nikki offered to partner with us, it was an easy decision to say 'yes.'

Over the next year, Chet and I became frequent visitors to the Governor's Mansion. It's rumored there may have been a few cold Coors seen on their kitchen table from time to time during our meetings. We spent a lot of time riding in Brad's Jeep up to the Governor's Mansion. Brad was integral to getting us in front of the Governor; we wanted to find a way to include him in our trip so we made a promise to Brad that we'd call in to his radio show whenever we could find a payphone to update him on how we were doing and what state we're in, figuratively and literally.

May 1986 was fast approaching. We had to make every day count. Chet and I were hard at work, getting every member of our team into the best shape possible. There was a reason no one in modern times had ever attempted to traverse the country on horse—it's not easy. We knew this trip was going to be a test on all levels, mentally, spiritually, and physically. We had to get our bodies right. I had begun my training in 1984, exercising three to four times a week for nearly two years. I worked out in the morning with Grand Master Charles Ferraro at his Tang Soo Do Mi Guk Kwan dojo. Then I met in the afternoons to work out with Chet. We began with a three to four-mile run in the woods, then we put on our boots and trained two to three hours on the ponies. We worked our Boys hard, particularly in the final three months. We had to prepare them for all the elements: rain, snow, ice, extreme heat, and high wind. Chet and I worked them on every type of terrain.

The pace of our equine work out was a mixture of trotting at different paces, jumping downed trees, and learning how to wade through water, from small puddles to small ponds as well as slogging through deep mud that often surrounds water sources. The trust we developed with the horses during our training would pay huge dividends on the trip. I knew there would be moments when a quick response could be the difference between injury and safety, maybe even life and death.

Our four-legged brothers took to the training like Olympic athletes. Rebel was the smartest of the group. He was a classy "sorrel" quarter horse from a strong quarter horse bloodline. He had four white stockings and a white blaze on his face. Rebel was extremely fast and had a very soft mouth, which meant he would stop or turn on a dime with only a slight pull of the bridle. Rebel and Chet were best friends. He followed Chet around all the time. They were both great athletes with an easygoing nature about them.

Big Red, on the other hand, was a big ol' stubborn hard-head. He was chestnut color with a white blaze on his face. He had a massive chest and stocky legs. Big Red didn't have a lot of personality, but I bought him because of his great strength and durability. Outside of Thunder, Big Red was the strongest of the bunch, but (being stubborn) he was prone to doing things his way. Sonny (aka Wizard or Whizzer) was a short Palomino mixed breed with a long white mane. He was small and quick but didn't bond with Chet and me as much as we'd hoped. He also tended to fight with the other three horses and liked to be left alone. Sonny was our lone wolf.

Thunder—Oh boy, was he special. He was our alpha male and leader of the pack. He was the first horse I ever purchased. A two-year-old Belgian-cross with a Palomino's color, he had a long blond tail and mane. He wasn't just a pretty boy though; he was a big and powerful horse who was over "17 hands" tall, with the thickness of a draft horse and the agility of a thoroughbred. He had a huge heart to match. There was no question he would be the lead horse on the trip, so I trained with him most of the time. I was counting on him to carry most of the load for us. I'd bought Thunder from a friend of mine who was a local horse trader. He came from a farm in Pennsylvania where he'd been abused. He was barely "rough broke" much less "green broke," so I had to finish the task. Poor fella was damn near afraid of everything when I got him. You could tell why. He had a big scar around his neck from being forced to obey simple commands and tasks. You sure can't outmuscle a horse as large as Thunder, so you better learn to connect with his mind, so I did; I knew with patience and a kind hand, you can gain a horse's trust.

I began spending a few hours with him every day for the first two months until he trusted me enough not to throw his ears back at me. Still, it took a month before I could get in the stall with him. He tried to kick me every time. But once Thunder saw I wasn't going to hurt him, he finally let me in. But he still wouldn't let anyone else into his stall, not the vet or even the blacksmith.

Thunder and I were becoming more simpatico with every passing day. I gradually introduced him to the "scary" horse blanket; then, he became best friends with my saddle. Then after some anxiety, he took the bit and bridle. I still hadn't tried to climb on his back, but I knew that "rodeo moment" was coming. I'll never forget the first time I attempted to mount him. First, I ran a steel cable from the D-ring on his cinch strap to the bottom of his bridle. This way, he couldn't rear his head up and flip over with me on his back. Thank god for that cable. For the next month, every time I climbed on him, he would buck up and try to rear me off him. He eventually stopped when he realized he couldn't get rid of me. Even with all the time we had spent together, he was still trying to figure out what role I was to play in his life.

In time, I taught him everything he needed to know: how to cross water, how to be around other animals in the wild, how to turn on a dime and most importantly, how to stay "ground tied," which meant I could get off him, drop the reins and he wouldn't run off. I also taught him to come to me when I called him. He was a smart horse.

All these "tricks" were important for him to learn. His knowledge would be vital to the success of our trip. I even taught Thunder how to drink out of a hose! It was quite a sight to see this massive 1400-pound horse with a hose hanging out of his mouth; the sound of him gently sucking water from a hose was amusing to many folks.

Preserving our horses' hooves would be one of the biggest challenges we would face on our ride. We were fortunate to have our local blacksmith, Joe Mantei, pre-form thirty shoes for all four horses. He coated each shoe with titanium that he melted and applied for maximum strength, toughness, and endurance. Titanium is one of the hardest materials on earth, having titanium-coated shoes helped to toughen up our horses' feet and protect their hooves for long periods.

Chet was a huge help training the horses. He had a natural way with animals. He had an unspoken kinship that created a quick bond with Thunder, Rebel, Wizzer, and Big Red. His strength and toughness were out of this world. He could toss a bale of hay up on the trailer like it was a feather, and when he was helping me break Thunder, he was able to calmly keep him from "blowing up" countless times. We planned to shoe all the horses ourselves on the trip, and if you haven't ever put a shoe on a horse, particularly a large horse, it can be backbreaking work. Often the horse being shod will "cheat' and rest much of his weight on you. Chet was better at putting shoes on the boys than I was. He used his strength to keep the horse centered, which cut down the leaning process significantly. I also entrusted Chet with a tall task that didn't involve horses. Some might say it was an impossible task, but it would be essential to keeping us alive on the road.

Once you got to know Chet, I didn't take long until you noticed he had a passion for cooking that bordered on obsessive. The guy could look at a half-empty refrigerator and find a way to cook a five-star meal from seemingly nothing. He could also make the best comfort food dishes I ever tasted. Seeing how passionate he was about cooking, one day, while we were eating a meal he had whipped up out of nowhere, I had an idea, "Hey, let's talk about food."

"My favorite subject!" he said.

"You want to be in charge of the food during the trip? You got the skills for it."

"Now you're talking boss," Chet's eyes lit up at the thought of all the meals he could cook over an open fire. "We could have steak and eggs and bacon and—"

There was one slight hitch to the deal. Since neither of us had much money to our names at the time, and I was financing the trip, I came up with a whopping food budget of forty dollars a week. Chet was flabbergasted, "Forty-dollars per week? For how many two-legged critters?"

"Four. If you count the two hands, we need to drive the truck."

"Are you trying to starve us to death?"

"That's all I can afford after taking my leave of absence from work," I said. "You can do it, man. I love your cooking no matter what's in the pan."

Chet kept repeating, "Forty bucks. Forty bucks." as we ate the rest of our meal in silence. Every few bites, he'd look up at me and shake his head.

Later in the barn, during our work, he'd occasionally shout, "Forty bucks? Forty bucks?" and look at me with a raised eyebrow. Since I didn't have a good answer why, I just shrugged my shoulders and slowly walked away. I could feel his cold stare on my back. Best Friends, I say.

In time, Chet heartily accepted my challenge to feed the entire CA86 team on a micro-budget. He even met with a local nutritionist in Hartford before he planned our meals. The nutritionist told him we needed to pack in at least 2,500 to 3000 calories per day to keep us from losing forty to fifty pounds each. Chet took the nutritionist's advice and used his creative culinary skills to plan all our meals. Every meal had to be high in calories and packed with nutrition. He planned to mix and match ingredients that were inexpensive, healthy, and gave us a lot of energy to burn. Chet had to perform a real balancing act to plan good meals on a forty-dollar budget, especially considering he'd be feeding not just us, but the two helping hands we were about to recruit for the trip. "I hope those boys you hire won't eat us out of house and home," Chet said as he passed me the menu he was preparing for the trip.

"I'll try to find two skinny guys," I said, "You can have their seconds every night."

"I'm holdin' you to that one, boss," Chet said, hunkered over his itemized food ledger, which made me crack a smile.

"Looks like your studying for college finals," I said with a chuckle.

"Maybe I am," he said. "You'll thank me later."

Chet was serious about studying for finals, food was that important to him, and would be for us on the trip—and he knew it. I sat back and watched his brow furrow while he crunched more numbers on his calculator; I admired his dedication to the task before him. I thought for a second that maybe I was unduly stressing him out by giving him an impossible task. Little did I know the old boy was going to work some culinary magic on the road that would go down in cowboy cooking history.

★ 2 ★

A PLAN COMES TOGETHER

"If you follow your bliss and put yourself
on a kind of track that's been there all the while,
waiting for you, then the life you ought to be living
will be the one you're living. Follow your bliss
and don't be afraid, and the universe will open
doors for you where there were only walls."
—*Joseph Campbell*

ALTHOUGH ONE OF the goals of the trip was to emulate the heroic pioneers who ventured West, I didn't want to risk our lives or the safety of our horses. I knew the odds were slim that Chet and I could make it to the Pacific alone without putting ourselves in jeopardy, so we decided to recruit two hands to tend the horses and drive my "rig," a Chevy Blazer that would pull my two-horse trailer. To enlist some candidates, I put an ad in the Hartford Courant and surprisingly got a big response. After interviewing around ten to fifteen people, I came across two young men who looked right for the job. The first thing that caught my eye about Dave Huntington was he looked the part. Ol' Dave showed up to our interview wearing his trademark black preacher hat, which he would wear the entire trip. "Nice hat," I said with an approving nod. "Not many people wear old Western hats to job interviews anymore."

"Thank ya, thought it was appropriate for this one," Dave said. He was a polite young guy (in his late 20s) with a beard who looked like he could have lived back in the olden times. After speaking with him, I learned Dave was a horse-man who liked the idea of unplugging from the modern world for a bit to see the country from the perspective of the old pioneers. It didn't take long for me to get a good feeling about him; he seemed reliable, thoughtful, and even-tempered, so I hired him, for no pay, of course, except for food and lodging during the trip.

"This is a big responsibility," I said, "The boys' lives will be in your hands."

"I won't let you down, Mr. Pappas," Dave and I shook on it. He accepted the responsibility of being CA86's official "Transportation Director" plus the "Personal Caretaker" and bodyguard for the four-legged stars of our upcoming journey.

Once we hired Dave, I went looking for someone to be CA86's second hand. That's when I met a feisty young fellow named Andrew. He was different from the rest of us cowboys. Chet classified him as a hippie, although I wouldn't call him that necessarily. Maybe he was just any artsy-type. "This one could be a loose cannon," Chet said. No doubt, Andrew was a bit "out there," but he seemed like a good enough guy, a bit cocksure maybe, but who wasn't when we were young?

"He does know the grey roads," I said.

Andrew said he knew a lot of the back roads from backpacking and hitch-hiking across the country several times. He was really enthusiastic about taking the journey with us, and his price was right (zero), so after giving it some thought, Chet and I agreed to bring him on. When I called Andrew, he hollered into the phone like he'd won the Publisher's Clearinghouse Sweepstakes. He was excited to be part of the team. I explained to Andrew that his job would be to assist Dave in his duties and be our primary scout, which appealed to him.

To make the best time possible, Andrew would stay ahead of the team during the day to scout out locations for us to camp at night, keep us informed about the weather ahead and make sure we were following our pre-set route.

With our team set and May just a week away, we were in full countdown mode. I was getting excited; Sue noticed my palms began to sweat with antici-pation when I'd never had sweaty palms before. Every day was full of activity. Chet and I were training the ponies hard and rushing around, getting every-thing ready to go. I was already having a hard time sleeping, but soon my sleepless nights would increase for a wonderful reason that came at the worst possible time. Life works out in strange ways sometimes. Sometimes there is no explanation for timing, good or bad.

I'll never forget coming home from work that day. I had cut the day short at the office so Chet and I could get some extra training in. After working the horses, I walked into the house and noticed Sue was already home from work. She had this funny look on her face like she was trying to keep a secret under wraps. I had never seen that look from her before. I took the bait and asked Sue what was up?

"Can I talk to you?"

I stopped dead in my tracks. I remember the words "ok" barely coming out of my mouth. Now, I don't know much about life, but I do know when a woman says, "Can I talk to you?" most of the time that means, run for the hills. I followed her into the kitchen, and she sat me down at the table and just looked at me for a few seconds. I wasn't sure what was coming next but knew it was serious.

She sighed and said, "Guess what?"

"What?"

"Well. I went to the doctor today."

"You did? Why didn't you—"

"I didn't want you to worry."

"You OK? What's wrong?"

"Well. I just haven't been feeling well."

"What did he say? What's wrong?"

"Nothing's wrong. I just. I found out why."

At the time, Sue and I had been married for seven happy years. We'd been trying hard to have kids, but it just didn't seem to work out. Sue had even miscarried a few years before. We had resigned ourselves to the fact it wasn't going to happen until . . .

"I'm pregnant."

I could barely register what she said through the fog of complete shock that washed over me. I felt numbness then a huge surge of joy. I stood up and grabbed her and spun her around the room. We stood there, hugging and kissing for a long time. There were many tears of happiness, as we both really wanted kids. I dried her tears of joy with my red bandana, and we both sat back down and looked at each other, wondering what the other was thinking. After a few minutes of pure dumbfounded bliss, my smile slowly faded; this pang of depression hit me. I thought, "Hell, that means I'm not even going to be here for more than half of her pregnancy?" I could tell she was thinking the same thing. I broke the silence. "I know what you're thinking hon, and let me just say now that I'm calling off the trip."

"OK. But don't be hasty."

"I'm not. The only thing that matters is you and the baby's safety."

"You know I will support you in whatever decision you make," she said.

I thought there was no other sane choice *to* make.

How could I leave her?

Later that evening, we both lay in bed, thinking about our new reality. After we shut off the lights, we had a heart-to-heart. While we talked, it began to dawn on us how much of a mess it would be to call off the trip after so many arrangements had been made. I didn't want to be selfish, so I kept most of my concerns to myself. I thought this wasn't her problem; I would handle it some-how. Well, Sue must have been reading my mind because it didn't take long for her to encourage me to "reconsider my decision."

"I'm happy you're willing to cancel the trip, but you have to go, Jeff. You spent all this time training and planning," she said. "Everyone's counting on you. There really is no other choice."

"But honey. Let's be sensible now. We've wanted to have a child for so long; I want to be here in case anything happens. I would never forgive myself if . . ."

"You can stop that talk right now. Don't start thinking negative on me. You're going to do this, and we are going to be just fine."

"You sure? You won't hate me forever if I do this?"

"I've never been more sure. And no."

"Aww, how did I get so lucky to have you in my life? I've got a big-hearted horse and a woman to match," I said as I leaned over to kiss her goodnight.

"I love you too, Jeff." She said. "But make that the last time you compare me to one of your horses," she said, clearly getting my goat.

I lay there watching Sue drift off to sleep; I was still in a state of awe, overjoyed to have a baby on the way but having a hard time wrestling with my conscience. I just wasn't sure if I could go through with it. I felt terrible just thinking about abandoning her at her greatest time of need, but to cancel the trip at this date would let a lot of people down. I tossed and turned, weighing the pros and cons all night. They say men sometimes have "dark nights of the soul," this was mine.

I woke the next day and looked over in bed. Sue was already up. I found her in the kitchen, making coffee, just beaming from ear to ear. She saw me stumble in, still half asleep and glided over to kiss me. I saw how happy she was. I realized that Sue's support was not just talk but unwavering. It was then that I truly decided to go through with the trip. I am forever grateful for her amazing attitude.

I carried a great deal of guilt around with me for many years about my decision. To this day, I'm not sure if I did the right thing. All I know is Sue is the hero of this story, just as much as the horses, for being so strong while pregnant and covering a good deal of my work responsibilities on top of everything else. They say, "behind every great man is an even greater woman" because it's so often the truth. I was extremely fortunate to have such a wonderful woman on my side.

Still am. Thanks, Sue.

I broke the news to Chet. "Hot damn, congratulations, boss! A Pappy! Wow! Soo, what does this mean for the trip?"

"Drumroll . . . It's still on," I said.

"Sue gave you the green light?"

"She sure did."

"Wow. What a lady. Your powers of persuasion are off the charts."

"I didn't persuade her; she persuaded me! But if anything happens while we're gone, we're canceling the trip, and I'm flying home."

"That's okay with me. Pops," he said, smiling as he slapped my back and handed me a little cigarillo he had in his breast pocket. We lit up the cigar to honor the occasion. Chet blew smoke rings, "Can you believe the day is almost here?"

"I can and can't. Nearly two years in the making, and it all comes down to this. This is what the good ol' boys call 'nut-cuttin' time."

"If we get er' done, think we'd set the world record or something?"

"According to Mr. Guinness."

"Yeehaw! Let's go make some history boss."

Our moment had finally arrived. I was up before the crack of dawn on May 3rd, 1986, raring to go. I looked up into the still night sky while loading the rig and saw the stars were still out. I looked at Sue and said, "They're aligned for something special."

She handed me a mug of coffee, "Alright, Aristotle, just keep your eyes on the road out there." The core team arrived at the house, first Chet then Dave—then Andrew appeared from the road on foot with a guitar on his back.

"Looks like we got a troubadour on our team," Chet said. "You play any Chris Ledoux?"

"Who?" Andrew replied, still sleepy and irked by Chet's ribbing.

"That's okay with me," I said. "Andrew can sing for the horses."

"Or for his supper!" Chet said. "You don't eat much, do you?"

It may sound strange, but we had two departures for the trip. Our first "unofficial" launch was May 3rd and very "hush-hush." Only the core team knew it was happening. The secrecy was due to the fact Chet and I had made a pact to go coast-to-coast and beach-to-beach. Our problem was starting from the beach didn't jive with the Governor's plan. He had scheduled our "official" launch for May 5th at the State Capitol in Hartford, with what we heard was going to be great fanfare. Since Governor Bill had organized a big ceremony to see us off, we didn't want to spoil his plans by telling him we had to leave two days earlier to touch both the East and West Coasts.

We kept it under our hats and drove the rig out to Long Island Sound on our own. When we got to the shore, it was a calm, overcast early morning. Chet and I walked down to the beach in our boots and left our footprints in the sand. We would have ridden Thunder and Rebel down there, but the beach prohibited horses.

"Get any shut-eye last night?" Chet asked as we looked out into the Sound.

"Not a wink," I said with a smile.

"Me either."

"Adrenalin will take us the first few days."

"Till it becomes a grueling ride from hell," Chet said.

"Crossing Nebraska's gonna be like the Bataan Death March," I said.

"I can handle anything, me strong like Bull. Just hope I don't get hemorrhoids the size of grapefruits."

We walked back up to the horses. It was finally time.

It was a nervous day, but Chet and I were pumped beyond imagination to do something no one had ever done before. I looked at Chet as we saddled up and said, "Transforming from one world to another. Giddyup!"

And off we went. The horses felt good beneath our chaps; Thunder and Rebel were in top shape and ready to ride like two ponies escaping a bank job. We started heading north from Hammonasset State Park just after the break of dawn. We planned to put in a long day then meet up with "the rig" somewhere in the Rocky Hill area. We plotted a course that began on Route 81 and took us up the back end of Route 9. No fanfare, just the beginning of some hard days of riding. With the help of Thunder and Rebel, we ambled our way up to Route 9 then off to Route 99 to keep a low profile. We didn't want folks to know what we were doing in advance of our big event at the State Capitol. ·

It was a challenge "sneaking around" on horseback. We tried not to speak to anyone and didn't indulge the few people that tried to stop us and ask us what we were doing. By the end of the day, we made it thirty miles north up to Rocky Hill. Andrew said we were clocking a little faster than a three-mile an hour clip, which wasn't bad at all.

From Rocky Hill, we trailered the horses, and, unlike any other day on the trip, we didn't pitch camp. Instead, I gave everyone the night off.

"Great work, men. Now everyone, go on back home and sleep in your soft beds." I wanted to give everyone (the horses included) an extra day of rest. "Get some sleep, boys. This was just a dress rehearsal, next time we do it for real."

I didn't follow my own advice. I couldn't sleep the night before our official departure. We were about to embark on a trek that would change our lives forever, but I wasn't sure how exactly. The uncertainty was keeping me up. We were as prepared as we could be. Our "unofficial" test run from Long Island Sound was a success, but I still couldn't shut down my brain. When I wasn't thinking about the trip, I was thinking about Sue. I truly believed in my heart that she strongly supported me leaving, but the needle on my moral compass kept wavering from "go" to "stay" up until the last minute.

Sue could tell. She could always read my mind.

"Can't sleep?" Sue whispered.

"Hard to when you're headin' into uncharted waters."

"You're not gettin' cold feet?"

"Naw, it's just—"

"Well, I hope you aren't worrying about me."

"I am."

"You stop that. I'll be fine. C'mere," Sue said as she held me tight. "This is the best night's sleep you're gonna get for a long time. Best enjoy it." After that, I managed to get in a few precious hours of shut-eye in Sue's arms; the love of a good woman sure can do wonders to help ease a furrowed brow.

May 5th, 1986, is a day I'll never forget. Yes, we were really leaving, but it sure didn't seem that way. I felt like I was walking in a dream as we loaded up the rig once more, this time for good. When Chet showed up clean-shaven, I realized this was no dream; this was happening. We had a date with a bunch of politicians and media members at the State Capitol in a few hours. Just the thought of it made me feel queasy.

We didn't say much on the ride down to the State Capitol. Chet and I were uncomfortable with the send-off Governor Bill and Nikki had arranged for us, but we knew it was good publicity for their "Care and Share Program, so we prepared to face a throng of their supporters. When we arrived at the Capitol building, boy were we surprised to see how many people showed up to see us off. It was quite a scene; for a second, I thought we had pulled up to the wrong event.

"All these people came to see us?" Chet said, dumbfounded. "There must be nothing else going on today," he laughed. Chet and I had never been to a "grand affair," but this surely was one. After all, we were just two regular guys that didn't fit in too well with Republicans, Democrats, and media folks.

"How do you act at one of these things?" Chet asked.

"No cursing into the microphone," I said.

Hundreds of people were gathering outside the Capitol steps. It was a beautiful Monday; the sun was out, and everyone was in a celebratory mood. I don't know why really, maybe it was because some of the people were on their lunch break from work.

Chet and I tied Rebel and Thunder to one of the mighty oaks that dotted the grounds and went over to check on Dave and Andrew. They were keeping a watchful eye on Big Red and Wizzer, who were both tied off to the trailer.

"Hey, boys. Everything ok here?" I asked.

"Sure is." Andrew said, "Some kind of sendoff, huh?"

"Didn't know we were gonna be famous," Dave said dryly as the crowd filed in.

"Don't worry, preacher man, Governor Bill won't ask you to take off your hat," I said with a smile, then pointed to Andrew, "But maybe he'll ask you to sing a song."

"I'm not singin' anything," Andrew said.

Chet and I left the boys at the trailer and headed to the Capitol steps. It didn't take long for us to run into a bunch of friendly faces. Both of our parents came down to see what their sons had been up to for the past eighteen months. Leading our cheering section was my Mom, Dad and sister Claudia, and Chet's parents, Jean and Mike Senior, playfully known as "Fatty" as well as his brothers Mike and future "super lawyer" Patrick.

After all this talk of riding horses across the country, many of our friends and extended family came down to ask us the same question, "What are you boys up to now?" We were happy to see all our loved ones as well as Brad Davis and Kathy Wyler amid the hundreds of other curious folks. I was proud of Mom and Dad for showing support, even though they had mixed feelings about the trip. When I told Dad about it, he was taken back at first just like my brother Brian (who did not attend).

Dad said he didn't understand "why I was doing this" or "how I could be away so long." But good ol' Mom, the saint, was always supportive. Her only concern was being worried about my safety. As we mingled before the start of the ceremony, Chet gravitated to his fiancée, Diane, who was bopping around, noticeably nervous. She kept joking that she didn't know if she was going to see "her fiancé" again. Chet just laughed and told her we "aren't running off to join the French Foreign Legion or anything."

Steady as always was Sue, my rock; I spotted her from fifty feet away wearing that bemused smile on her face, a look that fell somewhere between a wife, my best friend, and expecting mother. Right before the event was about to begin, Sue handed me a comb and said, "Get ready for your close-up." I took the comb, and Chet and I nervously combed our hair and tucked in our shirts. Chet looked at me and said, "You realize this is the best we're gonna look for a long time, boss."

"Your fly's unzipped," I said to Chet. When he looked down, I flicked him on the nose with my finger to ease our nerves.

"Gotcha," I said.

"You shit."

⋆ ⋆ ⋆

Then came the ceremony. We walked up to the steps of the Capitol Building and looked out at the sea of people. It was surreal. TV cameras were filming the event; the entire affair felt like we were two decorated soldiers being sent off to War. It was a bit overwhelming. On hand was the Governor's Horse Guard, a marching band, a group of State Senators, and several members of the State House of Representatives. Governor Bill O'Neil and Nikki got up first and said some kind words about Chet and me, as did our old pal Brad Davis. Even (then) State Senator Richard Blumenthal, who is now one of Connecticut's senators in Washington, got up and said a few nice things about us. After Senator Blumenthal sat back down, Chet leaned over and said, "Don't they know we haven't done anything yet?"

"They should be honoring the horses," I whispered back.

After the ceremony, a few reporters asked us for interviews, so we obliged. I have no idea what we said on camera. I only remember being nervous as hell. After our interviews, Governor Bill struck up the band and sent us on our way. Although we were grateful for the hospitality of our honorary Chairperson Nikki and her generous sidekick, Governor Bill, we were anxious to get on the road.

Media photographers snapped photos of Chet and me as we walked back to Thunder and Rebel. I stopped to say goodbye to Sue. I gave her one last memorable kiss.

"I love you, darlin'," I said.

"I know you do. You be careful out there," she said.

"You know I will." I rubbed her tummy, "Take care of yourself. I'll see you both soon." I swung up into the saddle and looked down into Sue's eyes one final time. I remember thinking this is what it must've felt like to say goodbye to your family before heading West in the old days. My eyes were misty, and so were Sue's, but we stayed strong. "Don't make any promises you can't keep!" Sue yelled as I rode off. "Love you!"

With all the months of training under our belts, every member of the CA86 Team had galvanized into one happy family, a bunch of two and four-legged best friends ready to hit the road for an adventure of a lifetime. Chet and I took off on Thunder and Rebel out to old Route 4, which skirted the northwest side of Hartford through our old stomping grounds of Farmington and Burlington.

Then we cut up to Route 18 in Litchfield, which was Chet's hometown. It was only fitting that we got to go through his old neighborhood.

At the end of our first day of riding, we were met by a news truck from the Hartford CBS affiliate, WFSB, which had followed us for a sunset interview outside the Harwinton Inn. It was exciting to have the Channel 3 news truck there.

Naturally, no rehearsal produced some pretty comical results. During the interview, Chet and I tried not to talk over each other when the anchors Don Lark and Denise deCenzo asked us questions. When we finally got some words out, we talked about the plight of the homeless and answered the most popular question we would get on the trip, which was, "Why are you doing this? And do you think you will make it?"

I told them Chet and my friendship would carry us through the tough times ahead. I also took the opportunity to honor Chet and talk about the importance of best friends. After the interview ended, Chet and I looked at each other and vowed we would be better prepared for the next one. "No excuses!" we said to each other and laughed.

Believe it or not, we were the lead story on the six o'clock news that night.

When the sun went down on our first official day, we camped in familiar surroundings a few miles from Chet's old family home. Our families drove out to meet us at our campsite. Chet said it felt good to see his Mom, Dad, and brothers one last time. We all had dinner around the campfire together and said our 'final-final' goodbyes to our families. Then Chet, Dave, Andrew and I all settled down with the horses for our first night's sleep under the stars. As you might imagine, we were still so full of adrenalin; it was a restless night for the entire team.

The next day, our team was itching to get on the road. Even though I was a "local," I was excited to ride through all the back roads of Connecticut. If you've never had a chance to experience "Connecticut horse country," you're missing something special; it's simply beautiful. We followed Route 18 to Bantam Road through Litchfield County and followed the Litchfield Turnpike headed for Route 202 in New Preston. Our route took us over many beautiful rolling hills lined with old stone walls from the late 18th and 19th centuries. "Will you look at this beautiful country," I said as we clip-clopped along the side of Route 18.

"Can you believe I've never seen most of these places? And it's been right under my nose the whole time."

"Me either boss," Chet said. "And I was born and raised a few miles from here."

We were faithful about sticking to our daily routine of riding Thunder and Rebel four to five hours in the morning. Then around midday, we'd look for Dave and the rig and switch to Big Red and Wizzer. We hoped this routine would keep our boys fresh every day and injury-free. As we rode Big Red and Wizzer in the afternoon, so many friendly folks stopped to talk with us. Some offered hay for the horses while others offered food for us two-legged critters. Some even offered lush grassy fields to camp in, which is exactly how we spent our second night.

On our third day, we made our way through New Preston and the New Milford area. As we began to head southwest, New Milford, and the many little New England towns, we passed through slowly became a warm memory. We were happy to finally be getting some distance from home. Yet we never looked back. Our sights were always set on the future and plotting the next day's route. We had charted our course for more than a year, but since we were riding on "grey roads," we knew some of the roads we saw on the map might not materialize in real life. Maps were fickle back in those days.

Our ability to improvise would be key to our survival. It was a daily lesson in paying attention to the small signs that led us to all the hidden back roads the country had to offer. We ended up using our "improv skills" many times on the trip, but the first time we did it was on Day Three after talking to a few locals about shortcuts and best routes. They suggested we take the back roads that paralleled Route 6 and Route 7, and we took their advice.

"'Depending on the kindness of strangers' ain't just words from a Tennessee Williams play," I said to Chet after the local's short cut not only saved us some time but got us off a busy road for a spell.

"That may end up bein' the motto of this trip, boss," Chet said. "If we're lucky."

After our third long day riding through the beautiful Connecticut landscape, we ended up bunking again in a friendly farmer's field. We tied up the horses for the night and fed them well. Then Dave and Andrew secured the trailer, and Chet whipped up one of his magical meals. Most of our nights were like this, and they all began to weave together, one into another. We sat by the campfire and talked shop. We figured once we had left the familiar roads of Hartford, we were about three days away from hitting New York. The plan was to take the back roads until we got close to Bear Mountain and the Bear Mountain Bridge that crossed the Hudson River.

It turns out we were close to being right on this one because, by the fourth day, we started seeing signs that New York was fast approaching. But crossing over into another state wouldn't come easy. We didn't know it then, but we were about to come face-to-face with our first major hurdle of the trip, which was crossing the Hudson River into New York on, you guessed it, Bear Mountain Bridge. Hurdles were a daily occurrence on our cross-country journey: big hurdles, small hurdles, and some in-between—they never stopped coming. Some challenges stretched out over a one or two-day basis while others happened at a moment's notice. We had to react quickly to them all, but this was a big one. We thought we were prepared for everything, but crossing the Hudson turned out to be harder than we expected.

"As much training as we've done with these ponies, can't say any of em' are 'bridge broke,'" I muttered to Chet as we surveyed the huge Bear Mountain Bridge, which was full of speeding cars and had to be close to 1,000 feet above the river.

"We never trained the horses to cross a bridge like this," Chet said.

Chet and I needed to talk about this one. We knew we couldn't swim across the Hudson with the horses. "Let's see if we can cross on the bridge," I said.

"Wing it?" Chet looked skeptical.

"What other choice we got? Let's just take it slow and see how far we get. Maybe the traffic will offer us a bit of cooperation."

"You're the boss," Chet said.

We took our first steps onto the bridge. I told Thunder to keep his eyes straight ahead; I didn't want him looking down and getting spooked. Thunder did as he was told, but I wasn't as smart. I took a quick glimpse down into the rushing water below and quickly noticed everything looks a lot higher sitting on a horse that's 17 hands tall.

"We're high up now," I said, trying not to startle Thunder.

"This is crazy. This is crazy," Chet said nervously.

Without any police escort, we started a slow walk across the bridge amid the cars and trucks. We tried to stay to the right of the road, but the vehicles didn't give us much room to maneuver. The cars zooming past us that day got to witness quite a rodeo. With all the traffic going by, Thunder and Rebel were soon stopping traffic, pirouetting around the bridge with no rhyme or rhythm.

"Whoa, you settle down now!" Chet tried to keep Rebel's cool. He looked at me, "So this is what 'horse dancin' means?" We got halfway across before we finally decided the horses just weren't prepared for this. We didn't want to end the trip at Bear Mountain, so as the head of the outfit, I had to decide: Did Chet and I want to risk cannonballing one thousand feet into the Hudson River or trailer our horses across the last stretch? I finally decided to load them into the horse trailer and get us all safely across the bridge. "Let's cut our losses, Chet, c'mon, Dave, let's trailer em up!"

Dave was driving in front of us and already had the good sense to have transported Big Red and Wizard to the state park on the other side of the river where Andrew was minding them. We loaded the horses into the trailer like a pit crew at the Indy 500 right there on the bridge. Only a few cars honked at us for stopping traffic. When we got into the truck and knew we were safe, we laughed.

"Phew!" Chet said, "Smart move, boss!"

"Could've been a lot worse," I said.

"This mean we're not setting any record?" Dave said.

"Oh. We'll tell ol' Guinness we didn't ride 'em all the way across the country, but some things aren't worth dying for," I said. "Here's to livin' to fight another day!"

"You said it," Dave said from behind the wheel.

"Ya' know, leaving Connecticut, I felt a little transformed," I said to Chet.

"Transformed, huh. That's a big word. I feel a bit peckish," Chet said as he looked back at the slowly disappearing span of steel, "Good riddance to that bridge."

We were happy to be safe and sound on the other side of the Hudson. We stopped in the park to meet Andrew, Rebel, and Wizzer and eat lunch. I remember feeling that crossing the Hudson was a symbolic accomplishment. It meant we were serious about this trip. No more "weekend warrior" tags for us, we were slowly transforming into a tight unit that was committed to a cause that was larger than ourselves. Our transformation started happening slowly after crossing the Hudson, and increased a little bit every day, in every town and every state. With every new state came a new challenge where we grew a little and learned a little bit more about ourselves and how to function like a well-oiled machine. We saddled up for our first ride into New York. We set our sights for Route 6 and Herriman State Park. I looked at Chet and said,

"Well. guess we're really gone now."

"Ain't seen nothing yet boss," Chet said and laughed one of his trademark laughs. "There's nowhere else I'd rather be."

"Me too, partner. Me too," I said. "Adios, Connecticut! Hello, New York!"

We both hooted and hollered. New York. I hope you're ready for us.

THE OTHER SIDE OF NEW YORK

"Life is not a journey to the grave with the intention of arriving safely
in a pretty and well preserved body but rather to skid in broadside,
thoroughly used up, totally worn out,
and loudly proclaiming—Wow—What a ride!"
—*Anonymous*

ONCE WE HAD wrangled the Hudson, we started the second leg of our adventure on a southward trajectory. Atop our faithful steeds Rebel and Thunder, Chet and I rode around the outskirts of Bear Mountain State Park on Route 9 West. The day could not have been prettier. When most people think of New York, they think of the hustle and bustle of Manhattan, but this was another side of the state entirely. The landscape was rural, quiet, and beautiful, full of rolling hills, lush mountains, and countless "grey roads," which, of course, appealed to a couple of cowboys like us and appealed to our four-legged friends. "This place musta seen its share of battles with the Red Coats," I said, pointing to some dilapidated headstones and an old stone wall that looked like it predated the Revolutionary War.

"Just think," Chet said. "If it wasn't for Paul Revere, we'd be riding on English saddles right now."

"Not me. Had enough of them in my younger years."

"Gotta have a horn for ropin' shit off," Chet said. "What they use English saddles for anyway? Jumpin' steeples?"

"They call it dressage . . . or polo."

"Did you just say you rode English?"

"Yep . . . playing polo as a kid. back in Manila."

"Playin' polo? In Manila?"

"Polo ponies are the best equine athletes in the world."

"Last time I checked, cowboys don't play polo in Manila."

"This one did."

"Gonna' try and forget I ever heard that about you, boss," Chet said, ribbing me.

We rode past Iona Island situated off the western bank of the Hudson River and decided to go looking for a more scenic ride a little more off the beaten path.

"Thinkin' we may wanna try some of these back roads," I said.

"It'd save time instead of goin' round the whole damn park," Chet said. "These ones ain't on any map," He pointed to a few country roads leading into the park.

"May as well cut through," I said. "Ok, let's do a little improvisin'.'"

We told Dave and Andrew we were veering off Route 9 W and would meet them later down the road to switch out horses. I instructed Andrew to scout a place where we could get some supplies for the night. Chet and I took a short cut on a grey road with no name. After a while, it led us to another nameless road inside the park. We didn't know if they would lead us to any towns, but after a while, we came upon a few.

Passing through, Chet mused, "Any of these little hamlets have names?"

"Beats me, Hoss," I said. "Some places just don't."

"Hoss?" He said, raising an eyebrow.

I just chuckled and kept riding.

"Always fancied myself more of a 'Little Joe,' type," Chet said, laughing.

"Only a few thousand miles till we get to the Ponderosa," I said, "Let's get it in gear, c'mon Thunder!" I gigged his flanks, and we took off galloping down a dirt road.

"You cheater!" Chet said as he spurred Rebel and took off after us.

About ten miles into the park on our way to Route 6, we had a strange and unique encounter. We were on a back road that was supposed to lead us to an old town on the map called "Doodletown," which is where I had sent Andrew to scout for supplies. We were getting hungry and didn't have the trailer around with our grub, so we started looking for a town that had some food. We weren't having much luck. "Looks like we're not gonna' find anything till we hit this 'Doodletown,'" Chet said. "Hey now. What's this?" We suddenly found ourselves in a two-block area of old buildings that didn't seem to have a name at all. The town was simply a small, one-pump gas station and a General Store. "General Stores have food?" Chet asked.

"Round here, I reckon it's our best bet," I said as we pulled up to a General Store that looked like time had passed it by. We got off Rebel and Thunder and tied them to one of the wooden posts that supported the porch.

"This place looks like it hasn't been open since the Civil War," Chet said. We walked up the porch, opened a swinging screen door, and heard the loud creaking of old rusted springs. "Must not have any WD-40 in stock," Chet said.

I knocked on the old door—no answer. I looked inside the window and still couldn't tell if the store was open or had ever been open. The musty smell indicated the place had been closed for years, if not decades.

"Anybody home?" Chet said loudly. Still no answer.

"Guess there's one way to find out." I turned the old handle, and the door opened easily, "They're open."

"Nothin' like a little light breakin' and enterin' to break up the monotony of the day," Chet said with a chuckle. We took a few steps inside and heard something scurry into the back of the store. "What was that?" Chet stopped.

"Varmint probably," I said.

"Sounds like a two-legged critter to me," Chet said.

Chet and I strode into the dusty little General Store and saw six lunch tables, a small lunch counter, and a couple of old Coca-Cola signs hanging on the wall. We peered over the lunch counter. Three old magnet menus hung above the grill that listed their Specials of the Day:

TODAY'S SPECIALS

PIMENTO CHEESE SANDWICH (15 CENTS)

ROAST BEEF SANDWICH (35 CENTS)

HAM SANDWICH (30 CENTS)

MOM'S MEAT LOAF (40 CENTS)

CHICKEN POT PIE (QUARTER)

COFFEE (NICKEL)

COCA-COLA (NICKEL)

I stood there, dumbfounded, "Would you look at that?"

"Doo-doo-doo-doo, doo-doo-doo-doo. We in The Twilight Zone, boss?"

"Those are prices from the depression era," I said.

"Wonder what a ham sandwich older than me tastes like?" Chet asked.

"Like a nickel and a dime, probably," I said.

"So hungry I could eat a forty-year-old slice of meatloaf," Chet said.

We waited for another few minutes but didn't see hide or hair of anyone.

"Yoohoo. Are you open?" Chet asked. Nothing. We gave each other puzzled looks then decided to sit down at a table, hoping someone would materialize to wait on us. No sooner had we sat down when a little old lady in a long, flowery dress puttered out from the back room. She had one of those old-timey Gibson Girl hairdos.

I looked at Chet and whispered, "If that's not Ma Kettle, I don't know who is."

The old lady got a bit closer then stopped puttering. She gave us a very strange look then disappeared into the back room again.

"That it?" Chet asked, "She think we're the James boys or somethin'?"

"Must be our getup," I said.

A minute later, Ma Kettle came out with what we surmised was her husband, and I'll be damned if he didn't look just like Pa Kettle. They were both in their late 70s (or 80s), and I don't think they knew what to make of us, but after seeing we were seated at a table, they figured we were customers, so they had to talk to us. They approached cautiously. Pa asked, "How can we help you, boys?"

"Howdy. We'd like to have some lunch if you're servin'," I said as politely as possible.

"What you boys hungry for?" Pa Kettle said.

"Well." I said, looking at the menu, "I reckon if we could just get a couple of sandwiches, we'd be on our way."

"Three sandwiches, one ham, two roast beef," Chet interjected, "And two ice-cold Cokes if you don't mind." He looked at me and shrugged, "I'm hungry."

"Okay then," Pa Kettle said. Once Ma and Pa Kettle deduced, we were only there to eat, they relaxed a bit, but not much. "Ma" quickly brought out the sandwiches and Cokes. "Now you boys eat em up and be on your way," she said sternly.

We ate our lunch in awkward silence. "Ma and Pa" didn't say much; they just watched us from a safe distance. It looked like Pa may have had his hand under the counter a few inches from a shotgun, but I figured I was imagining things. Every time we looked up from our food, we saw their eyes focused on our hats and chaps. Chet and I chuckled, "They think we're casin' the joint," Chet said under his breath. In hindsight, I suppose I understand why they were wary; it was obvious they were the only two people in the building. We assumed they owned the place but couldn't be sure.

Lunch hit the spot, even if we had to settle for sandwiches on Wonder Bread. When we finished, we paid our tab (with a generous tip considering the prices) and got up to leave. We could tell Ma and Pa still thought we might try to rob their store!

Little did we know this would be the first of many occasions that local folks thought we were bandits. Chet and I never figured out why so many people mistake cowboys on horses for criminals. Who in their right mind would rob a store then make a "quick" getaway on horseback in 1986?

We wrote it off to a lot of people havin' seen too many movies.

On our way out, Chet made small talk with Pa, "Jeff and I are riding our horses across the country. For charity."

"The county, huh. Well, ain't that-a something," Pa said.

"Actually, we're crossin' the entirety of the United States, sir, if you can believe that," Chet said. Pa Kettle just looked at him with a blank face.

"Coast to coast," Chet said.

"On a horse?" Pa asked.

"Yep," Chet said with a smile.

"You don't say," Pa said.

"Well, isn't that nice," Ma interjected.

Chet tried to explain, but Ma and Pa thought we were full of it; we could see it written all over their faces. We didn't bother trying to convince them; Chet and I thought it was funny. Ol' Ma and Pa were no doubt breathing a collective sigh of relief to see us "banditos" leaving their General Store. But as we swung open the screen door, something compelled me to invite them out to meet Thunder and Rebel.

The old man's eyes suddenly lit up with excitement while Ma Kettle wore a look of sheer terror on her face. She said, "Oh no, I don't like horses." I thought there was no way she'd come outside, but Pa somehow coaxed her onto the porch where Thunder and Rebel were. The Boys were hanging out and relaxing with back foot bent, so we brought Pa over to meet them. Ma kept her distance.

As Pa rubbed Rebel's noggin and stroked Thunder's white blaze just below his eyes, the Boys were doing their usual 'rubbing up against a new friend routine,' which many people think is their way of saying "Hi," but really, it's what horses do when they're sweaty and want to rub out an itch.

When the conversation died down, I started looking for Dave and the rig. They were supposed to find us around these parts, but we hadn't seen them yet. Chet and I checked the horses' cinches and were about to swing up into our saddles when, lo-and-behold, here comes old Ma Kettle puttering off the porch to meet the horses. She walked out into the sunshine like a timid little church mouse.

I held out my hand and helped her off the porch, "Must be losin' my cotton-pickin' mind, lettin' you talk me into this," she said to Pa.

"C'mon Ma," Pa said (he called her Ma), "Time you got over your fear of these animals."

"They won't hurt you, ma'am," I said as I slowly led her hand up to gently stroke Thunder on his nose and white blaze, "Is this the first time you ever petted one?" I asked.

"I'm not partial to pets," she said, which made Chet chuckle.

Ma looked happy, petting Thunder. She even got brave enough to inch a little closer to him. "He's a big boy, isn't he?" She said.

"Sure is, ma'am. Seventeen hands tall. Name's Thunder."

"Well, hello. Mr. Thunder," she said with a slight smile. "Can you do a rain dance for us? We need rain." Once it seemed like Ma was okay standing beside the horses, I slowly swung up on Thunder and was waiting for Chet to climb onto Rebel.

Then all hell broke loose.

To this day, I don't know what happened, but while Chet was tightening Rebel's cinch, something must've spooked him. Maybe Ma Kettle raised her hand, or a bird suddenly flew into his eyesight, or Rebel could've just seen a ghost (as is often the case with these four-legged critters). But before Chet could untie Rebel's reins and lead rope from the wooden post, Rebel went crazy and tried to break free.

"Whoa, Rebel! You cut that out!" Chet yelled to no avail.

Rebel snapped his leather reins and took off like a buckin' bronco.

"Arrggh!" Ma Kettle shrieked in terror and ran for the hills. Chet bolted after Rebel. D-rings and screws were flying everywhere. Since Chet didn't have a chance to fully tighten Rebel's cinch strap, his saddle had gotten so loose, and he was trying to buck it off. It didn't take long for the saddle horn to slip underneath his belly, which only made Rebel more frantic.

Watching the whole drama unfold, I was concerned at first, but the road we were on probably averaged a few cars per day, so I knew he wasn't going to run into traffic. Rebel was also usually so calm, I didn't worry about him getting too far. I must admit the sight of Chet trying to catch a full-blooded quarter horse in a full bucking sprint was funny. "You're only makin' him run faster!" I shouted, chuckling at the craziness of the scene. Ol' Chet finally gave up when he realized he'd never catch him.

As soon as he stopped running, Rebel did too, regaining his composure about 200 yards down the road. By this time, I couldn't contain myself; I sat on Thunder laughing uncontrollably at Rebel, who just stood there with his saddle hanging upside down, waiting for Chet to catch up as if nothing happened. Chet was so good with horses, especially Rebel—he slowly approached him from behind, softly stroking his rear flanks. Then he moved his hand towards his chest and gently put his arm around Rebel's chest to assure him everything was going to be ok. Chet slowly unfastened his loose cinch strap, so the saddle gently rested on the ground. Then he grabbed the lead rope and led Rebel back to us—a masterful job.

With Rebel under control, my attention shifted to Ma Kettle. Of course, her worst nightmare came true, and Rebel went crazy on her. I asked Pa if she was okay; he just smiled, so I knew she hadn't keeled over from fright. By now, Dave and Andrew had pulled up in the rig. Dave went and grabbed Rebel's saddle and hauled it back to the truck. "Guess I missed the show?" Dave asked.

"You guess right," Pa Kettle said from the porch.

"Rebel just saw a ghost is all," I said, "tore up the saddle and nearly gave a little ol' lady a heart attack. All's well." Dave cracked a smile.

"You dang fool," Chet said as he patted Rebel, who gave off a snort like he was laughing too.

After all the hubbub, we had to repair Rebel's saddle, so Chet pulled out our tools, and we went to work. There were a few missing pieces to replace. We used the extra leather straps and latigo we had brought along specifically for these purposes and replaced the screws and d-rings where possible. Twenty minutes later, we were on our way with the saddle almost as good as new. I took a final look back at the General Store to see if Ma Kettle was anywhere to be found. I didn't see her, but Pa was still on the porch. He never flinched or ran inside. He had stayed outside the entire time to take in the free rodeo. He held his hand up to say goodbye. Just then, I saw Ma Kettle poke her head out of the front door. "Well, I'll be goddamned," I said to Chet, who looked back too.

"She won't come close to a horse ever again," Chet said with a laugh. "No more Westerns for her after today!" Judging by the wry smile on Pa Kettle's face, he thought what he just witnessed was cool. Maybe he was thinking he was now one of us after living through that wild rodeo, up close? Who knows, but we tipped our hats to Pa Kettle. I saw Ma was still peeking out the door; I don't know if she realized we could see her, but we waved and tipped our caps to her, too.

Chet and I were on our way again, wondering what the next adventure would be. We were looking to make up for lost time after dealing with Rebel's outburst, so after sharing a few laughs about Ma and Pa Kettle, the conversation dwindled to nothing, and it got awful quiet for a long stretch. Adrenalin can only last so long. The only sounds we heard for a while were the continual clip-clop of hooves. The sight of Andrew down the road got us talking again. "Where's Dave? and the rig?" I said to Chet. We were supposed to meet the rest of the team in Doodletown to switch horses and get some more supplies. But all we saw was a barefoot Andrew strumming away.

"He's playing that damned guitar again, I see," I grumbled.

"The Pied Piper in bare feet," Chet said. "Jesus H."

When we got to Andrew, I asked him where Dave and the rig were. "He's a little ways down," Andrew said, still strumming. "He didn't like my playin'."

"Don't think I like it either," Chet said.

"Me either," I said. "Unless it's around the campfire."

Andrew frowned.

"You scout us out a store?" I asked.

"I did. We won't be finding any supplies in Doodletown. I can tell you that."

When we rode down to the rig, we found out why. Dave was parked by what looked to be a ghost town. "This place ain't nothin', not anymore," Dave said.

"Looks like it got blown away by a twister long time ago," Andrew said. We took a minute to read some of the historical landmark signs to find out what we were looking at. The signs said that Doodletown had been an isolated settlement that was founded before the Revolutionary War. From the 1920s to the 1960s, something called the "Palisades Interstate Park Commission" began acquiring all the property in town. Now, it's just a deserted landmark in Bear Mountain State Park that is a popular destination for hikers, birdwatchers and botanists—which made sense since trees, birds and foliage overran the place. It was quite a sight to see, like something out of a movie.

We got off our horses and looked around for a bit. There were no tourists or hikers around, so it felt a little eerie. All the town's buildings had been razed, leaving only stairways to nowhere, stone foundations supporting nothing, and a crumbled road overrun by nature. "Guess we need to find the next town," Dave said, looking at the map.

"Good thing no one's here to see our barefooted troubadour," Chet grumbled as he began switching out Rebel for Whizzer. "Or it'd be pretty damn embarrassing."

"What's that supposed to mean?" Andrew got his cockles up.

"You look like a hippie, and goin' barefoot ain't safe," Chet said, pointing to Andrew's bare feet and jean shorts.

"I can wear whatever I please as long as I'm doin' my job," Andrew said defiantly.

"Go ahead on," Chet said, shaking his head, "One day, a horse is gonna stomp your foot off."

Andrew kept talking back until I cut him off. "Now look, Andrew! We don't have to love each other all the time, but to survive, we gotta work together and be professional. You listen to Chet now. This ain't Woodstock. Capice?"

Andrew said, "Capice, whatever that means."

Once we hit Route 6, we crossed through Harriman State Park with our sights set on the border town of Port Jervis, New York, which would be our entry point to Pennsylvania. We decided to push through to the town of Chester before nightfall, which would leave us about 25 miles to ride until we hit the Pennsylvania border the next day. The team pulled into Chester around sundown to stop for supplies. We found a small market where Chet picked up some essentials for dinner. We were all excited to eat, and Chet was whetting our appetites for the upcoming feast.

He loved to talk about food as much as he loved to cook. He was always planning meals, which varied each week, depending on what he could purchase at a grocery store. But he had three signature dishes that he would serve us weekly, on whatever days he chose. They were: spaghetti with Chet's back-bacon flavored red sauce, beef Stroganoff, and cowboy chili. He didn't ask us if we were ok with these three meals since he was on a budget and had to make the best of what he could find.

Sometimes he saved some cash by buying meat that was several days old or cheese that was a little moldy or vegetables that had sat out a day or two. From time to time, he even slipped in some milk products that tasted a bit sour. But I never complained, even when I caught him scraping a "green colored substance" off the beef he had purchased one day. I just looked at him, and he looked back at me and shrugged, "Forty dollars a week," his eyes told me. So, I'd just nod and eat it with pleasure.

I've got to hand it to ol' Chet; he managed to stay faithful to the micro-budget I set for us, and truly did everything in his power to make sure we still ate like kings, as the old cowboys did. Tonight would be no different.

It was easy to find a place to camp for the night off Route 6 as there were lots of good ones in this beautiful part of the country. We settled on a quiet spot near a small stream a few miles down a state forest road. While Dave and Andrew tended to the horses' dinner, Chet tended to ours. Meal preparation was something special Chet looked forward to every night. For Chet, it was a welcome distraction from the grind and sometimes boredom of riding. I'd watch him whip up our food and marvel at how easy he made it look. For Chet, the joy of cooking extended through the meal. When a hearty dinner ended with full bellies all around, Chet was a happy man. He truly got pleasure from watching us eat his food.

On our only night in New York, Chet pulled out the twenty-pound side of back bacon he'd brought with us and carved up slices to use in our dinner. Chet seasoned all his cooking with bacon but was careful to make it last for 45 days before we had to restock. It may sound unhealthy to eat bacon every day since it's high in cholesterol, but it was a great source of energy, which we needed. Tonight, he served spaghetti seasoned with back bacon. My mouth had been watering at the sumptuous smells coming from his pot for the past half hour. When he served me up, I eagerly dug into my plate.

"Another masterpiece," I said with my mouth full.

Dave said, "Awful good, Chet."

"Thank ya'," Chet said.

"You woulda been in great demand on the Lewis & Clark Trail," I said.

"Woulda been the best Cookie on the Oregon Trail, boss," Chet said with a smile. "When I wasn't the best horseman!"

As Chet handed Andrew his plate, his smile noticeably faded, "Guess you earned it," he said, pushing the plate at the kid, who took it while barely looking up. I peered up from my food just in time to see Andrew sniff at his plate and say, "Don't like spaghetti."

Chet calmly sat down and dug into his food, never looking up from his meal. All he said was, "Tough. That's dinner, either you eat it, or you don't." Well, it turns out Andrew ate it all. Then asked for seconds. Empty plates tell no lies!

After dinner, Chet made a pot of his famous "cowboy coffee," and we sat around the campfire shootin' the breeze. Chet and I had the team laughing as we told our versions of the Ma and Pa Kettle story. We all laughed until it hurt, even Andrew. "What I would give to be a fly on the wall in their living room right now," Andrew said, smiling for the first time all day.

"Bet Ma's giving Pa the silent treatment!" Chet said. I wondered aloud how many more "adventures" like this we would encounter? We'd only been on the road for less than a week. Too early to tell, but our journey would turn out to be full of them. We turned in for the night. As I drifted off to sleep, I looked up into the sky and thought of Sue and our unborn baby. Would it be a boy or a girl? I didn't want to know. I wanted it to be a surprise. I fell asleep with a smile on my face.

We woke before the crack of dawn the next day to get ready for our final push to the Pennsylvania border. We were excited to be checking one more state off our list. Chet had his cowboy coffee already on the fire. When I took my first sip, all the cobwebs disappeared, and I felt alive again. "Damn fine cup of Joe. You could float a mule shoe in it. And that's a compliment."

"Puts hair on your chest," Chet said as he handed me a plate of fried bacon and a hunk of cornbread with real butter. Chet had drawn the line with me on that one, "No margarine, real butter, boss," he would say when he was buying the groceries. And he was right. Off we rode to Pennsylvania. It was a full day's ride of 25 miles till we hit Port Jervis at the border. Being the "Poppa Bear" of the outfit, the wellness of the team was always my top priority. I checked in with everyone frequently to make sure they were all right mentally and physically. It was important that we were all getting along and riding as safely as possible.

Along those lines, I'd, of course, noticed Chet and Andrew had been squaring off a bit. Chet had taken it upon himself to initiate the hands, and I gave him the green light all the way. It may sound like a fraternity hazing ritual, but it's a time-honored tradition some would call part of "The Cowboy Way."

Cowboys believe it's important to test the new hands to see how much ribbing and practical jokes they could take. You learn a lot about people that way. I had my share of jokes played on me as a younger man when I worked for outfits in Wyoming and Montana. You learn to grin and bear it. That's how the ribbing and jokes stop if you go along with it and are a good sport.

Andrew hadn't gotten the memo yet, so Chet kept on him about his bare feet and guitar playing. He hated being called "Pied Piper," but we kept calling him that, hoping he would get the message. No such luck, not yet anyway.

All we really wanted was Andrew to be the best hand he could be. We needed him, and I told him as much in our private conversations. I thought he was slowly getting it, but it was going to take time.

Dave, on the other hand, was more mature than Andrew. He rarely showed emotions, which was something Chet, and I liked about him. He would prove to be a steady hand and never "sick at sea." Chet and I bonded quickly with Dave. We were always calling him "Preacher" but out of respect. One of Dave's skills was he was great with knives. He had a fine skinning knife that he carried on his belt that we were always ribbing him about. "How does a Preacher afford a skinning knife like that? You must have a rowdy congregation if they got you carryin' that thing," Chet would say.

"What kind of preacher carries a skinning knife anyway?" I'd ask.

"Smart kind, I guess," Dave would say with a smile.

Dave seemed to enjoy the ribbing; he always took it with a smile. We also gave him plenty of "attaboys" for his good work, so he knew we appreciated what he brought to the team. He did such a good job from day one—he easily earned the leadership role between him and Andrew, "hands" down.

Our time in New York was drawing to a close every step closer we got to the Pennsylvania border. I decided to make some memories by enjoying the landscape. Being an outdoorsman, I get a lot of joy out of just being in nature, and riding atop Thunder. I had a front-row view that couldn't be beaten. Maybe it was the guide in me who always had one eye peeled for carnivorous four-legged critters, but I enjoyed pointing out the wildlife to Chet and the hands. In New York, we saw a menagerie of deer, eagles, bobcats, snakes, and even a snow owl. I kept my eyes peeled for black bears but didn't see any on this day. We would run into a few of their big "Grizzly" brothers later in the trip.

Other than spotting critters, our last day in New York was uneventful. Only daylight stood between the Pennsylvania border and us. Chet had gotten so comfortable he'd taken to napping in his saddle for spells. With nothing but verdant fields in my periphery and with no critters to spot, I turned my gaze inward to pass the time. As head of the outfit, I spent a lot of time calculating our mileage and plotting our course. When I wasn't thinking about the trip, I was counting the seconds until I was back in Sue's loving arms. I missed her something fierce, but I kept that to myself, mostly.

Atop Thunder, I was working out a whole mess of concerns in my head. I was concerned about making it to the West Coast, concerned about getting through the Rockies before the snow falls, and concerned that Sue's pregnancy might go wrong. I knew I couldn't solve any of the hypothetical problems in New York so after giving them some thought I'd fall back on my faith that if we just stayed the course then (god help us) we'd beat the snowstorm by a damn good margin and I'd get home to Sue safe and sound a few months before she gave birth.

Hopefully.

If I ever started to overthink a situation, I'd put it away for another day and spend some quiet time reflecting on all the people who inspired me to take the trip in the first place. Guess you could call it my "Cowboy Meditation." Sometimes I'd think about the lives of frontiersmen like Jeremiah Johnson and Jim Bridger, and other times I'd harken back to the heroic 187 volunteers who defended the Alamo. How they must have felt staring at 6,000 of Santa Ana's troops coming their way, knowing they'd probably never see their families again. Talk about relativity. I dedicated the trip to the spirits of those men, from Jeremiah and Bridger to that rascal Jim Bowie and the mythic hero Davey Crockett. If they could put aside their fears for "the cause," then I sure as hell could too.

On the trail and in life, sometimes it's all about getting your mind straight. There are moments in all our lives when you must dig deep and find ways to self-motivate, especially when you're fighting an internal war. Because, as many external obstacles as we would face on the trip, we were all fighting a "war of attrition" with ourselves.

Whenever the team ran into a "rough patch," and there would be a few, I would do my best to interject an ounce of relativity that I'd learned from my cowboy meditations. I'd look at Chet and smile and say, "Hey, it could be worse. Remember the Alamo?" Chet would chuckle and say, "Remember the Alamo, boss!" and we'd keep on going. *What did not kill us would make us stronger.* It had to. It may sound corny to some of you young-uns, but that's my life ethos.

Never give in to any challenge that lets you ride away with your life. Our time here on earth is too short to get down for long. As that ol' rapscallion Del Gue said to Jeremiah Johnson when times got tough on the frontier, "Keep your nose to the wind and your eyes along the skyline"—and you'll reach the promised land. Hell. Listen to me ramble. Now I'm the one that's preachin' now—aren't I? Maybe all the mind games I was playing with myself on the trail was me preparing life lessons for my unborn child. Shoot, now that I think about it, teaching the young ones how to live is part of The Cowboy Way too, ain't it?

★ 4 ★

WILD MERCY IN PENNSYLVANIA

"The eyes of the future are looking back at us
and praying we might see beyond our own time.
They are kneeling with hands clasped that we might
act with restraint, that we might leave room for the life
that is destined to come. To protect what is wild is to
protect what is gentle. Perhaps the wilderness we fear is
the pause between our own heartbeats, the silent space
that says we live only by grace. Wildness, wilderness
lives by the same grace. Wild mercy is in our hands."
—*Terry Tempest Williams*

ROUTE 6 HAD become our amigo.

It seemed like Chet and I rode on that familiar grey road for eternity. She had escorted us out of New York and into Pennsylvania and had fast become one of our favorites because she kept us out of the big cities and offered some of the best scenery on the East Coast. We spent so many days on Route 6 that thirty years later, I can still remember some of her cracks in the road and inaccurate mile marker signs.

"Route 6, you are a friend of mine," I sang to the melody of the old Shelly West tune, "I'd like to drink you a with a little salt." I stopped warbling when I heard Chet snickering on Rebel about ten feet behind me.

"Sing it, boss!" Chet said.

"Aww, you caught me," I said sheepishly.

"Must be missin' Sue if you're singin' love songs about roads!" he laughed.

"I reckon I could write a pretty good country song about this road, if only I knew how to play the guitar like ol' Andrew," I said.

"Maybe he'll teach you if you buy him some boots!" Chet said.

"I heard that," Andrew said from the open window of the Rig as it drove past us to our lunch spot ahead.

While studying our maps over lunch, Chet and I decided that staying on Route 6 through Pennsylvania would be the best way to go. It turned out to be the right move because except for a few detours, sticking on Route 6, let us put away our maps for a spell and soak up the scenery. Time-wise, we estimated if we kept our pace of 25 to 35 miles a day, we'd cross the state in nine or ten days, but we were never sure exactly. Chet and I were quickly learning maps could be deceptive, especially back in '86 when they weren't connected to global satellites like they are today. We'd find that out the hard way a few times on our journey.

Setting out on Wizzer and Big Red for our afternoon ride, I reminded everyone to stay aware at all times as every state "was full of surprises" and had their unexpected obstacles to overcome. Pennsylvania would turn out to be no exception.

As we rode through vast stretches of wide-open farmland, I thought of all the road trips I took across Pennsylvania in college. "Isn't it something," I said to Chet, "I've driven through this state probably thirty times, and none of this looks familiar."

"Nothing stays the same forever," Chet said. "You've changed too."

"Guess I never stopped to smell the roses, so to speak," I said. "A lot of this scenery just blew on past me."

"Like dust in the wind partner," Chet said.

"Reminds me of the line from that Chris Ledoux song," I said. Chet didn't need a reminder of which song I meant. We both just looked at each other and sang in unison:

"You can't see it from the road!"

We kept ambling on down the endless trail. I was determined to keep my eyes wide open, so I could enjoy the state, but as the afternoon sun started to set, my mind began to wander. It didn't take long until I was lulled into contemplation by the rhythmic clip-clop of horse hooves. Chet broke our silent meditation.

"Thinkin' bout Sue?" he asked.

"You're a smart one."

"Must be my feminine intuition. Y'all are like soul mates, huh?"

"Somethin like that."

"I envy you two."

"Nice to hear I guess."

"You're still all lovey-dovey after all these years. Wish I could say the same about Diane and me. And we ain't even hitched yet."

"Just need to find the right woman is all."

"Guess that's all there is to it," he said with a sigh.

"And I need to find a payphone here at some point, or she's gonna kill me."

We both looked around. There was no town in sight. Chet and I chuckled. "May have to wait on that one, boss. she'll understand."

Later down the road, I confided to Chet that I'd "been thinkin' bout how I'd get home in case something, you know."

Now Chet wasn't much of an advice-giver, but he gave me a good piece of it that day. He said, "You gotta stop tearing yourself up over this, boss. You know what a wise man once told me?"

"What's that?"

"Never fear the unknown. Cause 'fear' is a poor advisor," Chet said. "You gotta have faith we're doin' the right thing here."

"Guess so. You becomin' my therapist out here now, or what?"

"Something like that," Chet bellowed, "We'll both need one by the end of this trip!" which made Wizzer whinny. Chet patted Wizard's neck, "No courtesy laughs from you, Wizzer, you ol' turd!"

After several weeks on the trail, we finally found our first payphone at some gas station in the middle of east Jesus somewhere. That's what happens when you take the back roads, I guess.

"Your wish has been granted, boss. Look." Chet said, pointing to the payphone.

"Now there's a sight for sore eyes," I said. "Hope that thing works."

We tied up the boys, and Chet went into the gas station looking for two Cokes with ice. I pulled out a quarter and called Sue for the first time since we had left. Thankfully the payphone worked. The phone rang a few times, then I heard the operator come on the line and say, "Please deposit another two dollars for each additional minute."

"Shoot," I said as I checked my pockets. I didn't have that kind of change in my saddlebags, so I hung up. Now what? Since there were no cell phones in those days, I decided to call her "collect." Thankfully she accepted my call. It was an emotional moment for me to hear Sue's voice again, even though all she said was, "Hm" at first.

"Hey, honey."

"Who's calling?"

"Jeff."

"I don't know any."

"Your husband."

"Oh. Well. Look what the cat dragged in." she said.

"Sorry I took so long to call."

"I've only been worried sick. Are you tryin' to put us in the poor house calling collect? You know how expensive one of these things are?"

"Forgot to pack some quarters," I said.

"Well. What do you have to say for yourself?"

"I'm still alive. Haven't run off and joined the circus just yet."

"They thrown you and Chet in jail yet?"

"No, but half the folks out here think we're the James Boys," I said.

"Figures," Sue said. "Bet you smell terrible."

"Not as bad as Chet. Missin' you something fierce out here, honey. I'm singin' love songs to roads I'm so heartsick."

"You're still sweet, that's good to hear. I miss you too. Never realized how much I like you being around till you left me barefoot and pregnant."

"You trying to make me feel guilty?"

"Is it working?"

"Yep. Sleepin' with Thunder ain't the same as being in your arms."

"Well, I hope not!" she said. "Where are you, anyway? I was beginning to think you've been down at 'The Coach and Four' this whole time." I filled her in on the events of the past few weeks.

"Sounds like you're in Amish country," she said. "Seems safe enough."

"I guess. I've dreamt about you and the baby every night, you know," I said.

"Bet you say that to all the girls you knocked up."

"Only you. How ya feeling?"

"Pretty good, considering I have a tiny person growing inside me. I threw up on your side of the bed this morning."

"Nice to hear being pregnant hasn't robbed you of your sense of humor," I said.

"It hasn't. But that was no joke," she said.

This was how our conversations went on the whole trip. We kept things light. I never told her about any of our struggles on the road because I knew she would worry.

I tended to focus our talks on Sue's world by asking her how she was feeling and how the baby was doing. I wanted to keep her as stress-free as possible under the circumstances, which I could do for the most part.

After Sue told me about what was happening on her end, I said, "You know, I'll turn around and come home right now, just say the word."

"Promises, promises. You just get along lil' doggie. I'll be just fine here," she said. "Just don't get yourself shot."

"Don't worry honey. I got my posse in case we run into any outlaws."

We kept our calls short as neither one of us could say all we were feeling. It was hard for me to bare my soul with Chet, Dave, and Andrew within earshot, but there were a lot of "I love yous" involved, that's for sure. When we hung up, I felt a little pang in my heart, but I didn't let the boys know. Just hearing her laugh gave me the strength to keep going and made me feel good inside.

"All quiet on the eastern front?" Chet asked.

"Yep. Now, where's that Coke?"

Back on the road, we were bent to it again. Our team had settled into the Pennsylvania portion of our trek and got our routine down pretty good. We were fortunate not to run into any harrowing experiences as we would in some of the other states, but there were several unforgettable events that the "Keystone State" brought to our journey that I will never forget as long as I live. The first occurred on our second day when we couldn't resist the chance to ride through a farm town on the map called "Potato City."

On the way into town, we started to speculate on how the town got its name.

"Potatoes in Idaho. absolutely," Chet said. "Potatoes in Pennsylvania, who woulda thunk it?" It didn't take long riding on the edge of the rich-soiled farmland before we realized all we could see for miles around us were potatoes growing in the fields.

"That probably explains it then," I said.

We rode into town and noticed just about every local shop in the three-block hamlet had the word "potato" in their signs. Chet began wondering aloud what the locals call themselves, "Potato heads? Potato-ites?" Then he started in on a slew of potato jokes, which had me in stitches.

"Maybe we should check the phonebook and see how many locals have "Potato" as their last name?" I suggested.

"How much you wanna bet this place don't have a payphone?" Chet said.

"Good point," I said.

Our cowboy getups got a few curious looks from the locals until one Potato City business owner finally stopped us to ask a few questions that we had become quite accustomed to answering: "What are you boys doin'?" "Where did you come from?" "Where are you headed?"

The inquisitive local, whose name was Henry, had a white beard and smoked a pipe; he looked like he'd lived in Potato City his entire life. After we answered his questions, he was quick to share some of the local history with us.

"Well, you boys found an interesting spot on the map. This here town was built around the success of the potato farmer."

"You don't say," Chet said, pretending to be interested.

"Well, I'll be," I said as politely as I could.

"Safe to say, without potatoes, there'd be no town," Henry said.

Henry told us a story that seemed well-rehearsed about the town's most famous resident, "Lotta people don't know Dr. E.L. Nixon, who was President Richard Nixon's father mind you, founded this here town and lived here for the greater part of his life."

"Ol' Tricky Dick's former stompin' grounds, eh," Chet said.

"We don't call him that around here exactly, but you got that right."

Henry said he wasn't clear how long young Richard lived here, but he had given us an interesting anecdote that connected potatoes to presidents. Go figure.

It was getting late, so I asked Henry about the local accommodations. "We're looking for a place with some space for a horse trailer," I said. "Don't want to trespass on any potato farmer's land," I said.

"No, I reckon you don't." Henry said then he suggested since we were on the west side of town that "The Potato City Inn" might put us up for the night.

Henry said, "The Inn used to be the hottest ticket in town." It was originally built to serve the Pennsylvania potato industry. "Dr. Nixon did a lot of his work at The Inn cross-breeding new potatoes. Yes, sir, The Inn has hosted quite a few potato-related meetings, banquets, and functions in its day," Henry said proudly. "The Potato Heads sure had some fun there."

Chet looked at me and winked. Now we knew what the locals call themselves!

After Henry had run out of potato-related facts to share, we thanked him for the tip and moseyed on over to "The Potato City Inn.' I left Chet with the horses and went inside to speak with the lady at the front desk whose name turned out to be Linda. I told Linda what we were doing, and she smiled and excused herself for a minute to go into the back room. Standing in the lobby alone, I began to wonder if Linda was calling the cops because she thought I was going to rob the place. But then she reappeared with a smile on her face. "We'd like to offer you, boys, a night free of charge on account of what you're doing for charity," She said.

"Well, thank you, ma'am, that's awful kind," I said.

"Now, we don't have any standard rooms available, but we do have a banquet bungalow in the back that isn't being used," she said.

"That will be just fine," I said. She explained the bungalow was in the back near a secluded area that would be good for our horses. I thanked her mightily, and she gave me a key and pointed me in the right direction. Outside, I found Chet, and we went looking for our "secluded spot," which turned out to be surrounded by thousands of acres of forest that were part of nearby Denton Hill State Park.

"Will you look at this?" Chet said.

"A perfect spot to tie off the boys," I said, looking the place over. "Tell Dave to bring the horse trailer around, will ya?"

"That's one big hotel room, boss," Chet said, "Sure we can afford it?" He gave me a knowing smile. Ol' Chet would never let me forget the forty dollars per week food budget I stuck him with.

"Lady up front said we could bunk on the floor here, for free," I said.

"Never figured you for a sweet talker."

"I have my moments."

The door to the banquet hall was already open, so we entered and looked around, grateful to be out of the weather. Chet and I lugged our saddles and saddle blankets inside. I told Dave and Andrew they would have to stay outside to guard the horses, which Andrew didn't appreciate, but he didn't complain much. "Hadn't seen the inside of a room like this for weeks," Chet said. The bungalow was one big bare circle with lots of windows. Twenty or so round tables and metal chairs were the only furnishings. "Think of all the 'Presidential' potato banquets that took place here," Chet said as we fixed up two pallets in the corner. "Ol' Tricky Dick's ghost may still be roaming the halls."

"Think Nixon's still alive partner, and living in California," I said.

"What a shame," Chet joked. "Well, I suppose you boys will be expecting French fried po-taters with potatoes au gratin for supper tonight. But unless the kind lady up front's gonna deliver us a sack of spuds for free: Keep dreamin'," Chet said.

"I'll take what we can get," I said. "With a smile."

"You better," Chet said.

After another one of Chet's sumptuous spaghetti dinners in the horse trailer, the team was bushed, so we all turned in early. What I thought would be a quiet night of peaceful slumber turned out to be just that for Chet, but not for me exactly.

Before I relate the evening's happenings, you should know Chet is a very deep sleeper, almost impossible to wake up. Not only that, he talks in his sleep every night. His sleep talking is so loud and clear it's almost at the level of a storyteller.

It can be spooky to the uninitiated.

Also, it may sound strange to some of you good folks, but both Chet and I happen to sleep in our birthday suits. We didn't know this about each other before the trip. Now, why is all this personal information relevant? Well. Sometime around dark thirty that night, I woke with a natural urge that couldn't hold until morning. I hadn't used an indoor facility in over a month, so in the dark, my instinct was just to go outside as I had been. It seemed like a good plan.

As I tiptoed out the door in the nude, I felt the chill of the night air. 'No problem,' I thought half-asleep, it would only be a minute until I could climb back under my warm slicker and horse blankets. I quickly found a good spot to go. There was no moon to speak of (except mine), so I didn't wander far.

After doing my business, I crept back to our room and twisted the handle. It wouldn't open. The door had automatically locked from the inside. "Damn.

Damn. Damn!" I said as I shook the door handle. For a moment, I thought I had a bad dream. Then I felt a chill run up my spine. This was no dream.

Once I shook the cobwebs from my head, I realized I was stranded, naked and alone in Potato City in the middle of the night.

"We didn't train for this," I said as I started banging on the door. I didn't want to bang too loud and scare other Potato Inn guests who might happen to drive into the parking lot. I also didn't want to get arrested for wandering around naked, with no ID. I had a feeling my story that "I was just passing through town for the evening with no clothes on, officer" probably wouldn't hold up in a court of law.

I had to wake Chet before I had some serious explaining to do. I kept banging on the door, not too loud, so as not to wake up everyone, but after a few minutes, my soft knocking had done nothing. I knew Chet could sleep next to railroad tracks and not stir an inch when a train roared by, so I moved over to the windows and started banging on them. I peeked inside and could see Chet was still snoring away in a deep slumber. I had to start making some noise, "Chet! Chet!" I thought I saw him stir when I called his name. But he just rolled over.

The shivering continued.

The situation was becoming a race between who I could wake up first: Chet or an Inn guest. "C'mon Chet, partner, open up, buddy!" I yell-whispered, "I'm locked out! Let me in!" Still nothing.

My teeth were starting to chatter.

Suddenly, bright headlights illuminated the pitch-black parking lot adjoining our bungalow. 'Oh shit,' I thought and ducked down out of the lights. Still crouching, I kept banging on the door and calling his name in a semi-panicked yell. I praying Chet would somehow hear the desperation in my voice. It took several minutes of continued banging until I heard the jiggling of the door handle—what a relief!

"We don't want any," Chet mumbled through the crack in the door.

I have no idea how he found the door in the dark, but my eyes had adjusted enough to see his eyes were closed (and he was naked just like me). I didn't stop to wake him up. I jangled my way through the door and made a beeline back to my saddle blankets and rain slicker and lay back down. All I could think was, 'Thank god Sue couldn't see me now!'

Drifting off to sleep again, I couldn't help but chuckle. I knew Chet wouldn't remember a thing, and sure enough around coffee the next morning at the horse trailer, Chet acted as if nothing happened.

"Cup of Joe, boss?" he said, handing me a cup of cowboy coffee.

"You don't remember last night, do you?" I said with a smile.

"Remember what? What did I say or do?"

I told him the whole crazy story.

"You did what now?"

"You saved my ass partner," I said. "Literally."

Chet and I busted out laughing, and so did Dave and Andrew once I recounted the story to them. "You been sleepin' naked this entire time?" Andrew asked in disbelief.

"Yup," I said.

"And you too?" He pointed at Chet.

"Yup!" Chet laughed.

Andrew was in shock, "And you give me hell for not wearing shoes?"

"I was wearing boots!" I joked, which got Chet rolling again.

We all had a good hoot about it over breakfast. Pretty sure we got a few funny looks from some of the early birds who were filing out of their rooms at 5 am; they probably thought we'd been drinking whiskey all night. While I was still chuckling, I glanced over at the horse trailer and swear I caught ol' Thunder giving me a look I hadn't seen before; I even think he shook his head at me like he knew what I'd done.

Horses are smarter than you think.

We got back on Route 6 and kept heading west. It was time to get serious again; our focus turned to put in long days in the saddle until we hit the town of Kane. Chet and I rode for two days across the rolling hills and green farmland of Central Pennsylvania. We were fortunate to meet several kind farmers along the way who offered to let us camp in their lush hay fields at night. Thanks to their hospitality, we could turn the boys out at the end of a few long days and watch them chow down on clover and grass while we prepared to camp. Watching the sunset one night, everything felt right in the world. "I do believe we're starting to become a cohesive outfit," I said over a cup of Chet's cowboy coffee. "At least three of us are," Chet said with a knowing wink. We both looked at Andrew. He didn't take the bait; he just kept strumming away on his guitar.

The kid was learning.

Once the early adrenalin rush of the first few weeks wore off, it seemed life on the trail was finally starting to slow down for us. That's when we ran smack-dab into a moment in history. The next night, we had the radio on while we were preparing camp. Every FM station was talking about Hands Across America, a very popular nationwide event that was inspired by the Michael Jackson-produced song "We Are the World."

Unless you were living under a rock at the time, you'd heard about it. What we didn't know was it was happening tomorrow. Talk about serendipity. People from New York to California were going to hold hands in a human chain for fifteen minutes. The radio DJs said many participants were donating ten dollars to reserve their place in line and that the proceeds were going to local charities to fight hunger and homelessness.

"Hey, that's what we're doing," Chet remarked.

The disc jockeys said excitement was starting to build locally as—sometime the next day near the town of Kane—the human chain was to form along Route 6.

"We'll be right there," I said, "Wanna do it?"

"Why the hell not?"

We talked about it over dinner, and Chet and I decided it was important to be part of the event. They were raising money for the same cause, and it would be a symbolic show of brotherhood with the rest of mankind.

"Bet we'll be the only horsemen in line," I said.

"Why are we stopping to hold hands with a bunch of strangers?" Andrew asked.

"Do we have to sing?" Dave asked.

"Just hold hands. You got a problem with holdin' hands?" Chet asked.

"Maybe. With you," Dave shot back with a smile.

"Can somebody tell me what this has to do with horses?" Andrew said.

"I think, one day, Andrew, when we look back on the trip, we'll remember this as bein' an important part of our journey," I explained calmly.

"Okay with me," Chet said.

"Me too," Dave said.

"Whatever." Andrew grumbled, "I hate Michael Jackson."

We hit the trail at about 5 A.M. the next morning. At around noon, we ran into a noticeable build-up in traffic on Route 6. Many police cars and emergency vehicles were on hand, so we cut off the main road and rode through the back end of town in search of the business route called Route 6A. Riding

Thunder and Rebel allowed us to cut through back alleys and parking lots with the trailer following closely behind us. Once we got into town, we noticed hundreds of cars were parked in people's yards as far as we could see. We crossed some railroad tracks to get closer to the action and started to make our way through the sea of parked cars and countless gatherings of people.

As we got closer to Route 6, we could already see the human chain forming like dominos on one side of the highway. Numerous fields had been turned into parking lots.

"Think we found the party, boss," Chet said. "Hope somebody brought beer."

The crowd was quickly swelling around us. We decided to swing out of our saddles so the ponies would remain calm. We certainly didn't want to freak out any Ma Kettles in attendance. I looped Thunder's reins, and lead rope through the front belt of my chaps, and Chet did the same for Rebel. While we walked the horses through the crowd, we began to observe our presence was causing quite a stir. We found ourselves surrounded by packs of folks of all ages (from eighteen to forty) with some old-timers mixed in. We faced all the same questions, "What are you guys doing? Where are you going"? After we answered all their questions, the conversations quickly turned to what was happening around us. There was an indescribable air of peace and giving in the air. Hundreds of boom boxes were tuned into the local radio station and blaring, "We Are the World." "I haven't experienced this feeling since my college days," I said. "For the young generation, I suppose this is as close to Woodstock as they're gonna get."

"If this is Woodstock, where can I get a beer?" Chet asked.

We walked Thunder and Rebel down the road a bit until we saw a break in the human chain that was under a few shady trees. It looked awfully inviting.

"This looks like a good spot to jump in," I said.

"You said it," Chet said as he walked Rebel over to the shade.

Chet and I filled the gap in the line with Thunder and Rebel getting all the attention, and rightly so. It didn't take long before we struck up a conversation with our neighbors. On one side, we talked with a nice older couple about tractors, while on the other, we shot the breeze with a raucous group of twenty-somethings. "What a generational melting pot," I remarked to Chet.

The smell of burning joints hung heavy in the humid air. There were plenty of Bloody Marys, wine, and cocktails for all. "And whiskey for our horses!" Chet joked once he got the beer he was looking for. "Now this is my kind of party."

"I reckon someday I'll tell my kids about this," I said.

With Thunder's reins tucked inside my belt, we talked, drank, smoked, and made many new friends. Thunder and Rebel were having fun too. They enjoyed all the attention and face rubs from their new friends. Everybody was smiling.

It was truly a special day.

The moment neared. Chet and I remounted and took our place in line. The crowd began counting down the last few seconds like it was one big New Year's Eve party: "Ten, nine, eight, seven, six, five, four, three, two, one! Everyone joined hands and began to sing. "We are the world. We are the children." The song played on hundreds of portable radios up and down Route 6.

The moment seemed to freeze in time.

While everyone was singing, a spaced-out girl wearing a long flowing hippie dress turned to Chet and said, "Holding hands, I can feel the country healing. Can your horse feel it, too?" Chet smiled at her.

"Little lady. I think ol' Rebel sure can." Then he turned to me and said, "Whatever she's on. I want some." The unforgettable lyrics that practically the whole world knew by heart played across the United States—*"We are the ones who make a brighter day, so let's start livin'."*

After we sang the song a few times, I leaned over to Chet and said, "Watching this hullabaloo gives me hope that, with all the changes in the wind, we can still come together as a country.no matter what age, color or creed."

"Spoken like a true hippie," Chet said as more marijuana smoke wafted over us. "That may be the contact high talking, by the way," Chet laughed. "We're givin' back on horseback!"

"Now this is the time Andrew should be playin' his guitar," I said.

"You know he's flirtin' with some hairy-legged girl," Chet said.

"Wouldn't you be, at his age?" I asked.

"I'm not that old, boss!" Chet said, then he turned back to the gang of twenty-something girls beside us gave them a look that could only be described at the time as the John Belushi eyebrows.

And so it was, on the afternoon of Sunday, May 25, 1986, we joined hands with almost seven million people to form a line that stretched 4,152 miles from New York City's Battery Park to the RMS *Queen Mary* pier in Long Beach, California. Though there were breaks in the lines, the media reported if everyone who participated had been spread evenly along the route, an unbroken chain across the 48 states would have been formed. It was quite an accomplishment that raised millions for charity. When the fifteen minutes of singing ended, the party kept going on around us, but Chet and I knew it was time for us to keep moving. We said goodbye to all our new friends and then went looking for Dave, Andrew, and Big Red and Wizzer in the trailer.

We found the boys parked in a field down the road a bit. Dave was brushing the horses like a good hand. Of course, we had to pull Andrew away from some girls, but he didn't pitch much of a fit. Everyone was all smiles. It seemed we all felt our cross-country journey had taken on a new and special meeting that day. I looked at Chet and said, "Well, partner. We had fun and did some good at the same time. Sometimes in life, you can actually do both."

"Kinda like this trip," Andrew interjected with a smile. Chet liked hearing that; he put his arm around Andrew and gave him a noogie, "You finally said something positive, attaboy!" I think they were finally bonding.

We loaded Rebel and Thunder into the trailer and let Big Red and Wizard take us out of town. The team unity was stronger than ever. If you believe in such things, some might even say holding hands with a bunch of strangers was a magical experience that none of us would ever forget.

Even Andrew.

We got back to the business at hand.

Chet and I broke out our maps for the first time in over a week and determined that we only had three days left in Pennsylvania if we kept our 35-mile a day pace. Since we'd lost a few hours, we tried to make up some ground before sundown. "Can you believe we're gonna be in Ohio in three days?" I said as we rode on, westward bound.

"A new state, a new adventure," Chet said. "Can't wait to see what happens next." Pennsylvania wasn't through with us yet. We spent our last day crossing a wide swath of western Pennsylvania that we knew to be home to many Amish settlements. We finally said our sweet goodbyes to our mistress of the road (Route 6) and veered off to take an even smaller grey road (Route 62) to avoid traffic. Then we went south on Route 158 for a spell and looped through the northern edge of New Wilmington, less than ten miles from the Ohio border near Hubbard.

Heading south toward New Wilmington, there were scattered farms every few miles. If you've never been to western Pennsylvania, it's home to a wide variety of Amish folks, ranging from the ultra-conservative to the more progressive. Even though there's been significant out-migration in recent years, the Amish continue to settle here and in neighboring Ohio, with several new towns being founded in just the past decade. Amish and non-Amish neighbors have been living side-by-side in the farm country around New Wilmington since 1847. The Amish buy dry goods and other necessities from English stores, and the English patronize Amish tack shops, sawmills, furniture shops, vegetable stands, and nurseries. We rode into town; Chet and I agreed that New Wilmington had an old-time authentic feel to it. Founded in 1797, it was maintained as a rural province by the Old Order Amish families whose farms surround it.

We would learn from personal experience that New Wilmington had two claims to fame: the delicious sticky buns at the Tavern on the Square, a house-turned-restaurant that served as a stop on the Underground Railroad during the Civil War—and Westminster College, whose 1,500-student population boosts the town's population to a whopping 2,350. It didn't take long for us to see the entire town.

On the way out, we rode through an authentic Amish village and saw craftsmen and seamstresses who were advertising their wares with simple hand-lettered signs painted on scraps of wood that said things like: "Furniture," "Quilts," "Jams & Jellies" and "Harness Maker"—leaving visitors to discover the true quality of what's for sale behind a simple hand-painted sign. Exiting the village, we noticed the blacktop road we were riding on had become narrow with no "berm" (or grass on the side of the road) to speak of so we took to riding in single file down one lane of the road once we realized we'd have to contend with occasional car traffic.

We gazed into the many fields outside of town. We saw no tractors or any kind of modernized farm machinery anywhere. The few farmhouses we passed were modestly constructed. After passing the third farm, Chet pointed and said, "Look, the windows have no curtains. I'd say we're officially in Amish country, boss."

"You guess," I said.

Soon after Chet made his proclamation, we saw a tiny object in the distance coming our way. The road was so flat it was probably a mile or two ahead of us. "You see that?" I asked Chet.

"Yep. What could it be?"

"Beats me. But I have a feelin' we're gonna find out," I said.

Even though my eyesight was better than Chet's, it took me a while before I could figure out what we were looking at. As we got closer to the "Unidentified Moving Object," Thunder's ears started to rivet back and forth. Then they pointed straight at the approaching object. The horses smelled something.

"I'll be damned," I said to Chet.

"What? Suspense is killin' me," Chet said sarcastically.

"Appears we have a horse-drawn buggy heading our way."

It took a few minutes before the buggy came into plain view.

"This'll be interestin'," Chet said.

Thunder and Rebel didn't know what to make of the buggy, but they smelled a brother horse coming their way, so their interest was piqued. So was mine. I'd never met an Amish person before, so I wasn't sure what to expect. I looked at Chet and could see he had a strange look in his eyes, "Cowboys on horseback meets Amish in buggy," Chet said with a chuckle. "I'll try not to say any cuss words." I could see the driver was indeed an Amish man that looked to be in his 40s. He wore simple attire: dark work pants, a light blue cotton shirt buttoned to the top, long blonde hair, and a beard. Riding shotgun appeared to be his teenage son; they were both wearing traditional black Amish hats. When we got close, Thunder and Rebel slowed down, and so did the buggy. The dirt road was empty for miles both ways. Both groups were sizing each other up as if we had come from different planets.

It occurred to me, the Amish folks probably had no idea what to make of our crew. They probably had never seen a couple of cowboys like us in their lives. Maybe on TV, I thought but heck, they don't even watch TV. I tried to think fast, should we stop and say hello or just nod and continue? Thunder decided for us. In all his curiosity, the Belgian-Cross just had to stop to meet the stout draft horse that was pulling the buggy. This would be another first for us.

Before I could think of something eloquent to say, I caught myself blurting out, "How y'all doin'?" With that icebreaker, the older man introduced himself as Levi. "This here's my son, Luke."

"Pleasure meeting y'all," I said, "That's Chet, and my name's Jeff. These fellas here are named Thunder and Rebel."

"Pleased to meet you," Levi said. "Nice horses, you got."

"Thank ya," I said.

Of course, Levi asked what we were doing in these parts.

"We're just passing through on our way to the Pacific," I said. "Ocean, that is."

"What's that, now?" Levi asked and cupped his hand behind his ear.

When I explained what we were doing, I thought I saw Levi almost crack a smile. He seemed to grasp the magnitude of the trip anyway, and, unlike most folks who stopped us, he knew we were a long way from home. Levi said he'd never been past the county boundaries himself and was curious to learn more about such a journey.

"Jeff'll sure talk your ear off about it if you're riding our way," Chet said.

Levi said, "Well, I reckon I'm on my way to do some work now. I'm a carpenter by trade. Luke here's my apprentice." Hearing his name, his son Luke looked up from his bench seat on the buggy and gave us a shy grin beneath a fringe of cropped hair that was flared out over his ears. Levi explained they lived several miles "that-a-way," he pointed behind him, which happened to be the way we were headed. "Me and Luke are restoring an old barn down the road."

Levi then did the unexpected. Perhaps hearing that we were far from home, he said, "You and your horses can stay in my field tonight if you're looking for spot to camp," he said. We accepted his generous offer and told him we didn't need much space to camp, "a small corner of your pasture will do just fine," I said.

OK then," Levi said, then turned his buggy around and led us back to his home.

We followed Levi and Luke back to their farm and set up camp early, adjacent to his small shop. Dave pulled the rig in, and we began to unload and tend to the horses who enjoyed eating grass from Levi's field. Chet thanked Levi for the use of his pasture and said, "When you are done with your work, we'd like to cordially invite you and your family to eat dinner with us; I'm cooking. Our table is located at the end of the trailer over there," Chet pointed to the back of the rig.

"Much obliged. We accept," Levi said.

"Will beef stroganoff be okay?"

"It'll eat," Levi said, and then he tipped his cap and went on his way.

Later that night, Chet had dinner going early and lo and behold, walking down from the house came Levi and Luke. I looked at Andrew and said, "There's an unspoken rule to visiting Amish country: Be respectful."

"Yes, sir," Andrew said.

"That means leave the guitar in the truck," Chet said.

"What? Why?"

I put my arm around him in a calm, fatherly way and said, "No arguing tonight. The Amish way is best appreciated without interrogation." Andrew squinted his eyes and looked at me like I was speaking Latin then walked off. Not saying another word.

We sat down for another one of Chet's amazing meals. The team was on their best behavior. Of course, no alcohol or caffeine was consumed during dinner out of respect for Levi and his family. We found Levi to be a stoic man of few words, as I hear most Amish men are, but he had an air of genuine friendliness and modesty about him. There were lots of short questions and answers coming from our guests, but Levi was a good husband and father. I mentioned we would have enjoyed meeting his wife, but Levi said she was helping a neighbor for a few days, so it was just Levi and Luke at home that night. It was fascinating to learn about the Amish way of life and those in the New Wilmington community. Although he didn't say a whole lot, when Levi spoke, he spoke with sincerity. I could tell he had a real passion for his faith, his family, helping his neighbors, and doing good work. The closest he got to "tooting his own horn" was when he said, "Many fine Amish woodworkers and furniture makers live around New Wilmington." Then he explained that knowing where to find the finest Amish-made wares required a little luck and some local knowledge.

Levi said he rented a small space in the village where he did much of his work, but he also brought his tools with him to work on various jobs "like the barn I was working on today." Levi also had a small shop at home that he used for working on smaller jobs.

Levi was kind enough to educate us on the Amish way of life. We learned there are strict religious guidelines for all areas of life, from the colors Amish women can wear (no pink, red, orange, or yellow cloth) to the number and size of the buttons on the men's homemade trousers. He explained the rules in an "Old Order" Amish community are much stricter than those of other sects because they closely follow the teachings of 17th-century Swiss Anabaptist Jakob Ammann. Levi said a bishop governed each of the fourteen church districts around the New Wilmington community and enforced the ban on electricity, cars, and other modern conveniences.

"What happens if you break a rule?" Andrew asked.

Luke, who was sitting next to Andrew, responded with the only words he would say all night, "Those who disobey are subject to shunning."

The conversation steered towards our horses and how we came to acquire them. Levi was interested in the logistics of our trip, so we discussed our "grey roads" strategy as we made our way across the US. Being a card-carrying horse lover, I couldn't help but wonder about his horse's feet. I was inclined to feel sorry for all the horses the Amish use since they don't outfit them with horse-shoes, the wear and tear on their feet (with the constant pounding on the pavement) can only cut down their years of productivity.

I wanted to ask Levi if keeping his horse's feet healthy was a top priority, but I didn't want to push our way of life on him, so I held my tongue. Then Chet politely asked him the same question I'd been thinking, "How do your horses' feet fare with the heavy pounding on the paved roads?"

Levi admitted this "was a concern of many in the village" and was the main reason many Amish stayed on dirt roads with their buggies as much is possible. I asked Dave to pull out the extra titanium shoes that we brought along to show Levi. Dave handed one to Chet, who explained to Levi and Luke how our black-smith, Joe Mantie, had custom-made many extra shoes coated with the toughest of material, titanium.

"Those are mighty fine," Levi said. "But not allowed in these parts." Levi then opened up about his love of horses. To my pleasant surprise, he talked at length about how much the Amish cared greatly about their horses' health, particularly their feet, just as we did.

It was getting dark and close to 9 P.M. Over a table full of empty plates and full bellies, Levi mentioned it was almost time to go since he was an early riser, "We leave the house around five in the morning to get to the job."

"That's the time we'll be heading out, too," I said. Chet and I thanked him again for the use of his pasture, and he thanked us for a fine meal. "I say, that was some good cooking there," Levi said, and he shook Chet's hand. Then Levi and Luke headed up to the house for the evening. I would have asked him to join us for coffee in the morning, but we knew the Amish did not drink it. So that was that.

We had a restful night's sleep in the quiet solitude of Levi's Amish farm. I dreamt again of Sue and our unborn child. I thought I knew what sex the baby would be when I woke up at 4 am—but the smell of Chet's cowboy coffee got me thinking about the day and less about remembering my dreams. Rejuvenated, the team was "up and at 'em" before the crow flies, as they say. Dave was getting the horses fed and preparing for the day's ride, and Chet didn't even have to drag Andrew out of the sack. Saddling up at around 5 am, Levi and Luke came out to say goodbye and wish us well. They were by the barn, hitching up their buggy to their horse when Levi said, "Give the folks in the Pacific our best."

"We sure will," I said.

Chet and I mounted up and headed west.

We saw Levi's buggy had left his farm right behind us, except he was heading east down the same road. Chet and I turned back to see the tail end of Levi's buggy, churning up early morning dust on the dirt road. As we strained our necks for one last look, we saw Levi's black hat and long blond hair poke out from his buggy. He had turned to look our way one last time. I looked at Levi and gave him a short wave, and he waved back. He finally had a smile on his face. It felt like a scripted moment from a movie. "Finally got Levi to smile," Chet said. "He was a good ol' guy, huh?"

"Yes, he was. Yes, he was."

Thunder and Rebel rode on, as steady as ever. When the sun rose in the east, Chet and I felt the warm rays on our backs. Our destiny was just a few miles away at the Ohio border. When we made it to the "Welcome to Ohio" sign, we didn't stop to commemorate the event; we just kept on riding. "Time to turn that page, again," is all that was said. I can't remember which one of us said it. Though Chet and I never talked about it, I had a warm feeling leaving the Keystone State. I guess with all the people we met and "good vibes" we experienced, I felt a little better about mankind than I did when I entered. It seems as we mosey through life, there are some people you meet that you'll never forget and some experiences that you'll remember until your dying day.

Pennsylvania, you were one of those.

★ 5 ★

NEVER CROSS A BELGIAN CROSS

Horse Gods, Attack Dobermans, and How to
Survive a Buffalo Stampede

"I've often said there's nothing better for the
inside of a man than the outside of a horse."
—*Ronald Reagan*

NOSTALGIA CAN BE a funny thing—you never know who (or what) in life is going to make you look back, and smile. Who knew this cowboy would be nostalgic for two fellas wearing "funny hats?" Call me nostalgic or just plain curious, but I guess I wasn't ready to let go of Pennsylvania just yet!

I must have still been wondering about our new Amish friend's way of life, because I found myself looking over my shoulder all morning (just) in case we saw another horse-drawn buggy, but it was not meant to be. We'd seen the last of the buggy traffic, and Luke and Levi (at least in this lifetime)—but their pastoral way of life sure made a lasting impression. Not that I agreed with their religious beliefs—or disagreed, for that matter—but I wouldn't mind being transported back to the olden days to live off the land, even if it was just for a little while.

"Can you imagine taking this trip without all our modern gear?" I asked Chet.

"Yep. Half the damn team probably would've croaked on the way," he chuckled.

"Reckon I'd put my money on Andrew expiring, first," I joked just loud enough for Andrew's prying ears, "—Freak stampede or scarlet fever, probably."

"Ribbit. Ribbit," Andrew pulled up next to us, making his best bullfrog impression, "I'd put my money on you old boots, croakin' first."

"You have money?" Chet joked.

"Just giggin' you with some words of encouragement, son," I said.

"Don't you know our barbs are wrapped in love?" Chet snickered.

"Yeah, right," Andrew said, "More like wrapped in sarcasm."

That Andrew. I suppose every outfit has one. He had become the butt of our jokes for a good reason. The kid was already losing favor with ol' Chet, namely for his lack of focus, his "can't do" attitude, his highly questionable fashion sense, and (oh yeah) his infernal guitar playing. Andrew had been asking for a swift kick in the rear since day one, but I wasn't going to send the troubadour packing unless he seriously screwed something up. I've got a heart—besides, we had other things on our mind today. The outfit had reached another state line, which was always a cause to celebrate.

"Time to carve another notch in the old gun handle, boss, cause we're in buckeye country now!" Chet exclaimed.

We hooted and hollered when we saw the Ohio State Line in our purview, "Another state down pard—we did it!" I shouted.

"And a crapload more to go," Andrew interjected glumly.

Chet shot Andrew one of his looks, "Jeff, on second thought, I think Andrew would-a been killed by his own wagon train. Maybe by his own cookie!"

"See you boys later!" Andrew sped off with Dave.

Chet laughed, "That'll put a little giddy-up in his get along."

"Sure hope so," I said, chuckling, "You're like the team's 'Andrew whisperer.' Now, can you get him to put some damn clothes on before he gets us all killed?"

"You ask the impossible," Chet replied, and he was right. Andrew never did put on any damn clothes the entire trip.

Thunder and Rebel snuck us into the *Buckeye State* through a grey road called Route 62, north of the town of Hubbard. Our maps confirmed we were headed west toward a small town called Warren. Chet and I figured we could make it through Ohio in a week (or less) if we kept putting in twelve to fourteen-hour days, which had become standard for us. It didn't take long before we could see the terrain changing—from lush green rolling hills to flat as one of Chet's griddlecakes—as far as the eye could see. This would be the start of our long, arduous ride across the Great Plains of the United States, where Chet reckoned—even the anthills would be scarce.

"You'd think the man upstairs would have at least put a few goddamn hills in the Midwest, just to mix it up," Chet mused.

"Don't you know—hills are the devil's business?" I joked.

"Thunder's probably taller than anything we'll see till we hit Chicago."

"You may be right, but flat's just fine with me. Save the boys some work."

"Gonna be bored stiff staring at this same flat cornfield every day," Chet said.

"Reckon we'll have to make a game of it then," I said.

"Out of what—boredom?"

"Maybe, maybe," I replied.

Just then, a strong gust of wind snatched my hat off my head and blew it into some farmer's field. "Don't lose your head, boss. Better go get it!" Chet laughed. The wind had become a constant reminder to pay attention; if you lost focus for a minute, your hat could go flying into the next zip code.

"Goddamn hat thief!" I cursed the bitter wind. Then I had something akin to a brainstorm. I looked at Chet, "First one that grabs my hat wins?"

Chet stared at me like I was suddenly speaking Italian. "Aw, come on, boss. We're grown men. We don't play games out here in the open range—Hyaaah!" Chet didn't bother finishing his sentence before spurring Rebel to chase down my wayward hat. Seeing Chet was a rule-breaking hat wrangler—I gigged Thunder and gave chase, too. This is how our first "hat game" was born.

To keep some of us (I won't name names) from falling asleep in the saddle—we played the "hat game" every single day in Ohio, often many times a day. We quickly decided to stop racing to the hats (to keep the boys fresh) and turned it into a methodical game of skill. Scores were kept based on the number of times we got our hats blown away. The cowboy with the fewest points won. At some point, one of us decided you could no longer get out of your saddle to pick up your hat, which put me at a disadvantage, because 90% of the time I rode Thunder, who was taller than anything Midwest, at least according to Chet.

As you may imagine, this took a hell of a lot of practice, but since we had nothing but time on our hands, we had plenty of opportunities to master the art of the hat game. We'd tease each other whenever our hats got blown off and holler words of discouragement whenever someone was trying to reach for a fallen hat. We also made other rules like, whoever had the most hats blown off in a day—probably needed to wake the hell up, and pay more attention.

I discovered the trick to success was finding the right leg grip around Thunder's neck when lowering myself down to hat level. After a while, Chet and I were like two-trick rodeo riders, contorting ourselves in the saddle to grab our fallen hats.

All this time, I recall the horses just watched and wondered what the heck we were doing. I could read Thunder's mind on a few occasions when he'd look at Rebel and say—*What are these crazy humans doing?*

But maybe that was just the heat talking.

Win or lose, the hat game sure did the trick. It always gave me immense pleasure to watch Chet chase his hat into some ditch or off into some thicket, trying to rescue his lid without falling out of the saddle. I'm sure he'd say the same thing about some of the situations I got myself into—actually, I know he would! The hat game may seem silly, but it served its purpose. And ol' Chet and I would have tried any distraction to keep our minds focused on anything other than the thousands of miles ahead.

Besides chasing our hats for recreation, the outfit spent our first day in The Buckeye State searching for our next grey road, Chet had identified as *State Route 303,* otherwise known as Hudson Road. After scouring our maps, we opted to stick on 303 most of the way. We figured it would keep us heading west, somewhere between Cleveland and Akron, which is where we wanted to be. No way did we want any part of riding the boys through any big city. Cars can easily spook horses, and we'd get caught up in traffic, and (knowing Chet and me) *God knows what else.*

Well, as "FM would have it," once we picked up Route 303, we couldn't have asked for a more peaceful path. It was all farmland and cornfields as far as the eye could see. It was so quiet and still outside—I entertained myself by eavesdropping on Chet's private conversations. "You're no city boy, are ya?" Chet patted Rebel's neck, "This flat shit's boring as hell, but you like it—don't ya? Yes, you do. Yes, you do."

I never caught Rebel's reply.

During this "stretch of eternal boredom," as Chet liked to call it, all we could see were endless brown plowed fields, separated by rows of planted corn. Most of the cornfields were about six-inches high this time of the season. It was such isolated farm country we were fortunate to meet several kind farmers who offered us home-cooked meals as well as five-star luxury accommodations—which, to a cowboy outfit, was a night of shuteye in one of their haylofts.

"Now, this is penthouse living," Chet uttered one night while bunking in a loft overlooking a vast swath of farmland.

"You said it pard—Ow. Shit," I said.

"What's wrong?" Chet sat up.

"Somethin' just bit me," I said.

"Aw crap, boss.me too."

Oh, crap was right. I can't say what compelled us to stop worrying about ticks a few states ago, but that hygienic oversight would come back to haunt us right about now.

"Ever looked at a tick, up close?" I asked Chet while inspecting one.

"Nah—I just kill em, and let God sort 'em out," Chet replied.

"Probably for the best. Suckers look like tiny aliens."

The tick circus that, come to find out, had been traveling with us (for a good while, became part of our official team in Ohio. Hell, if Susie knew (back in '86) how bad our bug infestation got, she'd have never let me back in the house when I got home!

We really should have known better.

When the trip began, Chet and I took turns reminding each other to check our hair and beards for those little buggers—but then I reckon the itching must have stopped, so we got lax in our daily inspections. By the time Ohio rolled around, we had let ourselves go to total hell, hygienically speaking. We looked like two grizzled outlaws, our grooming regiment (if you could call it that) had been reduced to showering once a week, wearing our cleanest dirty shirts, and (yes) pulling those godforsaken ticks out of our beards whenever we felt an itch.

One late Ohio afternoon—Chet and I found ourselves in a café in some small town. We had pulled over to enjoy some free air-conditioning and a cup of coffee while Dave and Andrew found us a camp spot a few miles up the road.

Must say, it felt downright amazing to sit in that air-conditioned café with ol' Chet for a spell, just enjoying our cups of coffee, and being out of the saddle. While relaxing, I made the mistake of catching a glimpse of my haggard mug in the stainless-steel napkin holder, "Yeeesh, pard. Who the hell is that? I feel miserable, Chetter."

"That figures. You look even worse!" Chet said.

"You don't look so dashing either, Hoss."

Chet inspected his craggy mug in the napkin holder, "Daaamn. I look like Sasquatch. Someone call *Ripley's Believe it or Not.* We've spotted Big Foot in Ohio."

"Figures. You smell like a Yeti," I joked.

During this back and forth, I noticed Chet and I were both casually pulling tick after tick out of our beards, and depositing them in a worn-out black lacquered ashtray on the table. The ashtray was filling up fast.

"No tellin' what we're gonna look like by the time we reach the Rockies," Chet pulled another tick from his beard and deposited it in the ashtray.

"If we reach the Rockies," I said, "Sue may come due, and I'll have to get on back home. She'd give our table manners a big F, by the way."

"Speaking of pop, listen," Chet pulled out his lighter and lit one of those miserable little critters on fire. "Hear that?"

I did hear that. I can still hear that. Chet was acting like a kid doing a science experiment, "Look, they're like Rice Krispies—Snap, crackle."

"Pop. That's ugly, pard . . . yet, I can't look away." I didn't consciously realize what we were doing until Chet incinerated the eighth tick with his lighter, which made me chuckle for some reason. Then I looked up and noticed all the other café patrons were quietly judging us. I nudged Chet to let him know we had an audience.

"Are they calling Amnesty International?" He said.

"Do ticks have constitutional rights?" I smiled.

"Maybe we should start doing daily tick inspections, again?" Chet mused.

Hiss pop!

"Probably a good idea," I mused back.

Hiss pop!

To this day, I'll never forget us sitting in that café, nuking ticks with our lighters. We were entertaining ourselves like two deranged hobos, but we didn't mind, much. Chet and I wouldn't be coming back through this town anytime soon, and the locals would never recognize us even if we did. But after about the 13th tick was sent to hell by Chet (to let God sort out, I presume), we decided it was time to slow down on the bug executions, drink the rest of our coffee, and get back on the road before we offended some insect-loving sheriff or local clergyman. This would not be the last time Chet and I would hold a tick pickin' contest in public.

Maybe it was the boredom of the day, but riding away from that café—I imagined the *Legend of the Tick Pickin' Cowboys* would soon spread like wildfire (or Lyme disease, depending on how you look at it) across the Midwest. I imagined some old-timer in a rocking chair regaling his grandkids thirty years from now with a strange story—"Ever hear about those two cross-country cowboys who came through in '86? Few know they also set the world record for most ticks burned in ashtrays on that trip."

At least that's how I imagined the legend going.

Chet probably imagined it differently.

Sorry, you had to read that, Sue!

Ohio—no offense—but you're about as interesting as watching corn grow. Every minute began blurring into the next—until after a while—every day was the god-awful same. The thrill had gone, somewhere—I wasn't sure where or when—neither did Chet. But after keeping a solid pace for months, it felt like the boys were slogging through quicksand by our third day. I even found myself losing focus to daydream about Sue and our unborn child—or a steak dinner and a warm bed—which was not exactly good since I was the eyes and ears of the outfit (along with Thunder). It didn't matter how many cups of coffee I poured down me; the never-ending repetition had set in. I could predict every hour of every day like clockwork:

Chet and I would awake around four in the morning. We'd have our coffee, bacon, and cornbread around 4:30. Then Dave would feed, water, and saddle up the boys—and we'd be on the road by 4:45 to 5 A.M. We would usually ride for twelve to fourteen hours, then camp for the night. Chet would make dinner, Preacher Man would feed the boys, and Andrew would regale us with his incessant guitar playing—and we would go to sleep. Wake up and repeat a million times. Or at least it felt that way.

Luckily, for Chet and me, the riding part never got old. Being with the boys was pure joy, even when we were tired or bored stiff. But seeing the same cornfield on an endless loop for what seemed like an eternity? Not my favorite part.

The repetition had a curious effect.

When all you see are flat cornfields, and all you hear are the repetitive sounds of horses slowly plodding ahead—clip, clop, clip, clop—it can lull you into a dream-like trance. We could go hours without saying a word. Then someone (usually Chet) would break the silence with a joke, "Get a good look, boss. Map says those were the last of Mother Nature's 'dirty pillows' for about—let me check—a thousand miles. We're in bible banging flatlands country now! Best mind your P's and Q's."

"Leave it to you to bring up Mother's Nature's cup size," I chuckled.

"My mind is wandering, boss. I admit it! Been a long time since we've seen our ladies."

"I hear you, pard . . . it's been too damn long."

Once the rolling hills of Ohio disappeared for good—we were in an endless flat cornfield for the next thousand miles. You may wonder, how could we tell how far we'd ridden (in a given day) when every landmark looked the same? Good thing we had Dave to give us the mileage because our brains were beginning to have trouble calculating distance around this time.

To break up the monotony—every so often, we would come across a landmark, like a café, drugstore, grocery store, or grain silo—which was always a good reason to stir Chet back into consciousness. "Think fast, Chetter." I looked over, and he was snoring in the saddle, "Grain silo coming left!"

"Wha? Who—where's the fire?" Chet always seemed to wake from one of his catnaps completely disoriented, which never failed to entertain me.

"Just checking to see if you're still alive," I'd say with a chuckle, and he'd usually go back to sleep. I couldn't blame Chet for napping—I discovered it is damn near impossible to pay attention every minute in the saddle when absolutely nothing is happening. It didn't help that summer was finally upon us. Rather than opting to snooze in the saddle with Chet and leave our navigation entirely up to the horses (never a good idea)—I brainstormed other ways to keep our brains occupied.

The *Monty Python* game was little different than the others. It was created, not out of want, but out of necessity. Back in '86, Chet and I were both huge *Monty Python's Flying Circus* fans, which was a cult comedy TV show from the 1970s, in case you've never heard of it. I know—cowboys who love British comedy? I never said Chet and I were your typical cowboys. How did we come up with such a funny game?

Well, it's simple—we got tired of being asked the same silly questions by strangers we met on the trail—so we started giving equally silly answers. It's not that we weren't appreciative of peoples' interest in our trip to raise money for the homeless back in Connecticut—we were so thankful to have the support of so many good people—but after a while, some of the questions we were getting (over and over again) were pretty darn exasperating.

Our most popular question was, "How do you know which way you're going?"

Chet and I would usually glance over at each other with raised eyebrows, then politely explain (while pointing to the sky to illustrate our point)—"Now, if you look up, you will notice the Sun moves East to West across the sky. When all else fails, we just follow that." That was the pat answer we gave out for months.

But then one day in Ohio—when the mosquitoes and deer flies were swarming, and probably the 20th person had asked us that same silly question—something came over me, and I spontaneously replied in my best English accent, "I don't know Chet, what do you think?"

Chet looked at me and played along, "I don't know Jeff, what do you think?"

"I'm not sure," I'd say then turn to our new friend, "Why don't you ask us something we do know?"

"Yeah," Chet would parrot, "Why don't you ask us something we do know?"

This exchange (taken directly from a *Monty Python* skit) tended to stop the silly questions in their tracks. We'd usually keep the routine going for about two or three exchanges until our new friends would finally look at us, shake their heads, and leave—which was the desired effect.

There were only two people we met (during the entire trip) that got the reference—the rest thought we were crazier than two betsy bugs. Hell, there may still be some Ohioans out there regaling folks with strange stories about the two disheveled British cowboys who passed through town. Although it still gives me a chuckle, my belated apologies to all those good folks. Chet and I found out the hard way that never-ending boredom can do strange things to your head—really strange.

It can almost make you enjoy Andrew's guitar playing.

Almost.

If you've only driven through The Buckeye State, then you probably don't know about Ohio's impressive stable of attack dogs—but ride through Ohio on a four-legged critter, and you'll encounter quite a few of those two-legged ones running wild. Good thing I had my trusty bodyguard with me, and I don't mean ol' Chet.

As much as we tried to stay on the grey roads, there were times when riding through a city was unavoidable. By the time we were midway through Ohio, we were resigned to having to ride through some residential subdivisions. Many of the homes we passed had fenced backyards and dogs—some of the dogs we met were nice, while others were plain ol' vicious beasts. Chet and I never knew which type we were getting, so we just started calling every dog encounter "NDEs" or "Near-Death Experiences." Which, I admit, may have been a slight exaggeration—but it sure didn't feel like it at the time.

Chet and I kept ourselves on high alert (no sleeping here) as we rode through residential areas because we knew NDEs could happen at any moment. There were times when a charging dog would appear out of nowhere, and within a second, be attacking one of our horse's feet. Chet and I had trained the boys in many emergency situations, but it never occurred to us to train them to fend off an attack dog.

Good thing Thunder already knew how.

I was downright shocked the first time I witnessed a dog trying to attack a horse. I naively assumed that no dog in his right mind would challenge a much bigger animal to a fight. I was wrong about that! Our most thrilling "NDE" (if you could call it that) happened somewhere in central Ohio on Route 18, approaching the town of Findlay.

It was your typical Ohio summer day—hot, flat, humid, and (yes) pretty damn boring—until out of nowhere appeared an extremely large Doberman Pincher who decided he wanted to pick a fight with Thunder. A Doberman versus a Belgian Cross Horse? Doesn't this critter know what a Belgian Cross could do to him with one swift kick? I wasn't worried about my safety, since I was riding Thunder, a two-ton Zeus of a horse (who was over 17 hands tall). But then the Doberman got closer, and I could see he was one pissed off dog that meant business!

"Doberman at two o'clock, boss!" Chet said, "Shoot that son of a bitch!" I looked down at my rifle holstered in my saddle scabbard. Then thought against it, "I can't. He's someone's pet. He came out of that yard!"

I nearly regretted that decision immediately, because, seeing all that slobber flying, it was clear this Doberman had delusions of grandeur.

"Who cares? Plug him!" Chet shouted.

In hindsight, I probably should have plugged him because the crazy critter took a giant leap and latched on to my right leg like it were his last dinner on Earth. Fortunately, Chet and I were wearing chaps so the dog couldn't dig into my flesh. He just slid harmlessly down my leg, "No harm done! Except for the heart palpitations!" I said as the dog fell meekly to the ground.

"Whoa Rebel! Holy crap! Chaps work on dogs?" Chet shouted.

But the crazy dog wasn't done. He thought he'd try another attack. I couldn't believe it, "Is this S.O.B. rabid or just crazy?"

The Doberman circled back and made a second pass at Thunder's legs. Part of me wanted to pull out my Winchester 30-30 and end this game now—but I could tell Thunder had a better ending planned. It was time for my bodyguard to intervene.

"Big boy's done playing games now," I said, just as the dog prepared to launch himself again. Needless to say, the Doberman's second attack was short-lived!

He was met by a swift and devastating kick from a titanium hoof. We marveled as the Doberman was launched several feet backward like some chew toy flying through the air. "Holy shit, Thunder foot!" I yelled out.

"And the Doberman goes down!" Chet yelled.

The crazy Doberman yelped then ran away, shaking his head.

"Atta boy, Thunder!" I patted his neck, "The protector of all men!"

"That bastard'll never cross a Belgian Cross again," Chet howled.

We busted into laughter. Fortunately for the dog, Thunder's kick didn't catch him flush, or he may have been killed.

"That damn dog must have nine lives," I said. "He's lucky he's not dead."

After this run-in, you can be certain we paid a lot more attention to back-yards going forward. I remember just the thought of running into another attack dog served as a cautionary tale for the rest of the trip. Chet didn't even have to repeat the story; he'd look at me and say, "Stay on the grey roads, boss, remember?"

After this incident, I never forgot.

That night, while the team feasted on another batch of Chet's amazing spaghetti in the close confines of the horse trailer—due to a passing thunderstorm—Chet regaled the team with our latest NDE story, which had us in stitches. Good ol' Chet was such a great storyteller; he could turn even the most serious incident into a hilarious tale with real heart and humor. And this was a pretty damn good story, everyone agreed.

Everyone but that crazy Doberman.

By our sixth day in the Ohio cornfields, Chet was so thrilled to be near the Indiana border he could barely keep his damn eyes open. While he snoozed in the saddle, I speculated with Thunder (I had no human to talk to) on what wild encounters might lie ahead in Indiana. I figured we had probably experienced the last of our crazy encounters, but Ohio had one more surprise up its sleeve that would wake us up quickly.

By now, full disclosure, Chet and I had both learned the art of taking cat-naps in the saddle to keep us refreshed and (to) pass the monotonous days—but Chet had just gotten a little better at it than me! I remember on our last day, around late afternoon, which was the time of day when the boys tended to slow down their pace—Chet was catnapping as we moseyed our way through what appeared to be a giant ranch (or farm) that extended in a northwesterly direction for a great distance.

What was this massive land? There was no corn or any newly plowed rows in the fields. No ordinary fence protected it, either—this fence was reinforced—much bigger and stronger than the other fences we passed. My curiosity was piqued. I glanced back at Chet, but he was still sleeping—so I got out my binoculars. A few hundred yards off in the distance, I spied what looked (to me) like a herd of steers—a pretty good-sized one, too. After spying it a while, I figured this must be a working ranch of some kind.

Then, something strange happened.

Thunder's ears started flicking back and forth. He was picking up some new sounds. Then he started snorting, and out of the blue, suddenly picked up his gait. Now we were trotting toward the fence. "What do you see, boy?" I said, patting his neck.

Thunder's eyes were fixed on that herd of steers.

I knew what he was thinking—the leader of our pack, Thunder was always the first one to sense danger—so he was just doing his job and looking out for our safety. I patted his neck to slow him down a little—but Thunder would not stop trotting. I figured our increased pace must have woken Chet from his after-noon siesta because it was around this time that I heard him wake up, "What? Whoaaa! Where's the fire, Reb? Can't take my eyes off you for one minute!"

"He's just following Thunder," I said back at him, "He smells something."

A horse's sense of smell (and hearing) is vastly better than humans, so I knew Thunder felt something wasn't quite right with this ranch—so I let him take a good gander by trotting up closer to the fence.

This spurred the mysterious herd (in the distance) to come running our way, "Ever seen a herd of cows move that fast, boss?" Chet pointed at the oncoming herd, "Why would some cows spook him?" Just then, Thunder slowed his trot and settled into one of his patented Belgian Cross, fast-paced walks. I peered through my binoculars again to get a better look. I rubbed my eyes then looked again.

"Damn, Chet. If that isn't one big ass herd of buffalo."

"Uh. They know the fence is here, right?" Chet was awake now.

"Oh yeah. Unless they're blind," I said, "The American buffalo's a smart animal."

"I'll take your word for that," Chet put on his spectacles for a closer look, "They're huge! And fast! Must be all bulls!" Just then, the curious herd of buffalos emerged from a giant cloud of dust and arrived at the fence line to greet us. Thunder made his way up to the fence to greet the ten bulls that were pressing up against the fence to get a closer look, "They're just curious," Chet said, "Who are all these guys, Rebel?"

Rebel wasn't sure Thunder had the situation under control—the old scaredy-cat was tucked pretty damn tight into Thunders butt. This seemed logical to me since I wasn't sure what the hell was about to happen either!

"Never seen one of these guys before, have you?" I said to Thunder, patting him on the neck, so he knew he was among friends. Thunder greeted each of the ten bulls up close—which meant I was now nose-to-nose with them, too. "Never seen such massive heads in all my life," I said to Chet. Thunder went down the line, smelling them all and snorting intermittently, which I presume was his way of saying, "Howdy." I was so proud of Thunder for handling himself so well. All this time, Chet was transfixed, "This is amazing, boss. What's going to happen next?"

Chet must have read my mind because I was thinking the same thing!

Everything was going great until—Thunder had a sudden change of heart and decided he'd had enough of this encounter! Our fearless leader shocked us all by jumping back and taking a few steps away from the fence. This prompted the buffalo to follow Thunder, west along the fence line. I reckon Thunder didn't want to be followed, because he picked up his pace, and started trotting west. What surprised me was—so did the entire herd of buffalo. When Thunder saw he was being followed, he launched into a massive leap and hit the ground running—already in 5th gear. As we took off, I looked back and saw Chet giving me one of his "What the fuck?" looks as we tore away.

We were in a foot race with the entire herd! The only thought running through my mind was—We're about to find out if a buffalo could outrun a horse. The race is on!

I'm sure Thunder didn't realize there was a fence separating the buffalo from us—because he was running for his damn life. It didn't matter how fast he galloped; he couldn't shake the buffalo, which were running beside us neck-and-neck. I was amazed; these bulls were mammoth, many weighing more than 2,000 pounds, and fast as hell!

I can only imagine what the (few) cars thought as they passed us running away from a stampeding herd. I knew the American buffalo could run up to forty mph, and jump up to six feet high—so I knew the fence could be toppled if they set their minds to it.

Would they?

Were these buffalo really after Thunder?

I looked back, and Chet and Rebel were now running a distant third. I could see Chet had his hat pulled down tight, and was riding like the wind trying to keep up. As we raced west in a mad dash of dust, I spotted another dividing fence up ahead. I knew the herd would slow down before running through the dividing fence—but Thunder didn't know that! So even after the herd began to let off the gas as the dividing fence approached—Thunder continued galloping at full speed. I couldn't get him to stop, or slow down, which was the real shock of the afternoon.

"Whoaaaa! Thun! Whoaaa! You already won the damn race. Slow down!" But he would not stop. I couldn't believe it. Thunder and I were so close—I raised him since he was a colt. I trusted him with my life and thought he felt the same about me. What the hell was happening? I remember trying everything I could to slow him down, but nothing seemed to work. So, I thought of an emergency plan. I had never grabbed his mane before, so I grabbed it as far up his neck as I could and just started pulling and shaking his head to get his attention.

Thunder finally started to slow down. Not because of anything I did, I think his danger meter must have finally told him the coast was clear because—just like that—he came to his sense again, and slowly came to a stop. F.M. I say.

What a helluva ride!

I rolled out of the saddle and sat on the grass next to Thunder, panting almost as hard as he was, "What the hell were you thinking?" Thunder had nothing to say for himself. I looked back, and Chet (and Rebel) were still 75 yards behind us; I could see Reb had stopped running once Thunder did. As I sat on the ground, I remember hearing Chet shout—"I don't remember training for this, Boss!"

This would be the only time in our lifelong partnership that Thunder ever resembled a runaway horse.

When Chet and Rebel finally caught up, all four of us just stood there catching our breaths, trying to make sense of what just happened.

"Must have run with those bulls for 300 yards!" I shouted.

"Thun sure got his exercise for the day! You old scaredy-cat!" Chet busted out laughing. Then, a few minutes later, once the laughter died down, something compelled Chet and me to glance over at the road just as this large semi tractor-trailer passed by. I read the large letters on the side of the truck; it read: "Batesville Casket Company."

"Will you look at that?" I marveled, "Almost needed one of those, pard!"

Chet put on his glasses to get a good look, "Well, goddamn, take down the number, boss. We may need an undertaker yet!"

Chet and I busted a gut laughing.

"Was that a sign from our guardian angels?" I asked him.

"Nah. I'd say it's a sign from the horse gods."

"Horse gods?"

"Yep, the horse gods look out for the boys," Chet said, "And us."

Chet may have been kidding back in Ohio, but for some reason, that struck me as a profound statement. Now, all these years later—after riding horses my entire life, I reckon ol' Chet was right. The Horse Gods—they're real.

FM, I say.

The next morning around a fresh pot of Chet's cowboy coffee—the team's excitement level was sky-high. Border crossings always seemed to conjure a sense of wonder in most of the team (OK, probably not Andrew), which was part of that wonderful feeling of mystery that followed us the entire trip. No one knew what tomorrow would bring. And that was a great feeling. With everyone happy for the first time all week—Chet and I finally arrived at State Route 24, and rode it for about ten miles, until we crossed into Fort Wayne, Indiana. Adios Ohio!

Don't get me wrong, Buckeyes, I still love your state—but I doubt we'll be passing through on horse again. I attended college in Ohio, I met my beloved wife Sue in Ohio, and I enjoy visiting her family, most of who all (yes) still live in Ohio. But for a so-called boring state, you sure did surprise us with a few moments of high adventure. I think ol' Chet rather enjoyed the excitement—what he was awake for—but being an expecting father (and future family man), I think I've have had enough of this kind of "crazy" to last me a while.

"What are the odds, the weird is behind us?" I asked Chet.

Chet smiled, "I'd say zero percent. It's a weird country all over."

"Well. I do know one thing," I said.

"What's that, boss?"

"Our journey to the Pacific just got one state closer—" I finished that sentence in my head, "—*and one step closer to Sue.*"

But, I kept that last part to myself!

⋆ 6 ⋆

KNEE HIGH BY THE 4TH OF JULY

"Desperado. Why don't you come to your senses?
Come down from your fences; open the gate
It may be rainin', but there's a rainbow
above you. You better let somebody
love you, before it's too late."
—*The Eagles*

WE HAD TURNED another page on our journey West.

Our faithful maps told us the city of Fort Wayne was out there *somewhere* just off the cool morning horizon; Chet and I had to take their word for it. We saw no signs of life in any direction. The only visual evidence that told us we were in "Hoosier Country" was the sea of bright green and yellow that had supplanted the dark green pastures of Ohio. Freshly planted rows of corn, the staple of the United States agricultural universe, was as far as any eye could see. The only thing resembling a human in sight for miles was a skinny silhouette of a distant scarecrow. *We were out in it now.*

"Reckon' we're knee deep in the proverbial 'Rust Belt," Chet observed.

"Reckon you're right," I said. "Guess we'll be knee-high by the Fourth of July."

"Say again?" Chet said.

"That's farmer-speak, learned it from the Almanac. Means this year's crop's lookin' just fine."

"Closer to shin high, if you ask me," Chet grumbled.

We rode by endless rows of corn, which I suppose, were a bit punier than Chet had imagined.

"Patience young grasshopper," I said playfully. "What month is it?"

"Summer," Chet said.

"Gotta get you a calendar." I chuckled.

"It's all up here," he said, pointing to his head.

I knew Chet was playing dumb. We had nothing else to do with our time but talk about life, enjoy the beauty of our surroundings, and count the days of our journey.

Today was June 15th, 1986. Day 42, that much we knew.

As for exactly where we were in Indiana, no one rightly knew. All that mattered was we were in Hoosier Country now. The air around us even smelled different. We didn't pay the change in the environment much mind though—we just kept clopping ahead to the beat of our own steady drum.

Chet and I started talking about the bustling metropolis that was purportedly in front of us like it was Chicago or New York, which Fort Wayne sure as heck wasn't. But it had been quite a while since either of us had seen hide or hair of any signs of modern civilization. So, to us, a city of any size was a semi-event.

"You call ahead?" Chet said.

"Why would I do somethin' like that?"

"Hopin' a few long-legged members of the welcomin' committee's got a few cold ones lined up for us."

"Guess you're just gonna have to find out."

"Don't toy with my emotions, boss," Chet said with a chuckle.

"What are the odds a Hoosier gal would have any interest in an outlaw like you?" I said, ribbing him.

"A man can dream, can't he?" Chet said. "I'm so thirsty; I'd be happy with the cold one served to me in a gnarly old boot."

"That I can arrange," I said.

We got closer to the outskirts of town and pulled Thunder and Rebel off the road for a well-deserved morning breather. The boys were thirsty, and apparently so was Chet, for "wine and women," the way he was talking. He was practically licking his chops as we drank coffee and scoured the maps on the hood of the Bronco.

"Shoulda brought a map that listed all the saloons in town."

"We'll get you filled up. But first thing's first. We gotta suss us out a good route through town. Don't think we can go around this un."

"Boys may get spooked if we take em' through the city," Chet said, squinting his eyes into the morning sun. "There has to be a safer way."

We sipped coffee and examined our maps for a spell. Then as "F.M." would have it, I noticed a black and white Fort Wayne Police Cruiser parked at the gas station right across the road.

"Sue says I'm stubborn as a mule about askin' for directions."

"Join the club," Chet said, never looking up from the map.

"Maybe I'll take her advice, this time," I pointed at the police cruiser.

Chet looked up and spied the cruiser. "You go on ahead. They're bound to lock me up, the way I cuss."

I moseyed across the street and introduced myself to the officer. We shook hands.

"Howdy Officer," I said. "My wife says I never ask for directions, so I'm tryin' to turn over a new leaf."

"Well, howdy. You boys lost?" the Officer said.

"Reckon you might know the safest route through town. For our boys, I mean," I pointed to Thunder and Rebel and Sonny and Big Red in the trailer.

As it turned out, Officer Terry had read about us in the newspaper. "I tell you what. How about if I come find you a little further down the road and give you the skinny on the best route to take. How's that sound?"

"Mighty hospitable of you," I said.

"That's how we do it around here," he said. "Besides, you fellas are ridin' for a good cause. Okay then, I'll be catchin' up with ya."

Chet and I approached the outskirts of Fort Wayne a few hours later, and as promised, Officer Terry found us on the road. He stuck his smiling head out the window of his cruiser, "Good news; we talked it over, and you're gettin' a police escort clear through town. How you like them apples?"

"Well. We like them apples just fine if it ain't too much trouble," I said.

"It's the least we could do," Terry said. He explained the Fort Wayne Police Department appreciated our efforts to help the homeless so much that they even enlisted the Indiana State Police to ride along with us too.

"Now that's what I call rollin' out the red carpet," Chet said.

Officer Terry said we'd get an escort until we hit Route 24, which would take us clear across the state to the Illinois border.

"You're not gonna' arrest us if we stop off for a beer, will ya?" Chet asked the officer.

"Heck no, just don't drink and ride!" Officer Terry said. "I'd knock back one with ya' if I wasn't on duty."

"Maybe we'll catch you on the way back," I said with a laugh. "Give our thanks to everyone down at the station," I said.

"Will do," he said. "Now y'all don't let us slow down your routine. We'll be here if you have any questions about our beautiful town."

And off Officer Terry drove in his cruiser—just ahead of us.

I looked at Chet, "Well, that's one less thing to worry about.

"I guess," Chet said dryly. "Hope they don't run my license plate." Chet was never a huge fan of the police, after having a few scrapes with them in his formative years.

"Good thing our four-legged friends don't need one. Better be on your best behavior," I said, "Hadn't had a police escort since we left the Hartford State Capitol."

"I'll try not to rob a bank in the next few hours," Chet said.

By now, our unit was pretty road-hardened, so we didn't get too excited about the whole thing—but we sure were grateful not to have to navigate the city streets of Fort Wayne on horseback.

When we finally ambled the boys into town, you should have seen all the heads turn. To these folks, Chet and I probably looked like a couple of lost stuntmen from an old Western, because all eyes were curiously on us. People everywhere stopped to watch our procession of cowboys on horseback who (strangely) was important enough to have a police escort. "Who the heck were we?'

Shoot, we got that question about one hundred times in the few hours we were passing through town. Pedestrians and cars a-like stopped us to inquire.

"What may I ask is all this commotion about?" One red-headed woman asked from her car window.

Chet looked down from the saddle and said, "Well, ma'am, we can't find the rodeo. You know where it is?" Chet replied with a wink.

You hear of Hoosier Hospitality—well, it's true. Everyone was so dang polite. We talked to all kinds of people that day: children, old folks, girls of all sizes and persuasions, and lots and lots of men in suits.

A few even asked for our autographs—for their kids, of course.

We felt really special as we rode down Main Street then zigzagged through the other major thoroughfares of Fort Wayne. Ol' Rebel and Thunder handled the situation like the champs they were. They took in the scene with their ears constantly pointed forward, which indicated they were on alert and interested in what was happening.

There was so much new stimulus for them; I could tell by their demeanor that they were just as curious as the city folk were about what was happening. Sure, the boys were used to people stopping to talk to us (they did participate in the spectacle that was Hands Across America after all), but not among all these tall buildings. Not among all these loud city street noises and certainly not among the hundreds of people trying to get close to them. It was turning into quite a scene.

"I love a parade," Chet said.

"We're it pard," I said.

"Must think we're the real Butch and Sundance. Don't you start gettin' a big head," Chet said, patting Rebel on his neck. "You ol' turd." Rebel just snorted and shook his head.

A procession of cruisers took turns riding with us. Every so often, one would replace another. "Think we're the cush assignment for the day," Chet said.

Every time an officer peeled off the route to leave—they'd give us a wave, and we'd tip our hats to say thanks.

It sure felt great.

"This is the way the world's supposed to be," I said to Chet.

"Awww. It's just a slow crime day," Chet said.

Maybe Chet was right, but I like to believe that what I felt that day was true; there was a genuine feeling of wanting to help us get to the Pacific in the air.

It sure warmed this old cowboy's heart.

Looking at the response we were getting from people, I think we helped a few others vicariously live out their childhood dreams through us. What red-blooded American boy didn't want to be a cowboy when they were a kid?

I can't thank the Fort Wayne Police for the critical role they played in helping us get through town safely. They sure were hospitable folks who lived up to their reputation for kindness.

It was one of the best moments of the trip if you ask me.

Riding through downtown, we made our way to the southwestern outskirts of the city, where a whole city block of six-story glass office buildings came into view.

"I got an idea," I said.

"That's usually bad news," Chet said.

I signaled to Chet to ride up alongside me. We slowed down and waited for Dave and Andrew to catch up.

"What are you two plotting over here?" Dave said, pulling up beside us in the rig.

"Dave, we meet you in a few blocks," I said. "Chet and I are gonna take a little detour."

Chet looked at me quizzically; he wasn't sure what I was up to. I gave Thunder a quick squeeze of his flanks, and he bolted across the street onto the sidewalk in front of the glass buildings; Chet and Rebel followed suit.

We rode right in front of the office windows so that we couldn't be missed. Thunder peered into the buildings and preened for all the gawkers in their offices. I looked back at Chet and gave him a "time to have a little fun" look.

When we got to the middle of the block, Chet and I gave Rebel and Thunder a left rein tug. Now we were directly facing the office windows—two horses and riders staring down a bunch of businessmen sitting at their executive desks!

"Take a bow, boys!" Chet hollered. Chet and I couldn't stop smiling. I couldn't tell for sure, but I think the boys were smiling too.

The windows in the glass buildings started to fill with office workers. We were causing quite a stir without doing anything but just being there. People were pointing at us, trying to figure out what the heck was going on. Ol' Chet looked like a ripe old outlaw with his hat pulled down over his forehead. God knows what I looked like, but considering I was atop a 17 plus hand beast of a Belgian Cross draft horse—I probably cut a formidable swath.

There was nothing to be said. I looked at Chet, "Well. God damn."

"God damn is right," Chet said back.

"Glad we're on this side of that glass," I said.

"You sure said somethin' there."

We took a moment to reflect on the journey we were on. "Can you believe, just a few months ago, we were the men trapped in the office? Now here we are, living a different life," I said.

"Just a thin pane of glass separates us from them. But we're miles away, boss. That's freedom." Chet said.

"Wouldn't change a thing, Hoss."

"Neither would I."

We tipped our caps to all the onlookers then kept on moving. We ambled down the sidewalk and turned the corner. When we saw Dave and Andrew in the rig a few blocks away—I looked at Chet, and we busted out laughing.

"You two showboats!" Andrew said.

"Can't believe we just did that," Chet said.

"The looks on those office workers' faces were priceless!" I said.

The memory of it still makes me laugh to this day.

The outfit was energized after all that showing off. Even the boys had their heads held a little higher as they pranced along like a couple of show ponies. "Stop prancing Rebel—you ain't on stage anymore," Chet said playfully.

We didn't say a lot about getting the royal treatment after Fort Wayne disappeared in the distance. The small Midwestern city faded into our memories, just like every other town had behind us.

We kept plugging along.

You may not know this, but in the Midwest in the 1980s, there was no such thing as "the suburbs." Once you passed through a city like Fort Wayne, the rugged and real America that bewitched our ancestors was right back on you, always there to greet you like a rustic reminder of the past.

The ever-present cornfields, the grain silos and their mills, the dairy farms, and their pastures full of cows—and the straight-ahead railroad tracks became our default landscape once again.

It may be of little importance to the folks zooming by us on the back roads—but the team had several creative uses for the thousands of cornfields we passed through. They often served as shade, shelter, or a pretty darn good place to hide as the corn grew taller and taller. We even camped in a few. Don't tell anyone, but the fields also served as our own public restroom. More than a few times, I ended up squatting in a cornfield out of public view after Chet regretfully forgot to scrape the slime off some of our several-day-old meat he used in his stews and sauces.

"Knee-high by the Fourth of July!" Chet shouted as I ran into a cornfield to do my business.

"Where's Jeff goin'?" Andrew said as the rig pulled up beside Chet.

"He's going to see a man about a dog! Bend those knees when you're squattin'! The corn ain't gonna hide you!"

"You gotta start buying better meat!" I yelled as I ducked under the corn then pulled off my hat—hoping a passerby wouldn't see my old Stetson perched atop the sea of yellow.

"I need a bigger food budget!" Chet yelled back.

"Stop botherin' me!"

"You look like a wobblin' scarecrow out there!"

Ol' Chet thought that escapade was pretty darn funny.

But I survived. By the time we reached western Iowa and eastern Nebraska, the corn would be so high—we could all keep our hats on when we needed to duck in for a pit stop.

On this day, after the cornfield gave me some momentary relief, I climbed back into the saddle. My stomach felt better, but I felt a noticeable sinking in my heart. It was on this hot and humid Indiana afternoon as we plodded down state Route 24 that I officially got to missin' Sue something fierce. A minute never went by that I wasn't thinking of her, our unborn baby, and our happy home—but sometimes with nothing but your thoughts to keep you company, the melancholy hits you.

This time it did just that—like a sledgehammer to my achin' heart.

I was starting to realize how much I relied on sweet Sue for my happiness in life. She was truly the "light of my life" and "the fire of my loins." I was beginning to understand how those Apollo astronauts felt who got lost in space. I reckon the worst part of their journey was not knowing whether they'd ever see their wives again.

My heart sure did hurt.

I needed to hear her voice, but I knew that wasn't happening anytime soon.

Out here in rural America—opportunities to "phone home" were few and far between—and predicated on luck. You couldn't find one on any map. So Chet and I were as happy as two little kids finding an Easter egg full of chocolates whenever we were lucky enough to spot one in the distance. Usually, four to six days would go by in between sightings—but we never missed an opportunity to pull over and call our ladies.

Then we'd call into Brad Davis' radio show on WDRC in Hartford to update him on the trip. We were trying to raise a hundred thousand dollars for the homeless in Connecticut, so we needed to keep his listeners tuned into our journey.

Today. We saw nothing—so onward we rode.

I kept my eyes peeled for a day and a half—still no luck.

I was getting mighty restless. Then it happened. I found our "Easter egg" in the back of a small-town convenience store—next to a sign that said "Free Air."

"Never thought I'd be so happy to see a sign that said, 'Free Air,'" I said.

"You go on ahead first," Chet said as we both swung out of the saddle. "Know you're itchin' to be all lovey-dovey."

He didn't have to say it twice.

I made a beeline to the phone while Chet stayed with the boys.

"Tell Sue I said to send food—brownies and bourbon, preferably," Chet said.

"Will do partner," I could barely contain my excitement, even after all these years of marriage I still had butterflies percolating in my stomach at just the thought of being able to hear her voice.

I called the operator and made a collect call home, as usual.

While the phone rang, I wondered how she was feeling. She was in her third month of pregnancy, and I'd been gone for almost two of them. Would she ever forgive me?

Fortunately, Sue was home. I heard her familiar voice chime in. "Yes, I will accept the collect call."

"Can you hear me?" I said.

"Look what the cat dragged in."

"Hey, honey."

"Hey yourself."

"How's the sexiest woman alive?"

"Oh. Just barefoot and pregnant—beatin' my suitors off with a stick till you get home and claim me forever."

"Do I need to send a posse to guard the henhouse while I'm gone?"

"You might. Better hurry home, putting on weight pretty fast."

"Bet you're glowing."

"That's one way of putting it," she said.

I underestimated how much I missed her, but it all came rushing back when I heard her voice.

"Ain't no sunshine when he's gone," she said. "Guess I'll have to go to sleep with J.R. Ewing again tonight. I moved the kitchen TV into the bedroom."

"Thought you'd be more of a Bobby Ewing sort of gal," I said and laughed.

I focused our conversation on how she was feeling and what the doctor was saying about the baby—as well as what her days were like.

"Can't put into words how much I miss you," I said.

"How do you think I feel? You know how hard it is to tell people that my husband ran off with a horse?"

We both laughed. She was joking, I think.

I didn't spend much time explaining what Chet and I were going through. It was more important to keep our close marital ties going as best we could over the phone.

"Think you'll still find me attractive if the conquering hero ever returns?"

"Baby, you know I can't get enough of your sweet cheeks, no matter how big they get."

"Bet you say that to all your girlfriends," she said.

"Oh yeah," I looked around at the miles of empty cornfields around me, "Just look at all of 'em."

I was so lost in lovebird talk I didn't notice a vehicle had pulled up next to the phone booth. I could hear the engine running, so I turned around to look and lo and behold, this was no ordinary car. It was black and white—but it wasn't Officer Terry. This was a different officer entirely. He glared at me, then got out of his cruiser and walked over and stood next to me, arms crossed. I didn't know quite what to make of it, so I turned back to the payphone.

"Got some strange goings-on here."

"One of the locals flirtin' with Thunder?"

"We've drawn the attention of the local constable."

"Better hide, Chet."

I looked back. Now the frowning officer was giving our outfit the once over.

"Too late. Better go. The law's givin' us the evil eye.

"Love em and leave me, that's what I always say. Okay then." Sue said with a sigh.

"Call you again soon. Love you. Stay strong."

"Love you too," Sue said. "Don't let Chet get you arrested."

"I'll try. Can't wait to be back in your lovin' arms, darlin'."

"Promises, promises. You owe me one."

"I do. And you're gonna get it when I get home. Bye now."

"Okay, bye."

I hung up with a pang in my heart. I took a deep breath to keep my emotions at bay and exited the dusty phone booth.

My head was full of Sue, but that fantasy was soon erased. One foot out the door; there I was, face-to-face with an officer of the law who was downright ornery. I remember thinking, I hope Chet hadn't already pissed him off.

"Can I see your driver's license?" he blurted.

I smiled; I couldn't help it—but by the look on his face, I could tell the strangeness of the request didn't strike him as humorous.

"You want my driver's license or—my horse operating license?" I tried to lighten the mood.

"Not going to ask you again, your driver's license."

I pointed to Rebel, Thunder, and Chet, "Well, okay then—but my license won't account for them."

He asked me again for my driver's license.

Had he seen me illegally squatting in some cornfield? I was perplexed.

"Keep it in my saddlebag, can I go get it?" We walked over to Thunder, and I showed it to him. "This here officer wants to see my driver's license," I said to Chet, who gave me a strange look. He smartly kept his yap shut.

"I want to see yours, too," the officer said to Chet.

"Reckon' mines with Dave in our rig," Chet said calmly. "He's probably several miles up scoutin' a place for us to camp."

"So, you don't have yours?"

"Haven't needed it out here," Chet said.

"Can you tell us what this is about?" I flipped a look at Chet.

"Seems there's been a break-in at a private residence. Someone called it in with a description of two riders on horseback as the perpetrators. "

It took me a few seconds to process what he said, "You tryin' to tell me the burglars were on horseback?"

"That's the report."

"You don't see that every day," Chet said.

"No, you don't," the officer said.

"And you think we're the ones who did it?" I asked incredulously.

"I don't see any other horses around here. Think I'm going to have to take y;all downtown to answer some questions."

"This is the craziest thing I've ever heard," I said. "With all due respect, there's no way we robbed anybody."

I pointed to my license and explained we were from Connecticut and riding our horses across the country for charity. "You can't be stoppin' our progress here."

I could tell the officer didn't believe a word of my story, other than being from Connecticut. "Well, we'll just have to see about that," he said, which raised my blood pressure. I cut my call short with Sue to listen to this load of bull? Chet could see I was getting pissed, so he tied Rebel off and walked over to us.

"What exactly do you plan on doin' with our horses if you take us down?" I asked.

"They'll make a helluva mess of your jail cell," Chet said with a sly smile.

"We can't leave em unattended while you cuff us and stuff us, so we better figure out how to settle this here and now."

I tried to inject some rationality; I could tell this officer wasn't the sharpest tool in the shed. "Officer, if we burgled, where is all the stuff we stole? Search us!"

Chet chimed in, "We got nothing on us but two canteens and a tube of chapstick." He said, holding up his ChapStick.

"Look. We understand you have a job to do here. We support the blue; we even got a police escort through Fort Wayne two days ago," I said. "Perhaps you should call them to verify we're telling the truth here?"

"Police escort, huh?" He said skeptically, then clucked like a chicken.

"Hey," I said. "I don't like being accused of being a liar or a thief. You might want to get your commanding officer on the blower before you say something you're going to regret."

The officer got real quiet. We locked eyes; for a moment, I thought the entire trip could blow up in our faces. I looked over at Chet. I sure as shit knew he wasn't going down downtown without a fight.

This could get very ugly.

After a tense moment, the officer shook his head, "Alright. I'll call it in."

While he called it in, Chet and I agreed we weren't going down to any police station. When the officer got out of his cruiser, I could tell by his body language he didn't want any part of Chet and me or Thunder and Rebel.

"Spoke with my supervisor, and you are free to go. But I'll be watching you!"

I don't know what the heck he meant by that; he obviously didn't realize Indiana is flat as a pancake. Chet and I had no opportunities to hide out in the mountains!

But I let it go. We didn't say another word to him. We just swung back into the saddle and watched the cruiser pull away and fade out down the road.

"Man. This state is full of cops," Chet said. "Don't think I'll be moving here."

I looked at Chet, "Were you ready to rumble Hoss? Cause I was."

Chet cracked a smile under that thick mustache of his, "God damn right I was."

We rode past farm after farm, cornfield after cornfield, through a never-ending progression of checkerboard squares.

"Wonder if the entire Midwest's like this?" I wondered aloud.

"Riveting," Chet muttered. "Long-lasting stimulus, this ain't."

Looking back, I reckon ol' Chet and I didn't say a whole heck of a lot to each other as we trudged our way through the Midwestern territories. The monotony, the heat, and the humidity had shut us up good. Guess we both realized we were a long way from home and nowhere close to being where we wanted to be. With no end in sight, all we could do was keep our heads down and tough it out.

We kept close tabs on each other's disposition, careful not to intrude on each other when we were deep in thought. It was critical for Chet and me to be able to pull each other out of any moods that might make us lose sight of where we were. If we took our eyes off the prize, we could run ourselves into a helluva dangerous situation, real quick.

When one of us was having a "bad hair day," the other would pick him up. Sometimes we'd talk about what the "regular people" were doing with their day.

"Everyone back home ain't doin' any better than us," I'd say. "Here, we are doing what we love most. What do we have to complain about?"

That dose of relativity usually did the trick.

Usually. ˙

When that didn't work, and the guilt of leaving Sue weighed heavy on my conscience, Chet always found ways to keep things light. Finding humor in everyday happenings kept us loose—which was essential since what we were doing wasn't easy!

Hell, the longer we rode, even ol' Chet started to reveal more of his "internal life" to me, which was surprising—since he was always such a fun-loving guy, I didn't know he had a lot of deep thoughts. But he did.

I remember at one point, as we clopped along in a sea of Indiana green and yellow—he confessed that he wasn't sure if his relationship with Diane was going to end or lead to marriage.

"You just gotta follow your heart," I said.

"That usually ain't my best compass. There's a reason I'm not married. Don't tend to pick the right ones. Guess I'm just not lucky in love."

"Maybe you just haven't met Miss Right yet?" I said.

"That's the problem."

"Well, don't settle. When you know, you'll know."

"You mean like love at first sight?" Chet said.

"That's what happened with me and Sue. I knew she was the one."

"Like a lightning bolt, huh?"

"Something like that. Maybe the pounding of hoofs will reveal some answers to you, pard," I said. "Horses have a way of curing a man's problem. Just ask Louis L'Amour."

"This comin' from a man whose wife just scolded him for running away with a horse," Chet said, which made us both laugh.

Laughter sure is the best medicine. Our load was lightened once again, and we kept on trucking.

As fate would have it, "FM" would throw us another curveball somewhere just outside of a little town called Wabash. Maybe we conjured it from the heavens, but this time "FM" came in the form of a Cupid arrow. Who would have known that "love among the corn" was a possibility, but it nearly stopped us in our tracks. By now, we had become quite accustomed to folks waving at us from cars or pulling over to shake our hands and ask us questions about the trip. Since we'd attracted our fair share of media attention in newspapers and on TV, we started to welcome those encounters with open arms. We hadn't gotten all big-headed or anything. In fact, we didn't much care for the limelight—but the attention broke up the monotony of getting to the Pacific Ocean at three miles per hour. Our days had become so uneventful—we started napping in the saddle in the heat of the late afternoon. During one of our catnaps, something told me to check in on the trail—good thing I did. When I cracked an eye open, a red pickup truck pulled off the road right in front of us. The flash of red caught my eye, but what caught it, even more, was what appeared from the truck.

It was a damn fine-looking cowgirl walking our way.

Was I dreaming?

"Think fast, Hoss," I nudged Chet awake. "We got company." I nodded at the vision ahead. Chet sat up and set his eyes on the "looker" at twelve o'clock, as the old cowboys would say. I knew this Midwestern siren was nothing but trouble the second I laid eyes on her. We hadn't trained for this.

As she got closer, I admired the "roll in her brim" and tipped my hat.

I looked at Chet. I could tell he was admiring more than that.

"Where y'all headed?" she asked in one of those sweet Midwestern accents that'll melt a man's heart if you're not careful.

Chet, never at a loss for words, turned on the charm and filled her in. She said her name was Jean, and she owned a farm ten miles up the road. She offered to put us up for the evening, make us dinner and let us use her barn for our horses.

"Mighty kind of ya," Chet said, speaking for both of us. "Think we just won the lottery."

"Maybe you have, cowboy," Jean said. Sparks were flying.

"Guess we can't say no to that," Chet said.

"Guess you can't," she said.

I just nodded and watched the chemistry between the two unfold.

Jean gave us directions, and we visited with her a few more minutes—then we watched her drive off in her pickup—and kept on moving.

"Wow. Where you think she came from?" I asked rhetorically.

"Dunno," Chet said. "But I've been dreamin' of her for weeks. Nothing better than a pretty cowgirl in a pickup."

"Easy now," I said.

"Shit. I've been takin' it easy, boss—I was sleepin' in the god danged saddle drooling on myself before she dropped out of the sky," Chet said.

"Remember, you got a fiancé back home," I said, knowing that probably didn't mean a damn thing to him.

"Oh yeah, I know," Chet said. "But is she that Miss Right you were talking about? Not so sure."

We finally arrived at Jean's farm around sundown. We were grateful the boys would have a roof over their heads and their own stall for a night.

Chet and I quickly unsaddled by the barn. The smell of something quite tasty was drifting from the farmhouse.

Jean and her roommate Beth came out to say hello. Jean introduced Beth to us. We all tipped our caps.

"Just in time for the dinner bell," Jean said.

"You don't have to ring it twice," Chet said.

"Well, giddy up then," Jean said, then swung her dishtowel over her shoulder and sauntered back in the house with Beth.

Chet elbowed me in the ribs, "There's two of 'em, boss."

"You can have 'em both. I'm hopelessly devoted."

"Pinch me already, this must be cowboy heaven," Chet said.

"Don't forget, we got a job to do, Hoss."

"Don't worry," he said.

Chet wasn't worried. But I was.

Ol' Cupid's arrows kept flying across the dinner table. The conversation never lagged as we filled each other in on our jobs and our lives.

I apologized for the "ripeness" of our clothes. I couldn't remember the last time we had showered, but it had been more than a week. Jean insisted that we get cleaned up after dinner.

"Hope you got a large water tank for us," I said and pointed to Andrew and Dave, who looked like two dirty urchins wolfing down their food.

"Oh, we got hot runnin' water, soap, and everything," she said with a big smile.

After several second helpings of Jean's special meatloaf and endless "thank yous," it was time to do the dishes. Chet and I volunteered. Dave and Andrew would check on the boys then grab their showers first. I never thought washing dishes could be this much fun, but Beth, Jean, Chet, and I kept the dinner conversation going over the kitchen's double sink. The "kismet" between Jean and Chet continued. They couldn't stop smiling at each other.

After the dishes were cleaned and dried—I went looking for the shower. Jean's farmhouse had a real rustic charm to it; it sure felt homey and warm. The kindness coming from our new friends sure was genuine.

I ambled up a steep, twisting staircase, passed by two bedrooms and found the bathroom. The wood floors in Jean's old farmhouse creaked under my boots. No sneaking around the second floor in this place!

Once we knocked the top layer of dirt off our hides, Chet and I put on our cleanest dirty shirts. "Y'all clean up pretty darn well, I must say," Jean said when we reemerged less filthy than we had been in a coon's age.

"You boys interested in grabbing a few beers in town?" Beth asked.

Uh oh.

"You must've read my mind," Chet said.

"I don't know," I said.

"Then it's settled," said Beth.

"I'm drivin'!" Jean said.

"You comin'?" Beth asked me.

"I'm pretty bushed. It's a school night for us," I said, trying to exercise caution.

"Oh, come on, you're not that old!" Beth said.

"Alright. Just one or two," I said.

Trouble was a-brewin'. In more ways than one.

We left Andrew and Dave behind to watch the boys, and the four of us piled into Jean's red pickup truck. As we drove away, I wondered, "How is this escapade going to end?" We were about to find out.

The local watering hole was tiny with a distinct smell of stale beer and musty weathered wood. I found the jukebox and put on some Hank Williams. The bar was barely half-full, it being a weeknight. "A great jukebox always makes an old bar come alive, don't it?" I said as I sat down at the table and ol' Hank started warbling.

"You said it," Jean said.

We all talked and laughed as the second and third round of beers came and went. I watched Chet and Jean get real cozy while boot scootin' around the small, worn-outt dance floor that covered in sawdust and old peanut shells.

The suds flowed through the night. I could see everyone was having a little "too much fun," so I thought ahead and started nursing my beer. I didn't want to lose my bearings as we had an early day in front of us.

Once it officially started to get late, my internal alarm clock started buzzing. I sidled my way over to Chet and Jean, who were slow-dancing to George

Strait. I stopped to take in the scene. Man, I hadn't seen Chet look this happy in . . . I couldn't remember when. Maybe never?

I didn't have the heart to interrupt them, so I let them finish their dance. But my romantic nature only went so far. When they moved back to the table, I ambushed them, "Hate to be a party pooper, but I think it's time we moved the party back to Jean's."

As you know, Chet and I were best friends—but we didn't always agree on things. This would be one of those times.

"Aw, c'mon boss, we hadn't had a lick of fun in months."

"Tomorrow's gonna come real fast if we don't get some winks," I said.

"Come on, Dad! We want to party," Beth said.

"Jean, you wanna call it?" Chet asked.

"Never," Jean said, "Dance with me, Chet, or lose me forever." She grabbed Chet and continued their "party of two" on the five-by-seven dance floor.

I was outnumbered.

Chet and Jean had a few more beers and a few more dances.

Beth was a bit tipsy and starting to circle my table. She sat down beside me, "I guess you really are married."

"Yep."

"Happily? I suppose."

"Very. Even got a little one on the way, or my wife Sue does," I said.

"I just got one question. Shouldn't you be with your pregnant wife who you love so much—and not out riding fences?" Beth said with a smile.

The feelings of guilt came rushing back. "That is the eternal question I've been asking myself the past two months."

"She must be a special lady," Beth said.

"She sure is. She sure is."

When the clock struck midnight—I knew by the look in Chet's eye, he was falling hard. I was the soberest of the bunch, so I started to round up the gang. I paid our tab; luckily, beers were only a buck, so the tab was pretty small.

It was like herding cats getting everyone into Jean's truck.

I took the wheel. You could barely jam three people in the cab, so Jean conveniently ended up on Chet's lap.

Beth gave me directions back to Jean's. Jean popped in an Eagles tape, and everyone sang "Desperado" the whole way home.

I couldn't stop thinking about Sue.

When we got back to Jean's, the four of us laughed some more while visiting in her small living room. Then someone had to break up the party, so the old married guy finally chimed in, "Okay, okay, I reckon it's time we all turned in."

"Exactly what do you have in mind?" Beth asked suggestively, which elicited laughs from the room.

"We really do have to get an early start. How about I grab the couch?"

This was a signal to Chet it was time to turn in, but he blew past my warning flag going 80 miles an hour. Beth knew she had no chance with me, so she announced she was heading to bed, much to my relief.

Chet and Jean had no such intention, "Jean and I are gonna catch some late evening air and check on the boys," Chet said with a coy smile, "See you in the A.M. pard." They walked out onto the front porch hand in hand while I muttered my displeasure then grabbed some sack time. This old cowboy really was bushed. I barely got my boots off before I drifted into a deep slumber.

I opened my eyes the next morning to a sliver of sun beaming in through a crack in the curtains. I sat up and rubbed my eyes. Where the heck was Chet? I looked around the living room. He hadn't slept downstairs, that much was evident. I crawled out of my makeshift scratcher and went outside and roused Dave and Andrew, who were snoozing away in the barn. I asked Dave to put on a pot of strong cowboy coffee to get us all going. "Where's Chet?" Dave asked—barely awake.

"He get lucky?" Andrew said, "Jean's hot."

They were both good questions, but I pretended not to hear them. I turned around and walked back to the house. I knew where Chet was—upstairs, so I walked up the steep, creaky staircase to use the bathroom and get cleaned up.

I passed by Beth's room and saw her sleeping through her half-open door. Had she left that door half-cracked for me just in case I had a change of heart? I didn't want to entertain the notion, so I kept walking to the second bedroom door.

This one was closed.

I had my answer.

To announce the new day, I made a point of making some noise, hoping Chet would stir. Jean's creaky old farmhouse came in handy. When my boots hit those planks, it sure did the trick. I figured I'd give Chet about thirty minutes, then I'd go retrieve him if he wasn't up.

I went out to the barn to feed and saddle the boys. They looked refreshed and ready to go. I brought Thunder and Rebel out of the barn and tied them off to the trailer.

A few minutes later, Chet came out of the screen door and slow-stepped his way over to me. I hadn't seen him without his hat on in quite a while.

"You look like you got rode hard and put up wet!" Andrew cackled.

"Better get a brim back on that bed head, Hoss," I said with a chuckle.

"Ooh. Didn't get much sleep last night," Chet said and beat his chest comically.

"We guessed as much," I said, then we all broke out in laughter. All I could do was shake my head.

"What I wouldn't give for a camera to capture this moment," I said.

"Best you didn't. I'd have to destroy the evidence."

"Ready to hit the road?"

Chet got real quiet.

"Uh oh," I said.

"Well boss, it's like this"

"Don't even!"

"C'mon. I really like her. I think she could be 'the one.'"

"After one night?"

"I saw fireworks."

"So. What are you sayin', hoss?"

"It's just, Jean and I were talking."

"You're scarin' me pard."

Chet stammered, "She'd like to come with us."

"Jeessssusss, Chet."

"Well? What do you think?"

I had to look away for a few seconds to collect my emotions. "Have you thought this through? Cross America '86 is you, me, and our four-legged boys. No women were invited for a reason."

"What reason's that?"

"Are you kidding me? They're a distraction!"

"Well, yeah. But in a good way! Beats cat nappin' in the saddle."

"So much shit could go wrong, you don't even know this woman!" I said.

"I know enough," he said. "I feel like I know her. Or maybe I did in a past life."

"Past life?"

"She believes in soul mates," Chet said.

"Are you listening to how flaky you sound? You're engaged to get married to another woman, remember?"

"Not yet, I ain't." We both stood there, looking at each other. This was awkward. I was dumbfounded.

"Never should've mentioned the whole Miss Right thing," I said. "I took your eye off the ball."

"I'm glad you did. She won't affect my work."

"How do you know that? Think about the two years of training we put into this. Now we're gonna add a lady into the mix?"

"The plot thickens, boss," Chet said.

"I, for one, am all for it," Andrew interjected.

"No one asked you, Andrew!"

I looked back at Chet, "What happens if I say yes and somewhere in Wyoming, it doesn't work out and she has to go home? How will that work?"

"She'll just turn around and go home," Chet said.

"On a horse? With no truck or trailer? No way in hell. We'd have to stop everything and find a way to get her home safely. It would ruin the trip!"

Chet got quiet and looked away. Then he did something I'd never seen him do. He got emotional. His eyes welled up, and he looked me directly in the eyes, "Boss, I know this sounds crazy, but this might be my one chance for happiness. Girls like this only come around once. If I let her go, I may never see her again."

"Look pard, I don't have the luxury of caring about matters of the heart right now. I gotta look out for the whole outfit—so this is my decision to make."

Chet gave me a hard look then went back inside to talk to Jean.

I brushed Thunder to cool down and let the whole thing sink in.

Could this work? I loved Chet like a brother, but after I processed it, I felt Chet was acting irrationally. This was a terrible idea.

When Chet came back outside, I offered a compromise, "How about, if Jean rides with us for the day, and Beth follows us in Jean's truck and trailer?"

"Well. I don't know. I haven't—"

"Well, go talk it over with Jean. Quickly! We're burning daylight here!"

Chet kicked the dirt; then went back inside to talk to Jean. I sipped my coffee. I couldn't help but think about how crazy life can be. What twist of fate prompted Jean to stop and say hello to us in the first place?

Now our world was turned upside down.

Dave came over, wondering what was going on; I filled him in on our dilemma. Dave just gave me a blank stare. Andrew said he was all for her tagging along. "She's hot."

"Yeah, yeah," I said. "I'm not asking for your input, Andrew."

"You know you can be a real hard-ass sometimes," Andrew said.

"Tough," I said.

When Chet came back outside, he didn't say a word. All he did was give me a nod. Jean would ride with us for the day.

I gladly accepted the role of the bad guy, destiny destroyer, love killer, party pooper—whatever other names you want to hurl my way—but I was doing it for the good of the team. We were on a mission out here, and it had nothing to do with finding Chet's soul mate. The day Jean and Beth tagged along was one of the strangest of the trip—at least for Dave, Andrew, and me. I felt like I was watching a romantic movie unfold right in front of our eyes. Jean and Chet rode together and talked all day like two long lost lovers. I had no idea what they talked about all that time since they kept a good distance behind us. We let them have their privacy.

At sunset, we made camp for the night, and Chet pulled dinner together for all six of us. He made one of his great spaghetti dinners, and I was glad we could return Jean's hospitality with a little of our own.

After dinner, the sun cast its deep golden lines on the Indiana cornfields; it was time we all said our goodbyes.

I watched Chet load Jean's paint horse into her trailer. Even my heartstrings were feeling a little tug watching it all. Andrew was gawking at them, but I had to turn away from their long hugs and deep kisses.

To this day, I wonder if I made the right decision.

When Jean and Beth disappeared on the horizon in that red pickup truck, I looked at Chet, who was wiping tears from his eyes. "Only thing more painful than a burr in your saddle is a Cupid's arrow to your heart," I said. "You okay, partner?"

"I'll be fine. Just don't talk to me for a while," he said and turned away. I knew he was putting on a brave face.

Chet was true to his word. He didn't speak to me for a good long while after that. When we approached the Illinois border, I tried to pull him out of his mood by playing the "hat game" with him. He came around a little bit—but he couldn't bring himself to do the *Monty Python* routine with me.

Our last night in Indiana, Chet solemnly made dinner around the campfire. There was no way around it; the mood of the team had been dampened significantly. Andrew wasn't playing his guitar. Dave wasn't sharpening his knife—no jokes were being told. I'd look over at Chet occasionally, but he kept his head down.

He wasn't pouting or angry, just quiet.

I could tell the old lug was heartbroken.

Now I felt doubly guilty. For leaving Sue in the lurch, for pouring water on Chet's fiery romance—at least I hadn't let down Thunder. Yet.

No one announced it, but after our chili dinner, we all decided to turn in early. I remember it was a warm night. I thought I'd fall asleep the second my head hit my pillow, but I tossed and turned under the stars for a spell thinking about Chet.

As the leader of this outfit, I wondered if I had steered us wrong for the first time on the trip? I thought about how a certain woman can get scuttle a great friendship. Some of the greatest pieces of literature are written about just that situation.

Was Jean going to tear us apart? Was this the beginning of the end?

I finally shut down my brain and drifted off—I had mixed emotions, but I was at peace with my decision. All I could do was pray that a new state would bring a new "state of mind" to my riding partner.

If not?

I didn't want to think of the consequences—but if ol' Chet had taken a fatal hit to the heart and had permanently lost all the "hop in his get along"—then we were going to need a lot more "FM" to make it to the Pacific.

A whole helluva lot more.

★ 7 ★

COWBOY LIMBO & THE GARDEN
OF THE WEST

"Courage is being scared to death
and saddling up anyway."
—*John Wayne*

WE LUGGED OUR beaten bodies, broken hearts, and sore feelings over the Indiana border into the "Land of Lincoln" and the state of Illinois, just west of Kentland. We were in a new state but not a new state of mind. With Chet giving me the silent treatment, this part of the trail still felt like cowboy limbo to me. The burned bridge back to Jean's loving arms was still smoldering in Chet's soul. No hearts had been patched, no soul mates reunited, no conflicts resolved. The hotter it got outside, the thicker the ice grew between ol' Chet and me. An ice storm in summer? Who woulda thunk it? Even more curious was the "freeze out" came while the heat and humidity were in full bloom. The forecast was the same every day in the Midwest, "Hot and humid, highs in the upper 90s with a 70% chance of severe thunderstorms accompanied by strong winds and damaging hail." This lasted through August.

The thunderstorms were stalking us like a vengeful Comanche. The locals were right, two Connecticut Yankees like us had never experienced this type of weather. We hadn't trained for this shit; there's no way we could have. That was one problem. The other was team morale had sunk lower than a cricket's butt on a summer day. Even Thunder was snorting at me like I brushed his mane the wrong way. All I could do was shake my head and chuckle. Halfway through the trip and I had become the proverbial "black hat" of this story? I didn't have the energy to try to figure it out.

None of us did, I suppose.

I reckon Illinois felt like riding through some strange, silent movie. Every few hours, one of us piped up to prove we were still breathin'.

"It's a mirage. All of that." Chet pointed to the horizon. "Everything looks the goddamn same."

Chet was right. Illinois didn't look any different than Indiana. The only thing that changed was the Route 24 sign.

"We're officially in Illinois, by the way," I said, pointing at the sign.

"Think the State P.D.'s gonna roll out the red carpet?"

"Ain't you curious to know how I know we're in the 'Illini State?'"

"Nope. Curiosity killed the cat."

"Route 24 sign changed shape."

Chet didn't bother to look at the sign, "Guess you're smarter than you look."

We hardly said a word for the next two days. Guess the bucket o' laughs we brought with us from Connecticut had dried up somewhere over the Indiana border. This was not a good development; laughs were as valuable as any resource we had in our saddlebags. It was downright alarming to see that Chet and I could no longer make each other laugh.

I tried to come up with creative ways to add some humor to the overall misery that plagued horse and rider. I played the hat game by myself.

Chet wasn't having any of it.

"Lethargy is a dangerous attitude, pard," I said, picking up my own hat.

"Thanks for the advice."

After our coffee break, I got wacky and put my clothes on backward (including my boots and Stetson)—then I jumped on Thunder and rode for a spell.

"What in the hell are you doin'?" Chet remarked ten minutes into my silent backward ride.

"I left my keys in Connecticut. I gotta go back and get em."

"You finally strokin' out?"

"Can't feel the left side of my body. That bad?"

"Just keep on bein' an idiot, if you must."

"I must. I must." I stayed in character for fifteen more minutes before I finally got him to chuckle.

Think he only laughed to get me to stop.

Sparse chuckles aside, Chet and I were trapped in horseman hell smack dab in the middle of pastoral purgatory. Every town was the same, every field the same field, every step the same as the one that came before it.

Reckon too much of the "same" could turn a sane man near bat shit crazy.

"Think the corn's plotting to kill us," I said, half-joking.

The two-foot-high cornfields had us cornered on Route 24, a sticky two-lane blacktop that went on forever. There was nowhere to go but back home, or straight ahead.

Chet looked out at the cornfields, "Those little bastards? You wanna take a shot at 'em?" Chet pulled out the rifle.

I looked at the gun and thought about shooting the nearest scarecrow square between the eyes out of boredom.

Saner minds prevailed.

"Better keep our powder dry, Hoss."

I looked for signs of the next town to keep myself tethered to reality. I made a game of spotting the tall stacks in the distance that indicated another farm or grain mill.

No matter how punchy I got, I made sure to keep us on the straight and narrow, usually by keeping us parallel with a nearby train track. There were plenty of them.

Back in the days of the old West, the railroad companies built thousands of miles of tracks across the nation to connect both coasts. Only a few remained in 1986. Lucky for us, they paralleled much of our westerly route. The train tracks were usually thirty yards from the main road, so Chet and I rode along them whenever we could.

This was one of those times.

I glanced at Chet to see if he was going to complain about my executive decision to pull us off Route 24.

He was already snoring in the saddle.

Even though Chet was being a little shit to me, there was something about the sight of him snoozing on top of ol' Rebel that made me smile. I remember thinking, Chet can't hate me too much if he still trusts me with his life. Right?

We got off the road and found the tracks, but there were none. They had been ripped out, which was pretty common. We preferred the no-track variety; they let us relax with no fear of a car, truck, or train running us over. We could just put the boys in cruise control and let them follow along the dirt path, which is what we did.

I leaned back and dozed a spell, too.

I dreamt the ripped-up tracks led us through a string of ghost towns that afternoon. We rode by empty farmhouse after empty farmhouse—all with rotting roofs. I dreamt every shack that was once a home to someone sang a quiet song of sorrow.

When I opened my eyes, we seemed to be passing through a real ghost town.

The recession of the early 80s had put them all out of business. The only things left were fossilized reminders of fortunes lost all around us.

Where were the tracks?

The boys were clopping us along a half-brokenn sidewalk of a long-forgotten town. "Think fast, Hoss," I said. "Boys took us off course."

I saw no railroad in sight.

"Shit, man," Chet moaned.

The town (if you could call it that) had a spooky feeling; I remember wondering if squatters had moved in. I definitely felt a presence.

Chet must have too. "Feels like we're being watched," he said.

"Circle. The. Wagons." I said, still trying to be funny.

"Wake me when they got us surrounded," Chet muttered.

We rode by an abandoned bank across the street from a shuttered filling station café, then past an old hardware store whose crooked sign still hung sideways and swayed in the wind. "A reminder of good times," I said.

It was an eerie patch of ride that touched me emotionally. Maybe it was the heat or Chet being mentally checked out—but I stopped for a moment to soak it all in.

"No one will believe what we're seeing, Hoss. Whole town's disappeared, like everybody just packed up and left."

Chet wiped his eyes. "We in *The Twilight Zone*?"

The pain I felt riding through all these empty towns is hard to describe. "How do disasters like this happen in our country?"

"Shit happens in our country. America ain't fair. Life ain't fair," Chet said, coming to life again. "C'mon Boss, let's stop rubberneckin' and find the damn tracks."

Chet and I observed the summer storms usually came knocking around late afternoon, so every morning we were in the saddle by 4:30 A.M. to get a head start on them. We usually rode for twelve to fourteen hours a day. Dave and Andrew would pump electrolytes into the boys' water every few hours to keep them fresh, but the humidity was just too much for them.

The outfit would be holed-up most evenings by 5 or 6 P.M.

We loved camping in farmhouses, but most nights, we camped outside exposed to the elements—so we'd have to create our own shelter by finding a big tree on the inside of a farm fence and angling our rig and trailer into a protective "V" shape. It created a nice little windbreaker for us to cook in.

"Just like circling the wagons in the olden days," I said to Andrew and Dave while parking the rig in a V-shape (to show them how it's done).

"You're old," Andrew said unimpressed.

A storm was brewing dead ahead. This one looked like it had teeth. We tried not to push our luck with the weather, but today, we did. It all started with a short cut.

You city folk may not know that most Midwestern farmers rotate their crops to prevent their soil from losing richness. We encountered quite a few empty fields where crops once were. When we saw an opportunity, we'd cut across one of them to save time.

On this afternoon, as "MF" would have it, we were riding across a dirt field when we saw dark clouds forming in the northwest sky.

"That storm looks biblical," Chet said.

No way we were getting to Dave in the rig without getting wet. "Never a dull moment. Reckon we can't avoid this un," Chet put a dip in his cheek and scowled.

"This Mother Nature's way of sayin', we need a shower?" I said.

"This'll blow the ticks off real good!" Chet hollered, "The four of us just gonna have to ride this one out!"

"Good thing we brought our waxed Australian dusters!" I said, pulling mine out of my saddlebag. What were Chet's last words before the chaos began?

"Boss, this is going to be a mother fucker!"

He wasn't wrong.

The wind, man—the wind! Imagine a freight train from hell roaring by a few feet away, and you can imagine the force that was suddenly lording over us and our once tranquil scene. I never felt smaller in my life. The electricity in the air made our beards and hair stand on end. Thunder crackled across the sky. This was the moment when it dawned on me. "MF" was "FM" backward.

With no trees for miles, staying in the saddle was sheer stupidity. "You never want to be the tallest thing in a lightning storm! I yelled to Chet, "Put the boys together, and we'll squat in between!"

We faced Thunder and Rebel's butts to the wind. They crouched down to protect themselves. Chet and I hunkered down; our heads shoved right next to the boys' snouts. Long riffs of hot horse breath blew down my face.

"You could use a breath mint Rebel, you ol' turd!" Chet yelled.

The boys whinnied their displeasure.

Chet bellowed to the 'Big Guy In The Sky,' "Bring it on you bastard! You can do better than this! C'mon, bring it to us!"

"Bring it on, goddammit!" I screamed, "Bring it!"

The fury rained down. We asked for it. Sheets of driving rain and hail pummeled us. Then the uppercut, a huge explosion struck ten feet away, followed by a huge bang! I looked over at the smoldering hole in the earth. It took me a few seconds to realize that a lightning bolt had sprayed us with mud! Now, faithful reader, I'm not a praying man by nature, but I sure as hell was that day. Even crouching down, we were still the tallest things in sight. It just didn't make sense to wait for something worse to happen. I signaled to Chet. "We're gonna die out here! Let's ride, pard!"

I grabbed Thunder's reins, swung up into the saddle, and gigged his flanks. "Come on, boy! Ride for your life!"

Thunder and Rebel galloped into the teeth of the storm while Chet and I hollered at the top of our lungs, a litany of expletives I thankfully do not remember.

I hoped we might run out of the storm or get put out of our misery by another bolt of lightning, either way, it would be over quicker!

One thing I learned on our wild ride was Thunder was a mudder; when he got to full speed, he left Rebel and Chet in his wake!

Chet and I rode until we lost track of time. It might have been five minutes or fifteen, but the rain let up, and we slowed down. The boys were sucking air something fierce. Chet and I looked at each other with matching bug eyes. The rain dripped down the brim of our Stetsons onto our faces; we were beet red.

All we could say was," Holy shit. Holy shit."

The dark clouds gave way to a cool mist. We dismounted in a daze.

"Is this heaven?" Chet asked.

"Naw, it's Illinois."

Whatever just happened was transformative. "Guess the big guy's reminding us why we're here," I said.

"Why's that, again?" Chet said, taking a big swig of water from his canteen.

"Best friends, pard, till the end," I said.

"Amigos," Chet said, "Till one of us sinners gets hit by lightning. or sucked up by a twister!"

The thunderstorm had us buzzing the rest of the day. The good news was our little adventure proved that the ice was thawing between ol' Chet and me. All we needed was a little excitement to shake us out of the doldrums and get us back on track.

Shoot. After all these years, I still don't know how that lightning bolt missed us.

FM I say.

The next day we finally hunted down a working payphone in one of those forgotten towns. I was pining to talk to Sue. When I got her on the horn, she didn't disappoint. I told her about our near-death experience, which I thought would be the big news of the day. But she had other plans. "Sounds like you need a care package," she said mysteriously.

"I'm dyin' for one. We almost got blown up by the universe, hon."

"Too bad you don't have two cute girls to rub your neck and mend what ails you."

I knew something was afoot, "Just what exactly do you have in mind?"

Sue confessed she and Diane (Chet's fiancé, remember her?) were plotting a surprise visit. The plan was to fly to Chicago, rent a car, and find us on the road.

When Sue dropped her bombshell, "Goddamn," was all I could muster up on the phone.

Sue said they booked a Saturday morning flight.

"That's in two days!" I said.

"Don't sound too excited. Think you can handle us, cowboy?"

"You bet your boots I can. Hot damn!"

We broke out in uncontrollable nervous laughter. God, would we even recognize each other after all this time?

"Guess what? I've been 'moo-moo' shopping," Sue said.

"You been to a bovine boutique? Just for me?"

"They don't have a lot of sexy ones, but I'm determined to find one you will like."

"You could just forgo the moo-moo, entirely," I said. "Or maybe do a little hula dance for me?"

"Don't push your luck," she said, "I can barely walk in this heat."

"I'll take care of your barkin' puppies," I said. "Just get your cute little butt out here."

"I'm not stepping one solitary swollen toe in that state if you don't get yourself cleaned up. I can smell you over the phone."

"That bad, huh?"

"And no bathing in horse troughs. I don't want to smell like Thunder after one night with you."

"Guess I best warn you. I also look like warmed over shit," I said. "You might wanna trade me in for a younger model."

"Well. I guess we make a fine pair then."

"Guess so. They'll write a book about our love, someday," I said.

"Big talker. How on god's green earth are we gonna find you?" Sue asked.

"Mighty good question. I'd say buy an Illinois road map and get on Route 24. By the time y'all arrive, I reckon we'll be somewhere between the towns of Gilman and Chenoa. It'll be hard to miss us."

"Maybe we should just follow our noses to the smell of horse hockey?" she joked.

"If you get lost, just ask a local. We'll keep the light on for y'all. Chet is going to flip."

We said our goodbyes in hushed loving tones. I was over the moon—what a lady.

Just like that, Chet and I had dates.

We didn't have much time to prepare. I looked as rough as an unshorn sheep, smelled the same too. I hadn't felt a razor on my face in months. I had to get it in gear!

Chet didn't believe me when I told him the great news.

"You gotta be shittin' me," he said. "Is this some plot twist to get me to forget Jean?"

"I'm not that cunning, pard," I said.

Besides, Chet was the last thing on my mind. Sue's arrival got my adrenalin (and hormones) pumping. I wasn't sure how I would act when I saw her. I'd been so focused on keeping our outfit safe and moving forward that I couldn't imagine sleeping with her in two days. Even though I thought about her every second of the trip, I'd blocked the thought of making crazy love to her out of my mind knowing that it would be months before I saw her again.

All those feelings came rushing back now. I felt all tingly inside.

Easy now.

That night, we camped in a field somewhere west of Gilman. I didn't say much. All I could do was plot "her" arrival. I couldn't make Sue camp with us; I had to come up with a more civilized alternative. I rehearsed what I would say when I saw her.

My mind was in overdrive. I needed to calm down. I was thinking like a newlywed!

Life was good again.

Chet and I got an early start after a hunk of morning cornbread and some heavenly cowboy coffee. We were going to knock out as many miles as we could before the girls arrived. We had one of our better mornings. We spent the time advising each other on how to handle the impending female situation.

"You gonna invite Sue to ride along with us?" Chet asked.

"Don't even start with that."

"Just checkin'."

"You gonna confess to Diane?"

"Gotta be shittin' me."

"Just checkin'."

"It goes without saying—do not mention anything about Jean."

"Who's Jean?"

"Exactly."

Sometime late morning, I saw the rig heading our way. "There's the Preacher," Chet said.

"Hadn't planned on seeing him till lunch," I said.

We waited for Dave. He slowly ambled over.

"Met some nice folks up the road who offered us dinner and a place to sleep tonight," Dave said.

"I trust you, Preacher man. As long as you feel good about them," I said.

"Ok, then. Andrew's already there."

"He's calling it a day already?"

"You know Andrew."

"I know Andrew. As long as you can handle all his responsibilities."

"Heh! What responsibilities?" Dave joked.

"Good point," I said. Chet and I ate a quick lunch then kept on riding. We cut the day short when we arrived at our new friends' house about ten miles up the road. Dave pointed to the dirt road that took us to our new friends' home. "Real nice folks, husband and wife school teachers. named Steve and Germaine."

Their house was at the end of a long dirt road. It was a private spot nestled on three acres. We were all excited to indulge in a real home-cooked meal, but all I could think about was Sue. She was pregnant with no husband in the heat of the summer. This is not exactly how she envisioned motherhood; I'm sure! I snapped back to reality when we moseyed up on the porch. A kind-looking woman introduced herself as Germaine then she introduced her husband, Steve. "Dinners almost ready," she said. "Just baked two fresh raspberry pies with the raspberries from my garden—hope you are hungry!"

"Yes ma'am, I'd say that is an understatement," I said.

"We will definitely consume mass quantities, ma'am," Chet said.

I smelled the raspberry pies cooling in the open window. Had we traveled back in time to Mayberry R.F.D? The raspberry pie was my favorite. Don't tell Sue, but in all my years, I'd never had a fresh-baked pie like this one.

Steve and Germaine were great people, smart and funny, and extremely easy to talk to. They treated us like family the second we strode through their door.

The aroma of baked chicken and fresh raspberry pie could be found in every nook and cranny of the house, which was a good thing for several reasons. First, it smelled like the ambrosia of the gods. Second, it helped override the fact Chet and I had not bathed in a week! I sniffed my armpit when no one was looking, then immediately excused myself to the washroom to clean up.

Chet, Andrew, and Dave followed suit.

After we knocked the first layer of dirt off, all six of us sat around the dinner table and laughed about the absurdities of the world. We enjoyed Germaine's amazing cooking and exchanged stories about our lives. The meal was incredible (baked chicken, potato salad, coleslaw, corn on the cob, and raspberry pie). I was in hog heaven, but the happiest pig of all was Chet, who (as promised) was inhaling mass quantities of food that he did not have to cook.

Germaine and Steve were good eggs. They seemed so content with their lives and happy to be where they were; they made me happy to be alive.

After dinner, we moved our full stomachs into their small living room. Steve and Germaine sipped on a glass of wine. When Germaine found out that the girls were coming the next day, she offered her home and a bedroom for us.

"Well, thank you, ma'am, but I got us a motel room in town for the night," I said.

"Fear not." Chet interrupted, "I imagine Diane and I will take you up on your generous offer, ma'am."

"Oh, good. Y'all just stay as long as you'd like," Germaine said.

"Can we take a few days off to get to know the locals, boss?" Andrew asked.

"Nice try, kid," I said. I informed the outfit we would get back on the trail Sunday after the girls leave.

My eyes were getting heavy after just one beer. "Getting up at 3:30 every morning takes a toll," I told Steve in between yawns.

"It's after Jeff's bedtime," Chet said.

"One beer only accelerates the sleep process," I said and settled into a comfortable part of the couch.

By 9 P.M., it was dusk, and I was in a deep slumber on the sofa while everyone kept talking around me. I woke up alone on the couch a few hours later. I guess the party moved outside to the grassy front yard. "Hope it wasn't my snoring," I mumbled to myself half-asleep while I shuffled to my bedroom to cash out.

When day broke, Chet and I popped up like two kids at Christmas. Today was the day! Before the house began stirring, Chet and I took the rig into town and had breakfast at a local café. The plan was to wait for the girls while getting to know some of the locals. We sipped coffee and had a great breakfast, which ended up being on the house. Chet and I visited with several town folk about our trip; they made us feel welcome.

I'll say it again. Midwestern hospitality is a wonderful thing.

We were both full as tics after our luxurious two-hour breakfast. We walked outside, feeling like two kings and decided to hang out in the rig and wait for

Diane and Sue. We parked in the café lot just off the highway. I thought we would be easy to spot with "Cross AmeriCA86" written on both sides of the rig.

"Now, we wait," I said, handing Chet a newspaper I bought as a treat. We took turns reading interesting bits of news to each other and laughing.

"Any minute Sue will be rolling up!" I said.

"This is crazy, isn't it?" Chet replied, "I feel like a sixteen-year-old kid again."

"That's a good thing, Chetter. I'm an old married guy, but I haven't felt this excited about anything in a long time."

"Love is a splendid thing, ain't it?" Chet remarked, genuinely happy.

After waiting for an hour, a small white car pulled in beside us and honked. It was our special lady friends. I got choked up.

Chet and I looked at each other. We knew we wouldn't be talking much for the next day. "Well, good luck pard, with Diane," I said as I hopped out of the rig.

"Say hi to your wife for me, boss!" Chet laughed.

Sue was in the passenger seat. She had a huge smile on her face. She was barely out of the car when I got her in a bear hug. We hugged and kissed for several minutes; I couldn't stop. This was the longest we had ever been apart.

It felt like we were dating again.

I could tell by the way she was looking at me that she was adjusting to the new "me:" long beard, long hair, and skinny! Meanwhile, she was glowing and gorgeous in baggy white shorts, one of my long sleeve dress shirts and a new pair of gym shoes.

Sue announced she'd put on 25 pounds and showed off her feet and legs, which were swollen with water weight. "Look at my Miss Piggy legs," she said.

"Looks plenty good to me," I said.

Sue's embrace was so warm, I forgot about ol' Chet for a while there. At some point, I looked over and saw he and Diane were hugging it out too.

We all stood around the parking lot, laughing and catching up. Then Chet got in the rental with Diane, and Sue hopped in the rig with me.

Sue and I drove to Steve, and Germaine's talking a blue streak. Everyone back at the house was waiting to meet the girls. Naturally, Andrew greeted them like the insufferable joker that he is. "We keep your husbands safe," Andrew crowed, "They almost perished many times. I could tell you stories."

"Don't listen to him," Dave said. "He's just our mascot."

"You must be Andrew," Sue said with a knowing smile.

Steve and Germaine made us feel at home. It was such a wonderful day, after lunch, we all migrated outside to the porch and front yard.

Sue and I sat like two lovebirds in the green grass under a tree most of the afternoon, just lazin' around and catching up. We were in our own little world. Everyone ate leftovers from the night before and drank beer.

I noticed the women mostly ate salad. Sue said, "It's too hot for anything heavy." She mostly ate watermelon with sea salt on it instead. I insisted Sue have a piece of Germaine's home-baked raspberry pie. After some prodding, Sue went crazy for it and even helped herself to a second piece when no one else was looking. After all, she was "eating for two" as she kept saying in between bites.

I told her when I got home, "I'll be so hungry I'll be eating for four."

Sue laughed, "You'll have to fend for yourself," she said. "I'll be busy with my utters out for the next year, buddy!"

As the day went on, I realized that even with Sue here, I was so programmed to ride that it was painful for me to sit around and do nothing. I almost felt guilty. Then I remembered this was the first day off we'd had in a month.

"That puts us close to 400 hours in the saddle in June," I said to Chet.

"No wonder I got hemorrhoids," Chet said.

"Ugh. No more shop talk," Sue interrupted and slapped my butt. "Your skinny ass needs a serious time-out."

"That's the truest statement I've ever heard," Chet said.

That night, Steve and Germaine invited a few friends over and had a cook-out. It was fun to socialize with some new faces—but I found after a few pleasant exchanges, I was out of material and just wanted to be alone with Sue. The girls did most of the talking. Sue really hit it off with Germaine. "So Sue, let me get this right, you let Jeff ride his horse across the country—and a week before he leaves, you find out you're pregnant with your first kid?" Germaine blurted.

"What a pisser, right?" Sue added.

"And you still let him go?" Germaine was hooting up a storm.

"Yep. And I have to cover his job at work too! Guess I'm just a lucky girl."

The girls laughed a lot, often at Chet and my expense (mostly mine). Germaine made a point to tell Chet and me we were lucky to have such amazing and understanding women in our lives.

"I will admit I've got the greatest lady in the world on my side," I replied. "But this cowboy life ain't easy Germaine. Ain't that right, Chester?"

Chet just shrugged, he was trying to contain a chuckle.

He loved to see me squirm.

After dinner, Sue and I took a romantic stroll around the property. The tree frogs were kind enough to give us a lovely serenade. I took her hand sheepishly like we were teenagers—she put her head on my shoulder, we started feeling close again. Sue talked about how strange it was to be back after all these months.

"You know, I made a reservation at a motel for the night so we could, uh," I said.

"Look at you thinking ahead," she said. "Brownie points for Jeff."

"Don't think a pregnant lady would much like camping outside with a bunch of stinky, horny cowboys and their smelly ol' horses."

"Hate to break it to ya, but you still smell of horse," she said.

"I'll take another shower at the motel. I'll take two!"

"You're so romantic," Sue never lost her sense of humor.

Time flew by—at dusk, the mosquitoes invaded, so we went inside. Sue and I announced we were heading to the motel. Chet and Diane were nowhere to be found.

I grabbed a few beers for the road. Sue said her goodbyes to Germaine, "Gonna take this cowboy home and clean him up good!"

"Hose him down outside before you let him into your bed," Germaine said.

Everyone cheered our exit like we were newlyweds off to our honeymoon. On the way out the door, I leaned into Sue, "I'm sure everyone thinks we're gonna have sex."

"I just wanna take a bath and put my feet up."

"How about a foot rub?"

"You're still good for somethin'."

The hotel was as close to a rundown "flea-bitten" joint as you could find, fortunately without the fleas—but for 19 dollars a night, the price couldn't be beat. After the past few months, it felt like a four-star hotel to me—with a great mattress, a real bathroom, and a TV. I got Sue all propped up and comfortable. We spent the rest of the night just talking in bed. I rubbed her feet and neck. Sue said she didn't have anyone to talk to about the intimate details of being pregnant, so I was more than happy to let her share her feelings. I didn't yammer on about the trip, but I did give Sue a glimpse into what the "trail boss" was going through.

We fell asleep in each other's arms. We didn't even bother with a shower or bath. Both of us were worn out for different reasons. I think Sue went out before me. At least I hope she did. The next morning, I awoke with a double helping of melancholy in my heart. Why did she have to leave so soon? With no horses to tend to or wagon train to get moving, I stayed in bed and just watched Sue sleep. She was so radiant and beautiful. I lamented the fact it was going to be months before I'd see her again.

I had to get moving, so I took advantage of the real shower. I had taken two showers in less than ten hours. I was getting spoiled.

When Sue woke up, I walked down the street to get a coffee (for me) and an orange juice (for her) while she took her shower.

We sat around the room, talking for the rest of the morning.

I was afraid our bond would be vulnerable after all this time, but it turns out it wasn't at all. FM, I say. We were still as right as rain. Though she did make it clear that I owed her one—which I sure as hell did (and still do).

After a few hours, we decided to head back to Steve and Germaine's to have lunch. Steve and Germaine had invited a few friends over; it was nice to feel part of society again. Sue and I ended up on the same blanket under the same tree in the front yard, appreciating the shade in what was shaping up to be another 100-degree day. Sue and Diane's flight wasn't until early evening, so we had a few more hours to socialize before they had to leave for the Chicago airport. Chet, Sue, Diane, and I talked about what lay ahead of us down the trail.

Then our vacation time ran out.

It was time for Sue and Diane to head to the airport. "You two make me happy to be married," Steve said to us as we said our goodbyes. "You better treat Suzanne like a queen when you get home, cowboy," Germaine said, gigging me one last time out the door.

"You know I will," I said and dutifully kissed Sue on the cheek.

I thanked Steve and Germaine for their hospitality. We all hugged and promised to keep in touch. They were two more great people who had taken us in and treated us like family—just like so many other folks we met on the trail. We sure never expected it, but we were always mighty grateful to meet another gracious friend.

Outside by the rental car, Chet and Diane quietly said their goodbyes. I have no idea what they were talking about; it was almost like they weren't even there. I had tunnel vision. I had my eyes glued to "the romantic movie" playing out before me starring Sue.

Suzie and I found a spot by the big tree to say a proper goodbye.

I fought to keep my cowboy composure. I wanted to be stoic like John Wayne, but my heart wouldn't let me. My mind raced with questions. When would I see her again? How will she fare without me? What if I don't make it to the coast and something bad happens? I'd never forgive myself.

I kept a stiff upper lip and tried to push the uncertainty out of my mind.

"Think we're gonna make it?" She asked.

"Don't worry, dumplin'. This, too, will pass."

"Just wish it passed a little faster," Sue said.

"Miss you more than you'll ever know."

"I know you do."

I rubbed her back and patted her backside. I kissed her head then her soft lips. I couldn't bring myself to say goodbye. Only "I love you."

In her embrace, I felt all doubt leave my body. In my heart, I knew we would finish the trip in good health, and I'd be there in November when she had our baby.

"Our baby."

It felt incredible just to say those two words. Together they give me chills.

Sue got into the passenger seat of the rental car. I looked at her one final time, and she smiled. "Don't forget where you live."

"Got the address memorized and everything," I said. "Now watch that baby's head." I pointed to her tummy.

The car slowly made its way down the old farm road. She blew me a kiss out the passenger window. I carried that kiss with me for the rest of the trip.

Just like watching Jean drive away in her rig—Sue and Diane's cloud of afternoon dust got smaller and smaller until it slowly disappeared into the past.

With heavy hearts, it was time to hit the trail again.

Chet and I didn't talk about Diane's visit for a good while, but it seemed to me everything went pretty well. Chet was grinning a lot, which was a good sign.

"Sure are smilin' a lot more," I remarked.

"Think she may be Miss Right," he said.

"Diane?"

"Yep. think she's it."

"I dunno pard, you fall in love too damn easily."

"That's the fun part though; ain't it?

"You're the king of your own world, Hoss. We simpatico again?"

"Hell, you did me a favor."

"I did?"

"What if Diane had showed up and Jean was with us? How would I have explained that shit? Think Chetter, you gotta think!"

"You do gotta think," I said. "Glad I could help out, pard."

Chet and I didn't say much more about our disagreement; we just slapped each other on the back, called each other a name—and away we rode.

Guess that's how cowboys bury the hatchet.

The next two days, we were on the road to Peoria. I reckon our conjugal visits were like a serum because we officially got our third wind. The outfit started getting some breaks, too; the first being, we were lucky to dodge several nasty thunderstorms that passed through our parts.

I had gotten my trail boss routine down so well, we were regularly surpassing our 32 to 34-mile daily goal. I remember we were 100 miles from the Iowa border when our maps told us we could save time by taking this 'grey road' called SR 116.

I followed my gut, and we rode it all the way to Iowa.

I remember thinking I was surprised that we had almost made it through the state with no hassle from the Police.

I must have jinxed us.

Several miles before we were to cross the Peoria River, a Peoria PD police cruiser pulled in front of our procession and stopped.

I looked at Chet. "Should we flip a coin?"

A faint smile curled under his bushy mustache; Chet just shook his head.

"Heads, he's here to help," I said, "Tails, we get a night in the Peoria pokey."

We never knew what to expect from the local "boys in blue," but today, it was a good day.

As FM would have it, we flipped our coin and got—Heads, here to help.

"How you all doing today?" the Peoria officer (who was named John) asked us. "Where y'all headed?"

Chet filled him in, "Lookin' to cross the river on our way to the Pacific. Our rig's about half mile down, pulled off on the berm waiting for us."

Officer John shook our hands; he had to reach up to the saddle. "Don't pull over many horses," Officer John joked.

Chet and I got off Rebel and Thunder and chatted about our travels.

John said he had seen us on the news and asked if he could help us cross the bridge that spanned the Peoria River.

"Much obliged for any help we can get," I said.

Officer John said he would block off one lane with his cruiser. "Y'all can just ride behind me," he said.

Officer John also told us about a great spot to camp on the other side of the river. "It has trees galore, so you're guaranteed shade."

"John, that sounds just about perfect," I said.

Just then, Dave rolled up in the rig, wondering where we were.

I introduced him to Officer John then asked him to find the camp spot. "If you can, secure us a spot by the trees lining the river bank."

"I had some great times there," Officer John sighed with a hint of nostalgia, "The horses are going to love it." We thanked John for the assist. "It's what I do," Officer John said then hopped in his cruiser.

Chet tapped on his window, "Spaghetti's on the menu tonight. Come on down if you want to get fed." Officer John thanked Chet for the offer and said he'd join us when his shift was over.

Chet and I got back in the saddle and followed John's cruiser down the road.

Chet looked at me, "See? We're making progress. We got cops pals now."

"Sure beats the cuffin' and stuffin' kind," I said.

"I think our luck is changin', Boss. We got the media wrapped around our little finger. We eat free everywhere we go, we got cops pals, we got women flying in to throw themselves at us. We must be getting respectable."

"Only buildings and whores get respectable with age," I said with a chuckle.

"Maybe we're just gettin' smart," Chet said then let out one of his classic belly laughs.

When I heard that laugh, I knew Ol' Chetter was back.

At least for now. Hallelujah.

★ 8 ★

FAME AND F.M. ON THE IOWA TRAIL

Barbwire, Blood, and Fireworks on the Fourth of July

"They talk about big skies in the western United
States, and they may indeed have them, but you have
never seen such lofty clouds, such towering anvils,
as in Iowa in July."
—*Bill Bryson*

MAY I CONFIDE in you? I never told a dang soul on the trail (not even Thunder), but in moments of quiet contemplation, a part of me wished Sue would magically appear to take me away from all this *glorious adventure.* Being the ringleader of this outfit, I know it's not good to have these thoughts—but I did visualize the scenario many times, and dreamt about it almost every night under the stars. Now before Thunder starts looking at me funny—I didn't wish for Sue to drag me home for good. I reckon I just hoped she would bring a little home to me, and she did. FM, I say.

But after my "secret wish" came true, you can bet it was hard as hell for this old cowboy to move on (emotionally) from our moment of conjugal bliss—not to mention the state that rejuvenated our spirits with a little love, kindness, and hospitality. The downtime sure gave us a renewed sense of hope that we could finish the trip without losing our god dang minds. Thanks to Illinois, the whole outfit felt a little more human again, me included. To all the good "Illini" people who helped us along the way—I tip my hat in your *general direction.* That's a *Monty Python* joke, by the way.

Don't worry. No one else gets it either.

The team spent our final night in Illinois feasting on another one of Chet's sumptuous spaghetti dinners with Officer John, our favorite Illinois State Policeman. Even with the humidity and mosquitoes, sitting around the campfire on the banks of the Peoria while John caught us up on current events, made the strenuous day worthwhile. Chet, for one, was mighty curious to know what we'd missed in the world, "Something important must have happened since we left."

"You hear about that Hands Across America?" Officer John said.

"Reckon we know about that one, don't we pard?" I said.

"We were in it! Horses too," Chet said.

"Well now, that's a story," John replied, "Bet that was a heckuva experience."

"The boys got one helluva contact high," Chet said.

"Don't tell me that, I'll have to arrest 'em!" Officer John chuckled.

"What else you got?" Chet wasn't giving up.

"Well, let me think. Reagan's still president. Boston Celtics won the NBA championship again. And that *Top Gun* movie came out. Pretty popular."

"I prefer a good Western myself," I said.

"That's it? Normal life is boring," Chet sure was disappointed to hear nothing all that eventful had happened.

I told him, "Don't get too upset, Hoss. No news is usually good news."

"Yeah, yeah, I know," Chet grumbled.

Looking back, I was probably talking to myself here in Illinois.

To me, no news meant Susie's pregnancy was going as planned. No news meant the world wasn't falling apart, and no act of God was going to fall from the sky and end our trip. No news also meant that our secret weapon "F.M." might guide us to the promised land, after all.

At least that's how I viewed it at the time.

With our belts loosened and bellies full, Officer John said he had to get back to his wife and kids. We thanked him for his help and hospitality. I vividly remember telling him, "If I ever write a book about our trip, you'll be in it."

Well, now you are, Officer John.

That night, as we camped on the banks of the Peoria with the soothing sounds of the river serenading us to sleep—I thought about how far we had come and how far we had yet to go. Entering a new state always brought a fresh set of challenges, joys, and adventures—but reaching Iowa had a special meaning. Before we left, Chet and I would dream about how it might feel to cross the

Mississippi on horseback and to reach the Rockies, and ride into the Pacific surf after completing our mission. All were lofty goals, but crossing the Mississippi was particularly special for me.

I don't know why—maybe I just romanticized it since I was a little boy reading *The Adventures of Huckleberry Finn*. Aw hell, I know I did. I still do.

Chet and I had known this Illinois-Iowa border crossing would be a little different, a little bigger, a little more thrilling than the others. Shoot, it would be our biggest challenge yet. Crossing the mighty Mississippi River on horseback? It doesn't get any more cowboy than this. I don't know about ol' Chet, but I've dreamt of this opportunity my entire life. The only problem was I had no plan to safely accomplish it, yet. But I reckoned if the old pioneers could cross the mighty "Mississipp" with no maps, no trailer, no rig, and no modern gear—so can us city slickers.

Today was the big day. Thunder could smell "the River" from miles away. My sniffer took a little longer to detect it—but that earthy river smell sure brought a big smile to my face. I could feel the team's excitement level rising with the sound of every hoofbeat. Even young Andrew had some extra giddy-up in him today. I knew that once we saw the signs for Route 94 and Route 96 to Dallas City, Iowa—we only had a few hours till the Mississippi would be in sight. As for how we were going to cross that monster? It was still a mystery. Officer John told us there would be a major bridge in Dallas City we could take across into Iowa—which sounded like a good option—but after talking to some of the other locals in western Illinois; I got conflicting reports, so I still wasn't certain which way to go. I didn't tell Chet, but I kept having flashbacks to New York and our near-fatal crossing of the Hudson River Bridge. Could crossing this river be the end of our trip? Take the wrong approach, and you bet your boots it could—although my horseman instincts told me we would find a safe crossing somewhere. But being the head of this outfit, it's my job to be extra careful—so I wasn't taking any chances, especially today.

Well, I reckon as F.M. would have it, several miles outside of Dallas City—another Illinois State Trooper pulled us over. Chet and I weren't sure if this officer would be a "friend or foe" considering our inconsistent record with the Boys in Blue so far. But we quickly discovered this officer (named Walt) was one of the nicest people we'd encountered. After exchanging some pleasantries and giving him a summary of our trip, I asked him the $64,000 question. "How can two humble cowboys get across the Mississippi, if we want to stay on our horses, and not trailer them across?"

Officer Walt thought about it a minute, "Ever crossed a bridge on horse before?"

I looked at Chet, "The Hudson River Bridge in New York. But it was precarious." After telling Walt about our Hudson River experience, he directed us to a surefire way across called the Fort Madison Toll Bridge—which he said was "just up ahead," and was two miles long. "That's one long-ass bridge!" Andrew interjected before I shooed him away. "Hell," Chet said, "We may as well pack a lunch, we'll be on the bridge for damn close to an hour." Officer Walt saw the concern in our eyes and—just like that—magically offered to give us a police escort across the bridge.

"Tell you what. I'll even close down a lane, to save your horses some stress—how's that sound?"

"We'd be much obliged. Thank ye," I said, "The boys thank you too."

"We sure appreciate you rolling out the carpet for a couple of dirty, bearded horsemen like us," Chet said. "Sure, you won't get fired?"

"Doubtful! Unless you knock over a bank later," Walt chuckled, "You're going to need me to get across that bridge anyway." Officer Walt gave us instructions on where to meet him. The last thing he said was, "Cinch up your straps, you're about to cross the largest double-deck swing span bridge in the world!"

Chet looked at me, "Did he say 'the world'?"

F.M., I pray!

Another hour up Route 96, we finally came to the bend Officer Walt told us to look for—and there was Walt's police cruiser waiting for us next to the Illinois entrance to the Fort Madison Toll Bridge—which I learned was also called The Santa Fe Swing Span Bridge. I've ridden across my fair share of bridges, but this one was fairly intimidating. It was very long and had two levels: the bottom was for trains, and the top was for cars. We were preparing to ride across the top level with all of the cars.

"Holy . . . Whoa! It's taller than I imagined, Boss," is all Chet had to say about it. The bridge climbed several hundred feet in the air until it reached the swing span.

"They don't call it the longest swing span bridge on earth for nothin'," I said.

Chet gave me a nervous smile, "This should be interesting!"

The team huddled by Walt's cruiser to form a plan of attack.

I figured it best to ride ol' Rebel across the bridge today since he was our most laid-back horse, and less likely to get spooked—unlike our fearless leader, Thunder—who was still young and skittish. Dave and Chet agreed with my summation, so we trailered Thunder and got Rebel out for bridge duty. Chet decided he was going to ride The Wizzer across, who also had a calm demeanor. Our moment of truth was here.

Can horses walk on water? Can cowboys swim?

I prayed to hell we were *not* about to find out.

Chet shouted he was ready. So was I. So were the boys. I gave Officer Walt a nod, and he signaled us to follow him, "Remember, I've got your back. I'll be right behind you in my cruiser, just keep in the right lane!"

"OK! Here goes nothing!" Chet hooted as we took our first steps on to the largest swing span bridge in the world. Chet, who likes to joke he's a "recovering Catholic," didn't take any chances, making the Catholic cross before we embarked. I'm not a religious man myself, but I do remember uttering a prayer under my breath—promising the "horse gods" that I would be forever grateful if they just kept Rebel under control. Did the horse gods listen?

With the humid wind pounding our faces, we slowly traversed the bridge, "Just don't do anything crazy till we get off this thing," I implored Rebel. Not sure if the old fart heard my pleas.

But thanks to Officer Walt's one-man police escort—our traveling horse and pony show suddenly brought traffic (pretty much) to a standstill, which was a pretty surreal feeling. The bridge was packed with cars, now all magically stopped for us. It felt like the entire state of Iowa was watching, but I never confirmed that feeling, since I didn't look at traffic once! I was too busy monitoring Rebel's ears (and every step we took) while patting him on the neck, and telling him how much I appreciated all he's done for us.

I know this story may not sound like a monumental event to some city slickers, but (to me) crossing the Mississippi River on horseback was one of the most beautiful and exhilarating moments of my life.

The views from the top of the bridge were spectacular. The wind felt amazing as the Delta mud, and churning water filled our noses with earthy memories of our pioneer past. I remember wondering as we clip-clopped our way across—How many pioneers died trying to cross this river? It blew my mind to fathom it.

I tipped my hat to them all.

About halfway across, I must have gotten pretty comfortable in the saddle because I made the mistake of looking down at the Mississippi rushing by, which made me downright dizzy, so you can bet I didn't do that again.

The Wizzer and Rebel were the real professionals on this day. They would calmly glance over at the traffic or down at the Mississippi river every so often—but they didn't spook once—*thank you, Horse Gods.* Breathing in that earthy river breeze sure must have felt as good to the boys, as it did Chet and me. Once I felt we were probably going to survive, I kept telling myself to appreciate this moment—"*Be here now because it doesn't get any better than this.*" Now that I think about it, I reckon I stole that "inspirational" line from an "Old Milwaukee" beer commercial.

Doesn't mean it's not true, though.

P.M. I still say—about this whole day!

It turns out, Chet's internal horse pedometer was right—it took us about an hour to get across the Mississippi River. I know I didn't breathe a sigh of relief until I could see every member of our outfit had made it across the bridge.

"What a ride, huh, Boss!" Chet was all smiles, "The boys were real champs!"

"They sure were, Hoss,"

When we saw the "Welcome to Iowa" sign on the other side of the river, we pulled the boys over and thanked Officer Walt for the escort. What a godsend Walt was—I still have no idea how we would have crossed that bridge without him.

"Gotta tip our hats to you, Officer Walt, for helping us navigate one of the most dangerous parts of our trip. Can't tell you how many hours I worried about this. Really can't thank you enough."

"Jeff would have killed us, for sure," Chet said, "Thanks for the safe passage."

Chet grabbed Walt's hand and gave it a hearty shake. Like all of the other police officers that helped us, Walt replied with humility, "Aw shucks fellas, I'm just doing my job. You guys are the real heroes."

Which I knew was not quite true—but we didn't have time to argue over who was more heroic—the cowboy or the horse? We had an ocean to get to, so we thanked him profusely and then went on our way. Thank you, Officer Walt, wherever you are. I will always remember the hospitality we received from you, and pretty much every officer we met along the way. I won't bother mentioning the Indiana Policeman who nearly "cuffed and stuffed" us for crimes we did not commit (*we won't dwell on that one*).

Thank you, boys in blue.

These cowboys could not have done it without you!

We were suddenly in a new state—Iowa, corn country, which brought a new state of mind. We had to get serious now that we're smack dab in the middle of the Midwest, where the extreme weather can really bite you in the ass. Every day (from now until we hit the Rockies) brought a new potential weather threat—from thunder and lightning, to hail storms, to tornados, to killer windstorms, to some Biblical level flash floods that came out of nowhere.

Knowing what danger awaited us, Chet and I decided to call the "hat game" a draw—which was a brilliant move, in retrospect. Besides, it had become damn near impossible to keep track of who was ahead (anyway) since the game had been going for several states. But it sure was fun while it lasted.

"OK, listen up: we're in Iowa now—so no more games, and no more napping in the saddle," I told the team. "We have to keep our head on swivels at all times."

"Why do I get the feeling you're talking to me?" Chet laughed.

We could joke about it—but Chet and I knew if we got caught in a bad storm with no shelter to protect us, it could be fatal for us, or the boys—so we took turns keeping a close eye on the sky. We relied on Dave to keep us informed of the weather reports he heard on the radio. I told him not to venture too far on his scout missions, in case a storm hit, and we needed rescuing. "I won't leave you boys hanging out to dry," was his only reply. That Preacher Man, he's not a man of many words—but he meant every word he said. A good hand all the way around.

There were some positive effects of bad weather. For one—we got to see a slew of amazing *double rainbows* that would grace the sky after some of the worst hailstorms (I'd ever seen) had passed us by. It takes a special sky for a double rainbow to happen, and in Iowa, they were almost a daily occurrence. You can bet, ol' Chet, and I never got bored seeing God's beauty on display.

Due to the unpredictable weather, the team started having quite a few cozy dinners inside my spacious two-stall horse trailer. When the weather got dangerous—one stall transformed into Chet's kitchen, fully equipped with a prep table, which we created by flipping over one of the boys' red water buckets. The other stall became our recreation area, where the team could gather, eat, and yes, sometimes even sleep. Fortunately, we only had to bunk a few nights in the trailer, due to tornadoes. On those evenings, I wasn't the only one picking dried horse manure out of my beard.

I remember one night Chet rolling over and saying, "I'm using two dried horse patties as my pillow, Boss. Good thing our special ladies can't smell us now. We'd never hear the end of this shit." Chet wasn't wrong about that one.

Sorry you had to read about that, Sue!

One of the first facts we learned about Iowans was the entire state felt like one big small town. Everyone was connected, and news sure traveled fast. Even news about two bedraggled cowboys passing through seemed to spread like wildfire.

I reckon it took about two hours of riding before a local TV reporter pulled over to see what we were up to. After hearing our story, the reporter asked if he could interview us for the local news. "TV news? We might break your cameras if you put us on the air," Chet said. We hadn't given an interview since we left Hartford—so I felt it was about time to change that. After hearing his pitch, I said, "heck yes" to the offer, which made the team quite happy. I figured, at minimum, it would help break up the repetition of the day, and who knows, maybe Sue would see it, somehow?

That was my own little special wish I didn't share with the others.

We arranged the interview for around mid-afternoon. I recall the TV reporter set us up in a parking lot of some hardware store. Before we went live on the air, Chet looked at me and joked, "Are you ready for your close-up, Mr. DeMille?"

I smiled, "Let me just comb this cow manure out of my beard."

I can't recall exactly what we said during the interview, but Chet, Dave, and I didn't embarrass ourselves. I purposely left Andrew off the interview list just for that reason. The interviewer asked about our journey so far, as well as the horses, the cause we were supporting—and why the heck we were attempting this so-called "world record cross-country trip." We politely answered all of his questions without going into our *Monty Python* routine live on the air. I was proud of ol' Chet for showing that kind of restraint. After the interview ended, the reporter thanked us for our time, and told us we would be on tonight's six o'clock news, and maybe the eleven o'clock news as well, depending on how busy of a news day it was.

"Well, there they are," Andrew teased when we finally returned to the trailer. "It's the big celebrities. Why didn't they interview me? You let Dave say a few words."

"Maybe Andrew," I said, "—It's because you aren't wearing any shoes."

"Or a shirt," Dave said.

"Or any jeans!" Chet said, pointing to Andrews's cut-offs—"No shoes. No shirt. No interview!" Chet laughed, which did not make the troubadour all that happy.

But it made the rest of us smile.

After our interview break, we got back on the Iowa trail and rode west for the rest of the day. I asked Dave to scout up ahead to find us a bar or restaurant in Farmington or Bloomfield where we could watch our news story, which Dave did. By 5:30 that afternoon, the Preacher was pulling us around to the back of a local tavern in Bloomfield to park the trailer. I told Andrew to stay outside with the horses, which pissed him off even more. "Hey, it's outta my hands," I said, pointing to the "No Shoes. No Shirt. No Service" on the bar door, which sent Andrew back to the rig in a pout.

Chet, Dave, and I shuffled our way into the small, dimly lit Iowa bar, which I was surprised to see, was strangely half-full for a weekday. Chet ordered us three Schaeffer's and we made our way to the main TV area, near the pool table. We flipped around the dial and—goddamn—there we were! Chet, Dave, and me standing in front of the "Cross AmeriCA86" logo on the side of rig. Our story was two minutes long and featured a map of the United States with our route mapped out, which Chet liked quite a bit. "Fancy graphics. Wish our maps were that good!" Chet laughed.

"Hey, don't knock our maps, I paid a pretty penny for all those," I laughed.

Must say, it was pretty amusing to observe the barflies slowly recognizing us. I'd look out the corner of my eye and watch them as they looked at the TV, then back to us (then back to the TV), then back to us. It usually took five or six double-takes before one would get up and walk over to ask the familiar refrain we would hear throughout Iowa—"Hey, aren't you those guys on TV?"

"We sure are," I'd say.

"Hard to miss us," Chet would say almost every time.

Quite a few barflies came over to shake our hands, which was nice. Unfortunately, we didn't have time to drink all the free beers they offered, but we sure thanked them for the gesture, before hitting the road again. "All in all, a successful TV appearance," I said to Chet as we rode away. "Iowa has some good old guys, don't they?"

"Sure do, Boss. This could be our good luck state," Chet said.

I looked over at Chet and busted out laughing.

Chet was still sipping on a beer in the saddle!

"How'd you smuggle that thing out? And why didn't you smuggle me one?"

"Here, catch!" Chet tossed me a beer, "Didn't want to waste the free ones. The barkeep just nodded at me on the way out. Figured it was his gift to us!"

FM, I say!

Not sure if our reporter friend called his colleagues in the local media—but we ended up doing several more TV interviews in Iowa. After every one, we'd find a local tavern, and watch our interview as part of the ritual. It seemed like every day some nice Iowan would stop to ask, "Hey, aren't you those guys we saw on TV?" which made us feel good like we were doing something of consequence. The media coverage also gave us several more opportunities to bring attention to the $100,000 we were raising for the homeless back in Connecticut. I know those TV spots helped us raise some money because we got donations from all over Iowa. Now I don't reckon we got big heads or anything, but we sure got accustomed to people stopping to ask Iowa's favorite question, "Hey, aren't you those guys we saw on TV?"

"We sure are," We'd always reply, "Thanks for stopping to say Hi."

Then we'd tip our hats. *It beat performing the Monty Python routine.*

"Get the feeling, we're the two most famous cowboys in the state," Chet mused one day after riding away from yet another pleasant encounter with a curious Iowan.

"Don't they know the horses are the real stars?" I asked.

"Don't think Thunder'd be much of an interview. We speak way better English."

"You have got a point there," I chuckled.

Having somewhat conquered the medium of local television—one morning, somewhere between the towns of Farmington and Mount Ayr—we got another visit from the Iowa media. This one was a nice guy in his 40s who stopped on his way into work to ask us if we would come on his radio show. Radio? "We got the faces for radio, boss. Maybe we should do it?" Chet joked. It was hard to say no to this radio guy; he was very persuasive.

"Aw, what the hell, we'll do it!" I said after hearing his pitch, "What better things do we have to do to anyway?" The guy said his radio station was just a few miles up the road on Route 2, "You can't miss our tower. See you boys in about an hour!" he said then took off in his car. I chuckled as I watched him go, "Chet. If we can't spot a radio tower on these flat plains, there must be something wrong with us."

Well, true to form, it was impossible to miss that huge radio tower. By the time we pulled up to the station, Dave and Andrew were waiting in the rig. Chet and I tied Thunder and Rebel to the trailer, loosened their cinches, and drank some ice-cold water to wet our whistles, and lubricate our throats for yapping.

Chet and I then took a few deep breaths and walked through the front door—"Ready to be a celebrity again?" I said to Chet.

"What the hell," Chet said. "Let's get into character."

The receptionist led us into the glass-walled studio where our DJ friend was ready to interview us. It felt downright unnatural to remove our cowboy hats and don these strange headsets. Once we sat down, the first thing I saw was Andrew outside pressing his face up against the glass window to get a better look. He was still wearing his cut-offs. "Uh, may want to call the cops on that hippie—he definitely ain't with us!" Chet joked.

The DJ ignored Chet's joke. "No pressure fellas, but your voices are about to be broadcast live on the air to millions of Iowans. Who's excited?"

"I am? This will be a first," I gave Chet a raised eyebrow.

"Wish you hadn't told us that," Chet said, "OK, Pard, let's do this shit live!"

The DJ shook his finger, "No cursing or any blue language, please! This is a family station! And we're live in, three, two, one." I remember Chet smiled at me (sheepishly) as the DJ counted down. Here we go again!

It felt a little otherworldly to spend months on a horse speaking to no one—then suddenly being interviewed live on the air. But ol' Chet and I politely answered all of our interviewer's questions. It was a great interview. We even got to talk about some of our experiences on the trail, and some of the good people we met along the way. Chet also brought some depth to the conversation by bringing up the plight of the American farmer, and how painful it was to see all those abandoned farm towns in Illinois, which I felt was a nice touch. Then after a pleasant thirty minutes, the interview was over, "That was painless," Chet said, standing up. "Think I need a smoke after that!"

We thanked the radio personality and took him outside to meet "the real heroes of the trip" Rebel, Thunder, Big Red, and the Wizzer. The DJ gave the boys several pats and said, "We'll interview you guys on the way back."

Chet and I never got to hear our radio interview (since it went out live), so we never found out how it was received—but more and more cars kept stopping to talk to us, that's for sure. "Wonder if they heard the show, too?" Chet would muse.

"Which one? We're everywhere!" I'd marvel, which made us both laugh at the absurdity of it all. After this experience, Chet and I both agreed, we'd rather be in the saddle than in front of a microphone any day, but the media coverage in Iowa accomplished one key intangible—it helped to break up the crushing monotony and boredom that had become our biggest mental challenge. But don't tell the horses that.

They might get offended.

Around our makeshift Iowa dinner table, on the night of July 3rd, I reckon I had one of my brighter ideas. "You all have worked real hard. How bout we cut it short tomorrow and search for a farm that'll put us up? We can celebrate the Fourth with a little extra R&R!" The team hooted and hollered. I looked at the preacher man, "You up for some more scouting?"

"For the afternoon off? You bet," Dave said with a smile.

For the first time since Sue and Diane surprised us back in Illinois, our minds were on a little downtime. "Hey Jeff, you mind if I bring a woman back to camp tomorrow night?" Andrew asked.

"No women at camp," Chet and I said in unison.

"You had your ladies fly out here," Andrew groused.

"No, we didn't. That was a surprise," Chet said.

"And they're our wives. It's a little different than picking up someone at a bar."

"You're not even married to Diane," Andrew accused Chet.

"So, she's my FI-ANCE. Gotta problem with that?" Chet raised his eyebrow, and that ended that conversation right there! That Andrew, he's always looking for an angle.

He would not be getting it from us.

The next morning, we had ridden about a mile or so, outside the town of Corydon—when Dave showed up looking uncharacteristically happy. He told us he found a spot to enjoy the Fourth just a few miles up the road. Dave had met a nice farming couple (named Bill and Linda) that invited us to bunk in one of their fields. After logging only seven hours on the trail on July 4th—I pulled the plug and officially called it a day—telling the team to follow Dave to the farm for a little celebration.

While Chet and I spent an hour or so entertaining Bill and Linda with humorous stories about our adventures—Dave let the boys loose in one of Bill and Linda's fields to enjoy some horse R&R.

"Where'd you stick the boys?" I asked Dave later.

"In one of their fields, up by that corral we passed about a mile down. Bill says we can pitch camp *out there*," Dave pointed to the field across the road.

"That'll work," I said, "As long as the boys are safe."

Being the Fourth of July, I was pleasantly surprised to learn we didn't have to go seek out a local fireworks show to enjoy—we didn't have to—one found us!

"Look! You can see the Corydon fireworks from here!" Andrew enthusiastically pointed at the sky, like the kid that he still was.

"Well, will you look at that? Not a bad perch, if I do say so myself," Chet said.

"F.M strikes again," I said.

While watching the fireworks, the outfit relaxed and took it easy around the campfire. Andrew pulled out his guitar and serenaded us (rather poorly, but whatever) while we dug into another one of Chet's cowboy chili feasts.

After supper, Dave surprised us with a six-pack of "Iowa's finest and cheapest beer" that cost under a dollar, which was mighty impressive. Not all that tasty, but it sure did the trick. While sipping on a lukewarm beer, something about this moment struck me as poignant. I wondered what sweet Sue was doing this Fourth of July—was she having fun at some BBQ? Was she cursing me, and this trip to high heaven? Is she sending divorce papers my way (as we speak) via the Pony Express?

It had been a while since we'd seen a payphone—I felt so damn guilty. Would Sue forgive me for not calling to wish her a Happy Fourth? I imagine she must be very pregnant by now. My heart ached something fierce. We were more than worlds apart now, and I couldn't do anything about it—except keep plodding forward, further away from my wife, and my Connecticut home.

After the fireworks died down, the stars came out. The troubadour had talked a good game all day—but we all were beyond bushed—so the team bunked down for the night without much said. Andrew never went into town looking for love—the kid was asleep before his head hit his makeshift pillow. The tall Iowa grass sure was a welcome bed; it provided a nice soft cushion for our overworked bodies. As I lay under the stars, I told myself never to forget the heartache I feel on this Fourth, without my sweet Sue. I vowed never to miss another major holiday with her for the rest of our lives.

I'd be remiss if I didn't mention, right before I drifted off—a funny thought crossed my mind—*I hope the boys are OK.* This would turn out to be a premonition.

One I wish I had heeded sooner!

I stirred the Preacher Man around 4 A.M. the next morning to get the coffee perking—"No rest for the wicked," I said, nudging Dave awake. I let ol' Chet and young Andrew snooze a little longer. The first crack of dawn broke over the eastern plains; it was a picture-perfect Iowa morning. Over a fresh cup of cowboy coffee, I mused, "You know Dave, life is amazing. What a truly beautiful morning this is."

"Sure is tranquil. This is the best time of day if you ask me," Dave said, "Not too hot, and look at that sunrise." We gazed at the pink and orange sunrise and just sipped our coffee. Life was perfect.

Then the entire trip almost went to hell!

After coffee, I asked Dave to run down and check on the boys to make sure they were still kicking. Twenty minutes later—while I was rinsing my toothbrush in an old coffee can—I looked up and saw Dave rumbling the rig down the dirt road.

"Uh oh," I could tell something was wrong.

"Chet, get up, Pard! Think we got a problem! "

Just then, Dave slammed on the brakes, kicking up a cloud of dust, yelling—"Boss, boss, boss! Come here, quick!"

I ran over to the truck, "What is it?"

"Fireworks must have scared the boys. Tried goin' through the fence, get in! Thun's tangled in barbwire, and Red may have sliced a hoof off."

I got in the front seat in a daze.

"Jeeeesus!" I could hear Chet say, pulling on his shirt and hopping in back. I yelled over to the troubadour, who (somehow) was still sleeping.

"Andrew! Wake the hell up and pack up camp!"

Dave peeled out like he was in the Indy 500—no one said a word.

Dave was shaking with emotion.

One solemn "goddammit!" is all I could muster. *This was my worst nightmare.*

A mile down the road, we hopped out, and carefully approached the corrals where the boys had gathered. Thunder was standing in an unnatural position, next to Big Red a few feet away. Chet looked inside the corral, "Reb and Wizz are accounted for. They look fine!"

"That's good," I said, jogging to Thunder to assess the damage, "Thunder was the first one through. Dave, bring me the kit! I saw a long strand of barbwire was embedded in Thunder's torso, then ran down his flanks and wrapped around his hind legs. "Never seen anything like this," I yelled over to Chet, "Thun's standing here like nothing happened! How's Red?"

"Ain't good, boss, ain't good!"

I ran over, and Dave had been right—Red's right rear hoof was sliced in half and bleeding profusely. Chet and I jumped into action with our basic knowledge of how to care for scratches and bruises. "Stop that bleeding, apply pressure, Chetter." Chet applied salve and bag balm to Big Red's hoof. I took a deep breath, closed my eyes for a second to try to control my fear. I remember looking up at the sky and saying out loud, "Please, God, don't let him die."

"You're gonna live, boy!" Chet said, "You're too tough an old fart."

Dave showed up with more horse medicine and first aid supplies from the trailer.

"Keep him off of that foot, and keep him relaxed while I go untangle Thunder."

I went back and tended to Thunder myself. He seemed almost sedated; the big boy was clearly in shock. Fortunately, I had my Gerber tool on my belt, so I used it to follow the barbwire around Thunder's body to find some loose points where I could cut away small sections of wire. All the time, I patted Thunder and told him how brave he was. I rubbed him on his neck to keep him as still as possible as I carefully pulled away the long strand of barbwire embedded in his chest, flanks, and legs. After some careful surgery, I finally got it all off him.

"We've come too far to turn back now, old pal," I patted Thunder, and we locked eyes, so he knew his old friend was here to help. He stayed calm and still the entire time. I yelled over to Dave, "Will you ask Bill if he could recommend a good horse doctor? Hopefully, one that's close!"

"Good luck trying to find a vet on a Sunday after the 4th of July," Chet said.

"All of Iowa can't be at church yet," I said. "Pray a kindly doc takes pity on us."

Dave returned twenty minutes later with the name, address, and phone number of the nearest veterinarian who lived ten miles away in Missouri. Dave had called ahead to make sure the Doc would see us on a Sunday, which he would, thank God. When we pulled into the Vet's office, we unloaded Big Red first, since he was more injured.

I nervously shook the Vet's hand and thanked him for seeing us on such short notice. When I explained the situation, the Vet didn't seem too concerned with Thunder—he was more focused on Big Red's injured hoof, which made me worried about Red's safety. Both horses were like my children; it was heartbreaking to see them both in pain. After the Vet cleaned and treated Red's hoof, he said that's "one lucky horse," which was a huge relief. Although Red's hoof looked like absolute hell, the Doc seemed to think, "No tendons were severed so he should heal pretty quickly."

We had dodged another bullet—if Big Red had severed a tendon, I would have been forced to put the old boy down, right here in Iowa. Thankfully, it didn't come to that; having to euthanize one of the horses would've been like losing a son. It would also have ended the entire trip! But, as F.M. would have it, once again—it was just not meant to be. Bloodied and bruised, the outfit was still kicking*!* "Just clean his wound three times a day and apply this salve and bag balm, and in two or three weeks, you may be able to ride him again. Just keep him off that foot! " The Vet gave us penicillin and a syringe; I had given plenty of shots to horses in my past, so I knew how to treat them.

When the Vet got to Thunder, he looked at him a long while, "You really ride this big fella every day?"

"Yes, sir. He's faster and more agile than he looks. I trust him with my life."

"You're a big, strong, pretty fella, aren't ya?" the Vet said, "We're gonna get you all healed up."

"He's got a heart bigger than Wyoming and Montana, put together," I said, getting a little choked up, "Can't lose Thun—he's the most important member of our outfit, except for ol' Chet here."

"Never heard you say that before," Chet put his arm around my shoulder.

"What would we do without our cookie?" I patted Chet on the back to try to lighten the mood. Because I won't lie—I was genuinely scared! Fortunately, since I was able to remove all the barbwire, the Doc said Thunder was just covered in deep cuts that could be treated with antibiotics. The good old Vet, I wish I could remember his name, said if we gave Thunder three to four days off—he should be back to normal and OK to put back in the rotation, "There may be some scarring, but his breed's got pretty thick skin," the Vet said. "Thunder will live to ride another day! "

"You're easin' my mind, Doc. I can't tell you how thankful we are. I might cry."

"That's alright. Cry away. Cowboys are people too," The Doc said with a wink.

Which made me smile again, "How much do we owe you for saving our horses?"

"Let's just say—no charge," The Vet said coyly through his bushy white mustache, "It's for a good cause, am I correct?"

Chet and I were speechless, "Yes, sir, it sure is."

The old horse doctor pulled on his colorful suspenders and told us he appreciated "all we'd been through" and "would like to make a donation to our charity this way."

I was floored.

This good-hearted Veterinarian—like so many other good people we met—became an unofficial member of our team by offering to help us when we needed it most. We thanked the old Vet. I remember telling him (a few times) how grateful we were.

"Just promise, you'll have a cold Olympia beer for me when you reach the Pacific," the Vet said.

"You got it. I'll have two!" Chet replied.

Looking back on yet another FM moment, I know that good old Vet made a big difference in the boys' recovery time. He may have even saved their lives. If you're out there, Doc, I'm forever thankful for your generosity. Chet and I will most definitely drink a cold one for you when we reach the Pacific!

Chet, Dave, and I loaded the horses back on the trailer and slowly made our way back to the farm where Andrew, Rebel, and Wizzer were waiting to begin the day's ride.

"What was all the fuss about?" Andrew said, totally unaware of what just happened.

"Go back to sleep. You missed everything," Dave joked.

"What a relaxing morning," Chet said sarcastically, "You know Dave, our trip just almost ended, don't you?" Dave took Chet's cue to apologize to the team (and the boys) for "trusting that damn field" a mile away.

I put my arm around the Preacher's shoulders, "You're off the hook, Preacher Man. We'll probably need to camp closer to them from now on, but no one could've predicted they'd be spooked by some two-dollar fireworks. You're still a topnotch scout in my book."

"Means a lot to hear you say that, Jeff," Dave said. "I'll do better."

"We all will. I'll be sure of that," I said.

After dodging this near disaster, I truly feel someone is looking out for us. F.M. I say—now more than ever!

The rest of Iowa was a blur of gratitude. Rebel and Wizzer pulled double duty for the next seven days. We took precautions to make sure they didn't burn out, giving them extra grain (twice a day) to keep their energy up. As for us human cowpokes—there weren't a whole lot of words spoken the next few days. The team was focused on being extra cautious in everything we did to make sure Rebel and Wizzer stayed strong and safe.

Chet and I took turns carefully cleaning, treating, and wrapping Big Red's foot every day. Thunder used his time off to inhale as much grain as possible to get his (boundless) energy back. He still looked like hell—but his were topical wounds—so after about three days, our fearless leader was back at the head of the rotation, raring to go.

"Glad Thun's back, boss," Chet said.

"Me too, pard. Me too," I said, riding Thun for the first time in days.

"Perfect timing. Reb and Wiz were wearin' down," Chet said.

"That's one thing we'll never have to worry about with this-un," I chuckled, "Thunder doesn't wear down. *Not now. Not ever.*"

I thanked the "horse gods" for letting us gallop another day.

But being the team leader (internally), I reckoned I let the boys down by not staying on top of their sleeping arrangements, so I vowed to turn my senses to hyper-aware for the rest of the trip. I also vowed I would not see another drop of horse blood spilled on this trip. Not on my watch.

The boys meant that much to me.

Our outfit ended our Iowa tour by riding through the towns of Clarinda, then Sydney, then we headed south to Nebraska City. I couldn't believe we were going to make it to Nebraska, which was almost the halfway point of the trip.

Of course, being me, with another milestone comes more "deep thoughts" from the saddle—this idea had been ruminating for a while—*What have we become since the trip started?* I pondered this one for hours. I figured I wasn't sure what exactly we had become after all we'd been through, so far—but at very minimum—I'd say we've grown into one tough, smelly, mangy-looking outfit with a hell of a lot of heart—two-legged critters included!

Looking back, I reckon we didn't have much of a "team identity" until we were tested (repeatedly) here in the Midwest. We had already survived multiple bridge crossings and multiple dog attacks—but the near-fatal disaster with Big Red and Thunder galvanized us, and brought us all together. I guess it took a near disaster for all of us to realize how close we came to losing one of our family members and bringing our trip to an abrupt end. Even Andrew was showing some gratitude for all the good fortune (and good people) that helped us get this far.

"You know what we're doing that's unique?" Andrew said to me on our last day in Iowa, "I hitchhiked across the country once, and we're kinda doing the same thing."

"How do you figure that?" I said.

"We're depending on the kindness of strangers to get us through. That's pretty cool." Andrew said it right, for once.

In the heartland, we only "lived to ride another day" because the people we met gave in ways that transcended words. I can't explain it—but I've never felt as thankful for being an American as I did here in the heartland. With Big Red and Thunder on the mend, and out of danger, we had dodged another major bullet and learned something about ourselves along the way.

Chet figured it was a sign it was, "Our destiny to reach the Pacific."

"You might be onto something," I said, "Who knows what we'll learn about ourselves when we reach the Rockies?"

"I know what I'll learn—that I didn't pack enough warm clothes!"

Good ol' Chet—he would not be wrong about that one, either!

Good thing I packed enough for both of us.

FM, I say.

Chet and Jeff training for the trip.

More training.

With unnamed friend (center) during training.

Speaking to unnamed TV reporter at Hartford State Capitol.

Cameraman with Chet's brother; cousin; Chet's girlfriend, Diane; and Chet's dad, Mike (far right with white hat).

With Governor Bill O'Neill at steps of State Capitol.

With Governor O'Neill's wife, Nikki, and Chet's mom, Jean.

With Brad Davis (right), WDRC's morning drive radio personality—and still on the air!—in Hartford, Connecticut.

With Howard Morse (center), one of our PR coordinators.

Discussing details at the State Capitol.

Watching the news on first evening of our trip. We were the lead story!

Dave Huntington keeping watch over our rig while were on the road.

Taking a break in a small town just outside of New Preston, Connecticut, on Day 2 of our trip.

Approaching the town of New Milford, Connecticut, on Day 3.

Somewhere near the North Platte River outside of Ogallala, Nebraska.

Taking a shortcut through Togwotee Pass in the Jackson Hole Valley of Bridger-Teton National Forest near Grand Teton National Park in Wyoming while on our way to Yellowstone National Park.

Jeff at our campsite in the Frank Church-River of No Return Wilderness in Idaho.

Riders complete 4½-month trek to help needy

Three Connecticut men ride into the waves at Oyehut Friday afternoon as the finale to their 4½-month trek across America to help the hungry and homeless. Below, Chet Tomasiewicz, right, and Jeff Pappas on the last leg of a 3,300-mile ride. (Daily World photos by Greg Lehman)

The Daily World newspaper clipping of us riding on the shores of the Pacific Ocean at Oyehut Bay, Washington, September 12, 1986.

MYSTICAL NAVIGATORS, BIBLICAL STORMS, AND "BITING THE BIG RADISH" IN NEBRASKA

"America is not a country of immigrants,
we are a country of pioneers."
—*Mike Klepper*

NEBRASKA. JUST THE word itself sounded strange to the ear. To this cowboy, it felt a little unfamiliar, a little uncomfortable, and just a little, uninviting. Four hundred and thirty miles wide and hotter than the surface of the sun, our date with the treacherous lady they called the Cornhusker State was fast approaching, as intimidating as the turbulent weather conditions we were sure to encounter there. Memories of the games Chet and I played in the saddle to keep from losing our dang minds had melted away in the Midwestern heat like ice on the hood of the rig.

I'd alerted the outfit (repeatedly) that we were about to face the longest, most dangerous stretch of our journey, so we better be prepared to "cowboy up" from here on out. I won't lie, almost losing Thunder and Big Red to a freak accident shook me to the core. I was determined not to let anything, or anyone, sneak up on us again.

A day before we hit the Nebraska border, I laid out our mission to the team over a batch of Chet's cowboy chili. "Men, if we're gonna survive Nebraska, we're gonna have to overcome a mess of trouble, weather-wise. This means play time's over, for all of us—got that, Andrew?"

"When did playtime start, Jeff?" Andrew joked.

"Will you pay attention for once?" Chet slapped Andrew with his Stetson.

I can't say my "cowboy up" speech made the Troubadour all that happy, but happiness was the last thing on my mind. Lord help me, I wasn't going to allow any more bloodshed on this trip.

"What if the Troubadour spills his own blood?" Chet mused later that night.

I chuckled, "As long as the boys aren't involved, that's his responsibility."

Before sun-up the following morning, our outfit embarked from a kind Iowan's quarter horse farm where we had bunked in their bramble the night before, and headed west on Route 2. "Guess we're nearly halfway home. You spy the Pacific yet?" Chet asked.

"Not yet," I said, lensing the terrain, "I'm focused on the problems ahead."

"You mean Nebraska?" Chet joked.

"It's no joke. It's got no shade. It's hot and humid as hell, with bugs the size of Volkswagens, and twisters that come out of nowhere."

"You mentioned that."

"It's gonna get a lot worse before it gets better," I said, dead serious.

Chet (being Chet) lightened the mood with a timely chuckle, "To quote everyone's favorite space cowboy, Han Solo—Never tell me the odds!"

As F.M. (our mystical navigator) would have it, around mid-day, we pulled over near this neat-as-a-museum Iowa farmhouse and were quickly invited in for lunch. The kindness of the Iowa people will never cease to amaze me; these good folks were another reminder that F.M., the horse gods, or whatever you want to call the "powers that be," were still watching over us. Sitting on their front porch, the team feasted on a lunch of hamburgers, pickled vegetables, and pitchers of lemonade. Dessert was the ubiquitous Jell-O salad, a staple of the Midwest, made with ice cubes for quick service. Our lunchtime conversation with the farmer couple soon turned to the weather, which I learned was customary here on the open plains.

"You cowpokes best keep an eye on the sky," said Sam, the old farmer, over his toothpick. "Next state over's got some formidable weather—tornados, wind storms, dust storms, hail storms—every kind of storm you can imagine."

"So we hear," I said, glancing over at Chet, who was already scanning the horizon when (on cue) something ugly suddenly punctured the sky. Dave and Andrew had been so busy listening to (what Chet and I called) the "bizarre blues" in the rig all morning that they'd already failed to warn us of an oncoming storm. I watched the sky above us change from friendly to foreboding in the time it took Chet to wolf down his Jell-O salad.

"Hey Preacher, thought the weather report said we had clear sailing?" I looked over at Dave with a strategically raised eyebrow.

"Uh, it did before lunch," Dave said with his mouth full of hamburger.

"Not too sure about your police work," I pointed at the storm clouds coming our way. "Can you double-check?"

"I'll check again," Dave ran to the rig like a good hand.

"Do we have to check the radio every minute?" Andrew whined.

"YES," Chet and I both said, which made Sam chuckle.

I calmly gave our two young hands another friendly reminder to do their jobs or "We could all bite the big radish."

"Big radish? What's that?" Andrew said.

"Dirt nap? Tits up? What you will be if you don't shape up," Chet said.

I couldn't have said it any better than ol' Chet.

"Well. You fellas best be going if you're gonna outrun that thing," Sam said.

"Shoot, the boys ain't that fast," Chet replied with his eyes on the sky.

We thanked Sam and his wife, Adele, for a fine lunch, and they wished us luck on our journey. We met up with Dave by the rig; he told us the weather report now confirmed the storm we already saw with our eyes.

"Weatherman seemed as surprised as us," Dave said, and I believed him.

"They sure get paid a lot for being right half the time," I said, "OK, let's saddle up, and we'll see how far we get before all hell breaks loose."

Preparing to get soaked, Chet and I shook out our rain slickers, but not with the bravado of the past. The crackle of electricity in the air prickled my nerves; I felt danger looming. I think the boys felt it, too. "Don't like the looks of that one, Chetter. Not one bit," I said as we mounted up just as the first drops of rain began to fall.

"This shit could get ugly," Chet said, and he was right.

Five minutes into our afternoon ride and horizontal wind and rain nearly blew us off the road. The thunderstorm rumbled and rolled across the sky, then came hail the size of baseballs, which forced us to take cover next to an old abandoned gas station.

We watched in amazement as bolts of lightning crashed down around us, kicking up dust. Captivated by the electrical storm, I soon realized that staring too long at the neon crackles began to burn my retinas, so I stopped doing that.

"Never in my life have I seen the weather so fickle and furious!" I shouted.

"And we're not even in Nebraska yet!" Chet yelled.

"This ain't a good omen!"

"We need football helmets to ride in this crap!" Chet yelled.

Then, as quickly as the storm blew in, it veered east and—poof—it was gone.

Chet and I cautiously emerged from our shelter to make sure the rig wasn't damaged. It wasn't, thanks to Dave, parking it out of harm's way. Once we got the weatherman's blessing to continue, we got back on the trail and cautiously finished our afternoon ride.

A few miles down the road, Chet and I found the gateway to Nebraska we were looking for called the *Nebraska City Bridge*, so we pulled over and prepared to cross over the Missouri River. Considering all the trouble we'd had crossing bridges in the past, this one was a whole lot easier than crossing over into Iowa or New York. We timed it to avoid late afternoon traffic, and thanks to the "boys in blue" who always seemed to manifest when we needed them, we managed to get another police escort, this time by an Iowa State Trooper named Jack.

Big thanks to Officer Jack for getting us across in one piece.

We can only pray Nebraska will be as welcoming.

I'm thankful most of my silent prayers were answered on the trip—but not that prayer!

As advertised, Nebraska lived up to its nasty reputation and sucked the ever-loving life out of the team (pretty much) as soon as we crossed the border. Forget fun, forget games, forget setting any world records—this is the part of the story when we began to simply "exist" rather than "live." Shoot, I couldn't blame it all on Nebraska. After riding 2,000 miles on horseback, and living outside in the elements for three months, the outfit was worn out. Couple that with the 105-degree heat and humidity, the unpredictable storms, and the predictable swarms of mosquitos, and we had to alter our schedule, and stop riding at 10 or 11 A.M. to conserve energy, and avoid the extreme heat of the afternoons.

The team spent our first sultry night in Nebraska camping just outside its "mecca of monotony" as Chet put it, near the town of Unadilla. Dave had scouted us a safe campsite that had a picnic canopy for shelter, as well as a concrete foundation, to keep us grounded in case a rogue twister came to pay us a midnight visit. Our site was surrounded by freshwater and trees, and even had a place to put up the horses. "It's as sheltered as I could find, boss," Dave said, "Seems solid in case a big storm hits."

"You done good Preacher," I said as we unpacked our gear and set up camp.

It was on this night that we had our second curious encounter with a gift-bearing ex-muleskinner named Don Peterson. We'd met Don two days prior riding on an Iowa grey road. He was kind enough to bring us a home-cooked lunch, the likes of which we hadn't seen since we left civilization: fried chicken, mashed potatoes, gravy, mixed vegetables, rolls, and real butter, with ice-cold milk, tea, and watermelon for dessert.

Tonight, the old muleskinner took it up a notch and showed up bearing the gifts of eleven steaks, eleven baking potatoes, eleven ears of corn on the cob, plus fresh string beans, zucchini, and iced beer—which was deeply appreciated and thoroughly enjoyed. While we ate our supper, Don regaled us with stories of his mules and his life as a modern-day muleskinner. Then Don popped a surprise question on me.

"You think I could join your wagon train?" He asked me in front of the team, "I'd give it all up now, just to ride with you to the coast."

"Give what all up?" Chet asked, which was a good question.

I was touched old Don thought so much of our trip, but I was a little confused. Here was a 62-year-old, fit, well-spoken farmer who was married with four grown children—yet he desperately wanted to leave his happy home behind to join our smelly cowboy outfit on the most hellacious part of our journey?

"You got a death wish, Don? Reckon Nebraska's gonna be a helluva ride," I said.

"I know, I've ridden it. But I never rode all the way to the Pacific."

"Won't your mules, or your wife mind?" Chet asked.

"Don't worry about them. They'll be happy I'm gone!" Don said.

Don was a nice enough fella, but I got a strange vibe from him I couldn't quite put my finger on. This was the second person who asked to join our team in the last three states. The last one, Jean, was the lady cowboy in Indiana who had romantic feelings for Chet, of which I could make sense. But I wondered what possessed ol' Don to make a big decision like that so quickly? Was this old muleskinner trying to escape something, and saw us as a way out? I couldn't figure it. Of course, our resident "bearer of bad judgment" Andrew thought it would be fun to bring Don along—but I spoke for the party.

After dinner, I pulled Don aside and broke it to him privately. "I'm flattered you want to come with us, and we sure appreciated all your hospitality, but we just don't have the room. It's hard enough to find adequate water, food, and campsites for eight of us. I figure adding two or three more head of stock, a wagon, and another cowboy would present us with logistics problems of an enormity we could not deal with. You're a good old guy, but."

I reckon ol' Don left us that night at about 11:00 P.M., no doubt disappointed. After his departure, we sacked out early in our tents, Chet bedded down in the horse trailer (in case another storm crept up on us). As I drifted off to sleep, I had no regrets about Don. Young Andrew did, but that kid's never happy.

Tomorrow, we are on our way to Lincoln.

The next morning, Chet and I scoured our Nebraska maps for a grey road that suited the boys—but no luck. We couldn't avoid riding through the city of Lincoln, which is the Capitol of Nebraska—so Chet and I made a plan. First, we scouted a campsite just outside of Lincoln at the Nebraska State Fairgrounds, which Don Peterson said would be hospitable for our four-legged friends. Next, we needed to plot a safe route through Lincoln so, instead of winging it—Chet and I drove the rig up a day early to see if we could coordinate our route with the local police.

I knew lady luck was still riding with us when the first person we met at the Lincoln Police Station was a friendly officer named Katie, who just so happened to be born in Bridgeport, Connecticut—near me and Chet's current stomping grounds. When we told Officer Katie our story, she was quick to help us find the person in charge of horses. It turns out, the Lincoln P.D.'s biggest concern wasn't traffic jams or horses running wild in the streets—but surprisingly, public hygiene. While plotting our route with the city's resident horse expert named Officer Bill, he stressed several times that we had to "pick up what your boys leave behind," which we always did when riding through town, anyway.

"I think we can handle that," Chet said with a smile.

Perhaps it was because we hadn't seen hide nor hair of any town with a population of more than 1,000 in quite a while, but the Nebraska State Fairgrounds felt stately by comparison, much bigger than most of the towns we had passed through lately. It was so damn sprawling; we got lost inside. After we finally located their Fair Offices, we explained our situation to the nice fairgrounds folks, and one of their caretakers guided us to some of the largest horse stalls I'd ever encountered in all my days of riding.

"Damn, these stalls are bigger than my house!" Chet exclaimed.

"Pretty nice digs," I said, "Hope the boys don't get spoiled."

"Hell, they're already spoiled," Chet exclaimed, which made ol' Red whicker like they'd practiced their comedy timing for weeks.

"I reckon you two crackups are made for each other," I said with a smile.

With Thunder and Red safely tucked away in the Presidential Suite of horse stalls, we returned to the rig and rode Reb and Wizard into adjoining stalls. We fed and watered the boys, then dug into Chet's cowboy chili while Andrew stoked the open flame like a good hand. Guess the kid can still take some simple directions; if he keeps it up, Chet and I told him we wouldn't have to put him out to pasture, just yet!

After supper, our mangy crew decided to track down the nearest public showers, for humans. "Hot water, hot damn!" I could hear Chet holler from the stall next door. It was our first shower in ten days, and it was desperately needed. Chet and I knocked the first hundred layers of filth off us. I took a twenty-minute shower where I could see rivers of dirt coming off, as well as some hay, a few fleas, and, yes, a few dead ticks.

Once we'd cleaned up and were relaxing by the fire, Andrew had one of his patented mood swings, announcing his weariness of the entire project to the team, and wandering off on foot to see a movie in Lincoln. I suggested he see "Top Gun," but Andrew decided to see a movie that the rest of us never heard of—some French movie with subtitles. *Real artsy.*

With the Troubadour gone for the evening, all was quiet on the western front. The only thing left to do was watch the amazing light show the heavens were providing every night. As tonight's storm moved in from the southwest, we marveled at its majestic beauty. I joined Chet and Dave, who were sitting up against the trailer to watch the show, enjoying a cup of Joe with a healthy measure of milk, sugar, and bourbon for medicinal purposes only! "These are better than the dang fireworks," the Preacher remarked, still stoking the fire Andrew left to burn out.

"Good thing the boys aren't here to see this," Chet said with a chuckle, "They'd hightail it back to Connecticut!" Watching the lightning was entertaining enough—until the lightning bolts started slamming to the ground.

"Damn! That one was loud!" Chet shouted, clearly entertained. Judging by the three seconds between the flash of lightning and the thunderclaps, I figured, "Storm has to be thirty miles away, and coming our way, fast."

"Weatherman said it should move east before it gets to Lincoln," Dave said.

"It ain't gonna come this way. Wait—now it is?" Chet looked at me quizzically.

I put my finger to the air. Chet was right. The wind had suddenly changed course.

"Storms don't usually pop a one-eighty in the sky, do they?"

No one replied. Then Chet uttered the truest words he'd spoken on the trip.

"This is Nebraska, boss. Anything's possible."

Well, as F.M would not have it, at approximately 11:30 that night, the storm hit all right, and I mean, hit with a roar! We were awakened to a mess of thunder, lightning, and high winds with the craziest horizontal rain I'd ever seen that just about blew our tents back into Iowa. "So much for the goddamn weatherman!" I heard Chet yell as I scrambled to hold my tent down from the inside.

"It was supposed to miss us; I checked before bed!" Dave yelled back.

Chet and Dave began re-staking all our tents in the pitch dark.

As Chet recalled later, just at that moment, a bolt of lightning flashed down, and Chet could (suddenly) see Andrew sitting inside the rig, watching our campsite get blown all to hell. "What the hell are you doin'?" I heard Chet shout over the storm, which was so close now it sounded like a runaway freight train. It was so loud, I couldn't make out who, or what, Chet was screaming at out there, but I could guess! Chet was screaming because Andrew didn't bother to turn on the headlights so he could see what he was doing, or pull the truck around, so it shielded our tents from the wind.

He just sat there inside the rig, keeping himself dry, watching the rest of us struggle in the rain like he was back in the art house watching a movie, probably enjoying the hell out of seeing Chet run around like a chicken with his head cut off.

I remember peering outside my tent and seeing ol' Chet run over to the truck like an infantryman in a firefight to find a locked door. "Unlock the goddamn door!" Chet shouted. I think Andrew was scared Chet might drag him out of the rig and wring his neck right there because that door opened real quick.

"Can you give us a little help out here, Troubadour?"

"What do you expect me to do?" Andrew shouted.

"Your dang job!"

"They're your tents!" Andrew shouted back, which really pissed off Chet. I must say I was impressed by how Chet kept his cool, relatively speaking. I might have been inclined to give Andrew a swift kick in the soggy cut-offs, like ol' Thunder did to so many attack dogs on the trail, but he (fairly calmly) convinced Andrew to get out and help us batten down the hatches. Once the storm passed and our tents were secured again, Chet and I scolded Andrew again for not using his sense.

Then the adults had another medicinal bourbon (to unwind), before bedding back down, a lot "wetter for wear." I don't know about the rest of the team, but I caught a full three hours of dreamless sleep before waking at 3:30 A.M. to find most of our gear on the soggy side. We had survived our second hellacious flash storm. There would be many, many others. Drying out our gear, I thought, maybe one day, one of these storms will blow Andrew back to Connecticut? But maybe that was just wishful thinking on my part.

Day two in Nebraska was one of high cirrus, cirrus stratus, and cumulus clouds, following our outfit all day like buzzards circling their prey. "Lots of those puffy bastards look threatening, but none have dumped on us yet," Andrew said.

"Thanks, Captain Obvious," Chet replied as we entered Lincoln-proper for our morning ride through the city. The boys kept their molasses pace as we slowly made our way downtown, following the approved route. We got quite a few looks, but the citizens of Lincoln mostly left us alone until this old yellow pickup truck rolled up beside us, and a bow-legged cowboy wearing Ostrich boots hopped out to pay us a quick visit.

"You fellas lost?" the cowboy chuckled.

After relating our story, the cowboy, named Chris, informed us, "When you start a-gettin' to Grand Island, keep your eyes sharp for rattlers, now. The way you boys is headin', you'll surely see 'em."

Chet looked at me, "Just what we need; another thing that can possibly kill us?"

"You scared of snakes, Hoss?" I asked him.

"Uh, no comment," Chet said.

We thanked Chris for the tip and told him we'd watch out. Chris just nodded and hopped back in his truck, and that was that for Chris, the cowboy—and our uneventful ride through downtown Lincoln. As we left the city and ventured out into the great unknown, I could tell Chet still had snakes on his mind. "Don't worry, pard. Snakes are just another tourist attraction here," I said.

"I ain't attracted to 'em, if one gets too close, I'm taking that sucker out."

"With a garden hoe?

"If that's what it takes."

"Need my rifle?"

"You're the dead eye."

"Will you roast some rattlers for dinner if I shoot us up some?"

"Hell, boss, don't make me cook reptiles," he said with a shudder.

Who knew tough old Chet was afraid of a few little ol' snakes?

By 10 A.M. on Route 34, all visual stimuli had been reduced to one monotonous drone of cornfields and brown dirt vistas, as far as the eye could see. I reckon prolonged heat exposure, plus months of continuous hard work, can do strange things to a person's mind. Most people will accept their fate, grit their teeth, and bear the unpleasantness, which proved true for three of the human members of our party—the combination of heat and work created a certain internal numbness that allowed us to keep moving forward. But once the heat began climbing to 105 degrees daily, tempers began to wear thin. Chet and I made a real effort to keep a tight rein on our emotions, but biting my tongue was getting harder every day. I hate to pick on the young man, but the fourth

member of our party has decided, once again, that his mode of dress would be, how shall I say, as counter-cultural as possible?

Somewhere along the way on Route 34, Andrew decided the normal traditions of Western civilization didn't apply to him any longer. Maybe it was just the infernal heat, but he took to not wearing shoes, socks, a shirt, hat, or underwear. He began showing up every day in a pair of ragged cut-offs like he was stranded on some desert island. "Are you becoming a nudist?" I asked him one day.

"What?"

"Storm blow away your britches? Cause I brought some extras."

"It's none of your business how I dress, Jeff," Andrew replied. So once again, Chet and I had to explain that as a member of this outfit, we would appreciate it if he tried to look halfway presentable, "Just in case we ever run into another human being ever again." After our attempted pep talk, Andrew told me in no uncertain terms to mind my own damn business. Again. "I am a patient man," I said to Chet later that day, "But I'm getting less patient with his antics. Maybe it's just the heat?

"Nah." Chet said, "It's just Andrew."

Due to the heat and humidity, we continued to refine our daily regiment to keep both humans and horses from passing out from heatstroke. We got going even earlier in the A.M. to get in our morning shift, and before Mr. Sun told our bodies in no uncertain terms that we should hydrate, I'd pre-empt it by announcing to the team, "It's time to take a nooning, boys." A "nooning" became our midday pit stop where everybody on the team (man and horse alike) got pumped up with as many electrolytes and water as possible.

We began mixing baking soda and salt with the boys' food to help them retain fluids, and once a day, we also fed the horses a medicinal solution, which I took from (believe it or not) a cure for calf scours. So far, so good—but hell, it was scary to see the boy's tested to the limits of their endurance. We also had a heckuva time keeping dry (clean) blankets on the back of the boys. Clean was hard, but dry was even harder. Despite the slight breeze we'd get, at times, their blankets would stay damp with sweat all day, so we reserved a spare one for each animal, and made sure to rotate them, so their blankets were as dry as possible. "So far, no galls or hot spots. That's good." I said, checking the boys for damage.

"Think the consistent currying's paying off," Dave replied.

"All of our habits will tell the story at the end," I said.

"There's an end to this?" Chet joked.

Riding through Nebraska, this "all or nothing" land of extremes, I thought a lot about what it would be like if we had no rig, no maps, no air conditioning, and no technology to help us survive these conditions. My God, how supremely difficult it must have been to ride this trail a hundred years ago. The grit and determination of those early pioneers are just staggering. Looking at our bleak surroundings, I think of the human toll it took to open these lands. Five percent, or twenty thousand of the 400,000 pioneers who came this way reportedly died—which I now think could be an understatement. Incredibly strong and resilient people they were. I tip my hat to them all.

Besides the blast oven heat, unpredictable storms, and repetitive droll of nothingness that surrounded us every day, the outfit began to encounter swarming clouds of what appeared to be mosquitoes the size of quail eggs. Black and yellow-gray, these pesky critters were constantly attacking us en masse. They weren't your typical mosquitos either; these were armies of bloodthirsty critters, concerned only with bringing us misery. It didn't matter how fast we swept the bloodsuckers away with our bandanas (from us or the boys) they'd instantly regain the ground they lost. Even when we noticed no lumps had been raised on our skin, you could bet our tempers were raised all to hell.

Amid all these "natural wonders," you can probably imagine that our moods would eventually need a little pick me up, so Chet and I began distracting ourselves again, this time with an old café sign we could see on the horizon, promising some kind of soft drink heaven might be ahead. The sign read: "No Coke, only Pepsi."

Was it real or a mirage?

The entire outfit purported to see it, so Chet and I figured it had to be connected to a real café, so we kept riding toward our sweet carbonated oasis, dreaming of some ice-cold liquid heaven. When we finally arrived at the sign, we were overjoyed to discover it was real, and connected to an actual café that appeared to be open. Chet and I tied our horses (high) to the limbs of a young tree on a small greenway across from our objective—cold soft drinks!

Oh, the pure joy of air conditioning when you hadn't felt it in weeks—I thought as we wobbled our way across the street, like two Barnaby Joneses.

"Not many vehicles here, sure it's open?" Chet tried the door, which magically opened. Inside, the empty café was a 1950s style diner, with stainless steel everywhere, marble counters, and (most importantly) cold air pumping full blast. We were in heaven—until we heard (what has to be) one of the most horrible phrases in human history, "I'm sorry, but we're closed up."

"But ma'am, all we need is two of the largest Cokes you got and two huge ice waters," Chet laid on the charm with this nice waitress named Dottie, who was doing inventory in the back. Chet repeated the same story we had been giving people for months, telling Dottie who we were, where we came from, and why we were on these dang horses out in the middle of nowhere. Lucky for us, during Chet's story, close to a gallon of ice-cold liquid was consumed among us both.

Dot listened politely then said, "We're still closed."

Was Chet finally losing his mojo with the ladies? Who knew, but the good news was Chet's storytelling gave us time to convince Dottie to sell us the water, ice, and the Cokes we had been dreaming of all day. Then she politely shooed us back out into the blazing hot world, clutching our treasured cups of ice.

When we got to the rig, Andrew asked if we got him a Coke. "Cokes are rewards for a job well done," Chet said as we both carefully poured our cups of ice into the tepid water our canteens already held, to be savored later.

"Now you've got something to shoot for," Chet laughed.

"Well, you can't keep me from getting one!" Andrew said, running over to the café door, which was now locked. Poor Andrew banged on that door for a good long while, to no avail. Dottie, the waitress, never answered.

She must have known.

Riding away, I felt my mind slipping from the heat. Once again, we had forgotten to refill our canteens at the café. To understand why is to understand the numbness that was Nebraska. The heat prevented any attempt at making decent time. Our pace slowed even more as we headed toward a town called Tamora. "See you tomorrow, Tamora!" we'd shout to raise our spirits, but that didn't last long. Our pace was now that of men and animals who were nearing an abyss. To continue any faster would be dangerous. We couldn't even tell when we were dehydrated anymore, which sounds impossible—but with that light breeze we'd occasionally get, our sweat would evaporate as quickly as it came. "Hell, it can't be that hot out; neither of us are soaking wet," Chet said.

"Don't mean a thing, Hoss. It's like hypothermia. The effects are a little slower to catch up." With hypothermia, you're already miserable because of the combination of wet, cold, and wind. But with heatstroke and dehydration, you measure your misery differently. At night, one of the first signs is you'll have an insatiable thirst. It's not unusual for a quart of water to be consumed in one sitting. This usually happened two or three times in the evenings, for all of us. "First canteen never reaches the bottom," Chet said as he chugged water like he just won the Boston Marathon.

Our bodies felt like one dry sponge; you couldn't feel the water going in until full saturation had been reached. But once it did, you felt sated again, which brought a quick sigh of relief and a smile.

With all this daily torture being doled out by our host state—inevitably, a grim gallows humor evolved among the team, always deployed to cut the tension in the air. Whenever some strange country folks would emerge from the woods to pay us a curious how-do, or (ahem) threaten us with shotguns in the middle of the night—which happened a few times—Chet or I would break the tension by humming a few bars from the theme song of *Deliverance*, the ol' "Dueling Banjos" tune, to keep the mood as light as possible. One memorable instance occurred one night camping in Nebraska when a big bear of a man named Tom suddenly emerged from the darkness, claiming we had stolen his son's radio of all things. After we told him our story and convinced him who we were and that we had no reason to steal his son's radio, Tom lowered his twelve-gauge.

"Y'all seem genuine enough. Sorry, but we got horse thieves out here."

"And radio thieves, too, right?" Chet said.

"Shit, yeah. Can I offer you cowboys a turkey for sticking my gun in your face?"

"You got any turkey jerky?" Andrew asked.

"Pshaw, I'm talking about real turkey. My birds are the best in the state."

Tom explained he owned a turkey farm nearby, which we could hear gaggling off in the distance. I had brief flashes of having Thanksgiving dinner Chet-style over the campfire, but—how could we possibly pull that off? Ol' Chet, the resident cookie, cut my dream short, explaining to Tom that we couldn't cook the bird with our equipment. So, we thanked Tom for his kind offer, and Chet (sarcastically) thanked him "for not filling us full of buckshot," and strange ol' Tom, the paranoid Turkey farmer, disappeared back into the darkness with his shotgun. We think. Some people you just don't want to turn your back on. I may sleep with one eye open tonight. Just in case.

★ ★ ★

The boys gingerly approached the town of Grand Island like they were stepping through a field of landmines. Chris, the cowboy, had warned us Grand Island was "rattler country," but we hadn't seen one yet, which Chet no doubt was privately rejoicing. While he and Rebel whistled through the graveyard, I made the team pull over so I could call home from some desolate payphone to check in with my worried parents. This is when my Dad (Jack) up and announced he wanted to fly out from Connecticut and join us for a week.

A week? Out here? My Dad? The famous desk jockey?

"You're plenty tough, but trust me—no sane person wants to be out here on this trail of tears! The payphone I'm on is melting to my cheek, as we speak." I fibbed that part. "How about joining us when we get to the mountains in Wyoming, or closer to Washington when it's cooler?" I tried my best to talk him out of it, but Dad explained he had a wild hare about seeing "mythical Nebraska," which he romanticized since he was a boy, for some unexplained reason.

"I'm your father, and I want to support you when times are tough, what's so mysterious about that? You're on the toughest row to hoe right now, aren't you?"

"You're not wrong about that."

Hearing the sincerity in Dad's voice choked me up a little. As many arguments as we had when I was a teenager, the old man would still take a bullet for me. I don't know why I just now realized this, maybe it was just the desert sage in my eye, but hearing that he wanted to help me finish the ride hit my heart.

Still, I tried to talk him out of it. I promise I did.

Even Chet got on the horn and told Jack, "We're the walking dead!" and to "Send two body bags and some whiskey to Nebraska via Pony Express!" but our warnings fell on stubborn ears. Ol' Jack calmly listened to our pleas, then announced he would still be taking the next week off work to join us, my wishes be damned! This was a monumental event in itself. As far as I knew, Dad hadn't taken a real vacation in years.

"All right, I give up," I replied, "It's your vacation, but prepare to sweat. and bring mosquito repellent."

"And whiskey and women!" Chet yelled.

"Tell that Chet he'll be getting no such thing," Dad said with as much of a laugh as I'd heard from him in a long time, "All that's bad for his stamina. Maybe I'll stop by and pick up a care package from Sue?"

"That would be real nice. You remember how to ride a horse?" I asked. I honestly did not remember Dad, born and raised in New York City, ever riding a horse in all my life—but I asked anyway, which made him chuckle.

"Do stick horses count? You know your Dad's a desk jockey. How about if I just bring my walking stick and walk beside you? I'll get in the rental if I start stroking out."

I envisioned the soles of Dad's sneakers melting to the asphalt as he ambled next to us. "All right then. I won't try to change your mind. Just make sure your rental has plenty of Freon in the air-conditioning. I'll alert the team we got reinforcements coming." I hung up the phone. "How did this happen?"

My Dad was an honest and outspoken man who could be stubborn as one of Don Peterson's old mules—which is a trait Sue likes to claim I inherited (though I stubbornly refuse to admit it). So, I couldn't rightly blame Dad for refusing my advice—it's who he was! Looking back, I reckon Dad just wanted to support the cause in his own way. I think he was also a little curious about what we were doing out here. Either way, I took it as a generous gift of his time. Dad had spent his entire career working his tail off as an executive with the Exxon Corporation.

Years ago, when I began my first business, I remember Dad said he wished he'd tried entrepreneurship like me. I'm not sure he meant all that—he may have just been trying to make me feel good about the high-risk business I was jumping into. But when I hung up with him that day in the middle of Nebraska, I figured his surprise visit was his way of saying he wanted to see what would happen if he rolled the dice a little on this trip, and his son. Or maybe my worried Mom sent him out to check on us?

Knowing them both so well, it was probably a little bit of both.

"Jack's really coming? Holy crap, Jeff. Hide the women and the liquor!"

"We're old enough to drink. May want to hide *your* women, though," I chuckled.

"Does Jack ride, or, uh, camp?"

"He used to camp when he was a kid."

This gave the outfit a good laugh. "You tell him this ain't the place to rekindle his thrill for the great outdoors?" Chet asked.

"Yep, but he wouldn't listen. Said he wants to be here for the hard times."

"A real glutton for punishment must run in the family," Chet chuckled.

God rest his soul; my Dad was the classic 20th-century American father. If the adage "God loves a working man" is true, Jack is now a saint working double shifts at Heaven, Inc. Growing up, I thought he worked every day of his life. Quiet and stoic, but with a heart of gold, he would give the shirt off his back to help someone. I still remember the day he took my brother and me ice-skating at a local lake when a little girl fell through the ice. Dad was the first to run over and pull the girl out of the freezing water. Sometimes people ask where I got the courage to make this trip, and I always think back to that day when Dad courageously saved that little girl's life, and I just smile.

Three hot as hell days later, and Dad was finally due for arrival. His flight must be late, I thought as I checked my watch, and then the road from Omaha, hoping Dad would appear out of the desert in some tiny rental car. No signs of life so far. I was a little concerned since Dave announced there'd be more severe weather moving in tonight. I hoped to have camp set up and Dad safe and sound before the storm hit—but no sign of him yet. Did he get lost? Is his rental car broken down in the Nebraska sandhills?

We waited to find out while we pitched camp near this small hog farm just outside the little town of Aurora—when, as promised, my trusty Dad pulled up in this green rental car, at sundown—more than two hours late.

"Well look-e what the cat dragged in; the prodigal son returns," Chet joked as Dad hopped out of the rental with a wave.

"You bums looking for a new cookie? Chet poisoned you to death yet?"

"Almost," Andrew replied. Jack was not wired for public displays of affection, so I was surprised he gave me an immediate bear hug.

"Well, you sure smell like warmed-over horse hockey," he said, giving me the once over, "And you look even worse. You too, Chet."

"You should smell the other guys," I said with a smile.

There was something about having Jack around that instantly raised our spirits and made me feel more confident that we were going to reach the Pacific. Not that Dad came packing any particular horse or survival skill, but his calm demeanor and ability to bring people together was a boon, especially with young Andrew the "human monkey wrench" who was routinely mucking things up whenever we turned our heads.

I introduced Dad to the team, and we settled down to eat dinner, this time, a batch of Chet's sumptuous cowboy stroganoff. Dad made it clear he didn't want any special attention this week, "Don't mind the old guy, I'm just here to help out and blend in with the team," he said. I was worried I might have to spend as much energy tending to Dad as I did the boys or Andrew, but he turned out to be a vastly better hand.

After supper, we sat around the campfire, and Dad and Chet joked like the old friends they were. Chet had been part of my family for years, and both my parents loved him for his spunk and spirit. Dad caught us up on current events, then he and I decided to sack out early in my tent while everyone else bunked in an old empty garage that was nearby—which was the smarter move since another storm was due to hit.

But I thought I knew better. I had strategically set up our tent to survive the storm by wedging the truck and trailer in V position to block the wind, which seemed like overkill when I was doing it—but I wanted to make Dad's first night as enjoyable as possible. It felt oddly familiar lying down next to Dad for the first time since I used to crawl into my parent's bed when I had nightmares as a little boy.

"Ready for your first storm, big guy?" I asked Dad.

"You promised me a show. Let's see what Nature's got in store."

"Don't tempt the horse gods," I said, chuckling.

"Who's that? Trigger?"

"You'll find out. Just a matter of time," I replied, lensing the horizon from our open tent door, which had a stuck zipper that I couldn't lower. As thunder-claps rolled in the distance, I looked over and noticed Dad was visibly smiling. I thought—*he has no idea what's coming, does he?* After we settled down to sleep, I left the screen door open, thanks to the stuck zipper—but had positioned our tent, so it gave us some steady ventilation. At least that was the idea when we drifted off to sleep.

This is when I learned: never leave your tent unzipped in Nebraska.

We were both awakened around midnight when the wind suddenly shifted and blew sheets of rain into our tent. "The horse gods are angry! Damn side-ways rain!" I yelled as Dad and I were drenched before we could even sit up, "Damn zipper's stuck!"

I reckon Nebraska was eager to greet Dad with her typical flair: hurricane-level winds, thunder, lightning, and rain that belted us right in the face, along with torrents of golf-ball-sized hail that nearly collapsed our tent. At one point, a strong smell of pig manure came wafting our way. "That you?" Dad asked comically, trying to help with the zipper, "I smell pig shit!"

"We're right next to a pig farm!" I shouted as rain sprayed our faces. I'd camped in many bad storms before when I wondered if I would survive; this storm was no different, but Dad didn't know that! As it roared through, I remember looking over to see the look of sheer terror on his face. My brave Dad had never been in any shit like this—literally! Some quiet prayers were uttered, but Dad put on a brave face. I'm not sure at what point the child becomes the parent in life, but amid the howling wind, blinding lightning, and torrents of rain and hail, Dad asked, *"Are we going to die?"*

I patted him on the shoulder and said, *"*Not tonight, Dad. Not tonight!*"*

After wrestling with the zipper like my life depended on it, I eventually got the tent closed, and we both waited out the rest of the storm, huddled together like two wet Sherpas trapped in an avalanche, hoping sleep would come soon so we could put this nightmare to rest. The whole time I kept telling Dad everything would be all right.

And, thanks to F.M., eventually it was!

I never asked, but I believe Dad developed a new attitude for camping by the next morning. What a first night. The Horse Gods dropped him straight into the fire, and he still woke up the next day, smiling—what a trooper.

I reckon Dad will never forget who the horse gods are now.

After surviving our first night, I was astonished by how quickly Dad fit in with the team. He was great at finding water for the horses and scouting traffic and towns ahead of us. When it wasn't raining or blowing up a storm, Dad got used to sleeping out under the stars, or by the side of the road in the tall grass, where we often slept in Nebraska. I'll never forget how he'd wake up with me at 3:30 A.M. to help me get ready for our first shift and then hit the trail on foot (with his old walking stick) as we followed the Union Pacific tracks west. Sometimes it was just the two of us plodding along by the early morning light, me on horseback, and Dad on foot by the railroad tracks. We talked for hours about the trip, Mom, business, world affairs—you name it, we covered it.

As the miles rolled by with Dad on board, I wondered how many fathers would do this? Jack believed in me, and the trip, and was willing to sacrifice all the comforts of home, just to be with me in this hellscape. The funniest part about the week was we didn't shower at all, so for the first time in his life, Dad wasn't able to shave every day. "Hell, Jack, you look like Captain Caveman!" Chet hooted one day, "You mess up good!"

"I do? Hadn't seen a mirror lately. You're not looking too sharp either, bubba."

"You're one of us, grubby and smelling like an old Grizzly," Chet said.

"He looks good to me, smells good, too," I said.

"Not sure your mother would agree with that assessment," Dad smiled.

Then I got a whiff of him, "Hoo-wee! I take that back. Mom's gonna have to delouse you in the garage when you get home."

"De louse?"

I had to explain ticks to Dad.

It turns out, he wasn't a big fan of them either.

The week with Dad zipped by; he was never a rah-rah guy, but his positive attitude was infectious. Dad loved to joke around with Chet and truly enjoyed getting up at 3:30 A.M. every morning to help groom the horses. He even inspired Andrew to straighten up and fly right for a few days, which was a miracle in itself. That was the power of Dad. Just his presence made us a better team. When his legs got tired of walking, he'd hop in the rig with Dave and drive up to the next town to shoot the breeze with the locals at some café or talk to some kind farmer about using their hay barn for the night.

One time, I snuck up on Dad at some café, and (wouldn't you know it) he was talking Chet and I up a storm to a few of the local hayseeds like we were a combination of Lewis & Clarke and Butch & Sundance, which made me feel a little warm and fuzzy inside. Having two grown boys of my own (now), I've discovered that sons like to hear how their stoic dad really feels about them, even if they have to do a little eavesdropping to do it.

One day, Jack and I were standing in the middle of the famed Platte River to cool our proverbial "barking dogs," just chuckling with each other over some silly thing. The joke was Chet, and I had (once) hoped this river would be an emergency water supply for us. But here, in the dog days of summer, even with all of the flash floods—the Platte River turned out to be a muddy trickle (barely two feet deep) with the water temperature hovering near 100 degrees. Refreshing, it was not.

"Feels like water from a leaky radiator," Dad surmised.

"Too thin to plow and too thick to drink," I remarked, which accurately described the state of the Platte on this day. The flowing mud stream the Nebraska people like to call a river was not potable by anyone's standards. Hell, the boys wouldn't even get in it, but it still served a purpose.

The Platte pointed the way West for us—a way out of here! Standing together in the Platte with our shoes (and boots) off, I couldn't help but think of all the father-son pioneers that traveled through before us. Lost in my thoughts, Dad started running off fun facts about the state, "Did you know that the Sioux tribe named Nebraska? It means *Flat Water*."

Which made me chuckle, "Makes sense now. Platte's so flat, it's barely here."

Dad just let that line hang in the air.

Then he said, "Anyone ever told you—you got the heart of a pioneer?"

"No, but I sure do appreciate the compliment," I said.

"I never would have bitten off a challenge like this, but you're gonna do it."

"I hope so."

"I admire your persistence."

This interaction may seem like no big deal to families who "emote," but Jack didn't give out his "emotional stamp of approval" lightly, so that little comment might have been the kindest thing he'd ever said to me in my adult life.

"Means a lot to hear you say that, Dad."

"Don't get a big head now; you also got the foot stink of an early pioneer."

"Come on. These things?" I lifted a muddy foot from the river to illustrate.

"Remember that time when I had to pull over on our way to the lake to throw away your old tennis shoes cause they were stinking up the car?"

"Phew, those sneakers were sour as hell!" I laughed, "Had to wear flip-flops the rest of the trip."

"You've come a long way, Jeff," Dad said, "But, your dogs are still barking."

All these years later, I still remember how it felt that day, just standing out in the middle of the Platte River chuckling with Dad when he told me he was proud of me and my feet stank. Sue likes to say, "Fathers and sons sure have a funny way of bonding."

I wouldn't have it any other way.

F.M, I say.

After nine days of rough riding through the corn-lined cradle of Dante's Inferno, there was no end in sight to the Nebraska state of mind. Even with Dad riding shotgun, I began to feel like I was living in some movie, and all this pain would disappear when the lights were brought back up in the theater. "Wishful thinking," Dad would say, and he was right, "This land is bigger than any movie, or any one life.

Still, it gave off a mighty surreal feeling. It's like when people walk out of the desert, claiming they had a religious experience—how can they prove it to other people? How could you begin to describe the feeling of seeing so much sky that your eyes refused to take it all in? Or the feeling when the father becomes son, and son becomes a father? Or the terror of watching a rainstorm pop a U-turn in mid-air, just to come back and wipe you off the face of the earth? This cowboy is unable to put these feelings into words. I will say man has tried to domesticate the Wild West for hundreds of years—and is still trying.

Take the folly of fences—these barbed wire attempts to contain the concept of "mine" were all around us. They all seemed so ludicrous, and yet so totally necessary.

"I see all this flatland fenced off. But can you fence a mountain? Who owns those?" Dad asked one day.

"No one does for long. We're all dust in the wind as the song goes."

"What song?"

"Never mind. More and more, I think I understand the Native American's idea of land ownership," I said. "This land can't really belong to anyone."

"You may be onto something, son—guess some of these questions are not meant to be answered, just puzzled over. It's all part of life's rich pageantry," Dad replied.

"When did you get so profound?" I asked.

"Your mother has me watching Donahue, so I pick things up."

When the week was up, it was time for Dad to go home. The old man got a little nostalgic as he said his goodbyes to the team. He gave old Chet what remained of his flask of whiskey, and a bear hug—which was surprising since he'd been stingy with hugs most his life—but old Chet can charm the pants off a rattler, and he charmed Jack too. "Don't worry, Captain, I'll keep a close eye on your wayward progeny," Chet said.

"Who's keeping an eye on you?" Jack laughed, "Damn fine cooking Chef Tell, appreciate you keeping us all well fed."

Jack shook Dave's hand next, and gave him a pocketknife he'd been carrying, telling the Preacher, "You're going to be a good father" and to watch out for the "flower child Andrew, since you're gonna get blamed for anything he does, anyway."

Andrew was next. Dad gave him an Exxon t-shirt, which Andrew put on immediately. "Look, Jeff, it's the most clothes I've worn all week," Andrew said.

"I'll alert the damn media," I said.

Then Andrew gave Jack a silent going away military salute. Not sure if that was genuine, but Jack saluted him back. By now, Dad didn't look anything like his old Navy photo that hung in our family den my entire life; he looked like a filthy old hobo with a giant beard, so it was funny to see him salute Andrew in his current state.

"Sure, Mom will take you back looking like Captain Caveman?" I asked him.

"I can hear her changing the locks already," he said.

I chuckled at the memory of Caveman Dad saluting Andrew as I followed his rental car back to Omaha. We dropped his car off at the airport Avis, and he hopped into the rig. We drove over to the Radisson Inn by the airport, where Dad was going to stay the night. He said he felt as strange as I did walking into the air-conditioned hotel lobby after a week in the desert. The looks we received from the desk clerk confirmed my suspicions—we were strange, just like Nebraska. The state had changed us. Dad had spent his life "working the system," but now he was a misfit, an outcast, like me, and he seemed to like it just fine.

I checked Jack into his hotel room on the 8th floor, so he could rest up and make himself presentable before his flight back to Connecticut the next morning. I sat around as Dad showered then shaved his beard in front of the mirror while I read the USA Today and caught up on the world. "Your Mom said, 'Come back stinking like horse, and I'll divorce you for Tom Selleck!'" Dad shouted from the steamy bathroom.

"Thought Mom was more of a James Garner fan? May have to show back up with a Magnum P.I. mustache then. You notice all the looks we got at the front desk? Must have thought we were father and son hermits."

"I'd say we stung the nostrils most definitely. Was waiting for security to come escort us out the back door—How's this?" Dad popped out of the bathroom to show me his attempt at a Tom Selleck mustache.

I laughed, "Try again. You look like a snake-oil salesman."

We spent the rest of the afternoon reflecting on the trip. At one point, I decided, "Ya know what, how about I spend the night and see you off tomorrow?"

Dad agreed, so I hopped in the shower and got myself clean. Then Dad and I sat around the rest of the night, eating room service burgers in front of the TV, and talking about things he had never shared with me ever! Dad expressed some real emotions (as well as some regrets) about how he raised us kids and our family, among other things, which made me feel a lot closer to him and respect him even more.

And I respected him a helluva lot already.

Seeing Dad off (very) early the next morning, he was all clean-cut, and back to looking like himself again. We said our goodbyes at the airport gate. I thanked him, "Not just for being an unforgettable part of the trip. But for being an unforgettable part of my life."

"Proud of you, Jeff, you're living a more adventurous life than I ever did."

"But, you were in the Navy—"

"It was nothing like this," Jack said, "I never served on the front line, and this is some real frontier business you have going here. Don't stop riding till you hit the Pacific," he gave me a final hug, "Set the record.do it for your old man."

I thought our Platte River moment was special, but this was (now) the most heartfelt thing my Dad had ever said to me. It almost made me dewy-eyed— OK, shoot, it did! Under all this dirt and grime, this cowboy still has a heart, and I sure do miss my Dad (and Mom) something fierce today. I feel blessed to have been able to share my recollection of this special father-son moment with you, and with every generation of Pappas to come. I tip my cap to you, Dad, wherever you may be.

See you in horse heaven, big guy.

I returned to camp at the crack of dawn a little more emotional than I had left, and quietly parked the rig, hoping I could have a private moment to process Dad leaving. With barely a mouse stirring—I let the team get some extra shuteye, and decided to take Thunder on an early morning ride up to the nearest town to clear my head, and see if I could find a few sweet treats to get the team excited about our final push. The small town I came across had no sign, so it remains nameless (in my mind) to this day—but the town had an odd mixture of old and new. There was a cemetery next to a furniture store, a new car lot next to the bright lights of a convenience store, still closed for business. Shit, I thought, I may have jumped the gun and got us here too early.

"Was anything open?" I asked.

Thunder had no reply. So, I checked my watch, just as it struck 6:01 A.M.

Like magic, a flashing blue neon sign waved to me from across the street, that said—*Baked Goods*. I hadn't had a morning pastry in a coon's age, as they say.

I licked my lips—time to change that.

With Thunder tied to a light pole, I crossed the street and entered the shop, which had just opened for the day. Patsy Cline was playing on the radio, and the counter was U-shaped with a coffee station in the back. I walked over and checked it out. As I suspected, no damn milk again. The Midwest must have a cow shortage; every café seems to be out of milk. All I seemed to find here was powdered creamer.

Oh well, you can't have it all.

With four hot black coffees in hand, it was time to pick out some goodies. Being their only customer, I took my sweet time, perusing their collection of pastries like a starving kid in a candy store. Should I choose cookies or nut bars? How about donuts or brownies? My eyes scanned the top shelf until I landed on a group of beige, glazed treats that were a little bigger than my hand, and twice as thick. I questioned the sleepy young woman working the counter about the super-sized confections.

"What's this? A bear claw? Maple-filled, huh? Real light? You sure? OK, I'll take four. No, make it, five." She rang me up.

I gave Thunder a glance out the window and caught him snoozing in a three-legged nap, eyes barely open. Rather than disturb his horse nap, when I got outside, I just sat on the curb beside him for a minute and dug into one of these baked wonders. This must be where pastries go when they die—I thought, sinking my teeth into the delicious bear claw! As I chewed the pastry, I was surprised to feel something strange hovering above me. First, it was warm breath in my ear.

Then I felt my hat pushed off to one side.

I looked up and was suddenly face-to-face with the most inquisitive look I'd ever seen coming from two familiar brown eyes. *Thunder was trying to steal my bear claw.* "What's that? Can I have some?" The big boy was saying with his expression, "A horse needs some sugar too, ya know?"

I muttered, "Pain-in-the-ass won't walk at more than a creep for two weeks. But for half my breakfast, he'll run up the side of this building," as I tore off a few horse-sized pieces and fed them to Thunder. Better than any dessert or caffeine rush, I got quite the kick out of watching Thunder eat a bear claw—knowing that somewhere down the road, he'd probably try and kill me again with one of his ghostly sightings or crazy freak outs.

That's love, I reckon.

When we returned to camp, everyone was packing up, and wondering if some horse thieves had run off with Thunder and me. "Guess I need to surprise you boys more often," I said as I handed out bear claws to the team as rewards for their hard work.

"Everyone earned it. You, sort of, earned it," I said as I handed Andrew his.

"Yeah, whatever," Andrew replied, "Your Dad's funnier than you."

"Yeah, whatever—just eat your bear claw," I smiled.

With a new spark of optimism (fueled by sugar, caffeine, and the knowledge that Wyoming wasn't far off)—we left the 4-H Fairgrounds where we had camped the night before and headed northwest on Rodeo Road, Route 30. The day heated up quickly as usual. By our 10 o'clock remount, it was already pushing 80 degrees. I started my second morning shift on Rebel, leaving instructions for Dave to find us up the road in Ogallala in a few hours. This was when an exciting event took place.

There were no monuments to commemorate it, so we could only guess when it occurred—but "according to our maps," Chet said with a sly smile, "Welcome to the Mountain time zone, boss! We made it!" Chet hooted as enthusiastically as he could in the heat. Then we both looked around to check his map work. Not a mountain could be seen, just the long rolling monotony of brown dirt, with some sand hills peppering the horizon. "Well, it's the thought that counts," Chet said, and we both busted out laughing.

But Chet was right, just the mention of "mountains" jogged loose a whole bunch of invigorating memories of riding in all that crisp air, among all those green trees, and in all that clear spring water. Now, that's horse and horseman heaven.

But for now, it was back to the heat and the dust, the bugs, and the corn.

"We'll get there," I said, "It just takes time."

By the time we reached Ogallala, the "Cowboy Capital of Nebraska," for our "nooner," it was too damn hot to continue. Ogallala was a town of about 5,600, shown on the maps as a small yellow splash on the Platte River, just south of Lake McConaughy. I didn't tell Chet, but I felt quite the thrill when we entered town on horseback, and Buffalo Bill Avenue came into view. I couldn't help but find myself mentally transported back in time. As a student of the Old West, I knew we had been running on a parallel course with the old pioneer trails (pretty much all the way across Nebraska) right next to their literal foot-prints of history. But now, we were getting to share some of the same roads that once held the ghosts of cowboys and pioneers past.

Considering how beat up we were—I saw an opportunity to cut some of the day out of our throats and suggested that Chet and I pay a visit to one of their old-time taverns in the "Old West" part of town, while Dave and Andrew scouted us a spot to camp. Chet and I found water and shade for Thunder and Rebel, then we splurged on two buffalo burgers, fries, and iced water for lunch, just appreciating the cool, quiet darkness of an empty saloon. We did draw a few curious looks from the few tourists who entered the bar. "Reckon they think you're part of the town exhibit," Stan the barkeep said.

"It is a wonder of modern science, these cold beers," I remarked as Stan poured us two cold drafts for dessert. I prepared for it by inhaling more ice water, with one eye pitched toward the prize—the amber yellow nectar that had the ability to slake a thirst and get a semi-dehydrated man a little goofy. Our first frothy sip of cold beer was, in a single word, "Wonderful. Just wonderful," I said.

"Cold beer; there is no substitute," Chet replied.

Instead of hightailing it (like usual), Chet and I just lingered, enjoying the cool air and ministrations of Stan (the part-time school teacher/saloon keeper) as he told us about his life and worldly wanderings. It was a slow time of day, so Stan said he appreciated our company. After we told him our story, Stan began regaling us with Ogallala's rich cowboy history. Back in the old days, he said Ogallala had been the end of the trail for many of the cattle drivers and was the beginning of the trail West for many pioneers.

"The Mormon Trail, Oregon Trail, the Pony Express, and the Texas-Ogal-lala Cattle Trail all converged here," he said, "It was quite a rip-roaring little town, where lonely cowboys could come and have a little fandango." Which made sense, since Ogallala had a healthy tourist trade, as evidenced from the Old West part of town, which had hitching rails, a Dance Hall, a Saloon, and a Sheriff's Office complete with a Jail.

Later, Dave and Andrew showed up to tell us they'd found us a campsite outside of town. Maybe the beer was making me feel extra generous, but I felt like the whole team should have a chance to celebrate a little too—so I told our two young hands to come take a load off, which they happily accepted. For the rest of the afternoon, Chet, Dave, and I sat around sipping beer and discussing world politics with Stan, and the rising cost of chickens with a few locals while Andrew played video games. The whole time we were there, not one woman asked us to dance—can you believe it? "You just can't figure women, sometimes," Chet chuckled, sniffing his armpits. Naturally, he recoiled in horror.

When we finally got up to leave, I asked Stan where we might procure a few beers to go? He pointed us in the direction of a liquor store across the street. "Perfect," I thought. Then the idea got even more perfect when we saw their sign, which read: "*Special, Case of Schaefer Cans $3.99.*"

"Probably a typo, right?" Chet said, inspecting the sign.

"Some kid must've stole a number off it," Dave said.

Well, it turns out the horse gods were smiling on us. The beer really was that price. "That's one hell of a special," Chet said, "How can we say no?"

We emptied one of my saddlebags and bought a case of $4 beer to bring back to camp. The box almost fit in my saddlebag, halfway in, with the rest of it hanging out like it was waving to the world as we rode out of town. That night back at camp, I let the team kick up their heel a little, and celebrate around the fire, tipping our caps to Jack and all the old boys who passed through. For me, it was just the proper thing to do.

It was also fun, too. And I've learned that you have to have a little fun out here, or what the heck was this trip about in the first place?

FM, I say.

We left Ogallala the next morning with foggy heads (made worse) because we hadn't had more than a beer (or two) in months. It didn't matter—our hangovers were greeted by the same oven-baked cornfields and rolling brown hills. At some point, Andrew pulled alongside the road in the rig, next to a field of harvested oats for our "nooner" rehydration session. Chet and I got off our horses to clear our heads and walked up a small hill to see what was in front of us as we headed northwest to Wyoming. From that vista, a brown-beige quilt of irrigated farmland appeared with black irrigation piping spraying life-giving water in huge iridescent clouds. All the colors of the rainbow were visible in the irrigated mist, like huge aluminum insects, silently watching another growing season come and go. Peering down on that flat open field gave me an idea.

"Wanna rematch?" I asked Chet when we saddled back up.

"Hell, that again, boss? What about no fun and games in Nebraska?"

"Rules are made to be broken, Hoss," I said.

"You know Jeff, when will you ever grow—Hyaaah!"

Off Chet bolted on The Wizard—the joker had left me at the starting gate again!

"Hyaaah!" I shouted to Rebel, and we took off in a cloud of dust, chasing Chet and Wizzer, just like we were chasing our hats again. None of the boys had gotten up to a pace faster than a canter for over a thousand miles—so I felt it was good to stretch their legs a bit. I was glad I did. All the suffering the team had endured the past two weeks seemed to disappear as our four-legged heroes galloped at full speed. Neck and neck, we raced across the open field. God—that Whizzer can move—I thought.

So, I kicked Rebel into 5th gear.

In the end, I got the glory, but it was Rebel who deserved the crown of roses.

"Damn, that was fun!" I hooted at the finish line.

"I'll get you next time, boss!" Chet shouted, "C'mon Wiz! You let Rebel beat you? With that head start?" With that rush of adrenalin, Chet and I were feeling good again. I tell you, distractions can be small, and yet so good for the soul.

I think even the boys enjoyed this one.

Later, Chet suggested we take a short detour to Ash Hollow State Park. Chet hadn't ridden full days for a while now due to the heat, so he was able to get a taste for the local sightseeing—I'm thankful he pulled us over today. While Chet showed me around, he started talking up a storm like he was the Old West history buff (not me).

"This is where I felt the spirits of the 'old ones,' boss,"

I replied, "I feel it here, too, pard."

The lush park was a gorgeous contrast to the dust bowl we'd been slogging through for weeks. It was bursting with flowers and foliage; a sea of red geraniums and yellow marigolds surrounded the park's historical museum. Inside the museum, the air conditioning was almost too cold. We saw a few exhibits, illustrating what the "old ones" as Chet now called them, wore back in the pioneer days, how they traveled, and even what some of them looked like. We also got to walk around this historic spot called Windlass Hill. Back in the pioneer days, to get potable water into Ash Hollow, a steep hill had to be navigated.

That's where the Windlass part came in. To get fresh water into town, wagons had to be lowered up and down the hill, with the use of a "windlass," which was a type of winch. "A windlass winch, now I get it," I said, "Who says the pioneers weren't ingenious? Would you have thought of that?"

"I can barely find the water hose in the back yard," Chet said.

We also saw ancient pioneer footprints in the form of fossilized wagon ruts that were etched into the land (their grey-white imprints forever slashed across the flat prairie). Many ruts were cut deep into the side of the hill, never to be forgotten. Chet and I had no words for this experience. We just shook our heads in silent admiration of the temerity of the pioneer people. I remember thinking—if we've only got half the heart of those brave pioneers, we'll get to the Pacific all right.

F.M. I pray.

Chet and I had given Nebraska two weeks to show her affection for us, but she withheld her charms until the very end. Now that we were almost to the Wyoming border—the tough old lady finally began showing us some mercy with an occasional gentle morning breeze. But those didn't last long. Never-ending heat and humidity aside, now that we were finally in an area of Nebraska referred to as "the Panhandle" and almost free of this waking nightmare—I'm trying to conjure the feelings I had yesterday at Ash Hollow to keep me slogging ahead. It was a feeling of continuity with the past, and with the 'old ones' as Chet said, who were still watching over us.

I reckoned out here, we are not just travelers, but travelers in time.

Out here, we saw exactly what the pioneers did. For me, the feeling of having traveled here before was strong; I could still sense the hard labor involved in the lives of the people (of all nationalities) who passed through on their way to a better life. "The heat was the same 200 years ago. The insects and poor water were the same. The vistas? Looks the same. I get the feeling of the 'old ones' again and again," I said.

"F.M., we say," Chet parroted my catchphrase then pointed to the sky, which I like to imagine made the spirits of the "old ones" around us smile, just a little.

It sure brought a smile to my face.

We continued northwest along Route 26, along the Mormon Trail, not far from the Oregon Trail, which was on the other side of the North Platte River.

The more famous Oregon Trail didn't do much to make religious pilgrims feel safe; Mormons, like so many others, were persecuted on the Oregon Trail for the usual reasons—ignorance, superstition, greed or just brutal curiosity—so the Mormon pioneers eventually had to carve their own trail. Theirs wasn't as picturesque as the Oregon Trail; in fact, it was downright intimidating—but it kept them safe(r) and got them to their promise land. The Mormon Trail was marked with (quite a telling) road sign that had a weather-beaten buffalo skull perched on top of it for good measure. "This trail's about as inviting as that dang sign," I said. "May want to hop off, next chance we get."

"When the hell will that be?" Chet asked.

I had no answer.

We looked around. The Mormon Trail could be summed up as "desolation in all four directions." The only green in sight came from a distant irrigated field, while the other brown, water-starved pastures seemed to wave at our passage like ghostly memories. A rare pickup or tractor-trailer would blast by on occasion, barely acknowledging our presence. Sometimes, a probing glance answered ours, but not many folks bothered to stop to see what we were up. Our outdated method of transportation certainly meant nothing to Nebraskans. Except for a few locals like Don Peterson, Chris the cowboy, Tom the turkey famer, and Stan the barkeep—our journey through Nebraska had been about as noticed as the thousands of cowboys who came before us.

In other words: not at all.

"Iowans couldn't get enough of us, while Nebraskans couldn't give a single solitary shit," Chet observed, "Maybe if we were riding camels they'd notice?"

"Don't blame your lack of showmanship," I mused, "It's too dang miserable to get out of their air-conditioned cars to pay us a how-doo. I wouldn't do it."

"You wussy. Well, I reckon it's just different strokes for Nebraska folks," Chet said, "Wyoming here we come!"

We finally got off the Mormon Trail and headed northwest to higher country. The outfit was almost out of the flatlands, almost out of the monotony— almost out of here. With the towns of Chimney Rock, Courthouse, and Jail Rock in our rearview, the great feeling of emptiness we felt out on the plains was replaced with growing excitement for the Rockies. The fact the mountains were almost here served as some solace for the misery Nebraska had bestowed on our weary backs.

The little town of Scotts Bluff seemed to rise out of a huge cornfield like an optical illusion. We rode into town to little fanfare, much to Chet's chagrin, no one rolled out any red carpets—so we held a simple "nooning" along Main Street in a semi-shaded parking lot of a grocery store. While Chet hid the horses from the sun, I ventured into a nearby convenience store to procure the high carbohydrate treats Chet and I desired. I returned with a quart of Dutch chocolate milk, a pan of caramel nut swirls, half of a honeydew, and half of a muskmelon, all procured from the "day old" section. The caramel nut rolls were devoured first to provide the bulk the body required.

Next, Chet started cutting up the melons. "Now, that's one glorious fruit,"—I said as we ate the firm, musky chunks of flesh, dripping with nectar—the yellow pieces impaled on the business end of a buck knife.

Finally, we shared gulps of the slightly thickened chocolate milk.

"Slightly thickened?" I asked Chet handing him the carton.

"Jesus, this shit's sour!" Chet yelled while guzzling milk down.

"Think so? Let me have another swig," I said, giving the milk a cautious sniff. "You sure?" I took a big swallow.

"You crazy? Of course, it's sour! Here give it back, I'll show you," Chet said, tilting back and swallowing deep. "Hell, is it really that sour?" Chet took another drag of the milk. "Oh well, guess it must have been."

He handed me the last of the milk, which I finished off before my mind could stop me from drinking it. Who knew if it was actually sour or not? My taste buds were shot to hell by now. But this is how thirsty and dehydrated you can get in Nebraska. You'll chug a quart of sour chocolate milk so fast you won't even realize it until it's down your gullet. It's a miracle no one got food poisoning.

With our bellies full of delicious (possibly) soured chocolate milk, Chet and I kept pushing toward the Wyoming state line. We passed a giant cattle-feeding operation that was sprawled alongside the road. It was at the end of this fence line that Chet and I finally found Dave, Andrew, and the rig. Dave led us to our campsite, pointing to a small group of trees and a large irrigation ditch. When we arrived—I had to rub my eyes to believe it, but Andrew had snapped out of his self-adulatory reverie and was voluntarily making us dinner. "Who replaced Andrew's batteries?" I asked.

"Oh, I had Dave yank a knot in his tail," Chet said, "Don't forget the oregano!"

"Yes, sir," Andrew replied glumly.

"Andrew got the message," Dave said. "Now, are you ready for the bad news?"

"Don't tell me; a locust invasion is about to descend on us?" Chet said.

"Close, but." Dave explained tonight was going to be another fifteen-round slugfest with Mother Nature—"We already got two tornado warnings in effect."

"Better prepare for the onslaught," I said, "Just another day in Nebraska." We didn't let the oncoming storm ruin our evening. The spicy aroma of the boy's alfalfa hay mixed with our spaghetti dinner, plus the chatter on the FM radio gave us all warm feelings of being back in the land of the living. We were a day away from the border.

Life was good again until it wasn't.

Although the sky had gotten dark, it wasn't grey-black like all the other Nebraska storms we'd faced. This one came from the west and was a peculiar brownish-grey and green, like pea soup. "Airs too still; like the still that comes before a . . ."

Dave stopped short of saying it.

"Don't even—not a twister on our last night," Chet moaned.

The upside was we were in relative safety, under a small grove of trees with a ten-foot drainage ditch next to us. But when the rain poured, it felt hot to the skin like it came from El Diablo's watering can. Ten seconds after it started, Dave was already planted in the truck with Andrew, while Chet and I ran for shelter in the horse trailer. The wind trumpeted the storm's arrival, as golf-ball-sized hail rained down. Then it suddenly got cold—real cold. "Aw shit, this is gonna be the big one, time to bite the big radish!" Chet shouted, the lightning illuminating his face as hail pelted everything in sight.

The good news was the boys didn't seem to mind.

They just lowered their heads, and turned their tails toward the storm (a subtle horse insult), and didn't utter a sound. Meanwhile, hail rained down, making the inside of the fiberglass trailer sound like a snare drum. As the storm raged, Chet and I took a cue from the horses and just continued to eat our supper and talk to the boys, convincing ourselves we had a calming effect on them.

Then it was over.

No twister after all. Hot damn!

We peeked out of the trailer. Our world was dripping wet.

Over the feeder lot, a shaft of sunlight broke through. Andrew shut off the radio, climbed out of the truck, and said, "Four tornados had been sighted on either side of us—the closest five miles away heading East. We got lucky!"

"Now we know why. Look, it's a double rainbow, all the way!" Chet pointed at the double rainbow forming above us, which (to this cowboy) almost looked like it was pointing us West toward Wyoming. We greeted this colorful harbinger of good fortune with hoots and hollers, taking pictures while I quietly thanked the horse gods for letting the tornadoes miss us. "Will you look at that. The double rainbow's leading us out of here," Chet said.

"Maybe we're not as alone as we think out here?" I posited.

Chet and I turned our attention to the boys, who looked a little cold now, so I untied them to walk them around. I put on my slicker, but strangely, Chet couldn't find his. He searched the truck, no luck. Since North Platte, Chet hadn't needed it, so it had presumably remained where he stowed it, in the hurry-up area behind the passenger seat. Dave had gotten our permission to use our slickers as a makeshift "soogan" to sleep under, but no one had thought about "where" Chet's slicker was until this big blow.

Dave said, "I'll tear down the damn truck and find it."

"OK, Preacher, we trust you." Chet put on his yellow emergency slicker, and we began walking the horses around camp to warm them up and survey the damage. We fetched our pots and pans out of two inches of water. Then we noticed Andrew's tent was totaled, under approximately three inches of water. Even worse, one of the ridgepoles had collapsed, so most of his tent was completely submerged, including his guitar and cut-offs, which I had prayed on several occasions would be taken off by a rogue storm.

Had my prayers been answered?

Young Andrew took the news stoically—then not so much when Chet and I started laughing at him. "I'll say it again: if you keep pitching your tent far away from camp, these disasters will keep happening," I repeated to him over Chet's belly laughs.

"Thanks, Dad!" Andrew said.

I reminded him, "We'll be crossing the Rockies soon, and you don't want to mess with Grizzlies. You need to start camping with us, just cause it's safer."

Dipping water out of his tent, Andrew finally blew a gasket, "Well, I've hitchhiked across the United States and slept in a tent the whole way. I know what I'm doing, so don't tell me what to do or where to camp!"

While this philosophical discussion on outdoor living was being entertained, Chet and I cleaned up the remains of supper, which was scattered all over Shinola—then Chet made a fresh pot of cowboy coffee. Andrew didn't drink coffee—so on the rare occasion (like tonight) he decided to cook—he never made coffee for the rest of us, which we found a little passive-aggressive—but Andrew's coffee would have been underwater right now anyway. I guess the boy will learn the hard way or get eaten by a Grizzly.

Not sure which I would bet on at this point.

But it's coming to a head with him. That much I do know.

Our last day of riding in the state that had tortured us for weeks was surprisingly easy. Was the old lady losing her skills? The only memorable diversion we had before crossing into Wyoming occurred while riding through the town of Morrill. As we moseyed the boys down the town's Main Street—a tall cowboy with a big mustache cut us off at the pass, leaving his red Ford pickup truck still running on the street to come over and talk. We were so close to the border, I didn't want to stop for anything, but he stopped us in our tracks. Once we told him our story, the man introduced himself as Butch Sykes. Just his name sounded legendary, and we soon found out why. Like any cowboy worth his salt, the first thing Butch did was lavish praise on our fearless (sometimes skittish) leader.

"Mercy. How much you take for the Belgian Cross? He's a real beaut," Butch said, patting Thunder's neck and admiring his size and beauty.

"Sure is," I said, "Name's Thunder—he can be a pain in the ass, but I guess he's priceless. I can't imagine me ever parting ways with him. We're best friends." Butch liked that answer. This wouldn't be the last time someone wanted to buy Thunder right out from under me. Butch explained he'd ridden the rodeo circuit back in the day, and now, raised cattle, mostly, with some horses on the side.

It turns out, Butch's grandfather was one of Buffalo Bill Cody's close friends (and business partners) for a good part of their lives. I had a feeling we were talking to cowboy royalty, and we were. I was so taken with Butch; I forgot all about making good time. Instead, we pulled over and visited for a good while on the side of the road. Butch sure was a great storyteller; he regaled us with a few historical (and some, not so historical) happenings that old "Wild" Bill, and Grandpa Sykes had pulled off in their heyday. Butch had quite a few family connections to the old west pioneers.

He sure looked like a modern incarnation of one of the "old ones."

Then Butch mentioned he had a big spread, just a few miles up the road, and offered us a roof over our head for the night—a bed, a hot meal, and yes, a cold beer. "It'll suit your needs; the land's been passed down through my family for over one hundred years," Butch said, "Bill Cody himself used to hang his hat at my hacienda on occasion."

How could I turn down this offer?

As much as I wanted to stay, as the brains of the team, I had to think about the long-term ramification of losing a few more days. It sure was difficult to decline Butch's kind offer, but I felt it was my duty to keep us on track.

"Aw shoot, wish we could Butch, but we had a helluva time getting through Nebraska, so we're behind schedule and need to get through the Rockies before the first big snow hits," I said. "But we sure appreciate your kind offer." I shook Butch's hand. We said our goodbyes, and Butch wished us luck. The rest of the team was so tired they didn't put up much of a fight, but I still regret not taking him up on his offer. We were all so tired we just wanted to get the hell out of Nebraska as soon as we possibly could.

Riding away, I couldn't help but feel we just had a brush with history, and a man who embodied both the Old West (where cowboys could ride and rope all day) and the New West where raising livestock is a must for modern cowboys like Butch to survive.

Chet and I rode the final three miles to the Nebraska-Wyoming border with a feeling of pride in our hearts for our past heritage and a tremendous feeling of gratitude born out of thanks to F.M, our Maker, and the Horse Gods that we had survived Nebraska, and were finally getting closer to the Rockies.

Henry (Nebraska) was the final "whistle stop" town we passed through right smack dab on the Wyoming border. It had a grain mill and was next to the Union Pacific tracks. We rode the boys through town, passing the State-line Bar and Grill to find the legendary border sign that so many tourists still come to see, yet so few truly appreciate. The sign read: "Howdy, You're in Big Wyoming."

"Thank God we finally made it through hell," Chet said, seeing the sign.

"Or maybe a tornado sucked us up last week, and this is cowboy heaven?" I said.

"Either way, we're set," Chet chuckled as we dismounted to take some pictures in front of the sign, as well as shots in front of signpost for the Oregon Trail.

Once Dave and Andrew scouted us a place to camp on the Wyoming side, we called it a day (a little) early so we could repair our gear and do our horse chores, feeding the boys with barely a word spoken between us. I reckon sometimes, the achievement is its own reward, and silence between friends says it all.

After dinner, when the boys were safe and sound, Chet and I headed back into town to find a place to celebrate "not dying" in Nebraska. We came across a big Western saloon with a neon yellow Ranier beer sign winking at us from inside their window.

We walked in and sat down to try and forget how bad our bodies felt (pretty bad), and how far we still had to go (a long damn way). But the two icy cold drafts we ordered sure took the edge off as the faces around us nodded at the recognition of thirsty men the world over. "Well, boss, we are in Wyoming now—F.M., Jeff says—whatever the hell that means!" Chet smiled as we clinked glasses. His words were as soothing to my ears as the draft beers were to our dusty gullets.

"These cold ones are for all the 'old ones.' Thanks for showing us the way," I said with a tip of my glass to the sky. Afraid I was going to pour beer on the ground, Chet stopped me—"Wait, you're gonna drink that, right?" I answered Chet's question by taking a big draw from my ice-cold beer and wiping the foam from my mustache with a big smile. "The 'old ones' wouldn't have wanted it any other way." F.M., we all say.

★ 10 ★

POISON SPIDERS IN THE RED DESERT

"Knowledge is awareness, and to it are many
paths, not all of them paved with logic. But
sometimes one is guided through the maze by
intuition. One is led by something felt on the
wind, something seen in the stars, something
that calls from the wastelands to the spirit."
—*Louis L'Amour*

I RECKON' WE hightailed it outta Nebraska as fast as the boys would carry us. Nothing against the good folks living there, but it was one helluva ride that tested the limits of our endurance and, at times, our sanity. Can't say it was enjoyable, other than seeing ol' Jack for a spell, but the state that was a survival story unto itself graciously let us pass without any permanent damage. We were glad to come out the other side fully intact, but Chet and I weren't out of the woods yet. We only thought the horse flies, tornados, and sweltering heat of the Nebraska plains were bad. We had to pass through the eye of the devil next. Besides the danger of running into an early snowstorm in the Rockies, there was another obstacle standing between the Pacific and us.

We had to cross the Red Desert.

Not many people realize Wyoming has a desert, but you better believe it exists, and it's hotter than hell, even in the shade, and there ain't much of that. It's not quite as intimidating as its big brother, the grand Mohave, but 120-miles of wild, dusty death is nothing to sneeze at, despite what Chet had to say about it. "Look alive, hoss. Fun ain't over yet." I said. "This ain't no sandbox ahead," I pointed to the Red Desert on our Wyoming topo map.

"The Red Desert. You really know how to ruin my day," Chet said.

"Sorry."

"You got your pantaloons in a wad about it?"

"Hell no. You?"

"No dust pile's gonna stop this wagon train now."

"Hope you're right about that."

"What.me worry?"

I sighed, "Naw. Guess that's my job," I said.

Chet and I had read up on the Red Desert back in Connecticut, but we would soon find that no matter how much homework we did or bravado we espoused, we weren't properly prepared for the experience. Shoot, I'm getting ahead of myself, ain't I?

When Chet and I arrived at the Wyoming-Nebraska border, our date with the Pacific was still a long way off, but it didn't matter. We felt like we were halfway home. "Gettin' closer, boss! I can smell the ocean salt from here," Chet said, taking a big whiff of the dusty air around us, which made me chuckle.

"That's one helluva sniffer you got there," I said.

"First, we conquered the plains—now it's the desert. Next, we'll take the Rockies. Then we're on to the promised land," Chet said. "Nothing can stop us now."

"I like your optimism, partner. One step at a time, one step at a time," I said.

At this point, we were so damn excited to be out of Nebraska, a few members of our team were already dreaming of crossing the finish line. Not me, though. I did feel a sense of accomplishment for how far we had traveled. The only thing going through my head at this point was we were finally and officially in the Old West.

The Old West. Just has a nice ring to it, don't it?

I've dreamt of this place ever since I was a youngster. This is where the old cowboys made their name. It's where the pioneers traveled thousands of miles to reach—the *Old West*—an undiscovered, beautifully untouched, rugged stretch of endless land full of hopes and dreams and bounty. All those weekends spent riding in the Connecticut woods, this was where I wanted to be—bad weather, rough conditions, and all.

I was home.

We crossed the state line from Wyobraska into Henry, Wyoming. We didn't jump for joy or shoot our 30-30 into the air or anything, but I decided it was time to celebrate. Chet and I pulled the boys up to an old watering hole in Henry that was promoting a barbeque. Just seeing the word "barbeque" made our mouths water. We got the boys fed and watered, then we all sauntered into the bar looking to wet our whistles. The saloon held around fifty people. As we surveyed the scene, I could see the excitement swelling in the boys' eyes. "A barbeque?" Chet said. "I remember those."

"We're back in civilization," Andrew said. "Hell, yes."

"Men," I said as I sat back in my chair with a cold draft in my hand, "What do you say about us taking the night off?"

"Shit yes, boss!" Chet said, downing his beer in one big gulp. He wiped the foam from his mouth, "Another round on me this time!"

Chet, Dave, and Andrew hooted and hollered, which made me smile.

"Thanks, Jeff," Dave and Andrew said.

"Reckon you boys earned it," I said.

"We all earned it," Andrew said.

"You *barely* did," Chet said to Andrew, kicking at his chair playfully.

This was the first full day we'd taken off in a month, but a little R&R was the least I could do to help the team morale. Besides, my tank had "redlined" a long time ago. We talked about how we'd spend our day off. "I say we put on our best duds and venture out tonight for a taste of the local flavor," Chet said.

"I reckon I don't have any best duds," I said.

"I brought my tuxedo t-shirt and some 'smell good,'" Andrew said.

"You mean that stinky cologne?" Dave asked.

"It's catnip to the ladies," Andrew crowed. "I wanna take in some of the nightlife, know what I mean? Girls!"

"Think we know what you mean," I said. "I'm not that old."

"What do you know about girls Jeff; you're married!" Andrew shouted while slapping the table, clearly amused with himself.

"He's got you there," Chet said with a chuckle.

A few hours later, we set up camp just outside of town. The consensus was everyone wanted to attend the barbeque that night. I watched as Chet, Dave, and Andrew got cleaned up. "So that's what gussyin' up is these days?" I joked while they knocked off the top layer of dirt from their faces, necks, and armpits with a few old rags.

"I do what I can," Chet said, putting on his least-filthy shirt and combing his hair in the rig's side mirror. "Ain't you gettin' ready, boss?"

"Think I'm gonna stay behind. You boys go have fun."

Chet stopped combing his hair, "You gotta be kiddin' me."

"Nope," I said, "I'm sackin' out early."

"You really stayin'?" Andrew asked while dousing himself with cheap cologne.

"C'mon now, live a little," Dave said while sharpening his knife. "I'll stay behind and watch the boys."

"Na. You go have fun, Preacher Man. You earned it."

"OK then," Dave said. "We'll bring you back some BBQ."

"Thank ye," I said.

"You're sure missin' out on some action!" Andrew chirped as he sauntered around in his "best duds," which looked exactly the same as his other clothes except for his tuxedo t-shirt. The kid still wasn't bothering to wear shoes or long pants.

"I'm sure all the ladies will appreciate you dressin' up for 'em," I said.

The team got ready to head out. Chet gave me one final curious look and shook his head, "You are gettin' old," he said with a chuckle.

"Damn straight, I am," I said.

"See ya, boss," he said.

"See ya," I said back. "Y'all try to stay out of jail."

Chet was right. The exhaustion of the trip was getting to me. I was in desperate need of a good stretch of sleep, and tonight was the night. I told the fellas goodbye as they went off "honkey-tonkin'."

Alone with my thoughts, I was happy as a clam. Once I got the horses fed, watered, and settled in for the night, I crawled up under the front wheel of the rig, put my bedroll under me, and proceeded to sleep for fourteen hours without waking up or rolling over once. I didn't even hear the boys when they came stumbling back at late dark thirty.

The next morning came way too early for everyone, except me. I'd slept like a baby and rose a little stiff but was raring to go. We were getting ready to make a big push through Wyoming into Montana, so I let the rest of the team sleep. I got up and fed and brushed the horses, made coffee, and heated up some old cornbread in the skillet. I finally got a gander at the "fallen soldiers"—they looked pretty rough, to say the least. Didn't smell too good either. By the sound of ol' Chet, Dave and Andrew sawing logs, it appeared I missed one heck of a party. Chet was the first to rise. "You missed a rip roarin', good time, boss. What I remember of it," Chet said, rubbing his head.

"I bet," I said, handing him a cup of hot coffee.

"Think Andrew got lucky," Chet said, taking a sip.

"Oh, she was no beauty queen," Dave murmured, sitting up to scratch himself.

"Old enough to be his mother, if I recall," Chet said.

"I can hear you guys," Andrew said as he rose groggily from his pallet and staggered over to the rig for a drink of water. "She was nice, whatever her name was." We all laughed at that remark.

"When'd you get back, you ol' tomcat?" Chet asked Andrew.

"Round sunrise I think," Andrew said. "I feel like warmed-over horseshit. Itchy all over. Hope I didn't catch crabs."

"Better wash those jean shorts," Dave said.

"I don't wanna hear anything about your extra-curricular activities," I said. "Just keep it to yourself. And if it burns, see a doctor!" Chet and Dave chuckled.

"And if you give any of the horses crabs, I'll string your skinny ass up from the highest tree," Chet said.

"I'm really scared," Andrew said sarcastically.

For the first time since Sue surprised me with a conjugal visit in Illinois, I felt like a million bucks again. The horses were bright-eyed, and bushy-tailed too. At least some of us were raring to go. After breakfast, we loaded up the "hangover train" and headed west, a little slower than normal. Chet and I set out on Route 26. Our maps told us there were many grey roads around, but we didn't want to stray too far from our plan, which was to follow the North Platte River most of the way across Wyoming—so we stuck on Route 26 till we found it. As we rode, I regaled Chet with stories of the Old West while we zigzagged across the North Platte River a few times, which turned out to be a worthy test for our horses. "Riding in the North Platte," I yelped, "just like the old cowboys used to!"

"God, deliver me some aspirin," Chet moaned.

"I got some headache powder, here," I threw him a packet, which landed on the lid of his Stetson. Chet grabbed for it.

"Slow down, Rebel, you old son of a bitch!" Chet mumbled to himself as he ripped open the package and swallowed the headache powder with no water chaser. One of us was "playing cowboys" like a kid again. The other felt like warmed-over death. I was glad to be in my saddle and not his.

"Guess stayin' in last night wasn't such a bad idea."

"Yeah yeah," he said. "Don't rub it in."

"You're gettin' old, hoss," I said with a chuckle.

"My liver sure as hell is."

We rode through Mitchell and Morris. Then I noticed we were headed towards a town called Torrington. "Ain't that where you grew up?" I asked Chet, who looked up at the sign and had no reaction. Chet grew up in Torrington, Connecticut.

"Guess those horse thieves stole our name."

"Actually, a lot of the pioneers that settled out here renamed the settlements after their home towns."

"You're smarter than you look," Chet said.

"Reckon we should celebrate your homecoming."

"If you say so. I'm still recovering from last night's celebration."

"How bout I treat us to a little hair of the dog and a meal you don't have to cook?"

"Like the sound of that."

We arrived in Chet's "hometown west" around suppertime. To celebrate the occasion, I figured we should eat out for once. I suggested we have dinner at the local café. The team didn't need much convincing. We ordered burgers, fries, and beers all around and wolfed them down faster than you can say "hangover cure." Thanks to the graciousness of all the good people we met along the way, this was about the only time I paid for a meal the entire trip. I remember looking at the check and rifling through my pockets only to realize I had no money on me.

"Thank god for credit cards," I said, putting down my card. "Now, let's go get some shut-eye."

"Music to my ears, boss."

When the sun rose the next day, I had no idea last night's meal would be the last supper our team would have together. But as fate would have it, we would lose a team member by sundown. "This is the last goddamn straw," I whispered to Chet.

"You keep sayin' that," Chet whispered back.

"The kid broke the camel's back with this little stunt," I said to Chet. We crept up on our target (a rogue horse) slow as molasses so as not to spook him any further.

"This'd be funny if we weren't so pissed," Chet said.

"I ain't laughin'," I grumbled.

Chet wiped the crooked smile off his face. "Me either."

While Chet, Dave, and I were working on repairing one of the saddles, Thunder had gotten loose while Andrew was screwing around (again). Just as we were about to move out, I went looking for Thunder, but he was nowhere to be found. All I saw was a bunch of our equipment busted up and strewn from here to Shinola.

I went looking for answers.

"Where the hell is Thunder Andrew?" I asked.

"Uh, he's over." Andrew pulled off his headphones and pointed to the mess of equipment. "He was over there." It turns out Andrew had left Thunder tied to an old rotted railroad tie rather than the trailer, and of course, Thunder freaked out and took off. I was pretty heated, not at Thunder but Andrew. It took us all morning to finally track him down. We found Thunder wandering a half-mile away, slowly dragging the rotten railroad tie behind him. Chet was right; in retrospect, Thunder dragging around the railroad tie was kind of funny but also sad and infuriating all at once.

"I gotta send him packin'. Three hours we've wasted doing this," I said.

"It's about time," Chet said, "the kid's been nothing but trouble from the start!"

"Shh!"

The second Chet raised his voice; Thunder pricked up his ears and ran off again.

"Dammit!" Chet yelled in frustration. "Thunder, you get your ass back here!"

It wasn't about time to fire Andrew; it was way past time. His lack of attentiveness to our equipment, our safety, and our horses' wellbeing had become a detriment to the survival of the team. Chet had been trying to get me to fire him three states ago, but I kept hoping the kid would come around.

It just wasn't happening.

Andrew seemed more interested in meeting girls than doing his job. It had also become a regular occurrence for him to leave behind a piece of equipment every few days. When I'd notice something was missing, I'd send him back to retrieve whatever it was (a bridle, a jacket, a blanket, some cookware), and it would be gone. The most frustrating part was Andrew never bothered to clean up his act, wear shoes, or stop playing his silly guitar while on scouting duty. "As the old boys say, 'this dog don't hunt,'" Chet said.

"No, it don't. It's like one step forward, two steps back with him," I said as we tracked down Thunder grazing in another field.

"He's got to go. Got to geaux," Chet said. "He's been makin' us look like a bunch of Easy Riders from the get-go," Chet said, "and you know how I feel about hippies!"

"I'll do it tonight," I said.

"I second it, boss, and I know Dave does too."

After way too much effort expended, we finally got Thunder corralled. With some gentle maneuvering, I got close enough to him to get my hands around his neck. I rubbed his head, "You gotta stop running off like this." Thunder snorted and nuzzled me back. Chet and I gently bridled him up and led him back to the road. That's when Andrew and Dave pulled up in the rig.

"You found him, phew!" Andrew yelled out the window. I could see Dave behind the wheel, giving Andrew the stink eye. The kid had worn out his welcome with all of us.

"You can thank your lucky stars he isn't seriously injured," I said to Andrew. He just smiled sheepishly. I just stared at his silly expression for a few seconds. I wanted to slap that grin off his face, but I kept my composure.

After all the commotion, we didn't get started until 9 A.M., three hours late.

At the end of the day, I pulled Andrew aside and told him, "I hate to break this to you, but this was the last straw. I think it's time for you to go on back home. You're just not pulling your weight, son."

"C'mon Jeff." He said with a smirk.

"This ain't no joke."

"You serious?"

"As a judge," I said.

"But. You can't do this. I told you I was sorry. That railroad tie was rotten, how could I know he'd break loose?"

"Common sense. You don't tie a 1500-pound horse to a rotten railroad tie, then leave him unattended."

"How many times do I have to say I'm sorry?"

"You won't have to say it ever again. My decision is final. I'll buy you a bus ticket back home tomorrow."

He stood there, dumbfounded. After it sunk in, I could see his anger level rising until it spewed out in one long rant. For a moment, I thought I might have to get physical with him. "You can't fire me; I'm working for free!" he yelled, "This is a free country! I can stay on the trail as long as I want goddammit. I'll walk on the other side of the road and camp by myself if I have to! You can't tell me what to do, you jerkoff!"

I took Andrew aside and calmly told him all the reasons he had to go based on the safety of horses and his continued carelessness. I had previous business experience having to let people go, so I was no stranger to the situation, but Andrew took it hard.

Real hard.

"When we hit the Rockies, the trip is about to get very serious," I explained. "We can't afford to have anyone we can't trust with our lives and who doesn't take things as seriously as we do."

"Just 'cause I'm laid back doesn't mean I'm not serious! I'm more serious than Chet!" Andrew was determined to challenge my authority to the bitter end. He'd been doing that since New York in front of everyone. Every time he'd blow up on me, I'd watch Chet snicker like he was doing right now. Chet intervened, "Why don't you just haul off and knock him one upside his head? Want me to do it, cause I will!"

"Shut your big fat mouth, Chet! You stay out of this!"

Chet's smile evaporated. I could tell what was coming next.

"Settle down now, both of you. No violence. We're all grown men here," I said.

Andrew stormed off into a pasture; Chet went after him, "I'll talk to him, boss."

"Just keep it calm, will ya?"

"Don't worry," Chet said, "I got two brothers." Chet went after him while I switched out the horses and talked with Dave.

"You know what this means, right?"

"Yes sir," Dave said.

"You got all his responsibilities now. I know you can handle it," I said.

"Thank ye. I won't let the team down," he said.

"I know you won't. You're doing a great job, Preacher Man."

"Hate to say it, but it'll be easier without the pied piper around," he said.

"I know," I said. "That's why he's going home."

I looked out toward the pasture where Chet and Andrew were talking; Chet had his arm draped over Andrew's shoulder. Chet has a calming way about him that rubs off on people and horses, and he was working his magic on the young man. Eventually, I heard Chet laugh, then Andrew laugh too. Soon after that, Andrew came back over and said, "Ok, I'm ready to go home anyway."

"OK. I'll get Dave to drive you to a bus station when we get close to town. I'll buy you a ticket home. Appreciate your service."

"Yeah, thanks. But I don't want to go home. I want to go to Chicago."

"Alright then, I'll buy you a ticket to Chicago."

"I'll take care of it from there," he mumbled, packing up his guitar and possessions in his knapsack. The only problem was there was nowhere for Andrew to go. We were still a couple of hours away from any town with a bus station, and it was too late to drive him. It was an uncomfortable meal around the campfire that night. But Chet kept it light, and we tried to move past it.

By the end of the night, we were kind of joking about it—kind of.

The next day, we broke camp just west of Torrington. I asked Dave to drive Andrew to the nearest bus station in some small town near the Wyoming border. When we all said our goodbyes—Andrew shook all our hands like an adult, and we parted ways peacefully. We watched the rig drive away. "Think we made the right call?" I asked Chet.

"You know we did, boss," Chet said. "Finally!"

"I reckon I agree. C'mon, let's get going."

We rode across BLM (Bureau of Land Management) land, which comprises much of the open range in Wyoming and Montana. Our map showed our next major stop would be Casper—about a two-and-a-half-day ride. While Dave was driving Andrew to the bus station, Chet and I passed through the little town of Lingle then stopped for a couple of hours at the old Fort Laramie, a neat old historical landmark, especially for old cowboys like me. Fort Laramie was a major scout station for the cavalry in the old days. Walking the grounds, I had visions of all the old cowboys and pioneers that once passed through here. Located at the junction of the Laramie and North Platte River, it was founded in the 1830s to service the overland fur trade. It's trading post, and surrounding businesses were one of the biggest economic hubs in the region.

Situated just east of the steeper "High Plains" foothills that ascend to the Rockies, it sat on one of the few wagon-accessible roads that pierced the Continental Divide. It offered large grazing areas to rest draft animals; there were also places for people to camp, do laundry, and heal before embarking on the westward trail.

"What are we doin' here, boss?" Chet asked, pointing to tourist kids drinking root beer out of the bottle. "They got anything stronger than sarsaparilla in this here tourist saloon?"

"Na. Root beer's for the kids, hoss," I said.

"Damn shame," Chet said.

A kid drinking root beer approached us, "Are you real cowboys?"

I chuckled, "Young fella, I reckon we sure are," I said.

"Cooool. Can I have your autograph?"

"You sure can. If I can have a sip of your root beer," Chet said with a wink. The kid frowned and pulled his sarsaparilla away.

"Just pullin' your leg, we'd be glad to." Chet and I both signed his map of the fort, our inscription: "Keep riding West. Sincerely, Jeff and Chet, CA86"

We walked outside and toured the grounds, staying clear of the packs of tourists with their cameras. "Ya know, this here fort was a significant 19th-century trading post and diplomatic site," I said to Chet, "It was *the* primary stopping point on the Oregon Trail."

"You got an A in American History, didn't you, boss," Chet said.

"Yep, I did." I went on to tell Chet all I knew, whether he wanted to hear it or not. The plaques stationed around the historic site helped refresh my memory. They told the story of two men I was already familiar with. The first was Jacques La Ramie. He and a small group of fellow trappers settled here in 1815. One day, ol' Jacques went out trapping alone and was never heard from again. Arapahoe Indians were accused of killing him and dumping his body in a beaver dam. The river was named "Laramie" in his honor. His name would later be given to the Laramie Mountains, this fort, and the towns of Laramie, Wyoming, and Fort Laramie, Wyoming. "He must've been a bad hombre to have the whole damn place named after him," Chet said.

"Maybe, and maybe not. he was just an enterprising white man who got here first," I said. "Ya know, one of my favorite stories happened right here on Christmas night in 1866." I went on to tell Chet the tale of John "Portuguese" Phillips, who ended his historic horseback ride right here at Fort Laramie after riding 236 miles non-stop from the Powder River. "Phillips was sent to Fort Laramie to get help for Fort Phil Kearny, where Lt. William J. Fetterman's entire unit had been killed in a fight with the Lakotas, Cheyenne, and Arapahos under Chief Red Cloud."

"Sounds like ol' Red Cloud was the real bad hombre."

"Reckon you got that right. Portuguese crossed hostile Indian country during a brutal Wyoming blizzard. Legend has it, his thoroughbred horse dropped dead upon arrival."

"Damn. Better not do that to our boys," Chet said.

"That's what I call commitment to a cause," I said.

"Yeah. For the horse!"

Once Chet heard about Portuguese Phillips' horse, he insisted we rest the boys for a little longer before we headed out. When Dave caught up with us in the rig, we talked about Andrew's departure.

"Tryin' to figure out if I miss that little turd, or not," Chet said.

"I don't," Dave said with a crack of a smile. He wasn't much to show emotion or complain, but he'd been picking up Andrew's slack for a long time now.

"We won't bad mouth the kid now that he's gone, let's just move forward," I said.

"You got it," Chet said, "Good riddance to the kid. May the troubadour find what he's lookin' for." Now we just had Dave.

We embarked on our afternoon ride.

Chet and I decided we'd keep following the North Platte River. Our path wound us all around it. I knew somewhere along our way to Casper, we'd cross the Oregon Trail, but we hadn't spied it yet.

"Where's the Oregon Trail, boss?" Chet asked.

"As long as we keep followin' the North Platte, it won't be far off," I said.

When we got near the town of Guernsey, we went looking for a local that could tell us a good place to find some old wagon ruts from the Oregon Trail. As luck would have it or perhaps it was due to the genuine friendliness of everyone we encountered from Indiana and all points west, we struck up a conversation with a local grocery store manager.

"You boys look like you're thirsty," the manager said.

"Howdy. we sure are." We bought two big plastic cups of iced water and drank them down. I wiped my mouth, "Could you kindly point us in the direction of the Oregon Trail?" I asked.

"Well, sure. You boys look like you came from it already," the grocery manager chuckled. "When you get to Guernsey, ask someone how to get to Register Cliffs. If you watch out for historical markers, you should be able to find it on your own."

"Thank ya, we'll do it," Chet said.

"Good luck now," he said.

We approached Guernsey later that afternoon. The shadows were getting long by the time we saw the sign for the Register Cliffs Historical Site. Chills ran down my spine, just thinking about what the Oregon Trail might look like.

"I've been waiting my whole life for this," I said.

"I know you have, boss."

Dave was already parked about fifty yards ahead. We pulled Thunder and Rebel up to the rig and dismounted slowly, which was the only speed our bodies seemed to go after more than three months on the trail. It felt good to dismount for a bit and stretch. Chet and I unzipped our chaps and threw them over our saddles and headed up the narrow trail behind the sign on foot.

"Feels strange to walk," Chet said.

"I hear ya. Feels like I'm still straddlin' Thunder," I said.

"We got phantom horse syndrome," Chet said. We both chuckled as we walked up a small hill and looked out over the vast expanse of the plains.

"Wyoming, in all its splendor," I said.

Not far down the bottom of the draw, we saw what looked like two wide lines cutting through the fescue grass fields that were browned by the late summer heat. I glassed the area with my binoculars.

"Will you look at that," I said and handed the binoculars to Chet, who had to re-adjust the focus (he was blind as a bat). Chet didn't say a word, just sighed, smiled, and handed the binoculars back to me. We gradually made our way down the slope toward the open plains. Chet and I both knew what was ahead of us; they were the famous wagon ruts from the countless settlers that passed through this very spot more than 100 years ago. This was the Oregon Trail. Seeing it for the first time was one of those 'no-words' moments between Chet and me. Chills raced through my body. I felt a peace I'd never felt before; it was an experience that will stay forever etched in my soul.

The Oregon Trail begins in Missouri and extends to Oregon. The first expedition to the Pacific went this way. You may have heard of the fellas who did that, ol' Lewis and Clark. Their expedition was a huge success, but the Trail wasn't "wagon friendly" for many years. Still, countless people traveled this way, but it was so dangerous only the strong and the brave dared to do it. The sandstone rocks we found told the story of the thousands of brave souls to headed this way in the mid-1800s. You'll find wagon trails all over the west, but most of them pale in comparison to the ones we found here.

Here you can't miss them.

Here, they're carved in stone.

"Will you look at that? Some of these gouges are more than four feet deep!" Chet rightly observed. The deep ruts were from years of wagon wear as well as intentional cutting by pioneers who wanted better leverage for their wagons as they took the steep passage up from the level river bottom into the High Plains. Progress was often so slow due to bad weather, poor equipment, and illness that on some days, a family would look back and be able to see with the naked eye where they'd started that morning.

"Who were these folks who dared to do the impossible?" Chet wondered.

"I can only speculate partner, but mostly they were immigrants. Visionaries. Exiles. Grifters. Drifters. Conmen. Neophytes. Wealthy investors. Entrepreneurs."

"That's a lot of people, boss."

"Mostly, they were dreamers. Reckon you, and I fit into that category," I said.

"I reckon you're right about that."

Some of the early guides who led the settlers west chose different routes where better pastures, timber, and game could be found, while others headed west with no real plan. You can imagine this usually led to disaster. "Estimates are half a million people traveled on this here Oregon Trail. Nearly 100,000 of 'em turned around after being abandoned by their cash-in-advance guides," I said to Chet.

"You'd think the Tribes would have a problem with this 'highway' running right through their backyards," Chet wondered.

"They had an agreement with the white man," I said. "They let the settlers pass through, but straying from the trail was forbidden. Rule breakers paid with their lives but turns out very few died at the hands of Native Americans. Most succumbed to disease or from the accidental discharge of their own firearms."

"She-it. Rookie mistake," Chet said. Standing there, it was almost too much to take in, and too hard to believe.

"One day, I'll tell my kids about this."

"Me too, boss. Me too."

Chet and I removed our Stetsons and honored the timelessness of the moment. We both said, "Thank you to all the families who blazed a trail for us and helped build our nation." It was even more humbling knowing such a high percentage of families never made it to the end of their journey.

"Hard to believe 50,000 people died along the way," Chet said.

"Reckon we got nothing to complain about."

"You said it," Chet said, and he put his arm over my shoulder like two pals. He rarely showed physical affection besides his patented bear hugs, but this moment was emotional for both of us.

We walked back up the trail invigorated, swung back up in the saddle, and headed for Register Cliffs. It was a short ride from the trail ruts back through Guernsey to get there. We met Dave at the rig and dismounted again then walked the route to the fenced-off area. We took a deep breath and read the marker along the trail. Emotions were running high for me, and I could tell Chet felt the same. This was sacred ground. Register Cliff was once a key navigational landmark for the early pioneers. It stands a hundred feet above the North Platte River Valley on the eastern ascent of the Continental Divide. Parties heading west along the Platte River Valley checked in there, just seeing it let travelers know they were on the right path and not heading into impassible mountain terrain. It was a tradition among the immigrants who were splitting off to take the California Trail or Mormon Trail to inscribe or "register" their names on its rocks. They would spend the night at Register Cliff and chisel their names into the soft sandstone on the face of the cliff. The earliest signatures date back to the late 1820s when the trappers and fur traders passed through the area, but most of the names were carved during the 1840s and 1850s when the Oregon Trail reached its peak.

Chet and I wandered past the "No Tourist" sign and spent the next hour slowly moving from rock to rock, taking turns reading the inscriptions aloud. Sandstone is so soft; it was easy to read the names of the people and the memorable passages they wrote, including the month and year they made their eternal mark in history. Knowing many families never made it to their destination, some passages were difficult to read without tearing up.

We found a flat spot on one large-faced rock that strangely had no inscriptions but was surrounded by many others. I took out my skinning knife with its finely-honed blade and handed it to my partner. "I think you should do the honors," I said. "We're in good company. Scratch out something important."

"You got it, boss." Amid the pioneer inscriptions, Chet carefully carved: "Thank you, Jeff and Chet, Cross America '86," and added the date. When he finished, he stepped back, and we both admired his work. Chet's chicken-scratch looked like it belonged even though we weren't worthy of the sacrifice they made. We were honored to be a part of this heroic group of brave men, women, and children. One day, I'll go back and visit that spot with my family.

One day.

Back on the trail, as much as we wanted to avoid any interstate highways, there were a few times on our trip where there was no way around it. This was one of those times. We took Interstate 25 north for a short time, then exited off another grey road called Route 319 and rode west through the boomtowns of Aman, Douglas, and Glenrock. We passed through dusty little outposts like Cowhollow that only had a post office and a bar. I spent the day asking local ranchers their advice on the best route to cross the "Red Desert" of Wyoming.

Expert guidance was needed because there was no direct route from Casper that went west except to ride over numerous small mountain ranges. The other option was to go around them by heading north or south, but we didn't want to go 100 miles out of our way. There were very few marked roads on any map we could get our hands on, so we headed into Casper on Route 26, looking for answers.

Casper was pretty big by western standards; it's the second-largest city in Wyoming, so we were sure we could find some people who would point us in the right direction. As good fortune would have it, there was a rodeo in town, and the folks there were quite friendly. Hank, one of the rodeo hands we met, insisted we put our horses up for the evening in some of the corrals.

"Much obliged."

"Don't mention it," Hank said. "I respect what you two are doin'. Not many cowboys have the *huevos* to ride coast to coast. Bet you boys got some Texas-sized hemorrhoids." Hank laughed.

"No comment." Chet murmured.

"When's the rodeo?" I asked.

"Tomorrow. You got here just in time," Hank said, gesturing to all the cowboys and cowgirls who were pulling in trailers full of livestock. "There'll be some pretty little Phillies in town tonight, I reckon." We got the horses settled into Hank's corral, then we hoofed it around town and took in a bit of the local scenery. Whenever we got to bend someone's ear, the same subject always came up, "We're looking for the best way to ride across the Red Desert. You got any tips for a couple of out-of-town cowboys?" We got a lot of perplexed looks.

"You boys know what you're in for?" one of the local cowboys said with a squint as he spit a mouthful of chewing tobacco into a spittoon.

"Well, we know anytime you cross a desert, it's gonna be a pretty tough stretch."

"You got that right," the cowboy said.

One of the locals working at the rodeo heard us talking and came over, "Hey boys, all you gotta do is get on Poison Spider Creek Road in Mountain View, and follow that all the way 'till you hit the old Union Carbide plant at Gas Hills. Then you'll see a road that'll take you out the other side of the desert."

I looked at Chet, "Poison Spider Creek Road."

"What an inviting name," Chet said with a fake smile plastered on his face.

"You can say that again. It's a real bitch!" the local said, then he cackled like he knew something we didn't. It turns out he did.

We moseyed on back to the truck and met up with Dave.

"If that wasn't an ominous sign of things to come, I don't know what is," I said.

This was the first we'd heard of Poison Spider Creek Road. Back in 1986, there were no computers, so we had to rely on nothing but paper maps and locals' advice—and somehow, that name had never come up in any of our research. Chet broke out the topo maps and laid them out on the back of the rig and scratched his head. "There's no Poison Spider Creek Road on any of these, boss."

"It's one-a them ghost roads. Seen a few of those already, hadn't we?"

"Yep. Once again, we're counting on the good nature of folks for our directional. How could we go wrong?" Chet laughed.

The next day we set off for the mysterious Poison Spider Creek Road. We got an early start around 4:30 A.M. to try to beat the heat and the swarms of horseflies, deer flies, and mosquitoes that were sure to reach their peak by midday. The boys were rested, and so were we. The whole team minus Andrew, who was halfway to Chicago with his guitar between his legs, got to enjoy a little of the local flavor and some good conversation with the rodeo cowboys we met. It was a nice twelve-hour break, and we needed it to prepare for the next few days of misery. After riding west for an hour, we found our desert jump-off point in the town called Mountain View without any problem.

"Now, where's our poison spider hiding?" I wondered. The Casper cowboys said we'd see a sign, but one thing I learned on the trip is when you're out West, you never know how the roads will be marked. Lo and behold if we didn't find the poison spider we were looking for, sitting there in plain sight about a half-mile off the main road. The sign read: "Poison Spider Creek Road."

"There it is," I said.

"Well, I'll be goddamned," Chet said.

The directions from our friends in Casper had gotten us this far. Riding further into Mountain View, we saw another sign that read 'West Poison Spider Creek Road.'

"Guess we're in the right place."

"Well. You ready to do this, boss?"

"I reckon we got enough water for today, let's get it over with."

We knew to find water was going to be a challenge for the foreseeable future. By now, the good ol' North Platte River was a distant memory, so we carried a backup water supply in the trailer in the form of eight five-gallon water buckets (with lids) for the horses. We had smartly purchased more buckets in Casper, so now we had eleven. Those 55 gallons would last us for a day if we couldn't locate water.

I sent Dave ahead in the rig, "Your only mission is to find water."

"What about a place to camp?"

"Forget that we need water more than anything."

"OK then," he said, and off he went. We had no idea when we'd see him next; I just had to believe we would. Sometimes on our journey, belief was all we had, belief in ourselves and each other. The team was as prepared as we could be, so we braced for whatever was ahead and took a leap of faith into the unknown. We knew we could count on each other when times got rough. That's why we let Andrew go; we couldn't trust him to have our backs when it was, as the old ranchers used to say, "nut-cutting" time.

Now was that time.

Poison Spider Creek Road may sound exotic, but it wasn't much to look at. It was just an old dirt road that led into the desert. I'm no Ernest Hemingway, so it's impossible for this old cowboy to describe the terrain, but just the name hints at how wild and nasty it was. "Where's the creek?" I joked. "Looks like we're about to go hunting for the Treasure of the Sierra Madre."

"Badges? We don't need no stinking badges!" Chet said on cue then laughed.

"Just watch out for rattlesnakes, hoss," I said in all seriousness.

"Don't lose your sense of humor now!" Chet said, probably trying to negate his fear of dying in the desert with a little comic relief. Thunder and Rebel seemed to heed my warning. They slowly ascended Poison Spider Creek Road and tip-toed around a couple of its ridges to make sure it was safe. It didn't take long for the sprawling suburban homes of Casper to disappear in our rearview mirror.

On the back end of the ridge, we began our descent into "hell." There was nothing as far as the eye could see, no houses, no creek—only flat, dusty desert for miles and miles. The meandering Poison Spider Creek Road was its only discerning mark.

We were on our own now, literally in no man's land.

"Maybe we shoulda brought two camels for this stretch," Chet joked.

"Wouldn't trade Thunder for any camel."

Dave and the rig had disappeared into the western desert a long time ago. When the road flattened out, the wind kicked up, throwing sand in our faces. We pulled our bandanas up around our noses like a couple of bandits and kept them there. We were resigned to the fact we were going to be living with strong winds, extreme heat, and torturous conditions for the immediate future. Still, it wasn't any damn fun at all.

The wind stayed in the thirty to forty mph range for three straight days! No joke. We only thought we had escaped hell when we left Nebraska, but as fate would have it, we had landed in a new circle of hades. The sky was cloudless, and the hot desert wind was blowing right in our face. We were swarmed by horseflies.

"It's gotta be 105 degrees in the shade," Chet said.

"There ain't no damn shade out here unless you're the size of a rattler," I said.

"I have never seen a swarm of flies as thick!" Chet cursed under a dark blanket of bugs that followed us everywhere, like a black cloud. We buttoned our long-sleeve shirts to the top and pulled our hats down low; our bandanas covered our faces below our eyes. Still we were swarmed. Those bastards were relentless.

Thankfully after our fly attack in Nebraska, we were smart enough to bring some extra strength fly wipes with us this time. I pulled them out. Every hour we stopped and wiped down the boys from head to hoof, but it didn't stop the flies. Wiping down Thunder, I could see twenty to thirty little specks of blood on him just from the bites.

"Jesus H. Christ," Chet said. "This isn't heaven, this sucks!"

"And think, this is just day one," I said, trying to rally us with gallows humor.

"Maybe we should stop talking now," Chet said. The buzzing bastards had drained all his joviality. We didn't talk much in the desert. The only words that managed to escape our mouths the rest of the day were curses and the same pat response to our surroundings.

"M.F. deer flies!" Chet said, swatting them away. "Unbelievable!"

The only relief came when we camped at night. When we had a fire going, the smoke kept them away and gave us a brief respite from those miserable critters.

＊ ＊ ＊

I began worrying about Dave that afternoon. We were rationing water as best we could, but we only had a day's supply. We were already running low. I kept my eyes on the horizon. Every time Dave and the rig didn't appear, I got a sick feeling in my stomach. I knew I had to stay strong-minded out here, or a blanket of fear could smother you to death. I kept my anxiety to myself as Chet, and I slogged north of the Rattle Snake Mountains, another ominous name. "That there's the Rattlesnake Mountains.so heed that warning and look out for rattlers," I warned Chet.

"I would if I could see," Chet said, swatting flies away.

Rattlesnakes and horses do not make good partners.

"Look, those are rattlesnake holes all around us," I said, pointing to a few. Rattlers like to curl up in the shade of small sagebrush bushes during the day, and there were millions of sagebrush plants in the high desert. Some might slither from plant to plant during the day, but they're hard to spot.

"They'll blend in with rocks and sagebrush if you're not careful."

"That's all we need," Chet said. "Wake me when the locusts start invading."

I don't know how many rattlers we flushed out that day, but it was a lot. A few times, we tried to take a short cut off of the road, which was a big mistake. When we got out in the desert, there were thousands of rattlesnake holes around us.

"I feel like we're being watched," Chet said.

"Stay vigilant, hoss. Rattlers don't always rattle first," I said.

Suddenly, a rattler lunged out of the sagebrush and nearly bit Thunder's hooves. Thunder whinnied and jumped out of the way. "Get on, boy!" I yelled.

"This is getting ridiculous!" Chet said with his eyes glued to the sand, "How did the old cowboys get across the desert with no road?"

"They avoided it at all costs," I said, keeping my eyes peeled.

"It's a goddamn rattlesnake minefield out here!"

After our 7th or 8th rattlesnake sighting, we decided to cut back to the road and stay there. We were lucky none of the horses got bitten. On the road, we were able to see them better, and by then, we had our eyes glued to the ground.

"Think I'd much rather contend with grizzlies than rattlers," I said.

"Why?" Chet asked.

"An experienced horseman can better prepare for grizzlies."

"I'd rather us not run into either," Chet said.

"Reckon we'll run into both again, partner. Head on a swivel."

"You really know how to sweet-talk me," Chet said.

We kept slogging along in the miserable heat and wind—avoiding rattlers while being swarmed by horse flies from hell. I don't think Chet and I had truly experienced the sensation of being alone out in the middle of nowhere until this point of the trip. It was sobering. "Desolate as hell out here," Chet said. "This is where dreams go to die."

"Not ours, pard," I said, "Not ours."

We had no idea where Dave was. I knew we wouldn't see him till close to dark since he left us early in the day looking for ranches or farms. But still, the pit in my stomach got worse as the sun moved across the sky, and the late afternoon set in. When Chet and I stopped to wipe down the horses again, we got out our map and saw that the only town nearby was a town called Ervay. "There is literally nothing on Poison Spider Creek Road. No cars, no trucks, no Dave," I said. I put the map away. "Until we cross this sucker, we ain't gonna, see anybody."

"Didja hear that?" Chet piped up.

We heard a truck rumbling in the distance. After eight hours in the desert going at a pace of about 2.5 mph, it was a wonderful sound. It was our first contact with civilization all day. We waited with bated breath to see who it was.

It was Dave.

We hooted and hollered when he pulled up in the rig.

"You fellas thirsty?" Dave asked with his head out the open window.

"Well, it's about time!" Chet said, laughing.

We dismounted, grabbed a water jug, and gulped it down. Then we watered down the boys, grabbed a hunk of Chet's famous cornbread, and sat in the trailer out of the sun for a break. Dave had his own story to tell, "Boys, you are not going to believe how far I went to get water." Dave explained he had to drive four hours before he found a thing.

"I took the first side road I found, it looked like there might be a ranch up there, but by the time I found a place where I thought I might find water, there was no ranch and no people. So, I went looking around and found an old stock tank with a whole bunch of cows crowding around it."

"We're drinking water from a stock tank?" Chet stopped drinking mid-gulp.

"Yeah," Dave said. He said he noticed it in the distance thanks to the stock tank having a working windmill. "So, I filled up all of our buckets and caught up with you boys," he said, wiping his brow. "Now, I'm thirsty." Even ol' Dave had been moving at a snail pace, and he had the truck. The roads were that bad. Poison Spider Creek Road wasn't "wash-boarded" completely, so you could probably go about twenty to thirty mph, but some of the old ranch roads around these parts never got grated, so it was slow going.

For everyone.

By the time we had cooled off, it was starting to get close to 8 P.M., so we went looking for a good spot to camp. This was the end of another 16-hour day, and we were beat. Even Chet's usual cheeriness had turned to weariness.

"I'm hot, smelly, tired, thirsty, hungry, and bitten all to hell all over my damn arms and neck," Chet moaned. "This isn't heaven. this—"

"This sucks, yeah, yeah, we know," I said.

"You keep saying that," Dave interjected.

"This is the cowboy life, boys. You gotta have a little sour to enjoy the sweet."

"Screw the sour," Chet said.

"We probably need to stop jawin' and find a place to camp," Dave said.

"Alright. I really don't wanna sleep on the road or camp in the desert with the rattlers." I said.

"What other option do you think we have out here?" Dave asked.

Dave had me stumped.

"Sleep in the saddle?" Chet asked.

It didn't get dark until around ten, so we had some time to find a spot before it cooled down enough for the rattlers to come out to hunt for food. Just as it was getting close to dark thirty, Chet and I were starting to feel really nervous then I don't know if it was dumb luck or fate, but Chet noticed something out in the desert.

"What's that?" Chet asked loud enough to get my attention away from slapping horse flies off Thunder's neck.

"What do you see?"

"A black speck," he said.

As a former Montana guide, I was a little disappointed my "guide eyes" didn't catch it first. It looked like it might have been a quarter-mile north of the road. "Might be an old shack or some kind of structure we could camp in," I said. Well, I'll be goddammed if we didn't ride up closer to that black speck, and it turned out to be an old metal Quonset hut with one big opening on the east side, which was the side away from the wind. "F.M. I say. F.M." I smiled. "Good work, hoss."

"Thank you, God," Chet said, pointing up at the sky.

Dave had arrived at the hut first and was able to pull the whole rig inside. It probably could have slept 100 people in there. It was just one big open area—no sage, no snakes, and completely shaded from the sun and wind. We were so happy you'd have thought we were pulling up to the Ritz. "Is this a mirage? Why in the world is this thing even here?" Chet asked, looking around.

"Probably to house equipment and what-not."

"But this one is empty," Chet said.

"F.M. I say. Sometimes you just get lucky."

The outfit settled into our new home in the middle of the desert. I made a little fire by the entrance, and Chet made dinner—then Dave and I fed and watered the horses. The team was comfortable that evening being out of the wind. We could still hear it howling around us, which was a constant reminder of what awaited us when we left the next day. Before dinner, Chet noticed me strategically placing lariats around our campsite. "What you doin', boss?" Chet asked while seasoning the stew pot.

"Old cowboys trick. Snakes won't slither over a lariat due to the coarseness of the ropes," I said.

"You've tested this before, haven't you?" Chet said with a laugh.

We dined around the campfire on Chet's fabulous beef stew. After all, we had been through the past few weeks, we discussed the possibility of staying in our new home for a few days to rest in the lap of luxury. "I could get used to this place; but there's no place like home," I said.

"Home. Almost forgot I had one; it's been so long," Chet said.

"Sure do miss Sue," I said with a sigh.

"Wonder if Diane's left me for the milkman yet," Chet said. There's something special about sitting around a warm campfire that brings out one's inner feelings. We rarely spoke about home and our loved ones on the trip. I don't know why really; I guess we just kept those feelings inside. But on this night, things were different. We all spoke about missing our families back home. Even the Preacher Man talked about missing his little girl. Connecticut felt like a lifetime away from our newfound desert oasis. All we had was each other and our memories of home to keep us warm.

"Think they have any idea what's happening to us?" Chet wondered.

"How could they, we haven't seen a payphone in days," I said. "Can't believe I left my pregnant wife for THIS." Chet sympathized.

"You know Sue wanted you to go; don't dredge up that old guilt trip again."

"I suspect she was just saying that so I didn't have to cancel the trip. No way she wanted to go through this alone."

"You don't know that. Maybe she got tired of us always being in her hair. She's got some peace and quiet for once!" Chet said, which made us all laugh. Still, I wasn't too sure about Chet's line of thinking. Sue made it clear before I left that being pregnant in the heat of summer was not something she was too happy about, which made me feel pretty bad. I remember telling her next time, "better strategic planning on my part will probably go a long way in the marriage-longevity department, right?"

I smiled sheepishly, and she smiled back and hugged me, but in retrospect, I'm not sure how funny she thought I was, if at all. She's such a trooper, I thought. I wonder if she secretly thinks I abandoned her? I knew I had to stop tearing myself up over this. I pushed my feelings of guilt way down inside and tried to focus on the challenges of the next day. That was all I could do to keep going and not turn back and head east on the next bus, like ol' Andrew.

After supper, we all fell into a deep sleep that would've made Louis L'Amour proud. As I drifted off, I couldn't help but wonder how long we were going to be on Poison Spider Creek Road. Will we ever see anybody? Will the wind ever die down? Then I thought about Suzy again and wondered how she and our unborn baby were doing. I could see her sleeping in our bed alone. I could see her crying herself to sleep. I felt a pang in my heart I hadn't felt in a long time. That night, I dreamt I was back in her loving arms. It was a good dream.

I awoke the next morning as usual around 3:30 or 4. Chet fried us up some back bacon with a hot cup of cowboy coffee and some leftover cornbread. By 4:30, we were on our way again. We said farewell to our metal hut and hello to the harsh elements.

"Gonna be another long day," Chet sighed.

"Good thing we left early."

I always enjoyed the early morning; it's the most beautiful part of the day for me, but my appreciation for morning rides only increased in the Red Desert. It was the only time it was cool—about 65 degrees.

"Feels good, don't it?" I mused.

"In a few hours, it'll be hotter than H.E. double hockey sticks," Chet said. I knew if we kept riding, we would eventually hit the old Union Carbide plant. At least that was what the old cowboy in Casper had told us, and so far, he had steered us right.

We cut back onto Poison Spider Creek Road. Chet and I looked back into the cool morning sun and watched our cozy night's accommodations slowly fade into the rising sun. We never figured out how and why it was there or what purpose it served.

"It's one of the mysteries of life," Chet said.

"F.M.," I said.

"What does F.M. mean anyway boss?" Chet asked.

"You don't know by now?"

"Not. A. Clue." Chet said, "Never been too good of a speller."

"I'll tell you when we reach the Pacific. That's the ultimate F.M. experience."

"Whatever you say, boss."

By 9 A.M., we were sweltering again, the temperature was in the high 90s, and the deer flies were swarming—but at least we had a good night's sleep. The conversation died down the hotter it got. My thoughts drifted back to Sue, and the memories of her and Diane's surprise visit in Illinois. June seemed like years ago. I thought about the odds of them finding us on the trail in Illinois and the way she looked when she pulled up next to us with the window down and said, "Going my way?" It was a moment of pure joy. I'm still amazed Diane and Sue were able to track us down on a grey road that stretched for miles, and the only purpose was to connect farm after farm. F.M. I say.

The only thing keeping our heads up while the flies feasted on what was left of our weathered skin was today we were supposed to run into a slice of civilization in the form of the only town in the middle of this godforsaken desert called Ervay. We'd been dreaming about the place ever since we spotted it on our topo map. Chet and I started fantasizing about the large cup of real coffee that we would buy. "Maybe some nice folks will invite us to a barbeque?" I dreamt aloud. "Wouldn't that be nice?"

"Mmmm, BBQ. I could eat a barbequed horse right now. Sorry Rebel."

"Any place with a roof that serves food will hit the spot," I said.

By our estimate, we felt we should hit town just after lunch. We were already feeling peckish but were so excited we decided to wait to eat in town, where we were hoping to find some western hospitality.

"Where the heck is it?" Chet was getting anxious. The plan was to change horses in Ervay and look for Dave and the rig.

"Hold your horses, pard, just look for the rig in the distance." A little after noon, we had seen no signs of Ervay. We still hadn't seen a single car pass us all day.

How can that be with the town being so close?

When 1 P.M. approached, I knew there was a problem. We took a short break to look at the map. I yanked it out of my saddlebag, and Chet and I studied it again. We recognized the terrain on the map—it matched the area we just rode through. We determined we were exactly where Ervay was on the map. But there were no side roads, no signs of anything but dust, sagebrush, and sand. I glassed the area with a 360-degree look. I yelled over the wind, "I don't see a god damn thing in any direction for miles! Here, you take a look."

Chet looked through the binoculars, then shook his head and put them away, "These map engineers are idiots. I don't think there is a town called Ervay anywhere near here. Somebody screwed up!" We looked at each other in disbelief. "I guess that means no coffee in Ervay—no barbeque. No beer. No nothing!"

"Well, goddamn."

We were both pissed, then something came over us.

We looked at each other and broke out into uncontrollable laughter.

They say you either laugh or cry in these situations, so we chose to laugh—uncontrollably. We couldn't help but feel like fools, with all of our talk about what we would do when we got to Ervay—so Chet acted like one. He handed me Rebel's reins and went into a comedy routine. "Hello gentlemen, welcome to Bistro Ervay—on today's menu, we have twelve-ounce phantom steak with a side of imaginary *pomme frites*," Chet said in his fake French accent. "Please have a seat in our Corinthian leather recliner and let our lovely masseuse 'Fifi' rub your 'barking dogs' while you dine." Then he played the role of Chet in a French restaurant, "Actually Frenchy, I'd rather have a cheeseburger and an ice-cold beer," he said. "Beer? Beeer? We only have wine!" Chet was playing both parts and probably going a little crazy from the heat, but it was a perfect morale booster.

We got back on Thunder and Rebel and kept riding—what else could we do? When we finally saw our first vehicle three hours later, it was Dave and the rig. We stopped to switch horses and asked Dave if he could fill the water buckets, "once he hits Ervay." Then we broke out in laughter again and told him the story.

Dave rarely showed any emotion, but even he laughed. "You boys got suckered by a map," Dave said. "You just can't trust anybody these days."

Chet and I kept on riding until sundown. Nothing much happened but the same old desert routine. When we saw Dave again, it was 9 P.M. He already had camp set up for us just off Poison Spider Creek Road. "I'm beater than beat," Chet said.

"Figure we broke forty miles today—maybe 45." We both smelled dinner on the fire. I looked at Chet, "Dave's cooking tonight. It ain't Bistro Ervay, but it'll eat."

"At least I don't have to cook."

We dismounted and thanked Dave for setting up camp and finding another old stock tank in the middle of nowhere to fill our water buckets. "You are a top hand, Preacher Man," I said, patting him on the back. "Someday, I'll buy you a beer to thank you."

"If we ever see another town again," Chet said.

"Right. And that's a big 'if.'" Few words were spoken around the campfire that night—fatigue had set in. All we wanted to do was sleep, get up and ride out of this desert wasteland forever. "If our map don't fail us again, this is officially our last night on Poison Spider Creek Road," I said as we settled down after finishing the dishes.

"Hooray," Chet deadpanned. Then he started snoring immediately.

I lay down and stared at the stars for a spell, then my eyelids got real heavy. The last thing I remember was a mosquito buzzing in my ear as I drifted off to sleep.

By noon the next day, we finally came upon the landmark the old cowboy had told us about in Casper. It was a huge black pit we surmised was the infamous Gas Hills-Union Carbide Strip mine. It must have employed several hundred people in its heyday. Strangely, there were fifty old trucks still parked down in the pit.

"This place is like a ghost mine," Chet said. "Creepy."

"We've seen ghost towns but never this."

"Guess they don't have a soda machine in there," Chet said, pointing to the plant in front of us. Poison Spider Creek Road led us right along the edge of the deserted plant. We rode through the entrance to eyeball all the idle equipment and what was once a humming plant that created hundreds of jobs. We couldn't believe the devastation.

We didn't stay long.

We kept on riding and exited out of the other side of the plant. We felt we were getting close to the end of the Red Desert, then we saw a road marker that proved it. Poison Spider Creek Road had finally ended—it turned into Gas Hills Road for the rest of the ride to Riverton. "Well, what do you know? I think we actually made it," Chet said, unable to muster his usual enthusiasm for landmark events.

"I never want to see a desert ever again," I said. I'm not sure the exact number of miles from the start of Poison Spider Creek Road in Mountain View to Riverton, but I'm guessing we rode close to 120 miles. It took us three extremely long days to get there with two nights in the Wyoming Desert.

Thank God it was over.

Once we hit Riverton, we knew to follow the "Wind River Reservation" for a good stretch to our next stop, the town of Dubois. We had close to 80 miles to cover in that stretch. Once we reached Dubois, which sat at an elevation of over 6900 feet, we would finally be in the early stages of reaching the Rockies and eventually the Continental Divide and Teton-Yellowstone Park.

"I reckon a change of scenery will do us just fine," I said.

"I'll be shaking sand out of my boots for years. Bring on the mountains." We straddled the fence line of the Wind River Reservation along Highway 26. The ride was easy for the boys; the grass along the fence line provided a nice cushion, and it cooled their feet to boot. We could finally stop looking for rattlers, and the swarms of deer flies had subsided to a normal level with the cooler evenings.

We were happy again.

In Riverton, we were given some sage advice by a local, "If I was you boys, I'd keep on riding by towns along the rez," he said. "That'll keep you free of any trouble with the tribal police."

"Good tip. Thank ye," I said to the local and tipped my hat and kept on riding. We passed by Crowheart, by far one of the smallest towns we had seen. We didn't stop, but we saw a sign that said Crowheart's population was 141.

"That fits my definition of a small town," Chet said.

I knew something about the local history, so I started in on another history lesson for Chet to pass the time. "Just a ways off is Crowheart Butte—which was the site of a battle between the Crow and Shoshone American Indian tribes."

"You don't say," Chet said, half-listening.

"According to legend, after a five-day battle over who got the Wind River hunting grounds, Chief Washakie of the Shoshone and Chief Big Robber of the Crow agreed to a duel for all the marbles. Well, ol' Chief Washakie eventually prevailed—but he was so impressed with the courage of Chief Big Robber—rather than scalp him, he cut out his heart and stuck it on the end of his lance!"

"Damn, think it was a good idea to keep moving through Crowheart," Chet said.

"You reckon?" I said with a chuckle.

That night, we camped a few hours west of Burris. It was a quiet night; even the boys hardly made a sound. I knew they'd have to be at full strength to conquer the heart of the Rockies, and it was my job to make sure they were prepared. They were ready, but I could tell they needed more rest. We all did.

After another long day, we sacked out early. I drifted off under the stars once again and gazed upward to the "Chief's Highway," otherwise known as the Milky Way. As I stared at one of the true wonders of the evening sky, I gave a quiet thanks to the heavens for getting us this far. Then I gave Sue and our baby a mental hug and closed my eyes for some well-needed rest. Another day down.

Many more yet to go.

The next morning, we set out for the town of Dubois. We were hoping to find a comfortable spot to shut down the outfit for 24 hours and do what we had dreamt about for so many days now—nothing. We didn't have to travel far to find our sanctuary. We were a few miles outside of Dubois when, as luck would have it, or F.M. or whatever you want to call it—a pick-up truck pulled up in front of us.

"Hope that ain't the lynch mob," Chet said.

"Don't think so," I said as out of the truck stepped a forty-something-year-old blond woman rancher.

"This just may be our lucky day, hoss," I said.

"What are you cowboys up to?" she asked with her hand shading the morning sun from her eyes. When we told her, she introduced herself as Ginny Heiser. "You boys look like warmed over shit," she said. "Anything I can do to help? I got a ranch up in the foothills just a few miles off."

"You don't say?" Chet said. I looked at Chet, and he looked back at me with his bad poker face. "Well, thank ye. I reckon we could use a shower and a shave."

"Those duds you got on look pretty ripe, too," she laughed, "Let's get you all washed up. C'mon, follow me; I'll put y'all up the night—your horses too." Ginny gave us an offer we could not refuse. After she gave us directions to her ranch, I sent Dave ahead with the other two horses and trailer to begin the R&R process. I hadn't seen Chet smile in a while, but he was grinning ear-to-ear as we started up towards Ginny's ranch.

"Bath, shower, hot coffee—real bed? I don't have to cook today? Maybe a cold beer? Hot dog, life is good!" he hollered.

"I reckon you're right, old friend," I said with a chuckle. "Someone's smiling down on us today." Ginny's ranch was a lush twenty acres nestled up in the foothills with lots of fescue-alfalfa grass for the boys to chow on. "Are we in heaven?" Chet asked as we rode up to her little hideaway that looked like it came straight out of a dream.

"This ain't no metal hut in the desert," I said. It felt odd sitting at her kitchen table. Chet and I tried to remember our manners as we visited with Ginny while we drank countless cups of coffee and devoured the home-baked goods Ginny placed on the table.

"Now, you boys eat em up. I bet you could eat a horse," she said as she brought out a basket of muffins and dinner rolls. "Never heard of anybody crazy enough to ride clear across the country."

"Was about ready to eat a horse a few days ago, ma'am," Chet said.

"Please, call me Ginny," she said with a little flirty lilt in her voice.

"OK. Ginny," Chet said, grinning with his mouth full. I could tell she liked Chet, but after his fleeting romance with Jean in Indiana, which in retrospect probably broke his heart, it seemed by now he remembered he was an engaged man—so he acted accordingly and took Ginny's flirtations in stride. I reckon ol'

Chet was probably too tired to flirt back even if he wanted to. Not that Ginny wasn't attractive, but what was more exciting to both of us was her culinary skills. "I reckon this is the best home cookin' we've had since we started our ride," I said.

Ginny liked to hear that, so she kept rolling out more food. We didn't want to hurt her feelings, so we felt obliged to devour everything she put in front of us. Even skinny ol' Dave got in on the feeding frenzy.

As the morning turned into afternoon, we sat in her kitchen, just visiting with Ginny while she drank Tab soda. Chet and I kept binging while we answered the many questions Ginny had about our trip. She told us she lived alone and was a divorcee "from way back." Her love for horses (hers and ours) shone through from the first moment we met her. The hours rolled by as the four of us sat around, just shooting the breeze. It was true western hospitality. All day the sparks were flying between her and Chet.

I think if Ginny asked us to stay for the winter, we might have considered it—fortunately, she didn't. I reckon she would have liked ol' Chet to stay forever. She took an immediate fondness to him, as did many women along our journey. It wasn't because he was single, and I was a seasoned married man; Chet just had a magnetism about him that drew people in with his charm, wit, and infectious laugh. To meet Chet is to love the guy. But that's as far as it went tonight.

Once night fell, we got cleaned up and ready to turn in. Can you believe it was hard to sleep in a real bed? This was the first one I'd slept in since we left Connecticut more than three months ago. Since then, luxury had been an occasional rancher offering us his barn for the night. Dust, mice, and ticks were part of the accommodations—but not tonight. It didn't take long for me to sack out. Nothing could stand in the way of a good night's sleep. Not even a real bed.

I awoke to the distant crowing of a rooster and the smell of sausage and coffee coming from downstairs. Ginny had a sumptuous breakfast waiting for us and even packed us a lunch to take with us on the trail. "You are an angel Ginny. We'll never forget your hospitality," I said while we saddled up the horses. Before we left, we each gave her a bear hug—even ol' Dave, who wasn't too keen on that kind of thing, gave her a squeeze goodbye. Chet and Ginny hugged the longest. I could tell it was hard for Ginny to let him go. "Mighty nice meeting you, Miss Ginny. We'll send you a postcard from the Pacific," Chet said with a smile.

"Likewise, Chet. And you better. Y'all be careful out there now. You're about to run into some grizzlies."

"We sure will."

We grudgingly said our goodbyes to Ginny and her ranch. It was hard to leave heaven on earth, but leave we did. As we rode off her property and into the great unknown, we were as clean, fed, and rested as we had been since we left the East Coast. I had a renewed sense of optimism for the days to come, and Chet had an extra pep in his step too. "Off we go into the wild blue yonder," I said to Chet.

"She sure was nice, wadn't she?" Chet said.

"Sure was," I said. "She liked you."

"I know. Learned my lesson back in Indiana," Chet said.

"You're not still pissed at me, are you?" I asked.

"Na, Jean woulda slowed us down. And I'm an engaged man," Chet said.

We both looked back and waved one final time. I caught a sad look in Ginny's eye as she smiled and waved back.

"You sure can be a heartbreaker, sometimes."

"C'mon, boss, you're embarrassing me," Chet said with a laugh.

With our souls renewed, our clothes cleaned, and our stomachs full, Chet, Dave, and I kept heading west on our way towards our ultimate destiny. We had lost a team member, survived the perils of the red desert and recharged at a dreamlike oasis in the foothills—and somehow came out of it no worse for wear.

F.M I say.

★ 11 ★

TRUE COWBOYS OF WYOMING

"I told my Pap and Mam I was coming to trap
and be a mountain man, and they acted like
they was gun-shot. Mam says, 'Son, make your
life, go here, here's where the people is; them
mountains is for animals and savages.' I says
'Mother Gue—the Rocky Mountains is the
marrow of the world.' And by God, I was right."
—*Del Gue from Jeremiah Johnson*

TODAY WAS A brand-new day. Ol' Chet and I could feel it, and it showed. Our bodies and spirits had been renewed overnight. Ginny's ranch was just the medicine we needed at just the right time. It's wondrous what some home cooking; a good night's rest and a hot shower can do for a tired couple of cowboys' constitutions. It sure did the trick. Before Ginny's hospitality, I reckon Chet and I looked (and smelled) like a couple of overripe mountain men better suited for a hermit's cabin than any formal affair at a State House. When we saddled up the next morning, we smelled so good the horses didn't even recognize us. "Guess we can clean up, after all," I said to Chet as we rode out of Ginny's ranch through the cool morning air. "You were startin' to resemble the pioneer known as 'Grizzly Adams,' partner."

Chet smiled, "You were startin' to stink like Festus from *Gunsmoke*. Still are."

"Finally, understand why that cop wanted to 'cuff and stuff' us back in Indiana."

"For illegal use of a public payphone?" Chet said.

"Naw. For lookin' like a couple-a horse-thievin' vagrants," I said.

"Guess I'd a thrown us in the pokey just for stinkin' up the place, too." Chet said while rubbing his clean-shaven chin, "Sad to see my tick collection go. Almost had enough in my beard to start my own flea circus."

"Never heard of a tick circus."

"Coulda made a million bucks."

"Got a feelin' you may get another chance to rustle some more."

Our morning ride was perfectly uneventful. The cool, early morning mist that settled on the ponderosa pines filled our lungs with a lingering, unforgettable scent. I decided to let Chet and Dave sleep-in that morning, so we had gotten a late start, at about 9 A.M., which suited us just fine. We were still recovering from the trials and tribulations of the Wyoming desert, and I didn't want to push the team, knowing the Rockies were on the horizon. Not a whole lot was said that morning, so I passed the time thinking about life. I had gotten pretty good at that after all these months. I remember thinking back to the previous night, and the moment I first got a gander at my old mug in Ginny's bathroom mirror. Whoo-wee. Sue would've run for the hills if she'd gotten one look at me. I was one gnarly, weather-beaten hombre, but it wasn't my appearance that surprised me the most. It was my gruff demeanor I didn't recognize. Somewhere along the way, I'd acquired a crusty scowl that I couldn't erase, even after a hot shower. I remember thinkin'—Where had my smile gone?

Guess ol' Chet and I had lost our swagger.

Maybe the road had finally taken its toll. Or maybe it was just us being plain homesick. Or maybe it was the stress of having to let Andrew go or the never-ending stream of bad weather that had gradually wiped the naïve grins off our faces. Whatever it was, I made a promise right there in Ginny's bathroom that it was time to turn the page.

"Remember. This is supposed to be fun," I said to myself as I wiped the remnants of shaving cream from my face. Seeing a reflection, I recognized for the first time in weeks made me smile again. I vowed I would wipe my mental slate clean too, from here on out. That's why, on the high plains of Wyoming, I was a changed man, and although we didn't talk about it much, it seemed Chet was too. There was a renewed spring in our step and lots of smiles to go around. Even the horses seemed to have a newfound energy. "C'mon boys; let's put some giddy-up in our hop-along!" I hollered as Thunder kicked it into high gear. "You said it, boss!" Chet shouted as he gigged Rebel to keep up.

Part of our attitude adjustment was due to the fact we finally felt we were going to make it to the Rockies, which was exciting. We knew this would be the most fun part of the trip. Also, the weather was improving. Yes, the days were still warm, in the low 90s, but the nights were getting cool (in the 40s and 50s), which meant the horses were able to recover faster for our early morning starts. All these factors inspired us to pick up the pace. The cool high plains mornings and evenings, combined with the constant smell of spruce and pine, was a welcome pleasure from the dusty trails of the Wyoming desert. With each passing ponderosa pine and the frequent sightings of antelope and mule deer, our bodies seemed to be reawakened and our spirits at an all-time high, just like we planned it.

Leaving Ginny's ranch near Dubois, Chet, and I figured we could make it to Togwotee Pass before dark if we kept at a three-mile per hour pace. We had thirty miles to log, and we took the challenge head-on. I could feel Thunder's energy; the big boy inspired me to do some hard riding that day, probably closer to four or five miles per hour, which nearly doubled our slowest pace in the desert. On the powerful backs of Thunder and Rebel, Chet and I started our climb into the Rockies. We started the day in Dubois at 6,900 feet and by day's end, had ascended 3,000 feet to nearly 10,000 feet at Togwotee Pass. Not a bad day's work, and it didn't take much more effort from Chet and me since the real heroes of the trip, our four-legged friends, were doing all the heavy lifting—as always.

We reached the Pass by late afternoon, ahead of schedule. We stopped to have a hunk of Chet's famous cornbread and discuss our strategy for getting to Yellowstone Park, which was now less than a day's ride away. Chet and I munched cornbread and sipped some cowboy coffee while we studied our "topo" maps.

"Wonder if we could take a short cut through Togwotee Pass?" Chet asked. I pointed to a spot on the map, "Yep. This backcountry trail right here! Looks like we can cut through the mountains, and it'll shoot us out near the Yellowstone border."

"Any short cut is a good short cut, right?" Chet said.

"As long as it works. I'm not familiar with this country, so how about we give it a try for an hour, then reevaluate?"

You're the boss, boss," Chet said. "You gonna finish that cornbread?"

"I'm nuts, but I ain't crazy." I popped the last hunk in my mouth. "We can't be leaving any crumb trails round here. This is Grizzly country."

"Need all the extra helpings I can get, boss. Forty bucks!" he said.

"I know—C'mon, let's get goin' before it gets dark. Supper awaits."

I told Dave to drive the rig up "a piece" and meet us at the trailhead by the Togwotee Lodge at sundown, "See if you can scout us a place to pitch camp and we'll figure out a plan for tomorrow," I said.

"You got it," Dave said while loading Thunder and Rebel into the trailer.

Once Chet and I switched off to Big Red and Wizard, we went looking for our short cut. We found it just off Route 189 right before a sign for the Togwotee Lodge that was just up the road. I pointed to the entrance, "Reckon this is it. Let's hit it." We ducked off the road into a thicket and followed a trail that took us down to the Togwotee Basin.

"This sure beats the hell outta riding on the side of the road," Chet said, admiring the view. "The large snow-capped peaks of the Tetons and the Buffalo Mountain range began to rise around us. Chet was right. It was one beautiful ride. "We're finally getting to the essence of our journey, hoss," I said to Chet. "Life is good!"

"Rocky Mountain high," Chet said, "Bring 'er on!" Even Big Red and Wizzer were having fun navigating the more challenging terrain. The whole outfit was over the moon in our new surroundings. We were finally getting to use all of our "real horseman skills," and it felt great. What a change; it was a 180-degree turn from our experiences on Poison Spider Creek Road and Nebraska!

On top of everything else, our timing seemed to be good weather-wise. We had made it to the cusp of the Rockies by mid-August, and although there was still some snow on the ground, it didn't seem to be enough to cause us any trouble.

Seemingly.

"Snow in the summer," Chet said, pointing to the snow-capped mountains around us. "Guess you can't completely avoid it."

"Only in the Rockies."

Big Red and Wizzer were both "belled-up" as we rode through the Basin. The bells they wore were a precautionary measure you take in Bear country; they give notice to any Grizzly or black bears that might be around that people on horses were coming their way. Why would you want to alert bears to your presence?

You never want to surprise a bear.

By and large, bears don't want to mess with us. If they're hungry, they'd rather go looking for prey that's less trouble than us ornery humans. But if you were to "run up on one" and scare 'em well, they might lash out to protect themselves, or their cubs. On top of adding bells to our bag of tricks, our eyes became our most valuable instruments 'round these parts. I was constantly searching the surrounding area for any sign of bears, moose, buffalo, elk, or mule deer. My experience as a Montana guide sure came in handy here. Now that we had a whole new set of critters to contend with, as the lead rider, it was my job to signal Chet if I heard or saw anything out of the ordinary.

Didn't take long until I did.

As luck would have it, we weren't more than a mile or two up the trail when I heard a very strange and unique noise coming from the distant woods. I signaled to Chet by raising one hand. We both stopped. I silently put two fingers to my eyes then pointed to approximately two o'clock. Chet nodded. He heard something too. Now, you may not know this, but a horse's hearing is much better than humans, so when Big Red and Wizzer's ears pointed forward, it was a telltale sign something was ahead. So, we kept listening. What on earth was that strange sound? It sounded almost like jingle bells, or some type of bells approaching. Whatever it was, the sound was becoming clearer. "It" was coming our way. We stayed still, hoping to catch a glimpse of something. I noticed about thirty or forty yards ahead, the trail took a sharp turn north, so whatever was out there, we wouldn't be able to see it until it was close-up. I kept my 30-30 Winchester in my saddle scabbard; something told me I wouldn't need it in this situation. I had never heard any stories about any Grizzlies wearing bells around their necks!

Suddenly at the turn up ahead, we caught a glimpse of our mysterious visitor in the woods. Out of the trees appeared a cowboy riding a rather large mule. Trailing the cowboy on his pack mule was a string of four more mules, followed by a woman on a horse and a very small child riding a little mule. It was quite an unexpected sight. Chet and I had remained so still, I don't think the cowboy expected to see anyone. In fact, I know he didn't since his head was low and his hat was pulled down over his head. By the time he realized we were there, we damn near ran into each other head-on, "Whoa, now, whoa!" the cowboy shouted to his mules who got riled at the sight and smell of Big Red and Wizzer.

"Didn't mean to scare y'all," I said from our silent perch.

"Aw, shoot. You can't scare us," the cowboy said with a laugh while he pulled up his hat to get a good look at us. Chet and I pulled off to the side of the trail to avoid the wide sea of mules and horses. When Big Red and Wizzer saw the mules up close, they were "all ears," so to speak. All I could see were countless mule and horse ears going back and forth as the four-legged critters were checking each other out with all their senses. Chet and I looked at his gang, and they stared wide-eyed back at us. No words were spoken as we sized each other up. 'Why,' I thought, 'that little girl on that mule couldn't be more than three or four years old.'

"Howdy. Where you boys goin'?" rolled out of the cowboy's mouth.

"Washington. Pacific Ocean," I muttered in a low, scratchy voice.

The forest was deathly silent.

The cowboy's eyebrows bunched up, "What's that?"

"Washington. Pacific Ocean," I repeated.

Now he laughed," Well, you boys sure have a long way to go, I reckon."

"Bout another month, I'm guessing," I said and shrugged. The cowboy looked back and forth at Chet and me. The cowboy still couldn't figure out what to make of us.

"Well. Where are you comin' from?" he asked.

"Connecticut. Hartford area. Started on the beach in Connecticut."

"That's one trek you're makin'. Those are some big horses. They should be able to carry you to the coast." I knew I was confusing this cowboy, so I leaned over the saddle horn, extended my hand, and introduced myself. "Jeff Pappas. And this here is my partner, Chet Tomasiewicz." Chet leaned over, hand outstretched.

The cowboy shook both our hands. "I'm Mark White. And this is my wife, Jean, and our little girl, Brittany," he said through a crack of a smile. Chet and I nodded and tipped our Stetsons, "Nice to meet you," we said to Jean and Brittany. The tension in the air seemed to ease. I could tell Mark was processing what I'd said and was no doubt wondering what to say next.

"You boys really headin' to the Pacific from Connecticut?" Mark asked.

"As long as winter doesn't come early in the Rockies, we figure we have 'bout another month or so, maybe nine hundred to a thousand miles," I reasoned.

Chet interjected, "Where are you all headed?"

"We just come out of five days in the mountains. Supposed to meet one of our friends yesterday up in the hills, but I reckon he must've gotten sidetracked or somethin' because he never showed up!" Mark said emphatically. "So, we're headed to Togwotee Lodge to put up our animals for the night and wait for him to hopefully show. We'll probably end up getting a room at the lodge. You boys might want to consider doin' the same. They got plenty of corrals and hay for the animals, and the owners are damn nice folks." Chet and I looked at each other.

I could tell Chet was in favor of sharing camp with the Whites for the night. They sure seemed like nice people, and we'd already met so many gracious folks along the way. Mark and his family seemed no different than the others across the country that had left a permanent mark on our lives. "We'll follow you, Mark," I barked out.

"Well, OK then," Mark said. Our animals separated then headed out of the Basin in the same direction. I could tell our boys were happy to have made some new four-legged friends. They hadn't spent much time around mules.

We were now one big string of horses and mules, headed back to the Togwotee Lodge for the evening. What I didn't know was this night would affect my life for all time. Chet and I pulled up and unsaddled at the Lodge corrals. We said goodbye for now to the Whites and agreed to meet Mark later up at the bar for a visit. We went looking for the owners of the Lodge. They were as nice as advertised and welcomed us with open arms. We truly felt like we'd found another home away from home for the night. After visiting with them a bit, we thanked them for their hospitality and went out to get Big Red and Wizzer set up in their corrals.

"Appreciate you lettin' us use your corrals," I said.

"Don't mention it, we even got some alfalfa hay for your boys," the owner said.

The horses whinnied on cue. I went over to Dave, who was waiting for us by the rig with Thunder and Rebel. "We gettin' a room?" Dave asked.

"Na. Kinda like to skip that part." Dave suggested we set up camp just outside the corrals so we could "keep an eye on the boys." I thought that was a great idea, so I asked the owners if they would mind if we slept outside instead of getting a room.

"Oh, hell no, you fellas go on ahead," the owner said with a laugh. "You been sleepin' outside all summer; why stop now!"

"Thank the Lord," Chet said, "No hotel bed for me. They kill my back."

"Can't beat sleepin' under the stars."

"May never sleep in a bed again," Dave said.

"Me either," Chet said. "Though Diane may have somethin' to say about that!" I asked Dave if he would stay with the horses and watch all our gear while we went to meet Mark. He nodded. The Preacher Man had turned into a top hand.

After the three of us had another sumptuous supper (beef stew) from Chet's kitchen in the horse trailer, Chet and I said goodbye to Dave and sauntered up to the bar where Mark was already seated. "Nice to see you boys made it," Mark said.

"Wouldn't miss it," I said.

"I'm dry as the Mohave," Chet said. "Could definitely use a few cold ones."

"You came to the right place." Mark said, "Y'all pull up a stool."

"Think I'd rather stand," I said. "Feels good to be out of the saddle."

"I hear that," Mark said.

"How about I get the first round?" I asked. Over some cold drafts and a bourbon whiskey for Mark, the three of us started to talk about life. "Where you come from, Mark? If you don't mind me askin'."

"My family came from Big Piney, Wyoming. you probably never heard of it; it's a small town close to the Bridger-Tetons." After I politely inquired, Mark told us "by trade" he was an outfitter that took clients into the mountains for pack trips and hunting trips. Mark said he'd been riding his whole life, "I suppose you could say my old stompin' grounds are the Bridger-Teton Range—the Wind River Range—the Gros Ventre Wilderness and the Bear Tooth-Absaroka Wilderness in Montana," he said.

"That's a lot of ridin'," Chet said.

"Sure is," Mark said as he sipped his whiskey. "Got the bow legs to prove it."

"I know Bear Tooth-Absoroka," I said, "Used to guide in Montana myself."

"That right. Guess you're not one of those 'weekend warriors' then," he said with a chuckle.

"Though my wife might tell you otherwise," I said with a laugh, which got Mark to chuckling harder.

"Well," He said, "You fellas must know what you're doin' to be making a cross-country trip. Not sure I'd have the constitution for it, personally." Mark proceeded to regale us with the many Grizzly encounters he had during his trips into the wild. His explorations in the high country had taken him to places few modern men had ever traveled. "I reckon I've been lucky enough to have seen a rare brand of country in my day," he said with another sip of his whiskey. When Mark stood up, I noticed he was about six feet tall and 200 pounds of lean cowboy. He was as close to a modern-day Jeremiah Johnson as I'd ever met. Chet and I were captivated by Mark's storytelling and easy, laid back demeanor. I told him I admired him for giving up business opportunities to make a life for himself and his family in the mountains.

"That's always been a dream of mine," I said.

"The modern world can be a seductive mistress, with all her amenities and so forth," he mused, "Guess I prefer to live off what the mountains have to offer. Don't have a fancy way of living—never have—but I got a good life, good friends and a good family. That's all I need. That, and a good horse!"

"Here's to a good horse!" Chet said as he raised his beer.

A little later on, Mark mentioned that his wife, Jean, was a full-blooded Navajo. She helped him on his trips when she wasn't a part-time teacher at a Navajo school for children. And I had guessed it right. His daughter, Brittany, was indeed three-years-old. "Quite a rider for three!" I said.

"She better be in this family. Also got a son in high-school who rides."

"Who was it you we're supposed to be meetin'?" Chet asked.

"Aw, my friend Tom Wolfe. He's been on a pack trip. He's supposed to be coming up from just south of Teton Pass." Mark explained they were gonna meet somewhere in Togwotee Pass, which was the short cut Chet, and I were ridin' through. "He must've got a late start," Mark said, "He has to pass by the Lodge to get to the trail, so I reckon he'll see my mules in the corral and know I'm here." The vantage from the bar looked south towards Jackson Hole, "Keep a lookout, Tom'll be riding in from there," Mark pointed out the southern window, "Maybe we'll see him comin'."

Another half-hour passed, and we had another round. Chet and I told Mark all about the story of our cross-country horseback trip. He was fascinated with some of our encounters over the past three and a half months. "Sounds like you could write a book about your adventures," he said.

"Sounds like you could too."

"Suppose I could." he said, "If I could write worth a damn." Then something caught his eye. He pointed out the window due south, "Look."

"What do you see, Mark?"

"See those small dots?" he said and squinted. One of his eyes flicked back and forth. The old boy must have great vision because I couldn't spot the "dots" he was tracking, and I have so-called "good" eyesight. Mark ambled over to the window to follow the dots across the prairie. As soon as the group of "dots" drew closer, I could finally see what they were—one rider with five mules trailing behind.

"That's Tom," he said. "I can tell by that big old buckskin he's ridin'. You boys wait here. I'll go flag him down and help him unsaddle his gear. Be right back."

Chet said, "We'll keep your seat warm."

Fifteen minutes later, Mark came striding back into the bar accompanied by a younger, leaner, slightly more wind-burned version of himself—it was Tom Wolfe. Mark made the introductions—then we all moved over to the lounge and sat down on two old leather couches by a coffee table. We didn't know if this night was supposed to be a "rendezvous" of some sort for Mark and Tom— so Chet started the conversation by saying we "hoped we weren't crashing their party."

"You're not crashin' nothin," Mark said. "I've seen enough of ol' Tom's face to last a lifetime," then they both laughed. These two authentic cowboys seemed to like our company, so we kicked up our feet and spent the evening swapping stories like the old cowboys did. While we were talking, I gave Tom the once-over. He was about my height and age and had a "youthfulness" about him that came with an engaging smile. I noticed his old riding hat had a big eagle feather hanging off the side.

"That hat's seen some country," I said to him.

"Shoulda seen my last one," he said. "Got so tore up, one day it just walked off." Once Chet and I got to know Tom a bit, it turned out he had a unique history, too. He was also an outfitter like Mark, but he was "based out of the Red Lodge, Montana area," he said. Tom got to tellin' us about the time in

1981 when he drove a ten-husky dog sled across the Rockies from Alaska to Montana. "Took me eight months," he said. "Nearly got myself killed by wolves on a few occasions, but I made it."

"National Geographic magazine covered that one, didn't it?" Mark said.

"Guess so," Tom said humbly.

Chet and I were impressed. "Some company we're in," Chet said to me.

"F.M. I say," I said with a smile. Tom mentioned he paid for that journey by selling watercolors he painted of his dogs as well as the local scenery.

"You're an artist, huh?" Chet said.

"Hope to someday hang up my spurs for a paintbrush."

"Only draw stick figures, though some say I'm an artist in the kitchen."

"At least you can eat your art. Sometimes, I gotta sell my art so I can eat!"

"Chet's cuttin' out the middle man on that transaction," Mark said.

"Ol' Chet," I interjected, "he's the best chef I've ever known," I said. "A true magician. Been cooking for us the whole trip."

"On a forty dollar a week budget. For four people!" Chet said with a laugh, "Can you believe what this guy's been puttin' me through?"

"You've been giving me hell the whole trip. Still not sure how he's done it."

"Sounds like you're the miracle worker, Chet," Mark said.

"Saint me!" Chet said as he pulled on his mug of beer. "Or at least bring us another round."

As the night wore on, you could tell Mark and Tom were best friends. They were laughing and poking fun at each for not meeting up on the trail earlier. Their deep laughs filled the small bar. It was hard not to laugh along with them. "Me and this one have traveled a lot of country together. Shared many a campfire," Mark said.

"Too many," Tom said. When the waitress came over to take our order, Tom ordered, "Usual," he said, which was a blackberry brandy straight up.

"That's an interesting choice of drink," Chet said.

"Guess I'm an interestin' fella."

"What you got there?" Tom asked me.

"Oh, just a little Uncle Jim," I said.

"Jeff. I knew you were a good man before, but now I know for sure," Mark said as he raised his shot of Jim Beam and nodded to me. I nodded back, and we both took a sip. While Chet and I took-in more of Mark and Tom's adventure tales, it dawned on me these two men were the modern-day versions of the mountain men I'd always wanted to be before business and life got in the way. I felt honored to be in their presence. "Don't meet a lot of fellas like this in Connecticut," I said to Chet.

"Don't meet a lot of fellas like this anywhere."

We stayed put on the two couches, and all put our "barkin' dogs" upon an old wooden coffee table. The conversation became a round-robin of hilarious and somewhat embarrassing stories by each of us—stories I'm guessing were mostly true. I can't remember ever laughing so much or so hard. My sides were starting to hurt.

Our visit swung back around to Chet, me, and the trip. We both had gotten in on the ribbing action, poking fun at each other for some of the crazy but humorous situations we had endured. I enjoyed Chet's ribbing. It kept me grounded, and I knew Chet felt the same. Life was good. Or so I thought.

After another round of beers, bourbon, and brandy, we were all feeling no pain. I noticed Tom kept an old knife packed into the back of his jeans. "What kinda knife you got?"

"Thirty-year-old Green River knife," he said.

"That's a good un. Why do you keep it there?" I asked.

"Guess I like keepin' it hidden," he said somewhat mysteriously, "Helps with the element of surprise." Tom didn't show me his knife, and I didn't think anything of it. All I was thinking at the time was I knew what "Green River" meant. The mountain men who founded the West used the name "Green River" as a standard of quality for anything traded. Anything done "Up to Green River" standards signified it was first-rate merchandise.

Now, this is where the story takes a turn. While I was thinking about Green River knives—I failed to notice Mark and Tom's ribbing had gotten serious. They'd been ribbing each other all night, but it was all seemingly in good fun like the old cowboys did. But they kept digging and digging at each other until, at some point, it took on a darker tone. Once I realized what was happening, Chet and I looked at each other nervously. We weren't sure what to make of what was going on.

Then something unbelievable happened.

To this day, I still remember exactly how it went down.

Tom was ribbing Mark again while Chet and I watched. At the end of his story, Tom raised his voice to make Mark the butt of his joke. Just as Tom said his punch line, he whipped out his Green River knife like an Apache warrior and plunged the blade directly into Mark's left shin! The bar went completely silent.

I looked at Chet helplessly. His jaw had dropped to the ground. Everyone was staring at Tom's knife stuck there in Mark's propped up leg. I wanted to get up and do something, I could tell Chet did too, but the shock of the moment had glued us to our seats. We were like two deer in the headlights frozen in our tracks. I turned to Mark. He had an outraged look in his eyes as he slowly turned to look at Tom. I followed his glare; both of their friendly smiles were long gone. They were in some kind of old western "glare off." Then it happened.

Mark and Tom broke into the loudest, knee-slapping laughing fit I'd ever heard.

I thought—What in the hell's going on?

They were just about rolling on the floor with laughter. I couldn't stop staring at Tom's Green River knife, still plunged an inch deep into Mark's left shin. Mark didn't seem to care a lick. He felt no pain. Now, I knew we all had imbibed in quite a few drinks, but I didn't know we were that far gone. I sure wasn't. Or was I?

Tom finally said, "Can I tell them, boss?"

"What the hell, go ahead!" Mark replied.

"Well, ol' 'Packer' White, as his friends used to call him, once worked for the Wyoming Power Company down in the Bondurant area—'bout fourteen years ago. One day he was working on replacing one of those high-tension power lines," Tom recalled. "And someone back at the local switching plant didn't get the memo. So Mark ended up disconnecting a live line!"

"Shit, man," Chet mumbled, still agog at what was happening.

"Well, when that live line swung loose, it blew him clear off the pole. The explosion burned off his ear and damn near blinded him," Tom said.

"The current blew my left foot, clear off," Mark said matter-of-factly. "They found it about twenty feet away, still encased in my boot." I looked at Chet dumbfounded. We both had a numb, blank look on our faces.

"He spent twelve months in the burn unit in a cast, head-to-toe. Had to endure twenty-some-odd skin grafts and operations."

"Thirty," Mark corrected him.

"Right, thirty. They had to take off his left leg from the knee down," Tom said.

"Gangrene," Mark said.

"So now." Tom knocked on Mark's leg with the knife sticking out it, "Most of his leg's prosthetic. How many legs you gone through so far, Packer?"

Mark interjected, "Reckon I'm on my third, by now." Tom pulled his Green River knife out of Mark's leg and put it back in his jeans, "So there you have it. Helluva story."

"Whoa!" Is all Chet could say as he downed his shot of Beam.

"You got that right," Mark said. "Thankfully, Jean stayed with me the whole time. Nursed me back to life."

"Thank god for good women," I said as I downed my shot of Jim.

"Every day, the docs had to rip off the old bandages and re-wrap me. The pain of that alone damn near ended me."

"Jesus H. Christ, Mark," Chet said.

"Wudn't a pretty sight. Not for a long time. Without Jean helpin' the nurses and reassuring me I'd live—I'd be ridin' on the Heavenly Range, that's for sure. There were many times the pain was so bad; death seemed like the best way out. But Jean was always there. She made me understand how important my survival was to our family."

After hearing Mark's amazing story, there were no words spoken by Chet and me for a few minutes. I thought, 'that would explain his right eye flicking back and forth.' He was blind in that eye and had partial vision in the other. How the hell he could spot those moving dots from 1000 feet was beyond me.

All I could say was, "God damn, Mark. Next round is on me!"

After the crazy commotion, the mood picked back up, and Chet and I were officially initiated into the Mark White-Tom Wolfe clan. Tricks and ribbing were part of the right of passage for all cowboys, and we were the new hands. They got us good. Like we tried to instill into young Andrew on the trail. That's what you call the "Cowboy Way." I should have known these two characters were up to no good from my earlier days of guiding in Montana. What a story. Just good ol' cowboy fun, they say!

By the end of the night, we had exchanged addresses and phone numbers in hopes of getting together after the trip. We invited Mark and Tom to the corrals for coffee and breakfast, but when we told them what time we were pulling out (5:30 A.M.), Mark and Tom pointed out they'd both most likely be sleeping at that time, probably a bit heavy-headed also. I can't remember what time Chet and I finally dragged ourselves back to the corrals, but I do remember the bartender telling us the drinks were on the house. Apparently, we were the entertainment for the evening. Or at least Mark and Tom were.

My eyes closed the minute I hit my bedroll. As I drifted off, I wondered if I would ever see Mark, Jean, Brittany, and Tom again. Sure hoped so, I thought, although it would be hard to top the excitement of this evening at the Togwotee Lodge Bar.

As it would turn out, that chance encounter on a remote trail going over Togwotee Pass was the beginning of a 27-year friendship with Mark White and his family. I've lost many an item in my day, but I'm proud I managed to keep that small piece of paper with his number on it in my saddlebags for the endurance of the trip. Upon my return in mid-September of 1986, the phone rang at the White's ranch one evening.

Mark answered.

"Hey, Mark—Jeff Pappas. Remember me?" No drinks, No Green River knives, no Tom Wolfe.just an hour of relating the rest of our trip. We agreed to get together in Jackson sometime before the snow starting flying. I have ridden the high country with Mark now for over 27 years. We have explored the Yellowstone country together, the Gros Ventres, the Wind Rivers, the Bridgers, and the Spanish Peaks of Montana. You name it. I've learned more about packing, exploring, and surviving from Mark, and shared too many high-country adventures with him to relate here. I owe all this "life knowledge" to Mark and his brood. They are my second family. We've shared countless campfires, including Grizzly and moose encounters. We've also helped each other through some tough times in our respective businesses over the years. I consider Mark to be one of my best friends to this day. As for ol' Tom, he gradually pulled himself out of full time outfitting in the early 2000s and became a very popular outfitter-turned-artist with his own studio. His paintings are so inspiring he now makes a good living from just painting. To this day, Tom and Mark are still best friends and get together regularly.still on horseback or mule. I see Tom every few years, too, and we always bring up the story of the time we all met. Good friends, I say.

The next day, Chet and I woke up a bit fuzzy-headed and got back to the task at hand. After some cowboy coffee, we remembered what Mark said was the best route to Yellowstone Park. His advice was to stay on Route189 to

Moran Junction then head into the park from there. He advised against trying to navigate the Togwotee Pass. We wisely took his advice, which meant we'd only have a short day's ride to the south entrance of Yellowstone Park. So off we rode, out of camp at 6 A.M. We didn't say much all morning; we just reflected on the previous night and wondered what new adventures might lie ahead for us in the Yellowstone country.

We were about to find out.

★ 12 ★

INVISIBLE RIDERS OF YELLOWSTONE

Butch: "Ah, you're wasting your time;
they can't track us over rocks."
Sundance: (binoculars) "Tell them that."
Butch: (looking for himself)
"They're beginning to get on my nerves.
Who are those guys?"
—From *Butch Cassidy and the Sundance Kid*

SOMETIMES, A MAN and his horse have to be invisible to survive in the wild. If you're not the "top of the food chain" in this world, and one man never is, when the going gets rough, every once in a while, you gotta just flat disappear before the bigger dog takes a bite out of your hide. There have been a bunch of movies about invisibility over the years, but one of my favorites is *Little Big Man*, where Dustin Hoffman's character, Jack Crabb, and his mentor, Old Lodge Skins, learn how to become invisible.

We didn't know it at the time, but ol' Chet and I were about to make the same discovery out of necessity. The following pages will document the circumstances that surrounded this achievement. It all started around the time we finally reached the footsteps of the Rockies; it had been a long time comin'— three and a half months to be exact. On the sturdy backs of Thunder, Rebel, Big Red, and Sonny, also known as "Wizard," we made our way over Togwotee Pass. Zigzagging our way north by northwest, Chet rightly observed we weren't traveling in many straight lines.

"This crooked ass trail ain't helpin' my hangover. How's your head?"

"Can't say I'm feelin' too chipper, but I'll abide," I said.

"Geez, Louise. Think there'd be a faster way," Chet said. "You sure Mark ain't pullin' our leg again with this cockamamie route?"

"When ridin' the Rockies. There's no such thing as a direct route," I said.

Chet grumbled. "Guess that ol' son of a gun ain't takin' us on a snipe hunt. Sure feels that way, though."

"Shouldn't have drank so much blackberry brandy last night, hoss," I ribbed him. "Map said the other route would take us an extra two weeks. Dontcha remember?" I said.

"This mornin's map discussion was kinda fuzzy," he said.

"Guess you gotta trust ol' Packer White then. This jig-jag route's no hangover cure, but it's our best bet," I said.

"Alright-alright," he grumbled, "All I know is I'm never drinkin' blackberry flavored anything, ever again."

"Not even blackberry pie?"

"Not even."

"Gonna hold you to that. Next time Sue makes us one I'm gettin' your piece!"

Ol' one-legged Mark wasn't pulling our leg despite Chet's skepticism; his advice was tried and true, so we kept at it, ambling over the only crooked route that would take us through both Grand Teton National Park and Yellowstone National Park. We planned to stay on it all the way and emerge (after a few day's ride) out of Yellowstone's west entrance and into the little town of West Yellowstone, Montana, where we would cut a straighter path through the southwestern part of the state. It sounded like a good plan but we had to navigate the parks first. We rode on the glacial side of the majestic Tetons with Mount Moran and her big brother, Grand Teton, thrusting their way upwards into the heavens. I pointed to the peak of Grand Teton, "That right there is thirteen thousand feet of sheer beauty and might," I marveled, head craned.

"Tell me we aren't goin' over that thing," Chet said.

"More like around it."

After a while, we decided to get off the crooked road Chet had been complaining about and pick our way through the forest—always staying within earshot of the road, so we didn't get lost. Though Mark had led us down the right path, Father Time had narrowed it over the years, so there wasn't much room for us and the occasional vehicle that happened by. The scenic route we took through those steep canyons was spectacular. Everywhere we looked was another gorgeous vista. We rode north through valleys engulfed in bear grass, Indian paintbrush, and dotting by emerald ponds full of clear drinking water for the boys. I still had my "guide eyes" on, so I saw everything. I hadn't spotted any Grizzlies yet, but it had become a regular occurrence to catch a glimpse of a moose or elk disappearing into a juniper thicket, only to reappear with a mouth full of foliage. Taking a pit stop, I noticed an abundance of one of nature's little known delectables called tubular thistles, which Chet had never heard of. "What the heck you doin' over there?" he asked as I stripped off the thorny skin of a thistle.

"Eatin' off the land. This here's a tubular thistle. Good stuff?"

"Can't you wait for dinner?"

"Nope. Pretty good little liquid snack, kinda like celery." Chet watched me chew on some, "Lemme try some of that rabbit food." He peeled some thistle of his own.

"Won't fill you up, but tastes good," I said as I fed a bit to Thunder.

"Tastes pretty good," Chet said with a smile, then cut a whole mess to chew on.

"Looks like everyone's havin' veggies for lunch," I said, pointing to an elk with a mouthful of greens.

"Sure we didn't ride into California?" Chet joked.

The next day was beautiful, clear, and dry. The fresh morning dew filled my olfactory senses with the smell of crisp, chilled pine. It was 5 A.M., and the sunrise was just about to take center stage. "When God created beauty and freedom, he must have done it right here," I mused.

"You been sayin' that every morning since we hit Wyoming."

We ate our traditional morning breakfast of back bacon, Chet's homemade cornbread, and famous cowboy coffee. Then we packed up our camp we had pitched just outside of Yellowstone and headed towards the park. After talking about it for nearly two years, we were excited to finally explore the nearly 3,500 square mile park that straddled the corners of Wyoming, Montana, and Idaho. I could tell even Thunder and Rebel had a little extra pep in their step. "You know Yellowstone's bigger than Rhode Island or Delaware?" I said to Chet as we headed out.

"Do now. You tryin' to intimidate a Connecticut boy? Cause I ain't scared."

"Just don't get lost, or you might end up grizzly bait."

"Just lead the way, boss," Chet said with a smile.

We moseyed the horses up to the south entrance gate, where a redheaded ranger with shiny black boots stopped us immediately. "Welcome to Yellowstone, how y'all doing today?" he asked.

"Just fine, and you?"

"Alright. Nice horses. What you planning on doin' with 'em?"

"Thank ye, we're on our way to Washington State," I said and explained the whole trip to him like I had done to so many others.

"Sounds like quite an adventure." The park ranger looked through his clipboard, confused. "Can you hold on a minute? I need to call my supervisor to see how to proceed."

"Proceed?" Chet asked.

"Don't you just let us in?" I said.

"In theory, but I need to check. Never ran into a situation like this before!" he said. "But don't worry, don't think it'll be a problem." We tied the boys off in the trees and waited for the ranger to call his supervisor. We watched other cars drive through the gate into the park. While we waited, we waved at a few kids who were rubbernecking us from their station wagons and recreational vehicles (RVs). "Look at that little rascal stickin' his tongue out," Chet said then gave him a raspberry right back.

Ten minutes later, Ranger Bill finally waived us over and explained we had two choices, "Either you get a backcountry permit or trailer out of the park each night to camp. You can't camp in the park, sorry." He said. I tried to imagine the reality of what he was proposing: Spend the entire day riding in the park, then trailer the horses at sundown and drive back to where we started to camp outside the south gate. Or get a backcountry pass, which meant we'd have to trailer the horses several hours up to a remote part of the park and continue from there. We'd have to carry more supplies, which was impossible, and camping would be difficult, not to mention more dangerous.

"Dunno," I said, "That's heavy Grizzly country up there, and we only got one firearm."

"Um. firearms are not legal in the park, sir," Ranger Bill said.

"What, are we supposed to just use our hands like Davey Crockett?"

"I don't—"

"Look. Ranger Bill," I interrupted, "Pardon my French, but what you're sayin' is goin' over like mule shit in a bucket of grease."

"Believe me, I'm sympathetic to what you gentlemen are doing, but I also have a boss to answer to here," the Ranger said. "And I'm telling you the powers-that-be will not allow you to ride through the park without a backcountry permit."

"This is gonna take an extra week out of our trip," I said.

He was very polite, "That's just the way it is."

We didn't want any part of his plan, but I didn't let him know that. I told Ranger Bill to sit tight; Chet and I needed to confer before we let him know our decision. We climbed back off our weary mounts and tied them to a makeshift hitching post outside the entrance gate. We looked around and saw a huge line of traffic backed up behind us. Everyone had their heads out their windows wanting to know what the hell was going on—mostly RV Winnebago's packed full of folks with varying looks ranging from understanding to anger to fear.

We smiled at them, tipped our hats, and sat down on the nearest embankment to discuss the situation. "So, if we don't do the backcountry, the only other option is to trailer the horses out of the park every damn night? Is that what he said?" Chet was trying to figure out exactly what Ranger Bill was telling us. "It makes no sense," I said, "Either way, it'll be takin' two steps forward and three steps back. And we don't have time to jack around with these guys."

Chet knew what I meant. Even though we'd finally entered the home stretch, time was not on our side. We were still under the "weather gun," and with September rapidly approaching, we had to make it through the passes of Idaho and Montana before the first snow. "You can't predict the weather in the Rockies," I said, "I've seen snowstorms in June here."

"So we won't change our plans," Chet said. "We got no time!"

"As long as we're in agreement. They probably won't throw us in jail if they catch us, but they may fine us."

"I'll just tear that shit up, boss, you know I'm never comin' back here."

"Alright then. Let's give Ranger Bill a little decoy."

"Now you're talkin'," Chet said with a sly smile.

We went back to our ranger "buddy," and I offered this, "We talked about it, and how about we ride through and trailer our horses out of the park every night?" Ranger Bill said that "sounded agreeable" then he got back on his walkie-talkie, "I gotta call my supervisor to confirm." So, we waited another few minutes until Ranger Bill came back and said his supervisor had "O.K.'d" our plan. We thanked him and got back on Thunder and Rebel and went on in. We had succeeded in the initial phase of our plan.

"They bought it," Chet said as we rode on in.

"Must've been our honest faces."

We rode through Yellowstone Park all day. The sun was starting to set, so we stopped for the day and waited for Dave and the rig. Like we promised, Dave met us inside the park and we trailered the boys—then we turned around and went back the way we came in. We drove the horses out of the south entrance and even waved to the park rangers as we passed in the rig. They waved back.

"That should do it," I said to Chet.

We figured by doing this once, they would think we were following the rules.

That night, we camped a few miles back from the south entrance near a dude ranch by the side of the road. We managed to pull off next to one of the forks of the Snake River, tie the boys to the trailer and throw our bodies down for the night along the riverbank. At dusk, we saw a cow moose had wandered in the river upstream about fifty yards. Of course, we had to warn a few tourists at the dude ranch not to get too close if they wanted to live to tell their friends about their vacation.

"Y'all don't be messin' with that cow moose, or it'll charge you," I yelled.

The tourists just smiled and waved at us, taking pictures of the animal.

"Thinning the herd through pure stupidity," Chet said as he made us dinner.

After dinner, we settled into a few hours of sleep. 3:30 A.M. comes very quickly when you're tired, and tomorrow, we were to start our real plan for going through the park. We calculated if we hustled, we could make it through in two days and one night if we kept on the move and left little trace of where we'd been. "Dare I say, it'll be just like ol' Butch and Sundance did," I said to Chet.

"I wanna be Sundance," Chet said as he drifted off to sleep.

"Okay. You're Sundance. like Butch better anyhow." I said.

"Night, Butch."

"Night Sundance."

"You guys are crazy," Dave said.

We were kids again.

The next day, the real adventure began. Chet and I woke up early feeling like two schoolboys about to be set loose to play cowboys and Indians in the biggest playground on earth. We scarfed down breakfast and started our drive through the south entrance. I told Dave to drop us off at the same spot we had ended yesterday. "Come check on us at five at this spot," I said, showing him a point on the map, Dave nodded, "Then hightail it outta the park for the night," I said. "We're gonna stay off the roads and try to avoid any green men." Dave looked at me as if to say: 'But don't you need me to come back the next morning to change horses and bring supplies?' but he read the look in our eyes and got the message. His look of disappointment was more from wishing he could be part of whatever was about to happen with us.

"I'll be there, you can count on me," Dave said.

"You're a top hand preacher man," I said, "now skee-daddle."

The great hide-and-seek game with the park rangers was afoot.

Man and horse against green uniform and truck. Who would win? Only time would tell, but ol' Chet and I had a twinkle in our eye and were up for the challenge. Thunder and Rebel were too.

We started off at 5 A.M. riding through Lewis Canyon. The northwesterly route was narrow and flanked by steep hills on the north and 500-foot cliffs on the south. The "Winnie brigade" hadn't awakened yet to start their daily park migration, so we traveled in silent mode for a few hours except for the distant sound of the Lewis River pushing its way through the canyon to join the Yellowstone River.

A few hours into our ride, we came up to a little turn out in the road and saw an unexpected sight: an oversized Winnebago was parked illegally. Next to the RV was a large sign that read, "No Camping. No overnight parking."

"Rules seem pretty straightforward to me," I said to Chet.

"And the worst part is they're sleeping-in," Chet said. "Have they no shame?"

Maybe the rangers just "overlooked" the small vehicle, but we weren't about to. I looked at Chet, we both smiled; I could tell the same thought was flashing through his head, "Time for a little fun," Chet said.

We rode up to the Winnie.

Chet dismounted and circled the suburban land yacht to make a visual inspection. "Well, what do we have here?" he said in his best park ranger voice. He pretended to use a walkie-talkie. "Home dispatch: Looks like we got some illegal campers here, in a Brown Winnebago with an Illinois license plate— 5-W-X-J-A-Niner. Gonna need to send a tow truck down here. I'm gonna arrest the driver, need backup—over."

We heard some rustling around inside.

Once Chet mentioned the word "arrest," a curtain pulled back for a brief moment then whipped shut. Chet circled the wagon a few more times, kicking the tires and pretending to be a ranger, "Violation here, Violation here. Gonna need a tow truck, over." We couldn't see inside, but you could tell the RV inhabitants were in a panic. After a few minutes, we got back on our horses and rode away, chuckling.

"We scared the hell outta them," Chet said.

"Maybe they'll think it was all just a bad dream."

"Or maybe they'll park in the designated area next time!" Chet said. "If the rangers won't let us improvise, why should they?"

"I hear ya, pard. I'd like to give whoever's makin' the rules around here a piece of my mind."

By 10 A.M., the Winnies were out in full force; the roads were full of them backed up for miles. It felt more like we were riding through some recreational version of downtown Manhattan than the undiscovered God's country I had hoped to explore. We decided to get far away from the roads for good and stay there, which we did, but we couldn't avoid them completely. Around noon, we made an appearance near a road and immediately got busted by a park ranger driving a truck. This guy was decked out in full regalia: radio, automatic weapon, shiny boots, and even a summer trainee. "Ranger Scott" and his trainee didn't pussyfoot around with formalities—they informed us we were to go no further until he radioed ahead.

"Is there a problem, officer?"

"I'm a ranger, sir. And I suggest you gentlemen turn back right now."

Chet and I looked at each other and smiled. We did that a lot.

"But what for, young man?" I asked.

"You can't ride horses on the roads inside the park without supervision."

"That's alright," I said. "We're keeping out of sight; only occasionally crossin' a road."

"Well. That's good to hear, but crossing a road is still 'on' a road."

"We're only on em' for like two seconds," Chet said.

"Two seconds is still two seconds," the Ranger said.

"Look, we already got approval to ride through as long as we pack out at night," I said, even though we had no intention of doing so again. Ranger Scott didn't believe me and told us to stay put until he got clearance. He ordered his trainee in the truck to call it in. This got Chet's goat. His eyes got wide like saucers; I could see steam coming off his head. I knew he was hungry since all we'd had for lunch was beef jerky, and for a moment I thought he might devour both the ranger and his trainee, Grizzly-style.

Watching the trainee fumble with the radio, Chet finally exploded, "What do we got, a trainee trainin' a trainee here? C'mon, you gotta be effin' kiddin' me," he wailed and threw his head back.

"Now just simmer down there," Ranger Scott said in his most authoritarian voice, even though he was no older than 25 tops. I tried to calm Chet down but found myself approaching my boiling point too. These young rangers were beginning to try my patience, and I'm a patient man.

"Ya know, after spending twenty-four hours in your park, I'm convinced someone around here's lost their cotton-pickin' mind."

"What do you mean?" Ranger Scott said.

"Look at the mob scene," I said, pointing to the backlog of RVs clogging every road around us. "You mean to tell me Winnebago's are an acceptable way of traveling on these narrow roads, but horses are not?"

"Well, the rulebook says," Ranger Scott started to say, but I interrupted him. "Rulebook? I wonder what Jim Bridger would say about all these damn rules."

"Who the heck is—?" Ranger Scott asked.

"Exactly my point. You boys don't know your ass from a hole in the ground."

"Sir," the trainee interrupted, "I'm not getting a signal."

Ranger Scott left us to stew while he went to help the trainee work the radio.

"By the way, Jim Bridger discovered this damn place!" Chet yelled at the Ranger, who just smiled politely. I stood there thinking: One thing about park rangers, they're great as long as they have their truck and weapon, but if they have to walk on trails and deal with the elements, you might have a problem. A line from a Jimmy Buffet tune rang through my head. 'They're ugly and square, they don't belong here, they'd look a lot better as beer cans.' Chet looked at me, "What would Butch and Sundance do?"

We both knew.

Chet mounted Rebel, and I swung back on Thunder and told the rangers, "We don't have time to be hagglin' with you fellas every few miles. Either come to a consensus or let us be on our way. If your boss thinks we're doing something wrong, you can come find us. We ain't goin' anywhere."

Ranger Scott said if we were going to go without supervision, we "really should take Antler Creek Trail—that's more of a direct route to where you're going."

When we questioned him about Antler Creek Trail, he admitted he wasn't quite sure where it was or if it "had been cleared." Was he trying to get us killed? I knew Antler Creek Trail took us through the heart of grizzly country, and we'd left our rifle in the truck. I don't think he had much sense at all. We thanked Ranger Scott for the information and went on our way. Riding back into the thicket, Chet looked at me and said, "Butch and Sundance are smilin', boss. Screw these guys."

I looked at Chet, "Never trust a ranger with shiny boots, Sundance." We could hear Ranger Scott on the radio, frantically trying to reach his boss while we slowly dissolved back into the trees.

Invisible again.

We didn't make very good time on our ride across Yellowstone with all of the stops for ranger questioning. But we did get a brief glimpse of what it must have been like to be running from the law a century ago. Chet and I zigzagged Thunder and Rebel all over the park, darting up and down ridge after ridge, sidestepping pitfalls, and jumping across downed timber. The heavily wooded forest was lined with lodgepole pines that looked like oversized toothpicks. Navigating the many trails and turns of the forest at top speed had a hypnotic effect. It was as if the spirits of all the "old boys" were inside us, making their way to Robber's Roost where they knew it would be safe.

"Just like The Wild Bunch!" I shouted as Thunder jumped a downed tree. Chet hollered back, "Yeeehaw!" as he went soaring over with Rebel. We were having the time of our lives. For a few days, we were two modern-day outlaws on the run. And we liked it. Not bad for two frustrated cowboys who hung their hats in the East but whose hearts forever lie in Montana. The pounding of hooves and the fresh smell of horse sweat and leather filled the air around us. The trees whipped and scratched us all to hell as we galloped our way across the rough terrain known as the Continental Divide, but we didn't care. Our job was easy, but the real heroes of this story (the horses) were tested to the limit. Reflecting on it all thirty years later, I realize this moment in time was the essence of the trip. It was what all the years of preparation were for.

All to get right here.

I'm no "horse whisperer," but I felt Thunder, my faithful four-legged companion, was also gripped with the "specialness" of the moment. He used every ounce of his strength and agility to navigate me through the park. I'll never forget the look in his eyes; they were filled with pride, strength, and determination. This was the moment Thunder and I truly became one, bonded together with love and trust. It took nearly 2,200 miles to build, but only a moment to realize. I had two best friends with me on the trip, and one of them was this big boy, a horse with heart.

The terrain began to change. Chet and I rode across more basins with fewer trees. The wind picked up on the other side of The Divide. It whipped our faces and made our skin feel like old rawhide, but it helped the horses cool down, which was more important, so we didn't mind a bit. After four months outdoors, my skin could handle just about anything, especially a mirror that lies! Following the lay of the land and the contour of the various ridges and trails, our ride turned into a gallop across rolling meadows and fields of waving bear grass. I could feel the presence of elk, bear, and moose. We had our bear bells on the horses, so we became increasingly dependent on our horses' keen ability to pick up a scent. Occasionally we crossed a road, but we didn't worry about being seen. We were hidden in plain sight.

We'd stop to take in views from several ridges that looked straight down on some of the main thoroughfares. We wanted to give the horses a quick breath and dry out. The air from our perch was cool and dry at 9,000 feet. A few times, the vantage point was perfect. All the vehicles below were heading uphill directly towards us while we sat comfortably on our steeds with one leg crossed over our saddle horns. I thanked the Lord I was on horseback and not in one of those four-wheelers below us. One time while we were stationed on a ridge about fifteen to twenty feet up, it hit me: "We're in plain sight of all these vehicles, and nobody can see us!" I couldn't believe it; neither could Chet.

"It's official. We've become invisible." Chet said.

"Amazing. They'll never catch us now," I said.

"Those greenhorns never had a chance, boss," Chet said.

My "guide eyes" had become so used to spotting movement in the outdoors, it was easy to look inside the passing vehicles and observe all the tourists. It was fun for a while, peering into another world. I was amazed to see all the card games, eating, and drinking that was going on inside the Winnies. Outside in the wild, our lives depended on paying attention to what was going on around us. Chet and I had to be wary of every sight, sound, and movement or possibly end up some predator's dinner. Conversely, it seemed the tourists were only interested in what was going on inside their vehicles.

We were living on two different planes of reality.

What stunned me was the Winnie brigade seemed to have no appreciation for all the wildlife they were passing by. Atop that particular ridge, I could see herds of elk, a moose and her calf, a family of grouse, a flying squirrel and a fox—all blurs when you're blowing by them in an RV. Even if a kid in the back of a car wanted to see the wildlife, they were moving too fast.

"I swear some of these people are lookin' right at us," Chet said. "Their minds must be elsewhere."

"Look, but not see. That's an old Indian way of describing many white men."

"They were sure as hell right about that."

While the horses rested, Chet and I decided to play a game and see how many people noticed the two cowboys and horses right in front of them. Would you believe eight out of every ten cars whizzed by us? And by the looks on the faces of the other twenty percent who did notice us, they weren't quite sure what they saw.

After about twenty minutes of being invisible, we decided it was time to get moving. We waited until traffic was light, then we dashed down from our perch, galloped across the road, and rode up another small hill until we disappeared into the forest once again. Chet and I were emboldened. We felt this was a good omen of things to come. We were convinced we really could be invisible until we got out of the park. The day was winding down. We waited at the designated area for our support vehicle to arrive; we made sure to stay out of sight. I had instructed Dave to meet us about 32 miles up the road right around Gibbon Falls. The plan was to quickly saddle up two fresh horses, grab our bedrolls and head back into the woods. "Guess we weren't making such bad time after all," I said. "We beat Dave here."

"There he is," Chet pointed, "Right on time." Chet emerged from the trees and waved him down. Our plan worked like a charm. No one saw our quick change; we did our business like a professional pit crew in The Indy 500.

Afterward, I told Dave thanks and patted the side of the rig. "Good work. See you tomorrow. Look for us around Firehole Canyon at noon, and stay out of the park tonight."

"Roger that. Have fun. And don't get yourself killed," Dave said with a smile.

"We won't. Unless Chet tries to wrestle a Grizzly for dinner."

"I'm dumb but ain't stupid," Chet said, "But, what are we doin' about dinner?"

Dave chuckled as he drove away. Chet and I ducked our fresh horses (Red and Wizzer) back into the trees.

We went looking for a place to set up a dry camp. There wasn't much daylight left, so we had to get a move on. We got off our horses and started to poke around on foot when we heard a large rush in the distance. "Beef jerky? That's all you packed?" Chet was upset about my insufficient dinner planning.

"It's just one night. You hear that?" Chet stopped to listen. I looked at Chet, and we followed the sound.

"Years ago, the Indians stayed out of Yellowstone," I said as we walked toward the rushing sound.

"Why's that?" Chet asked, "And what does this have to do with dinner?"

"They thought the Great Spirit lived here . . . with all the geysers and massive thermal areas in the Yellowstone Basin. They were afraid to enter," I said.

"I'm experiencing that mystical feeling, too, boss," Chet said. "But that may be hunger." The distant roar grew louder with every step until there were no more steps to be had, except one that dropped 100 feet down into a deep ravine.

We stopped just in time.

Below us was Gibbons Falls, thundering like a freight train through a narrow passageway. We stood there frozen in our tracks, looking down at God's beauty while the warm, misty breath of our horses warmed our necks.

"Looks like the Great Spirit led us to a damn good camping spot."

"This'll do. Thank you, Great Spirit," Chet said. "Wish we'd brought a rod."

Chet and I looked skyward and tipped our hats to the Great Spirit, then we tied up the horses for the night. We braced our saddles up against a row of small pinion pines that had grown along the edge of the cliff. We couldn't have asked for a better campsite. Our saddle blankets served as a great under-sheet; we used the saddles as a pillow and the trees as a temporary wall. Knowing it was going to be a cold night, we climbed under our slickers and bedrolls to get warm. I pulled out some beef jerky and some old leftover cornbread, and we sipped on a beer given to us by a friendly tourist earlier that day. I gave most of my jerky and bread to Chet, which satisfied him for the night.

We gazed up at the clear starry night of Big Sky Country. "It's great to be alive, ain't it?" Chet mused while sipping on the beer.

"Sure is, pard. Right here, right now? I'm perfectly at peace in the world," I said. "These are the moments we'll remember."

"And to think most people are sleeping in their land yachts," Chet said. "They're missing the show."

"It's a strange world," I said, then pulled my hat over my head and slipped into a world of deep slumber.

We were awakened by force of habit at 4 A.M. It was a cold morning, a thick layer of frost covered my slicker; I had icicles on my mustache. The temperature was somewhere in the high 20s to low 30s. As I shivered over to the horses, I had the warm feeling inside that I was living life properly, right at that moment. With the stars still twinkling brightly above us, I brushed off Big Red and Wizzer's frosted backs and turned them loose to graze a bit. Then I woke Chet and went through the motions of getting my bones ready to function for another day. I did my stretches and deep knee bends while rubbing my hands to get warm. All the exercises I'd done for so many years in my Tang Soo Do class helped me to work out all my aches and pains.

We went looking for water and found a seep in the woods from one of the many underground springs in this thermal area. Boy, ice-cold spring water at 4:30 A.M. on a 30-degree morning definitely awakens every nerve in the skeletal system!

By 5 A.M., the horses were grazed, watered, and saddled. We walked the horses a little over a mile to give them a chance to stretch and build a little more body heat. We were only a few miles from Geyser Basin, which featured Old Faithful, complete with souvenir shops, refreshment stands, restrooms, and a lodge.

I reckon it's one of the more touristy areas in the park; if you have to pass through, the best way is by horseback at 5:30 A.M., when most folks are sleeping, and the only critters around have four legs instead of two. Chet and I decided to ride up to the lodge with our slickers on, and hats pulled down low; we were in search of a "cup of ambition" in the form of hot coffee.

"I'm goin' on a recon mission, hang tight," Chet said.

"Don't stop to talk to any park rangers!"

We tied the boys to a decorative hitchin' post, and Chet strolled into the lodge while I sauntered over to a nearby restroom. A real toilet! I almost forgot what it was like to use one. I felt out of place being back in civilization. Instead of trees, downed timber, and rocks, I was suddenly surrounded by tile flooring and four walls. I wasn't used to this kind of luxury. I didn't stay too long.

I went back outside to check on the horses when I saw Chet emerge from the lodge with an ear-to-ear grin. He had procured two hot cups of coffee and two cinnamon rolls for us, all courtesy of the U.S. Park Service, unbeknownst to them.

"You are a magician," I said as I took a swig of the hot elixir. It wasn't as stout as Chet's cowboy coffee, but it was just what I needed to warm up and shake off the cobwebs. "Thank Katie, the pretty girl at the front desk, she insisted we have them."

"Your powers of persuasion never cease to amaze," I said, taking a big bite of a cinnamon roll. Talk about hitting the spot; we inhaled the coffee and rolls. Our presence hadn't been detected except for our new friend at the front desk, so we quit while we were ahead and slipped out of the tourist area. The sun was just beginning to cast a golden prism of color into the eastern sky as we rode through the thermal areas of Yellowstone. We were careful to follow the numerous game trails, so we didn't damage the delicate balance of mineral-based earth surrounding the different geysers.

The landscape was littered with dried up geysers, each one surrounded by burnt wood and stone that had been steamed for years by the dark depths of the earth. Moose, elk, and buffalo scat was everywhere. We weaved in and out of the thermal area. At one point, I waved for Chet to stop. I heard something. We turned around to see a family of elk following us, not an uncommon sight while on horseback in the high country.

Nonetheless, it was nice to make new four-legged friends. The family of elk followed behind us for a mile or two at about twenty to thirty yards. We must have been on one of their trails. Then, as quickly as they appeared, they ambled sharply back into a meadow in search of long green grass. It is impossible to describe the beauty of watching my riding partner and best friend disappear into a faint cloud of thermal steam ahead of me. The sunbeams illuminated his shadow self with every color of the rainbow. His spectral silhouette had a glowing multi-colored aura that was almost otherworldly. Few people get a chance to experience such a moment. I was and am forever grateful to the "Great Spirit" for allowing my partner and me this mystic glimpse of nature.

It was like riding through a beautiful dream.

By mid-morning, we reached the famed mud pots and paint pots where the earth boils up mud. In other places, it created bottomless hot turquoise pools. I felt like we were tiny specs of life riding through God's giant paint palette with his masterpiece being the canvas of the park. After passing through the mud pots, we were suddenly in a clearing that had to be a two-mile stretch of open land. We could see another heavily forested area in the distance. As we began to ride through the large meadow, Chet and I both had the same thought. With nothing but open land in front of us, I said, "C'mon, let's give the boys a chance to fire up their lungs!"

"I'll race ya!" Chet hollered as he gigged Wizzer to "get on his horse." The horses dashed across the meadow, jumping streams, stopping, turning, and sprinting again. This was the first time in over four months Big Red and Sonny (aka Wizzer) had had a chance to put it in high gear. Their eyes light up while they galloped across the beautiful pasture. While we were racing, I could see a road in the distance full of Winnies that were lined up to see what was going on in the field. Hell, they were lookin' at us! The tourists probably weren't sure what to make of us. Probably thought we must be two large elk on the run. Invisible, I say.

By noon, we'd ridden through the 500-foot rock walls of Firehole Canyon past a slew of cascading waterfalls. We were looking for Dave to meet us with two fresh horses (Thunder and Rebel). We made our way back to the road and shortly after that spotted the black Blazer pulling the horse trailer. Chet and I quickly emerged from the woods near the trailer and dismounted and re-saddled. This time, we were relaxed enough to have a cup of hot coffee Dave brought us.

"Did the rangers stop you on the way in or out of the park?" I asked.

"No," Dave said.

"Good."

"We just might do this," Chet said with a smile.

"You old guys are a couple of rebels," Dave said.

"You're a good hand," I said, "Now meet us outside the west entrance at sundown, in West Yellowstone." Dave said a quick goodbye then departed for West Yellowstone, the little town that was our day's end rendezvous, which was about 100 yards outside the west entrance of the park.

We only had ten to twelve miles left until we reached the promised land.

"Well, Butch. Think we can make it to the west exit without getting cuffed and stuffed in some godforsaken ranger's pokey?" Chet asked.

"Only one way to find out," I said. "We should be there by late afternoon."

"Let's get her done!" Chet said. I could see the excitement in his eyes, "C'mon Rebel, get it in gear!" And off we went on a race to the finish line.

We headed toward West Thumb Geyser Basin and "cheated" by taking a quick shortcut through an official tourist campground. We rode by all the tents, Winnies, and bathhouses, much to the astonishment of all the campers. "Wonder if these folks think we're actors playing cowboys?" I said as we paraded ourselves in front of all the tourists.

"We stink too much to be actors," Chet said with a laugh. "Especially you." From there, we followed a fork of the Madison River toward the west exit of the park. We spent a good amount of time riding through the middle of the river. The rivers in Yellowstone rarely got deeper than three to four feet, and the sandy, cool river bottom was a welcome relief to the horses' feet. We were getting excited; we were going to make it through the park. "Hot dog; we really did it! We're gonna beat the rangers, boys," Chet said as he patted the horses. "Yee—hah!"

Then, I swear the second Chet started celebrating early we came into view of a road where we were immediately spotted by a green ranger truck. "Well god damn, will you look at that," I said. "It's an ambush." We were only twenty feet from the ranger and had no choice but to stand our ground. The ranger slowed down his truck, and we looked him right in the eye. It was a tense moment.

"So close," Chet said under his breath.

We all stared at each other like gunfighters at the OK Corral. No one moved an inch. I was about to say something, then something amazing happened. I thought I saw a faint smile come across the ranger's face. The smiling ranger tipped his hat to us, almost as if to say, "Good luck." We smiled back and waved at him. I looked skyward again. I knew we were going to be okay.

"Thank you, Great Spirit," I said.

Within half an hour, we could see the west gate ranger station.

"Well, Sundance. I reckon we made it."

"You reckon," Chet said.

"Should we be so bold as to ride right on through?" I said with a wink.

"If we want to be cowards, we could pick our way through the woods undetected," Chet said.

"What the hell, let's ride right through the damn gate!"

"Damn straight, we ride through." Chet and I moseyed Thunder and Rebel up to the Yellowstone Gate, tipped our caps, and passed on through. I couldn't tell if the smiles we caught from the "green gate people" were smiles of "good luck" or "thank God they're out of here." Probably a little of both.

We didn't see Dave and the rig until we got to West Yellowstone. It was parked by a General Store and an Old West saloon. We said our hellos to Dave as we tied Thunder and Rebel to a post across from the saloon.

"Guess they didn't throw you two outlaws in jail, after all."

"Guess not," I said, "Wanna grab a beer?"

"Guess so," Dave said.

"You guess so? You guess?" Chet said, "I sure as hell do!"

"I'll watch the horses from a window seat," Dave said.

"Always thinking about the job; you're a top hand preacher man! Top hand!" I said, patting him on the back. We sauntered into the dimly lit room and took a deep breath of the cool air-conditioned air. I ordered a round of beers and three large waters for our table. Chet and I grabbed our water glasses like we'd just come in from the Mohave Desert. As the ice-cold liquid flowed down our parched gullets, we looked out the window at our trusted steeds and smiled with gratitude.

Then Chet and I raised our beer mugs, and I made a toast, "To our boys. And the old boys," I said. "And Butch and Sundance."

"To Butch and Sundance," Chet said.

"To Butch and Sundance," Dave said, raising his mug. He was a little less enthusiastic than we were, but he was getting into it. "You guys are still crazy."

"Cheers!" We clinked frosty mugs.

Invisible, I say.

★ 13 ★

CROSSING BIG SKY COUNTRY

"Eventually, all things merge into one,
and a river runs through it. The river was
cut by the world's great flood and runs over
rocks from the basement of time. On some
of those rocks are timeless raindrops.
Under the rocks are the words, and
some of the words are theirs.
I am haunted by waters."
—*Norman Maclean,* A River Runs Through It

A **WISE MAN** might assume Chet, and I hightailed it out of Wyoming like two outlaws after playing hide-and-seek with the Yellowstone Federales—but a wise man would be wrong about that! No, I reckon once we evaded those pesky Park Rangers, and whoever else might be looking for us, we decided to stay awhile and soak up our victory (and a few cold drafts) at a West Yellowstone saloon. I don't know why we lingered around the so-called crime scene. I guess we just wanted to hold on to that "invisible" feeling as long as we could. Our Butch and Sundance thrill ride must have awoken the inner outlaw in Chet; this was the most energized I'd seen my running mate since we left Connecticut. Soaking in the glory over suds, he said something I found pretty profound.

"Ya know, Jeff, I think I could get used to being invisible here."

"Pard, if it weren't for Suzie Q, reckon I could too."

"Maybe in the next life," he said.

"Maybe in the next life," I repeated.

I'm still holding out hope for that one.

With the dog days of summer behind us, the outfit figured our upcoming date with "Big Sky Country" of Montana and Idaho was going to be the best part of our trip.

"Think: less Bataan Death March, and more Jeremiah Johnson," I explained to Dave (our last hand standing) who had never been this far northwest in his life.

"What the heck are those?" Dave said.

"Don't they teach you anything in school?" I chuckled.

"I majored in Calculus," he said.

Preacher, you're smart as a whip, but you're a proverbial babe in the northwestern woods," I explained to Dave what Chet and I already knew. "This here final push we're about to embark on is gonna be the most energizing and challenging part of our trip. It's what Chet and I dreamt about most during our two years of training."

"—And now it's here," Chet said.

"If we get outta here without getting thrown in the pokey, that is," Dave said.

"What's that phrase you like Chet—never tell me the odds?"

"Y'all didn't tell me I'd be riding with the dang James Boys. Should ask for a raise for driving the getaway car."

"Shit Preacher, you got morals? We'll give you a cut of the loot, just keep driving," Chet laughed, downing his suds and shouting "Let's ride!

With bellies full of ceremonial brew, we saddled up the boys in West Yellowstone and got back on the trail, heading west to the promised land. We following Route 26, en route to the Wyoming-Montana border, making sure to stay on the wide grassy berms to avoid traffic. This was God's country—our ride took us through glorious wide-open expanses, surrounded by snow-capped mountains like jewels on Mother Nature's crown. We rode past a series of large ranches, which led us to a shortcut.

I was anxious about not missing Targhee Pass (the northernmost turn off) that would take us up around Henry's Lake, one of the deepest and most beautiful fishing lakes in all of Montana, which I told Chet all about from my time living here as a Montana guide. "How'd on earth did you end up out here after graduating college in Ohio, again?" Chet asked as we clopped along the trail.

"Good question," I smiled, "Ol' Jack sure wasn't happy; he said I put my degree to no use—he probably hoped I'd join him at Exxon, but I was a rebellious colt and chose to move to Montana to pursue my career as a guide, taking folks on rides all around the Gallatin National Forest, Lion's Head, and Two Top mountain ranges, which all just so happens to border this here road we're on right now."

"Must be a real homecoming for you," Chet said.

"Yep."

"Anything change?"

"Nope."

"Your folks ever forgive you for going native on 'em?"

"Nope. Guess Dad's trip out here was his way of finally forgiving me, though," I chuckled. Thirty years later, I reckon I was right about that.

Since we'd taken a short cut into the deep thicket, we never saw an official "Welcome to Montana" sign, but we hooted anyway when I announced we had made it to "Big Sky country." That night, we camped in the Gallatin National Forest about a mile from the trailhead, where I used to guide nearly ten years ago at the base of Lion's Head Peak.

"You sure the Gallatin Federales won't mind us being here?" Chet asked while preparing another sumptuous batch of his famous chili as Dave, and I groomed the boys.

"Think we're safe out here, though I should remind you again, this is a 'Bear Management 1' conservation area," which got everyone's dander up. I might have spooked Dave with my warning, but I was so excited to revisit some of the trails, lakes, and streams that used to be my home, I was talking a blue streak.

"Say what again?" Dave stopped grooming Thunder to ask.

"Well, when I lived here in '76, grizzlies weren't protected by the Feds like they are today, but this land was their home. Nobody had to tell them they were protected—brother, they knew it."

"So, you're sayin' we can't plug one that invades camp?"

"You can, but you better have a good aim."

"Hell, we got a 30-30, and I'm still scared shitless," Chet said, while Dave walked around hanging every bear bell we brought with us around camp like a black hat wearing Christmas elf. He even hung one on Chet's kitchen fly. Seeing their trepidation, I reassured the team that I wouldn't let them get mauled. "Y'all settle down, spotting Grizzlies was my job. They're the easiest bears to track cause they're the only bears that don't have retractable claws."

"How does that help us when we're asleep?" Chet asked.

"That's what the bells are for." To make them feel better, I told them about the time ten years ago when I had a Grizzly bust into my cabin in the middle of the night to ravage my kitchen.

"Shit, boss, don't tell us that! What chance do our tents have?"

"Well, just don't leave any food out, and we should be OK."

"*Should?*" Dave asked with a curious eyebrow.

"Luckily, that bear didn't get into my bedroom where I was sleeping (buck naked) with my 30-30 beside me—"

"Hell, boss," Chet interrupted, "That's too much information!"

"—and my guide dog, Buff," I said.

"Did ol' Buff, sleep in the buff too?" Chet laughed.

"Reckon he did, too."

"I'm sleeping in my clothes till we get outta here!" Chet said.

"Me too," Dave said.

"You city slickers." I smiled, "Consider that your ghost story for the night."

Lion's Head Mountain, perched on the southern end of the Gallatin Mountain Range—loomed in our shadows as we headed west through the foothills the next morning. We were finally in Montana riding on the Forest Service dirt roads that ran parallel to Route 20 and Route 26. We spied Two Top (mountain) to our south approximately three to five miles away, which I pointed out. "You're looking at Idaho over there, pard."

"Thought you said we were in your old stomping grounds?"

"Wyoming, Idaho, and Montana all kinda converge here."

"Whatever you say, boss, just point us in the right direction."

Traversing the Gallatin's sure can make a cowboy feel insignificant, but also dang lucky to be surrounded by such beauty and grandeur. Surrounded by snow-peaked mountains and cool crisp mountain air, the outfit got another glimpse of what ol' Jim Bridger and the "old ones" must have experienced while riding on this same pristine, dare I say Holy, terrain. All these years later, I was honored to ride this sacred country, no longer as a guide, but as a guest. Timeless is the word! To this cowpoke history buff, it doesn't get any more thrilling than this. Chet, who seems to be fiddling with Rebel's bear bell whenever we hear a broken twig off in the distance, might disagree.

I reckon some benevolent force was smiling down on us as we navigated Targhee Pass. Plenty of things could have gone haywire, but the weather was perfect, and I was privately amazed we hadn't had any Grizzly sightings yet, and (more importantly) no Grizzly encounters. Had they all run off to Canada? "Where are the bloodthirsty bears with the razor-sharp teeth?" Chet joked, fixing Rebel's bell again.

"Maybe they're as apprehensive of you, as you are of them."

"I'll be just fine if we don't see bear one."

"Don't you want to fight one like Davy Crockett?"

"Shiiiit."

"Sure are seeing plenty of elk and moose tracks, though. See, right there?" I pointed to some elk tracks on the Forest Service trail. "Those are fresh."

"Where are they though?" Chet wondered, "They invisible too?" Chet was right; we hadn't had a single wildlife encounter yet.

"Let's just say, this is a good thing. We don't want tempt fate!"

"Stop scaring me, boss!"

I just chuckled.

We got to Henry's Lake turnoff by midday. What a view; it gave me chills just seeing it. Imagine crystal clear water, glassy as you'll ever find in nature that's protected by snow-capped mountains on all sides like it was our secret watering hole. We stopped to soak in the view and let the horses get a drink. Besides the breathtaking beauty, Henry's Lake was an important landmark for us, especially out on these grey road trails. From this point forward, I knew we'd be heading north until we hit the famous Madison River, which should be a half a day's ride from here if recollection served.

Once we got to the Madison, the plan was to cross Route 287, a two-lane highway, and ride west, following the river for the next sixty miles, through a good part of Montana. "The Madison's gonna blow your mind!" I said, unable to hide my excitement.

"What mind?" Chet laughed, "I can only think like Rebel after all this adventure."

"May want to learn how to think like a trout when you see this river."

"As chef of this outfit, you have my attention," Chet said, licking his lips.

If you love the outdoors and haven't treated yourself to the sublime experience of floating, fishing, or swimming in Montana's famed Madison River, put it on your proverbial bucket list. Some say it's the most prolific, trout happy river in the world.

"It's full of the smartest trout I've ever seen, tons of species, you'll love it."

"Aren't illiterate trout easier to eat?" Chet joked, passing me a hunk of cornbread. I spent the rest of the afternoon whetting Chet's appetite for some fresh trout, regaling him with stories about how fishermen from all over the world come here to experience this river because of its combination of fast-moving water, quiet eddies, and crystal-clear side creeks teeming with trout of all persuasions—cutties, goldens, brookies and rainbows—you name it, they got em. "All these rivers up here spawned from Yellowstone," I explained.

"You should teach Montana history, boss," Chet teased.

"I did on the back of a horse when I was a guide." I explained that once we crossed the Continental Divide, all the rivers from here to the Pacific originated from Yellowstone—"Like the Yellowstone River, the Madison, Fire Hole, the Jefferson, the Gallatin River, and the Boulder River," I stopped talking and noticed Chet shaking his head. "There gonna be a test? You're hurting my head with all those names."

"Sorry, just a little excited, I guess."

"You're a real renaissance guide, Jeff."

"I am?"

"You know all the hoof, paw, and gill routes round here. Why'd you ever leave?"

"Good question. Had a date with destiny, with a girl named Sue, I guess." I said, fully expecting Chet to give me hell for being sappy, but he didn't.

"You need to call your pregnant wife, and tell her that."

"You're right 'bout that. It's been too long."

"Wish I loved someone so much that I'd be willing to give all this up." From this conversation, I got the feeling Chet's fiancé, Diane, hadn't exactly been on his mind—was he getting cold feet? Was he thinking about a certain Indiana cowgirl? I never asked, but internally, I started kicking myself. I should have let Jean ride with us—I thought—How hard could it have been? But I didn't tell Chet that. Let sleeping dogs lie—I say, especially here on the trail when it comes to matters of the heart! I needed Chet focused on Grizzlies, the boys, and getting us to the Pacific. Privately, I vowed I would make it up to him (somehow) when we got home.

I'm sad to say that never happened.

The next day we arrived at the glorious Madison River. The weather had cooled down to almost perfect conditions, so we were able to ride full days again. With their ears and noses twitching, I could tell the boys could hear and smell the trout jumping from a mile away. It was Christmas morning for horses and outdoorsman. I could tell Thunder was ready to call it a day to splash around the river, bobbing for river trout—but we kept the boys dry and just kept following the river bank until we found a suitable campsite to spend the night. Riding along the river, Chet and Dave were stunned by the Madison's beauty. Chet said he was "overwhelmed" by the untouched splendor of the river and surrounding wide-open basins and green valleys.

"You been talking this place up for two years, boss."

"And now we're here."

"It's even more beautiful than you described."

"Sometimes, dreams do come true, Hoss." I looked down at Thunder, who turned his head to (try to) steal another treat from me, "Doesn't mean I'm giving you the rest of my cornbread."

Through the valley, surrounded by snowcapped mountains on all sides, we passed by several "rich man ranches" and a slew of historical landmarks, marking the migration of settlers with "gold in their eyes" to Montana during the late 1800s. We had a date with Virginia City, once the epicenter of the Montana Gold Rush. According to our maps and my memory, it would be on our radar soon. Chet began expressing a hankering for seafood once we started passing a succession of "Fishing Access" signs. With my stomach rumbling, I was tempted to pull over too.

"Guess what we'll be eating for dinner tonight?" I teased.

"Don't mess with a man's appetite unless you're gonna deliver."

"Pole's in the rig," I said, pointing to the fisherman casting their flies into the river, "They're bitin' all right." The plan was to camp by the river as many nights as we could. Not only would it be gorgeous, but it also gave us the gift of bountiful resources like fish, water, shade, grass, and cover from the curious masses!

In other words, we could avoid people; the team had decided it was a key to our continued sanity. As much as we enjoyed getting to know all the nice folks we met, who were all so gracious to us and the boys—I felt such a personal attachment to Montana, I wasn't interested in discussing our trip with every curious person who approached us—neither was Chet. Is that selfish? Or anti-social? Call me some nature boy, but I felt our ride through Montana was about honoring this patch of land to show my gratitude for the "old ones" who came before us.

The weather could not have been better, with days in the 80s and the evenings in the 40s. We didn't have to worry about the boys anymore with all the rich grass along the banks of the Madison, and abundance of fresh water. The horses loved the cool evenings. Camping that night by the riverbank in the most picturesque spot you could imagine, I was one happy cowboy, and an even happier fisherman when I got out my fly rod and rustled us up some fresh dinner from the Madison. I caught six trout (two apiece for each cowboy)—and Chef Chet was beyond elated to fry em up for supper. No offense to Chet's trademark "dish du jours" or any of the home-cooked feasts strangers offered us—this was, by far, the tastiest meal we had on the trip. I don't know how Chet does it, but he seasoned up that fish better than I could at home.

"There is something really satisfying about cooking up a fresh catch right by the river, huh?" Chet mused clearly proud of his work.

"Sure is," I said, "You put a damn good scald on that trout," I said.

"Yeah, awful tasty, and I normally don't eat fish," Dave said, still eating.

"Fish and fowl's heart-healthy son, you're a convert now, Preacher," Chet said, "And it's hard to mess this up!" Chet gestured to the glorious setting around us that looked like something you'd see in a postcard.

"Feels like the dog days are behind us," I mused, "With the boys all healed, and the Pied Piper causing trouble in Chicago, I reckon we're one tight outfit now."

"You mean—you don't miss his midnight warblings and guitar pickin'?" Chet asked with a sly smile, which caused the outfit to titter with laughter.

"Reckon I prefer me a little Merle Haggard instead."

We were up early the next day, on our way to the sleepy town of Ennis, about fifty miles downstream. It was breathtaking to see the size of all the working "rich man" ranches we passed like Sun Ranch and the actor Stephen Segal's ranch, located on the west side of Route 287 bordering Wolf Creek. "Amazing that bad movies can pay for all that," I said.

"I love his movies," Chet said.

I chuckled, "Gotta get you into Westerns, pard."

True to form, the mountains followed us. Today our backdrop was the backside of Big Sky ski area, which was closed for summer, though we could still see snow on the 10,000-foot peaks that served as our backdrop. "Just another day in paradise," I said. As we rode, I started talking about the town of Ennis, which was on our route, "Their claim to fame is their City Limits sign; want to know what it says?"

"Got a feelin' you're gonna tell me anyway."

"Welcome to Ennis: Where There are two Million Trout and 786 People."

Chet bellowed, "These country folks are pretty funny."

"Gotta have a sense of humor out here. That's why I brought you."

"Who? Thunder ain't cracked a damn joke in weeks," Chet laughed.

"You—you joker," I said.

Out-of-the-blue—our conversation was interrupted by a large herd of mule deer and antelope that came racing toward us. "There we go! You wanted a critter sighting! There's a hundred!"

"Hope that ain't more buffalo steaming our way," Chet said.

"Settle down Thun, they won't get you," I informed Chet they were mostly deer, which was obvious when they started bounding across the field like they were on springs; playing games, chasing each other, easily hopping over all the ranchers' fence lines that were in their way. I was curious to see if they would get close, and they did. "These pronghorns are friendly as hell," I said. They ran up to the fence line to watch the horses amble by, just like that herd of buffalo, way back in Ohio.

"See?" I told Thunder, patting his neck, "They just want to say howdy." Then, in the blink of an eye, the herd bolted away at an unbelievable speed, then circled back to approach us again. "They really want to make friends with the boys," I said.

"Some of my best friends are venison," Chet replied.

"Shh, don't tell 'em that," I smiled. These "Antelope drive-bys" would continue several times a day until we hit Ennis.

"Look at them go!" Dave marveled from the rig.

"What happened to our runaway horse?" Chet looked over at Thunder with a raised eyebrow. "You getting fat or something?"

"Maybe Thun's growing wise beyond his years? I said, patting his neck.

✦ ✦ ✦

Ennis was finally upon us. We tipped our hats to the eight-foot bronze fly fisherman statue just before passing through its downtown, which was one block long. Even though we had retired our half-day schedule, we had a "nooning" anyway to plot our next move and study our Forest Service maps. Unclear of the fastest route, we asked around town, inquiring with a few of the locals to see if we'd have to cross any major ranches to get to our next stop—Virginia City. "Ain't no towns 'tween Ennis and Virginia City," A local rancher told us, "You'll probably get there in half-a-day on those horses—Route 287 will take you there."

I checked my watch, "With some luck, we'll get there before sunset," I said to Chet and Dave, who agreed we should go for it—so we thanked the friendly local for the information, and saddled up again. "Always wanted to say this: let's ride to Virginia City—Hyaaah!" I took off.

"Wait up, boss, I'm still finishing my lunch. Hyaaah!" Chet followed with a mouth full of something messy. He and I had talked about riding to mythic Virginia City ever since we cooked up this crazy trip two years ago! People we met on the trail kept telling us it was the only real Old West town left in Montana, which got me even more excited if that was possible. "You know more gold was mined out of Virginia City than just about any other western city, except those in northern California?" I explained to the Preacher as he cruised beside us in the rig.

"Can't say I did," Dave replied.

"Had ten thousand residents at its peak but—after the boom went bust, it was nearly abandoned, last I heard. Will be interesting to see how it's holding up."

"Yeah, boss, real interesting," Dave said. Little did the Preacher Man know, but our time in Virginia City would be one of the most memorable moments of CA86.

Cresting a rocky ridge just south of where the town of Virginia City was located on our maps, I used my binoculars to spy what looked like an old western town sitting at the bottom of a gulch beside a hill, just like I envisioned it.

"That hayseed wasn't kidding, it's still here, boys!" I shouted in glee at first sight of the city I had romanticized since I was a kid. Seeing that Virginia City hadn't been turned into a giant shopping mall or a used car lot thrilled Chet and me beyond words. We rode our way into town with a few hours of daylight left, even though it was almost 8 P.M. "Feels like we're entering one of your Louis L'Amour novels, boss," Chet said. "How's it still so light out?"

"Part of the beauty of Montana in the summertime is—days are eternal."

"Kinda like Alaska," replied Chet.

"We're closer to Alaska than you think."

Stepping the first hoof into town was like going back in time. I was elated to see Virginia City had been restored (fairly recently) to look exactly like it did in the 1800s with the same wooden plank sidewalks lining the streets, the same General Store, the same Saloons, and shops you would have seen back in the olden days.

"Only difference is, they paved the roads," I noticed.

"And look? They finally got electricity," Chet said, nodding his head to the electrical poles around us.

We rode by an old Blacksmith's Shop and Old Hotel that had been meticulously restored.

"Feel like I belong here," I said, "Feels funny seeing cars tooling around."

"When are they gonna outlaw those horseless carriages?" Chet said, tipping his cap to a group of tourists who gave us a good long stare, no doubt, trying to figure out where we fit into this town. "Heads up. All eyes are on us, again," Chet said.

"Prolly think we're part of some wild west show again."

"Guess we are if you think about it," Chet replied.

"Except we're a traveling revue like ol' Wild Bill had."

"Does that make me the rodeo clown?" Chet smiled.

We went looking for a place in town where we could put up our horses, and spend the night. We passed the Bale of Hay Saloon; next to it was an Old Livery Stable that had a nice little open space beside it that was calling the boys' name. The only problem was it was roped off. "Should we try here, and just see if we get the boot?" I asked Chet.

"I'm all for breaking the law, but you'll have to pay the fine."

I looked around to see who might care. I saw no prying eyes. I spied the old Hotel (turned museum) across the street to see if anyone was watching us from an open window. "All's clear, so far. We could risk it and stay here, or go check out Robbers Roost up the way a bit," I said, unsure if Chet remembered it was once a well-known gathering place for thieves and criminals.

"Leave me out of Robber Town," Chet laughed, "I'm still on probation!"

"This ain't no saintly berg Hoss. Outlaws also 'vacationed' here. Story goes Butch and Sundance were frequent visitors."

"Shoot, you didn't tell me that," Chet said, "So you're saying we're in good company if we break a law here?"

"I reckon. How about this? If we get a ticket, I'll take it out of your pay."

"What pay?"

"Exactly!" I smiled. Considering we only had a few hours of daylight left, I made an executive decision to test our luck and camp in this cordoned off spot. I asked Dave to move our gear next to the Livery Stable. Chet couldn't believe my brazen decision.

"Hell, you've gone full horse thief on us, boss," Chet laughed at my wild hair.

"I know we're probably breaking some city ordinance, but Robber's Roost is too far. Just act like you own the place, and they'll probably leave us alone."

"Chet said, "If there's no one around to ask, is it really a crime?"

"You're full of cockamamie wisdom today," I chuckled as I directed Dave, who was angling the trailer up to the Stable. Chet began setting up camp like we owned the dang place and, believe it or not—no one said a word! Once I felt we were safe, my imagination started running wild. I imagined highwayman eating across the street at the Old Cafe then moseying over to the City Jail to collect their reward for the gunslinger they'd captured. I got so curious, I asked Dave to keep an eye on the boys so Chet and I could explore the town a little. "Ain't going nowhere," Dave replied, feeding the boys alfalfa hay. "I'll holler if they start hauling Thunder to horse jail."

Chet and I sauntered a block uptown to the Bale of Hay Saloon to see if we could rustle up some grub and a cold draft. Maybe I just wanted to play cowboy for the night because I still remember the sound of our spurs jangling as Chet and I pushed our way through the swinging saloon doors. Inside, it felt like we had stepped back into the 1800s. To our right was an Old Dance Hall with a four-foot high stage and red velvet curtains where (in the evenings) they put on a live Old West stage show for five dollars. The Saloon was to our left. There weren't many towns in America where Chet and I could venture out looking like two dirty wranglers and not feel like everyone was staring at us. We thought this would be one of those towns. We were wrong about that. All eyes were on us the moment we entered the bar. "Awk—ward," Chet joked as our spurs jangled past tourists in their baseball caps and Hawaiian shirts. Not a single other cowboy was in the bar.

"I guess times have really changed," I remarked.

Once again, we felt a little out of place and most certainly smelled pretty dang ripe to be among civilized folks, but Chet and I didn't mind. After perusing the crowd, we took a couple of seats at the bar and greeted the tall bearded bartender who furnished us with two drafts to quench our dusty gullets. I reminded Chet, "Gotta pace ourselves Hoss and stay out of trouble. My alcohol tolerance is for shit."

"Relax, Jeff, if there's any place we can let our hair down, this is the place."

"You mean you still got hair under that stinky hat?" I joked.

Halfway through our first draft, a gentleman who called himself "Dick" approached us, identifying himself as a reporter for the local Virginia City newspaper. A curious fella, Dick wanted to know what our getups were all about. "Getups? These ain't costumes!" Chet bellowed, which took Dick aback until he realized Chet was kidding him.

As usual, we told the curious stranger all about our trip. Dick listened intently, taking notes in a little green moleskin notebook. He seemed quite interested in us and asked if he could ask us more questions.

"Sure, shoot," I said, "Chet'll keep sassing you, though."

"I'm full of piss and vinegar," Chet joked, "And now beer." He downed his.

"Let me get the next round," Dick said, "On the paper."

"We will never say no to that question," I chuckled and thanked him.

For the next hour, we entertained Dick with our story, complete with all the bells and whistles. The usual questions flowed—so did the drafts, a little too quickly. After a while, Dick put down his pencil and said he'd "gotten his story," and warmly shook our hands, wishing us luck, and thanking us for speaking with him. Dick said our story would be in the paper in a day or so, which was long after we'd be gone.

"Will you mail us a copy?" I asked him and gave him our information.

"I'll read it when we return. If I can still read when I get home," Chet said.

"If we make it back home," I chuckled, "The jury is still out on that!"

Around this time, a rough and tumble group of what appeared to be bikers caught my eye, five barstools down from us. They were impossible to miss. One was a big bearded guy with a ponytail sitting on a stool next to a small Native American looking woman with long black hair, who appeared to be his wife. I remember the big man giving us a silent nod, and we nodded back. I don't know what it was about this dude, but I couldn't stop staring at him. It seemed obvious he was the leader of their group. But I stopped staring once Chet alerted me to the fact they were all wearing Hell's Angels jackets.

We had no interest in starting a biker brawl our first night in town.

But I reckon I must've been sending curious vibes his way because, a few minutes later, the big guy made his way over to us. I was surprised to see the big man was in a wheelchair. He spoke in a deep, gruff tenor, and introduced himself as simply "Ford."

"Mighty nice to meet ya, Ford," we said, and introduced ourselves, tipping our caps in his general direction. Ford gestured toward the black-haired woman, and she came over, and Ford introduced her as his wife. To this day, I cannot remember her name.

Then a second Hell's Angel walked over and introduced himself as "Indian Jeff."

"Nice to meet ya Jeff—That's my name too," I said, "Except for the Indian part. We're just a couple of Connecticut Yankee cowboys on our way to the Pacific."

Ford's eyebrows raised when he heard that. "You gotta be shittin' me?"

"We got the worn tread to prove it," Chet chuckled.

Ford wasn't sure what to make of us. While discussing the trip, he looked Chet, and I square in the eyes to see if we were trying to pull a fast one over on him. But once he halfway believed our story, he warmed up to us and kept curiously asking questions. His wife was very friendly too; they had a familiarity about them that indicated they'd been together for many years, finishing each other's sentences, and so forth.

Seeing how close they were made me miss Sue something awful.

"Indian Jeff," as it turned out, wasn't Native American at all. He was Dutch-Irish. He said he got his nickname because of his collection of vintage Indian motorcycles, one of which was parked outside the saloon. In his "other life," Jeff said he was a "life insurance salesman from Chicago." Which blew our minds.

"Hey, who's bullshitting who?" Chet laughed, so Indian Jeff took us outside to show us his 1960 vintage Indian motorcycle. We admired its bespoke beauty but politely declined when Indian Jeff offered to take us for a spin around the block. "Hell, we're so used to horses, we may fall off," Chet chuckled.

"Y'all sure come a long ways on four legs," Indian Jeff said, "Not many horses can make that trip anymore." Then Jeff went back to talking about his love for bikes, telling us he had ridden his Indian all the way here from Chicago to visit his old friend, Ford.

"The two of us represent the Illinois and Montana chapters of the Angels," Indian Jeff said and turned around to show us his jacket emblem representing the Chicago Chapter of the famed Hell's Angels motorcycle gang.

"Dang, Jeff. We need some 'Cross AmeriCA86' jackets like those," Chet said.

"I gave you my emergency slicker. What else do you want?" I laughed.

For the next several hours, Chet and I became fast friends with Ford, his wife, Indian Jeff, and his entire biker gang, swapping stories and laughing non-stop. At one point, Dick, the local reporter, who turned out to (also) be the publisher of the Virginia City News, pulled me aside. "Just so you know: your food and drinks are on the house."

This didn't process. "Uh, thank ye, but what's the occasion?"

"Drinks aren't on me, they're on Ford, so—they're on the town!"

"Come again?"

Dick proceeded to tell me Ford "owns the town of Virginia City."

This was another mind-blower.

"Never known anyone that owned a whole damn town," I said.

"It's irregular, but ever heard of the Bovey family?"

I had not—so Dick proceeded to tell me a story about how Virginia City came to be restored to its original glory, and how, after the Gold Rush was over, the town nearly went bust. Guess who the heroes of this story are? Ford's parents—who were successful real estate investors named Sue and Frank Bovey. They purchased every piece of property in the entire town (sometime in the late 1940s, early 50s) and restored it. When they passed away, Ford, their only child, inherited the Bovey fortune, which included the town of Virginia City. "Not only does he own the buildings and the land, but he runs the whole place," Dick whispered, trying not to be overheard.

"You mean, that scruffy Hell's Angel is the mayor?" I asked incredulously.

"Did I stutter? He owns the whole damn town!"

"Well, ain't that a show stopper," I said, "We never had a town pick up our tab before, but it's OK with us. Thank ye."

"Thank Ford," Dick said, then disappeared.

After Dick left, I pulled Chet aside to tell him the news. "Newsflash pard: Ford owns the whole damn town." The look on Chet's face was classic; first, shock, that soon turned into a big grin, ear to ear.

"Well, goddamn Jeff, no way we're getting arrested now!"

The stories continued to roll.

A little later, I asked Ford, "Word is you're picking up our tab?"

"Aw, it's the least we could do for a couple of real cowboys like you," Ford said. Chet and I thanked him for his generosity. By now, a big crowd had gathered around us, since Ford was everyone's friend. Ford seemed to have no interest in speaking with anyone but us stinky cowboys—probably because he knew everyone else in Virginia City. We closed down the Bale of Hay Saloon that night—talking with Ford about cowboys, relationships, old Virginia City, and what it was like growing up in this neck of the woods. Ford was more interested in our trip and why we decided to ride horses cross-country. He spoke of a "brotherhood between Hells Angels and cowboys" and the kinship between people "that ride motorcycles seriously and serious horsemen."

I let that sink in, "I never thought of that before." But agreed with his comparison.

After four more hours at the Bale of Hay (maybe longer), Chet and I got fairly haymakered, being unaccustomed to drinking. It became a challenge to remember our subsequent conversations with Ford, his wife, and Indian Jeff. We ate plenty, but as much as we paced ourselves, there were thirty people in our party, all wanting to buy us beers, and help us any way they could—so we got more than our fill of everything.

After we shut down the bar, we all walked outside and exchanged many hugs. Chet and I said we wished we could spend several days here, just hanging out with Ford and getting to know him and his town a little better. Before we embarked on our slow stagger back to our camp, Chet said, "All y'all good people are invited to join us for a real cowboy breakfast over the campfire, tomorrow morning, 9 A.M., at our horse trailer! There, you can meet our four-legged friends!" Everyone cheered Chet's offer; a few of them even honked their Harley horns in celebration.

Then we got a surprise question.

"Where you got your boys?" Ford asked.

Uh oh. When I told Ford we set up shop in the open field by the Old Livery Stable, he looked at me with a cracked smile, "Well, you know you're not supposed to stay there?" Chet gave me a guilty glance then walked away, comically whistling, "Gotta go see a man about a dog!"

Abandoned by Chet, and left to face the music, I stammered over my words for a second, then Ford said, "That's off-limits to everybody. But don't worry about it!" he said as a big smile broke across his heavily bearded face.

"Shoot, that's awful nice of you," I said, apologetic. But Ford wasn't having any apologies. "You picked the right spot to go rogue. Many a thief and robber spent the night some hundred years ago, in that very spot you made camp."

"Like who.?" I had to know.

"Butch Cassidy and the Sundance Kid, to name two."

You should have seen Chet's eyes light up after hearing that. He went from guilty dog eyes to hooting and hollerin' like he'd just been named MVP of the Super Bowl.

"Don't mind Chet. He's got a thing for Butch and Sundance."

Wandering back to camp, I felt pretty good knowing nobody would dare mess with us tonight. Hell, we had the blessing of the Hell's Angel who owned the town.

The end of the evening was sketchy—I don't recall returning to camp, or what time we left the saloon, but it was dark as hell out, and it didn't get dark till after 10:30, so you can do the math on that. But I reckon that evening was one of the best nights of my entire life that didn't include Sue!

Breakfast with the Hell's Angels was scheduled for 9 A.M.—I rolled out of my sleeping bag around 8:30, groggy but enticed by the smell of Chet's cowboy coffee perking and the sizzle of back bacon frying in the skillet. Chet, looking no worse for wear, said he had been awake for a while. Dave was helping him prep for breakfast, a bit confused by it all. "How exactly did this breakfast with Hell's Angels and Mayor of Virginia City become a reality again?"

While Chet filled Dave in, I helped prepare breakfast as much as I could— but I learned to stay out of Chet's way when he was prepping a large meal. I remember barely splashing water on my face before the roar of Harley's filled the air of Virginia City, shortly after 9 A.M. Chet looked up from his prep table and said, "On-time Hell's Angels? Never heard of such a thing." We watched Ford and his wife roll in, followed by Indian Jeff and six other Hell's Angels whose names I wish (to hell) I could still remember.

It was quite a sight.

"Looks like a pack of hungry marauders," Dave said.

With our rig and trailer in a quarter circle, Ford and his friends pulled in and completed the circle with their motorcycles. I reckon Ford partly showed up for breakfast, just to make sure our story checked out—because the first thing he said after taking one look at our filthy rig and well-worn gear was, "Well, I'll say, you weren't kidding Jeff. You must've been on the road a long damn time!"

The Hell's Angels entered our camp hooting and hollering.

Had they even been to bed yet? I wasn't sure.

They all grabbed makeshift seats around the campfire as Chet and Dave served up a feast of cowboy coffee, slabs of back bacon, scrambled eggs, fried potatoes, and some leftover Chet's cornbread. What a gathering this was—horses and bikes, cowboys, and Hell's Angels—all congregating around the campfire (and an awesome home-cooked breakfast) on an illegally obtained plot of land where Butch and Sundance once laid their heads. To quote that commercial again. *Life doesn't get any better than this.*

Over breakfast, we tried to piece together last night's conversations. None of us could remember what time we left the bar. The whole time, four sets of ears were curiously pointed at Ford and his friends. I could hear Thunder thinking—*Who are these hairy humans, and what are those strange metallic steeds?* Ford took an immediate liking to Thunder, fawning over his golden mane and palomino skin, like all the other strangers we met on the trip. "You ride this statuesque bad boy?"

"Sure do—Thunder and I are best friends."

"Shoulda named him Zeus, but Thunder'll hunt. Look at you. This golden boy's one of the largest horses I have ever seen in my damn life."

"He's our diva," Dave said.

"No Thun's our bodyguard when the bears come calling," Chet said.

"He's fended off some attack dogs, that's for sure," I laughed.

The unusual "Summit meeting" between the cowboys and the bikers continued as we just sat around the campfire, eating breakfast and reminiscing about what a great evening we had at the Bale of Hay Saloon. Once Chet had cleared the plates like the gracious host he was, Chet and I thanked Ford for buying our rounds, and also, "For not throwing us in the pokey. For uh, *you know.*" Ford just laughed.

"Shit. Any other greenhorns who pulled that move woulda gotten strung up by Toad over there," he said, pointing to his 300-pound Hell's Angel named

Toad, who nodded in silent agreement. "But not you boys. Y'alls special," he laughed.

Then Ford blew our mind again, announcing he and his Angels would be giving us a "personal escort out of town." Chet and I didn't know what to say except, thank you again. After several pots of coffee to shake the cobwebs from our heads, we packed up and got ready to go. Ford sure had a curious look on his face watching us break down camp, saddle up Thunder and Rebel—and be on our way.

I reckon horsemen and bikers are kindred spirits, after all.

"Let's see if you got the horsepower to keep up with this! Hyaaah!" Chet shouted dramatically only to have Rebel take off in the slowest cantor this side of the Pecos, which made Ford and his boys erupt in laughter. That Chet will do anything for a laugh.

Experiencing Ford and his motley gang of Hell's Angels escort us out of Virginia City gave me chills up and down my spine. The gang took turns making sure the two-lane road out of town was clear while a few Angels rode ahead of us. For the next two hours, we took turns waving and tipping our hats to each other, having the time of our lives. Seven miles later, with Virginia City in our rearview, the last of the Hell's Angels gave us a big wave and turned around. Chet and I raised our hats and waved one final time. It was another truly unforgettable memory, one of many we had along the way.

I tip my cap to old Ford Bovey, his wife, and his Hell's Angels friends for showing us a good time. I sincerely hope I will get an opportunity to see them all again someday. If not soon, maybe in the next life.

Hung over as we had been all trip, Chet and I kept our 20th-century wagon train moving west on Route 287 toward the town of Twin Bridges and Route 43. One of Ford's Angels suggested we take a short cut called Melrose Road once we neared the town of Twin Bridges, which we did—thanks for the tip Ford! We filled our water buckets in Twin Bridges, and Chet and I rode alongside each other on this old dirt road for the next day and a half—reflecting on the trip and missing our families back home, both of us wondering how they were getting along. "Diane's probably given up on me ever returning by now. She calls me the runaway fiancée!"

"That nickname fits, shoot. At least you're disappointing one person. I'm disappointing two," I said.

"I think your unborn child will forgive you, boss."

"Suzie must be cursing my name up a storm. We're so damn close now, can't turn back at this late date."

"Not unless we get mortally wounded. Don't worry. If she gets too lonely, she'll just run off with her Lamaze instructor," Chet chuckled. Maybe he was right? Last time we spoke was when Jack was in town, and I called to thank her for the care package she sent (stuffed with goodies that Chet and Andrew mostly ate.) Sue has always been a self-reliant, practical woman who can take care of herself, run our business when I was away, and do it all (and then some). So, I knew she'd never let on that she missed me, or needed me to come home now—she just isn't that type of personality.

Maybe I need her more than she needs me? If I'm being honest, that thought might scare me more than anything else.

Chet and I were on our final leg of Montana—plowing 90 miles west to our penultimate milestone: the Montana-Idaho border. This would take us into the most rustic and remote part of our adventure. Chet and I found our shortcut (called Madison Road) and got off the beaten path to ride through one of the most gloriously untouched spots in all America called Big Hole Valley. We didn't see hide or hair of civilization for days—no cars, no houses, and only one-bearded traveler on a bicycle to keep us company—and he wasn't much company at all. The story goes, after a long day riding, we were looking for a place to camp for the night, and came upon an old, dilapidated farmhouse, with a partial roof that was barely hanging on for dear life. This was the most cover we'd had in weeks, so we pulled the rig into the old dirt driveway to check it out. "Looks creepy, boss. I like creepy," Chet said as we swung down from the saddle and tied off the boys to the trailer.

"No, you don't, you're scared of the dark," Dave laughed at Chet.

"You shut your lying mouth," Chet joked right back.

"Well, I like roofs," I said as we cautiously entered the old farmhouse and checked the place out. It looked suitable for our needs, with three-quarters of a roof on it that didn't necessarily look like it would collapse on us in the middle of the night—so we settled on staying. Just as we were throwing some gear into the house, I was startled to find a man already inside, lurking in the corner of a darkened room.

"What's all the ruckus?" A voice shouted.

"Who goes there? Show your face," I inquired, barely making his silhouette out. I approached the stranger, looking around to see if he had other friends lurking too. He didn't. For a moment we just stood there staring at each other, with both of us probably wondering—What the hell is *he* doing here?

I think we scared him as much as he startled us.

"What in tarnation? Who goes there, yourself?" the old bearded hermit said.

"Name's Jeff. This here's Chet. What's your name?

We got no response. So, I showed the old-timer that we carried no weapons (except for the Winchester in the rig, that is), and the hermit let his guard down a bit and led us into his room where he showed us he had no weapons either—all he had was a rucksack and some canned food. Once I felt there was no danger—I got a little curious about him. It didn't take long to realize this fella with the scraggly white beard was a little "different." The first sign was he refused to tell us his name. I tried striking up a conversation with him a few times, but he wasn't talking. Then I told him our story and old-timer finally perked up, saying, "I'm just passing through too" and that we "could have the other room" that he was not sleeping in.

I looked at Chet and shook my head yes, and said, "Okay?"

"Works for us," Chet said, "But Jeff is a big cuddler, so watch out."

The hermit did not get Chet's joke. At all.

I tried to start a conversation with him, "You have any family?"

No response.

"Where do you call home?"

Crickets.

"Okaaaay, then, good talk."

We left him alone to unpack our gear. The hermit did warm up (slightly) after a few minutes, saying he "didn't live anywhere, per se," but was a "migrating snowbird of sorts"—who flies from East Coast to West every year on his bicycle. "I stay there in the summer, then turn around and peddle back West before winter hits, which is what I'm doin' now, if you haven't guessed."

"All the way on a bike?"

"You got it right, buster."

"We're riding across country too," Chet said.

"Your cowboy pal—the cuddler, already said that," the hermit remarked with a little dry sarcasm.

"Heeey. He's got some spunk after all," Chet smiled at me, "I like this old fella! Reminds me of Yoda!" I hoped the hermit didn't get that reference.

He didn't.

I asked the hermit where his bike was, and he walked us around to the back of the house and showed it to us. It was a white Schwinn twelve-speed from the 1960s probably, that was fashioned with several baskets filled with canned goods and camping equipment. "Don't be running off with my wheels now, or I'll have to." the hermit trailed off.

"Don't worry, old-timer, we got four horses and a truck," I said, which didn't seem to comfort him because he immediately began moving his bike into his room!

I looked at Chet. "Not the trusting type."

"His story seems sound, though, right?" Chet wondered.

"Shhh, I'll get the 30-30, just in case," I said.

The sun was fading fast, so once we unloaded our gear and got the boys watered and fed, we "retired" to our respective rooms. After our brief interaction, Chet and I just let him be, which is what he wanted—being a hermit, and all.

"Feels like we're back in college. Ya know, when you got a weird roomie?" Chet snickered later that night, trying to keep his voice down.

"Had a few of those," I smiled, "One locked himself in his room all semester."

"Should we play a prank on him? Like a couple of college kids?"

"I'm sure you'd like that, but I wouldn't—though I reckon, we could offer him a plate of warm food. He's so dang skinny, bet he hadn't had one in a while."

"You're a good man Charlie Brown," Chet said. "A little boring, but good."

During dinner, I did offer our new friend a plate of Chet's spaghetti, but he declined it through his closed bedroom door.

"He turned his nose up at my cooking?" Chet asked, surprised.

"Some people you just can't reach. Here." I handed Chet his plate.

"Thought we had stuff in common, with the cross-country thing and all," Chet said, quickly finishing off the hermit's uneaten spaghetti. Dave and Chet were a little nervous as we bunked down for the night. Dave said he almost slept in the trailer because he didn't trust the "crazy guy." Almost.

"We got a loose cannon in the house. How can you sleep?" Chet whispered as we laid down for bed. Ol' Chet must have had bigger trust issues than me.

Or maybe I just had the gun.

"Got Mr. Winchester here, don't worry," I said, tapping my rifle that I had slept with the entire trip. After much talk about our safety, the rest of the night went just like all the others that came before it. Nothing happened.

We slept soundly, and that was that.

When the sun came up the next morning, the old-timer on the bicycle was gone.

"He's gone," I woke Chet with the news.

"Did he steal the rig?"

"Nope. Just stole your heart," I joked.

Chet smirked, "Was he ever even here?"

The outfit mused over Chet's profound question over breakfast, before we broke camp and were saddled up by 5 A.M. to catch the cool weather of another Big Hole Valley morning. Chet and I kept an eye out that day, but we didn't see our bicycle friend again.

Hope you made it west old-timer, whatever your name was.

We spent the day crossing Big Hole Valley. With no other signs of life around, it was like our own playground. It truly felt like we had traveled back in time into the late 1800s. The old dirt road we were on bisected several small mountain ranges that dotted the Big Hole basin. It was easy riding, with no people or vehicles. It gave us a chance to enjoy the weather, admire the wide-open spaces of Montana, and allowed me time to drift back to thoughts of home and Sue, my very pregnant wife, and how far we'd come since the Connecticut shoreline. By midafternoon we finally reached Route 43 at the small town of Divide. There were many Kodak moments and hair-raising adventures on the trip, but I reckon this stretch here might have been my personal favorite.

The beauty of Route 43 was staggering. The land was completely untouched by civilization. Only true fisherman could even find this beautifully remote spot that housed the Big Hole River, fewer than 2,500 people inhabited this entire 2,800 square mile area. While we rode, Route 43 never took us more than thirty to fifty feet from the Big Hole River, a tributary of the Jefferson River, and still a popular destination for fly-fisherman.

"You know this river is the last habitat in the continental U.S. for native Fluvial Arctic Grayling?"

"What is a Grayling?" Chet wasn't a big fish man.

"If you didn't like that fact, how about this—Did you know when Lewis & Clark "discovered" this place, it was a buffer zone between rival tribes like the Nez Percé, Shoshone, Coast Salish, and Blackfeet?"

"Take me to school, professor!" Chet replied, humoring me.

Riding past historical markers, I explained to my unwilling student how "this site along the North fork of the Big Hole is what they call the Big Hole National Battlefield." At my request, Chet and I dismounted, gazing out at the battlefield, trying to imagine how this peaceful country was anything but that, back in 1877, when U.S. troops under John Gibbon fought Chief Joseph and the Nez Percé right here in the Battle of the Big Hole. "Leave it to the white man to turn this pristine country into a battlefield," I said.

"You got something against battlefields?" Chet joked.

"This is sacred country," I said, and I meant it! Call me a clairvoyant, but I felt the spirits of the Old Ones (again). I tipped my cap to them all. We camped that night somewhere between Wisdom and Wise River, with the sound of the rivers lulling us to sleep under millions of bright stars. "That's why they call this Big Sky country, boys," I said as we drifted off to sleep.

Dave said, "More like Big Night Sky Country."

Then he and Chet chirped in unison, "It doesn't get any better than this!"

I'm riding with a bunch of jokers.

"Pray for Me. I Drive Highway 93"—were the prophetic words that spoke to us like an oracle from the bumper sticker of an old yellow Ford pickup, soon after we arrived at the junction of Route 43 and Idaho State Route 93. I reckon someone should write a cowboy song about this stretch of road; it's so memorably treacherous—just don't write it while driving down Route 93 or you'll go careening off the cliff and into the great beyond.

Usually, the outfit made a point to celebrate a border crossing, but not today. According to our maps, we were officially in Idaho, but we weren't hooting about it. Chet and I were in survival mode for the next leg of our journey—a thrilling (Chet would say harrowing as hell) two-day ride that would take us high up into the alpines 9,000 feet in elevation, and into the famously rugged "River of No Return Wilderness" that has been written so much about in cowboy lore. Riddled with steep, rugged mountains, deep canyons, and wild and wooly class-five rivers, we were in adventure heaven, or hell—depending on how you looked at it! Our biggest challenge wasn't the mountains, but the narrow, winding Route 93 itself. The road crossed so many mountain passes it had virtually no berm for the boys to navigate, so it felt like we were riding (smack dab) in the middle of the damn road—and we kind of were. The cars and trucks going our way got so close to the boys, they blew Thunder's mane up every time one passed. I thought my left spur was going to get caught on some car's rearview mirror as it sped past us.

Gazing down at the scenic Big Hole Valley, now thousands of feet below us, I uttered, "We're not in Kansas anymore, Hoss."

"Yeah, no shit!" Chet replied, "This berm sucks!"

Although our view was amazing from here, this was no grey road, nor ideal riding, even if we'd been on a couple of miniature Shetland ponies. "Whose bright idea was this?" Chet yelled, "They should sell bumper stickers that say, 'Pray For Me, I'm Riding Horses On Route 93!'" I think ol' Chet just about stuck his thumb out and started hitchhiking from the saddle.

"Just don't look down, and you'll be fine," I said, trying to convince myself more than anyone.

"This wasn't in the brochure!" He complained, half-joking.

"We got no choice Hoss, there's no other option," I said. "This berm is goddamned ridiculous though—we got three feet tops."

"Thunder's fat ass barely fits," Chet rightly observed.

"Don't you make fun of my horse's ass," I said, trying to break the tension.

Dave pulled the rig behind us to give us some temporary cover, "Hate to be the bearer of bad news, men—but you're looking at riding this dragon tail 25 more miles till you reach the next cutoff.

"Game over, man!" Chet shouted.

"We barely fit, we gotta get off this damn road," I shouted.

"Best find that unmarked cutoff then, it's a dirt road called Forest Road 473 if they ever put up a sign for it," Dave said.

"Great, we'll be roadkill by then," I said.

"Want me to pitch camp early so we can trailer the boys?" Dave asked.

"Got no damn room up here, we'll meet you in Darby," I said as a string of impatient motorists behind us started laying on their horns at our horse conference.

"Get moving Preacher. You're backing traffic up to Wyoming."

"10-4," Dave shouted, then sped away. Chet and I had no choice but to survive.

I looked up at the sky, "F.M.—don't fail us now."

Reflection time was over for now—no more dreaming of Sue, the baby, or the Old Ones—Chet and I had to buckle down and keep our heads on constant swivels, gritting our teeth every time a pushy semi blasted by a hair's breadth away from us, cursing every time we got debris in our eyes. It wasn't a cakewalk—but we got 'er done, as they say—careful to keep the boys as far off the road as we possibly could. We climbed all day to 9,000 feet—then (thankfully) descended a bit through a series of little mountain towns named Darby, Sula, and Connor, on our way west into the (Frank Church) River of No Return Wilderness. Neither of us knew where the mysterious cutoff 473 was exactly—but the Preacher kept us on track. Once we finally arrived in Darby and had some lunch and fed and watered the boys, Dave pulled out the maps and showed us the general area where it should be. "Not sure if it'll be marked," I said, "But we can't miss it."

Finding this short cut was essential—not only would it get us back on a grey road and out of harm's way, according to our maps, it would also shave five days off our trip.

"Keep a lookout now, Chetter, we need this one bad," I barked as we got close.

"Way ahead of you, boss—keep your eyes peeled, Reb!"

Besides the time and safety factors, I also didn't want to miss this shortcut because I knew it would lead us to one of the most spectacular routes of our journey. When Dave pulled up in the rig to inform us we were "getting real damn close now," it didn't take long until we found the blessed shortcut called Forest Service Road 473, otherwise known as the West Fork Road cutoff. Turning off Highway 93 after holding our collective breath for 25 miles, brother, you can believe we hooted and hollered. I think I even heard Reb and Thunder, "our wide load," doing a little celebratory whickering, too.

The long-awaited turnoff was a small dirt road that didn't have a car, truck, or person on it for miles. "Hallelujah," is all Chet could muster once we realized we were all alone, except for some woodland critters. We told Dave we'd meet him at the next town and began riding past several large high-altitude ranches that eventually disappeared as the road took us south on to the Nez Perce Trail Road. This was rugged and daring country that very few modern souls have ever seen—except guides, loggers, outfitters, and hard-core outdoorsman dared to navigate. But the Old Ones sure knew all about it. We encountered numerous ancient artifacts in this wilderness, like old arrowheads and cobbling tools that proved Native Americans had traveled this mountain path long before pale faces ever did. While scouting for bear tracks during a pit stop, I showed Chet a few arrowheads, "Bet these are from the Shoshone or Nez Perce," I handed him one. Later, we rode by remains of early miner and homestead settlements. "And there's where some old homesteader once lived."

"This forest should be in a museum," Chet said, "And you really should be a guide again, boss," Chet joked while marveling at the remnants of pioneer history all around us.

"This was sacred land to them and to the wildlife, too, including—"

"Don't say bears, boss."

"Bears."

"Told you not to say that."

I explained to Chet, "Because of its sheer size, this stretch of wilderness provides a secluded habitat for a wide variety of animals, including some rare, vulnerable species like mountain lions, gray wolves, *black bears*—as well as lynx, coyotes, red foxes, bighorn sheep, mountain goats, elk, moose, mule deer, and whitetail deer.

Pretty full of critters, the old cowboys would say," I said.

"Just tell me we can hunt something small for dinner. I'm hungry!"

"We may get grouse up here. We could try hunting one for dinner later. You a good aim with a rock?"

"Hell, yes. Let's hunt caveman style," Chet said, salivating for some fresh meat.

We were riding south of a massive mountain range called the Salmon River Mountains that dominate the Idaho Wilderness. Salmon River Canyon is the home to the famous "River of No Return," and is one of the deepest gorges in North America, deeper even than the Grand Canyon. It doesn't have the sheer walls and towering heights, but it's famous for its wide variety of landscapes visible from the river—like slides and solitary crags, wooded ridges shooting to the heavens, and a series of huge eroded monuments and bluffs. "Why do they call it "The River of No Return?" Chet finally asked.

I explained, "The Main Salmon River was called "The River of No Return" back in the early days because boats could navigate down, but could not get back up, due to the crazy fast water and class-five rapids."

"Oh, that makes sense. Who the hell's Frank Church then?"

"Frank Church just got attached to the river's name, as a memorial to a man who helped preserve this wild central core of Idaho."

"Damn, you know everything. Ever thought of moving back?"

"Well, yeah, pard, I have. I did. But I'm no genius. I read that on that historical marker we passed back there," I chuckled.

You won't find Elk City on many maps. There's no route to Elk City, Idaho. You either have to know about it or bring a damn good Forest Service map and four to five days of supplies. This last stretch through Idaho would be a real test of our outdoor skills and our ability to follow forest service maps. We weren't worried about water since the forest was teeming with pristine mountain streams and many natural springs. But we put our bear bells back on the breast collar of our saddles, and I tried to calm Chet's nerves again—which I did. But it didn't last long. I knew were in black bear country when we were greeted by a traditional black bear welcome right on the path we were riding—a steaming pile of bear scat dotted with freshly consumed berry seeds.

I dug my skinning knife into the scat, "Welcome to the backcountry, Hoss. We got ourselves some bear scat."

"Oh shit."

"Yep."

We climbed and descended countless peaks and valleys to get to Elk City, now riding on a trail called Forest Service Road 14. For the second time on the trip, there were no people, no cars—just sixty miles of sheer mountain beauty. We took the boys into one of the many creeks that paralleled the road for a quick drink of probably the best water they'd ever tasted in all their horse lives. That night, we camped on top of a 9,000-foot mountain with a 360-degree vista of the surrounding rugged mountain ranges. This was living—even with the bear scat.

Chet and I decided we would hunt our dinner that evening. I told him sage grouse are common in the Rocky Mountains, so throughout the day, we had spotted several small flocks of sage grouse, which only whetted Chet's appetite. Once we made camp, Dave stayed with the horses, and Chet and I set out to get us a grouse for dinner with our trusty weapons (one large stick and several good size rocks). The only firearm we carried was my trusty Winchester 30-30, which I would not use to hunt since it would blow any grouse into a thousand pieces. We didn't have a .22 with us, and practically speaking—it's easy to kill a grouse with a rock and a stick since a grouse only flies about five or six feet up into the air. Once we spotted one, it would only be a matter of who had the most accurate throw. We made a game of it, of course—with Chet and I spreading out twenty feet apart and traversing through an open field full of tall grass, in hopes of scaring up a grouse.

After thirty minutes of hunting, I heard Chet yell out, "Got one!" I wish I had video of Chet chasing that grouse through the field—it would have been a hoot since grouses have a weird way of evading hunters, using their quickness to fly up in the air six feet, then coming back to earth, again and again. All I could do was follow Chet's voice through the tall grass until I spotted him.

When I caught up, we took turns firing rocks at the frightened grouse, but in our excitement, we couldn't hit the broad side of a dang barn! "Aren't you a famous college pitcher, boss?" Chet laughed.

I looked at Chet, "Aren't you a famous football legend?"

We couldn't help but laugh at our bad aims—but we kept gathering rocks, and trying, chased this one grouse all over the damn countryside. It was a real comedy review. I'd like to think my experience as a pitcher had something to do with the fact I nailed the bird first, which stunned it enough, that we found it lying in a daze next to a stand of pines. "Say hello to my little friend!" Chet yelled, in his best Scarface impression, knocking the bird cold with a stick, and breaking its neck to put it out of its misery. "It's dinner time, baby!" I shouted.

"You're still a dead eye, boss! After twenty tries," Chet picked up the bird carcass and held it high (in triumph) as we stood there huffing and puffing. We were jacked up on adrenalin, just like the "old ones" must have felt when they had to hunt their dinner every night. I remember we gave each other high-fives, which was probably not the way the old ones would have celebrated it—but oh well.

We can't be period authentic all the time.

That night, we made a spit over the campfire, just like the old ones. We skinned our first dinner of the trip (if you don't count scaling a fish), and Chet seasoned up that grouse to be the tastiest dang dinner we'd had since our fresh trout dinners in Montana. Maybe it was the thrill of the hunt or just all the exercise we got chasing that bird—but that night was one of the best night's rest I'd had a long time.

Dozing off with a sated appetite while staring at the millions of bright stars under the biggest (night) sky you could ever imagine, I felt at peace, nestled warmly in my sleeping bag in the forty-degree air, the steady jingling of bear bells on the horses faded another day into night.

F.M I say. Again.

We'd built a big fire the previous night to roast the grouse, so we still had some coals in the morning to warm us up before we embarked on another day. As much as we loved getting lost in the wild, I was looking forward to encountering the town of Elk City sometime in the early afternoon.

"Your grouse just got me hungry for other food, pard," I said.

"You saying you don't like my normal cookin'?" Chet gave me the eye.

"No, but I bet you'd like to have a break," which perked him up.

"I'll never turn down a restaurant meal that's for dang sure," Chet licked his chops. Neither of us had a clue what restaurants would be in this remote mountain town, but it was a town—so we figured it had to have some food somewhere. With hungry hearts, we made our way through the one block town of Elk City; there sure wasn't much to it. While we passed horse trailers and tractors parked on the side, I imagined how inaccessible this town would be in the winter. "Bet snowmobiles are popular winter vehicles round here," I observed.

We settled on the only café in Elk City, where I hoped we could order something a little different for once, like maybe a dang vegetable, but I didn't tell Chet that since he would bring up our forty dollars weekly food budget again and blame me for any "scurvy" (as he liked to say) that we might get from our limited diet. Although we tried to pay for our meals (I had meatloaf and vegetables, Chet had a turkey pot pie, French fries, and a salad), the café owner named Randy came over and, after hearing our story, said the magic words we (somehow) heard the entire trip—"Your money is no good here. Lunch is on the house." We thanked Randy profusely and went on our way.

"You got a velvet tongue, boss," Chet laughed, "every time you tell the story, we get a free meal." I just winked at him, which made Chet bellow. Before we left, we made sure and checked with a few locals, just to confirm that our maps were current and Forest Service Road 14 would take us to the outskirts of the town of Grangeville. Once our route was confirmed, we had a long row to hoe until we got to Grangeville, so we didn't linger much longer in Elk City. Chet and I saddled up and sent Dave up ahead to scout, in hopes of finding a place to camp for the night. A few hours later, Dave came rumbling back in the rig to say, "Found us a quasi-town about five miles up the road."

"Well, is it, or isn't it?" I asked.

"It's a one-horse town if you ever saw one," Dave said, "Only got one building as far as I can see—but they got a café, a bar, and a Post Office in that one building, and it's next to this little campsite nestled by a large creek. Lots of campers."

"Sounds like a good plan, top-notch work, Preacher Man," I said and asked Dave to wait for us there.

We pulled into the one-horse town (called Golden, Idaho) around dinnertime. As Dave promised, the town was one solitary building that housed the town café, post office, and bar. "How can this be a whole damn town?" Chet asked.

"Reckon, cause of the Post Office," I said, "Without it, it'd just be a building in the wilderness." Dave was waiting by the horse trailer with Big Red and the Wizzer tied off in the shade. "Fancy meeting you boys here," Chet said, swinging down from the saddle and tying Rebel next to the boys. "Look at all you loafers just sitting around getting fat," Chet joked and patted the boys, who loved Chet's joshing. I didn't spend much time with the boys. Once I smelled what was emanating from the nearby café; I had a crazy idea. "Hey, y'all wanna set a world record? Two cafes in one day?"

"We must be getting soft, boss," Chet said.

"You only live once, pard."

"Me too?" Dave asked.

"You too, Preacher, come on, let's eat."

We walked into the aptly named Golden Café and greeted the elderly lady behind the cash register with a hearty "How-Do?" The lady did not reply—I think she was hard of hearing, which was kind of funny. Inside, the café had an intriguing screen door leading to a small deck in the back, which I had to investigate—so we walked out onto the deck and looked down into a valley where a raging creek had cut its swath over the eons.

Makeshift tents dotted the creek banks, as far as we could see.

"Lots of campers, strange," I observed.

"Hadn't seen that many clumped together since our trout feasts," Chet observed.

No sooner had we sat down in one of their blue booths that we got a visit from a round, hair-deficient man who introduced himself as "Sonny, the owner of the Golden Café." We chatted Sonny up for a while and told him our story, which were the "magic words" once again.

"You cowboys come so far, you can have anything on the menu. On the house."

"That's mighty nice of you, Sonny, we're much obliged," I said for probably the 50th time on the trip? I stopped counting, but I never stopped being grateful. Dave and I didn't need to look at a menu before we ordered a round of cheeseburgers and French fries. You see, Dave and I had been guilty of sitting around the campfire dreaming of cheeseburgers for the past week—which Chet (our ace cookie) did not appreciate all that much. Chet was (rightly) annoyed he couldn't make burgers on the trail—why? Because buying fresh ground beef wasn't in our forty dollars (a week) meal budget. This had been a running complaint of Chet's the entire trip, so I was careful not to look at him while Dave and I had that discussion. But you better believe I could feel Chetter burning a hole through my head with his scowls every time we talked about our mutual craving. I think I could even hear Chet's "forty bucks, boss?" lament echoing in my head. But all that didn't keep me from ordering a cheeseburger. Even Chet succumbed to the aroma and ordered one too. Hunger trumps pride, every time.

While we ate our glorious burgers—Chet said, "Manna from heaven," as he wolfed his down. Curious about the campers out back, I asked Sonny, "What are all those tents and temporary campsites doing on the creek?

"Aw, those are starry-eyed idealists, panning the river for gold."

"You mean you still got some of that up here?"

"Not nearly as much as the old days, but you'll still find some gold dust—hence the name of the town," Sonny said, "Some folks come and go, but many are here for the summer trying to strike it rich." I wondered aloud what Sue would say, "If I told her I missed our baby's birthing 'cause I was out here, panning for gold?"

"She'd say I'm calling my lawyer!" Chet laughed.

After chatting up Sonny some more, it turned out, the elderly lady behind the cash register was Sonny's mother. Sonny looked like he'd been ridden hard and put up wet himself—so none of us could figure out how that made any sense, but we didn't ask any questions. Sonny went on to drop another strange bit of news on us. He casually mentioned that he was the mayor of Golden—which made chuckle because we hadn't seen any homes or buildings except for the café. But I wasn't about to question the mayor. "That is amazing, Mr. Mayor. This is the second time in ten days we made friends with somebody who ran a town."

"Well, we got plenty of one-horse towns 'round these parts, so ain't surprised," Mayor Sonny said. Over at the town bar, five feet away from the café, Chet, Dave, and I washed our dinners down with a few cold Rainiers, which got Chet talking again. Sonny saw us walking out of the bar a little later on, and said, "Y'all don't worry about getting a campsite, you can just camp here in that grassy area next to the café if ya want."

We thanked good old Sonny for his generosity, and Dave backed the horse trailer up and squared it off at 90°. We had our own little private campsite. After exchanging some more stories with Sonny, we thanked him for his hospitality. We didn't build a fire, but it was a cold night since we were camped 25 feet from the creek—but we had full bellies to keep us warm as we fell asleep with echoing sounds of the gushing creek running by our campsite. Thanks for the hospitality, Sonny.

The wagon train got an early start the next morning. We brushed the boys down quickly, saddled up, and were back on the dirt road by 5 A.M. I never asked Chet, but I was sad to leave the River of No Return Wilderness, and privately wished the rest of the trip could have mirrored the past two days. We calculated it would be around 280 miles (or one week's riding) until we hit Grangeville, Idaho—not a lot happened but that 280 miles sure did fly by.

Once we passed through Grangeville, we rode through the heart of the Nez Perce National Forest for several days, which was more amazingly rugged terrain. Then we emerged from the forest and rode west toward the Idaho-Washington border, and the warmer (more arid) region of Washington called the Yakima Valley.

Our journey through the Rocky Mountains was coming to an end. As much as I yearned to return to Sue and our new baby—it was hard to let this moment go. The terrain had been rugged as all get out and the roads harrowing, at times—but it had been a sublime experience riding through all this untouched land.

My old home had provided us with a renewed sense of accomplishment, a regenerated spirit, and just as important—four horses that were gaining weight (instead of losing it), and striding through the mountains like the trip had just begun. Despite all the pitfalls, alpine cliffs, and bear traps we could have stepped in (or stepped off of) in the past three states—the outfit was in good shape for the final two weeks of our ride to the Pacific. I didn't know what to expect from these final few days of our epic trip—but I sure was grateful for the Big Sky country's long days at high altitudes.

"Can't believe we're almost there. We're actually gonna make it," I said to Chet our last night in Idaho. I had never said that out loud before, until now.

"You mean you ever doubted us?" Chet chuckled as he prepped another batch of cowboy chili. "Never doubted us, Hoss—but I still can't believe what we did. This is a major accomplishment—one of a lifetime."

After dinner, we had time to sit back and enjoy the ever-changing light show called the Milky Way, one final night in Big Sky country.

"One thing I know for sure," I said, staring at the infinite stars above.

"What's that?" Chet replied in a soft sleepy voice.

"Couldn't have done it without our mystical navigators."

"Sure got a lot of ten-cent words coming out of you lately. You gonna start going to church when we get home?" Chet said with a yawn.

I smiled, "I reckon, this land is my church! Soak in this moment, partner. It may never come again." I looked over, and Chet was already asleep by the fire.

With Dave in his tent, I went back to gazing at the Milky Way and thanked whoever it was that had been looking out for us, and Suzie (and the baby) back home—be it God, the Old Ones, the Horse Gods, the Old Pioneers, Chief Joseph of the Nez Perce, Fucking Magic, or hell, even the conservationist Frank Church. I offer my gratitude to them all. Washington, here we come!

See you soon, sweet Sue.

★ 14 ★

WASHINGTON STATE OF MIND

"No memory is ever alone;
it's at the end of a trail of memories,
a dozen trails that each have their
own associations.
—*Louis L'Amour*

THE FINAL PUSH to the promised land was on—it was a bittersweet "hallelujah!" I wanted to shout from the highest mountaintop. For five of the most thrillingly repetitive months of my life, Chet and I blazed our way across this roughhewn trail called America. Our four-legged heroes, Thunder, Rebel, Big Red, and Sonny, aka "The Wizard," carried us up, over, and through every type of treacherous terrain imaginable to get us to this here spot at the Washington Border, the 11th and final state on our cross-country adventure. The outfit had sacrificed a team member, and nearly lost two more—but all that existential pain and suffering was behind us now. No more blistering heat, surprise storms, terrifying twisters, or pummeling hail was going rain down on us. No more attack dogs, horse flies, or turkey farmers with shotguns were going to rise up and bite us in the keister. All physical obstacles had seemingly fallen away.

Now the only hurdles left were mental.

And I won't fib, a little emotional, too.

Our new surroundings were suddenly so dang lush and gorgeous that I wondered if we hadn't already stumbled across some secret border into the mythic land of Utopia?

"Have we crossed into heaven, Hoss?" I said, gazing at Washington before us.

"Depends on what an apple symbolizes to you," Chet chuckled. "Could be hell!"

I fantasized about riding across the United States my entire life, and now the opportunity to fulfill my dream was here, just waiting to be picked like a fresh Washington apple. The satisfaction felt heavenly. I won't lie.

Though privately, I was a little shocked we had made it this far without someone getting seriously injured, but Chet, whose been our beacon of light and wellspring of confidence all trip, told me, "Always knew we'd get here."

"Shoot. You must be the Amazing Kreskin, pard," I chuckled.

"Aw, just had faith that—when you make a plan, it's gonna come together."

"Means a lot, you believed. This was our trip. We planned it for two years!"

"Hell, has it been that long? Diane's gonna be pissed!"

Looking back, maybe that's one reason why I enlisted ol' Chet for this adventure—he believed, sometimes more faithfully than even me! Now with only a few hundred miles left between us and our goal of riding from the Atlantic to the Pacific Ocean—I was a true believer now. Why shouldn't I?

We had already achieved what so many told us was impossible.

I don't know what Chet, Dave or the Boys are thinking—but whatever individual dreams were running through our heads, the outfit agreed on one thing: we were determined to be here right now, living in the present, of what we knew would be one of the most impactful moments of our lives!

But as overjoyed as I was to be "here now"—I must say, by this point, my mind kept returning to sweet Sue and our unborn child. I kept telling myself if the outfit arrives back home in one piece, and Sue is waiting for me at the finish line (and hadn't left me to elope with some Lamaze instructor like ol' Chetter likes to joke)—then it will have all been worthwhile. I reckon we'll still have to see about that.

F.M.—don't fail me now. We're so close!

People tend to think of Washington as a rainy state, but I reckon that's only half true. West of the Cascade Mountains, you're going to get damp. But few folks seem to realize that on the eastern side of the state (where Chet and I just entered) is mostly dry and sunny. Perhaps spreading this misconception was a way to keep the carpetbaggers from flooding into their bountiful land? I don't know, but you won't hear us complaining about good weather after all we'd been through.

"Weatherman said we got smooth sailing ahead," Dave said.

"You sure 'bout that?" I asked.

"He said zero chance of rain. So, yeah."

"The Horse Gods strike again," Chet said. "No need for slickers today. Did we ever find mine?"

"Hell, we may be able to retire them now. The old-timer back at the border told me this region ain't rainy at all," I said.

"I learn something new every day," Chet said. "If I never see another dang storm or tornado again—I won't mind a damn bit."

"I'm gonna have a helluva hard time sleeping under a roof again," I said, "Think Sue or Diane will mind if we replace our beds with haylofts?"

"That may tear it," Chet chuckled.

"We've put them through enough," I said.

"Damn Boss, with the way me and Diane are goin'—Rebel's stall may be my home when we get back," Chet said with a sigh, which surprised me a little. He had not mentioned Diane, his fiancé, in a while. I didn't press him for details, but it was the first inkling that one of our relationships might not survive the trip.

Will the Jean decision haunt me for the rest of my days?

Reckon we'll have to see about that, too.

Thunder and Rebel moseyed us into Washington from the southeast, and we made our way across the state, north by northwest to our pre-ordained "finish line" located in the coastal town of Ocean Shores, where Thunder and Rebel were scheduled to do their equestrian wave dance for the cameras to celebrate their achievement. "How many other horses have ridden across the country? Can't be many, I guarantee," I said.

"Probably none in a hundred damn years," Chet mused, "These boys are the Horse Gods we've been talking about all trip. I'll be the first to pour champagne on all their heads! What about you, boss? How you gonna celebrate?"

"After we ride into the waves, you can pour a bucket of Gatorade on my head."

'You're getting wet, one way or the other!" Chet laughed.

While we planned our victory dances, the majestic snow-capped mountains that had been riding along with us since Idaho, finally gave way to smaller rolling hills and valleys, populated with lush, eye-popping vegetation. The mild sunshine sure was a welcome surprise. I'm no theologian, but if the Garden of Eden was in America, I bet it would resemble southeastern Washington. All we saw were ripe, bountiful orchards as far as the eye could see.

After all the shit we'd slogged through, it was like riding through a dream.

"All this fruit's making me a tad peckish," Chet said, "Do we dare steal a nibble?"

"Why not? They call this area the 'Fruit Bowl of the Nation.'"

"Thought San Francisco was the fruit bowl of the nation?" Chet joked, grabbing an apple off a tree and taking a crunchy bite.

"Guess it'd be rude not to take one, then," I said, pulling an apple off a tree and taking a bite, "It's an apple, all right."

"Forgot what one tasted like," Chet said.

"We could use some roughage after five months of cowboy chili," I said.

"Stop moanin'—I couldn't afford to buy fresh anything on your crazy budget."

"I know. I'll take the blame if we all get scurvy," I chuckled just as Thunder took it upon himself to grab an apple for himself.

Unlike Chet and I, the big boy swallowed his whole.

Our cowboy outfit stuck to a gray road called State Road 12, which took us around the city of Lewiston-Clarkson by the Snake River, then led us through the small towns of Pomeroy, Kennewick, and Pasco—before we let the boys get their feet wet a little, crossing over the Columbia River—and riding through several gorgeous valleys that were blanketed with fruit trees that produced bushels of peaches, apples, pears, nectarines, cherries, and apricots.

"Never seen so much fruit just begging to be plucked!" Chet exclaimed.

Ripe fruit was dropping all around us. We could smell the fructose in the air. For two hungry cowboys who hadn't eaten something sweet in months—the fruit began calling our names. It was mighty tempting, since, at any time, we could ride over to a fence line and pluck a piece of fruit off a tree, or stop off at one of the hundreds of roadside Fresh Fruit stands and buy a bushel for a buck.

We didn't resist the temptation. We didn't even try!

Besides, we wanted to support the local farmers. There were so many stories in this fertile soil; riding through, you could almost feel the history of the pioneers who had first farmed this land. If you ever stop at a fruit stand in southeast

Washington, chances are good you'll get to talk to a professional "orchardist" whose roots go back multi-generations. "We like to say our fruit will give you a refreshing taste of our past," said one nice fruit stand lady named Jenny, who was a 3rd generation orchardist we met.

"You should put that on your sign," I said, "It's a good marketing slogan."

"I tried, but we ran out of space," Jenny said, pointing to her wooden sign that read, "Fresh Locally Grown Fruit." When I asked her about her business, she told us that the oldest fruit orchards 'round here dated back to the mid-1870s.

"This is the land where the old pioneers (who came west to farm) rather than prospect for gold—put down their stakes and established their settlements."

"So, your family is one of those old pioneers?" I asked.

"Yes, sir. Apples and other fruit trees were introduced by my family and many others, perhaps more by chance than by design," Jenny laughed.

"How so?" I asked.

"Well, the family legend goes, my people brought saplings along for personal use. But we started planting them, and they took off, so—here we are 100 years later, selling fruit my family only brought for personal use."

"Sometimes, a plan just comes together," Chet joked.

"Or not," Jenny laughed, "The man who founded his orchard, my great great great grandpa, came to the West Coast to be a dentist. Not a pear farmer."

"Oh, the irony," I said.

"Though fruit is good on the teeth, I suppose." Jenny went on to tell us how her family's saplings "took to the semi-arid climate and the mineral-rich volcanic soil"—so well—that her family set up nurseries to sell what they could not eat themselves.

"Just like that, an industry was born. The first commercial apple orchard was right here in Chelan County," she said.

I mention all this to highlight the sheer volume of fruit in this area before telling you about our fruit thievery. So maybe you won't judge us so harshly. Maybe.

I'm not exactly proud of it—but for the next three days, Chet and I were treated to a smorgasbord of the most amazing stolen fruit we had ever tasted. I will admit, at this point in the trip, we were feeling pretty invincible, and decided it was OK to have a little fun. We got hooked on fruit, first by stopping at a few local fruit stands (like Jenny's) and gorging on the fantastic fruits on display. Then we decided, since we were on a limited food budget, we would live off fallen fruit for the next several days.

"Live off fallen fruit? Is that even a thing?" Chet asked with a raised eyebrow.

"Sure is pard—ever heard of a herbivore?"

"Is that a Herbie Hancock fan?"

"Who? No, we're gonna be *fruit-avores* the next few days, it'll clean us out!"

That's when I got a bright idea. I had noticed the orchards extended for miles, so it would not be difficult for us to ride through some of these orchards, instead of riding on gray roads. It would save us time, and these orchards were so massive that no one would even notice we were there. "Speak of the devil. Someone must've left this gate open for a reason," Chet said with an impish grin.

"Shoot, let's do it—no one's bound to miss a few apples," I said.

"If we get busted, you know, the other prisoners will laugh at us."

"I'll take all the abuse if we get imprisoned."

"You hear that boy?" Chet said to Rebel, "OK, let's nab some fruit!"

We rode through that open gate, and many others, as we moseyed through countless orchards the next few days. I spied the landscape for pickers, but we saw no farmhands at all, so we reckoned—we were in the clear. We sure got spoiled rotten like the fruit on the ground (around us) as we passed through miles and miles of sweet land. Chet and I are law-abiding citizens in our normal lives, but the opportunity to sample some of the world's best fruit was just irresistible.

Up to now, we had hardly consumed any fruit on the trip (none, unless you count that Jell-O fruit salad Chet inhaled in Iowa)—so I was hoping our "fruit cleanse" (as they call them today) would make up for the months of lack of vitamin C and vitamin E in our diets. We stuffed our saddlebags daily with apples, plums, apricots, pears, cherries, and nectarines. Naturally, with this radical diet change, came increased frequency of bathroom stops, but I was happy to give our cookie a break from making dinner for a few days. And it also didn't hurt our health!

I wish we had taken photos of the gigantic apples and pears that grew in this arid climate. Talk about a diet change—we went from three-day-old produce and meats to a fresh-picked variety of fruit that would make the King of Siam blush. We were able to stuff enough in our saddlebags for Dave and the horses to eat the rest of the night. The funny thing was I never had to get off

Thunder's back to pick fruit. Our Belgian Cross Adonis was the perfect height for apple trees.

"Who would've guessed this would be another one of his skills?" I said as Thunder snatched another apple from a tree and swallowed it whole.

"He's full of surprises, now if you can teach him to change channels on the tube."

"Not a bad idea, though I bet Sue wouldn't approve of our new horse butler."

In the end, I felt a little guilty for taking fruit without paying. We would have pinned a few bucks to the trees if we could, but that just seemed silly. So I would like to take this opportunity to express my gratitude for the all-natural nourishment Mother Earth provided us in a time of great need. I pray our good intentions (and this written confession) made our fruit thievery a little less dastardly. I hope you, the reader, will understand. To all the orchards purveyors of southeastern Washington, we sure did appreciate the sweet tastes of your gorgeous land.

Thank you for the sweet gift. I'll never forget it.

Neither will Thunder. He sure did love your apples.

Once we left orchard country, we rode through the Yakima Valley on our way to the city of Yakima. Looking at our maps, it appeared there was an unavoidable stretch of Interstate in front of us that we would have to navigate. I wasn't sure how we would figure it out (yet) as I downed another juicy apple. But in a relaxed "Washington state of mind," I left it up to F.M. to lead the way.

We followed Route 12 all day until we hit the city of Yakima, where Route 12 and Interstate 90 became one road for a stretch of about ten to twenty miles. I can't describe what a strange sensation it was to be suddenly navigating an interstate on horseback after three blissful days of frolicking in the fruit orchards. The smell of highways fumes and car pollution was shocking to our senses. There were several places on I-90 where we had no choice but to dismount and walk the boys across an exit ramp.

We even had to temporarily take down a few stretches of fence so we could navigate through the maze of the highways, by-ways, and its many interchanges.

"Is this an omen of what's to come when we get home?" Chet said as we rode beside a long line of rush-hour commuters honking their horns at each other.

"I don't want to think about commuting ever again," I said.

"Thunder should be your ride into work from now on," Chet chuckled.

"Maybe I need to get an urban horse operating license when I get home?" Still considering that one.

It took us a long four hours to finally weave through Yakima's urban obstacle course. It wasn't a bowl of cherries, but it wasn't the pits either (sorry for the pun, blame the fruit for that one), but we left I-90 and the four-lane cement world behind, and escaped back to Route 12. The boys were sure glad to be off the only piece of interstate they'd have to ride the rest of the way. "Feels good to be invisible again," Chet said.

"Enjoy the peace while you can. Cause we're about to be visible as hell!"

A few miles west of Yakima—we got one final treat, riding through our last stretch of mountains on the trip. Our maps told us Route 12 would cut us through the heart of the Gifford Pinchot National Forest and its fast-rising mountain range until we reached the city of Olympia, Washington. This was another relaxing stretch that winded us through a series of sleepy mountain towns. Keeping our twelve to fourteen-hour daily riding schedule, we rode the next 170 miles on Route 12, enjoying the mild warm days and cool nights. With the change of weather, the horses had plenty of energy, and with green grass and sweet alfalfa hay all around—they ate like royal steeds every dang day. With all the apples they ate, you'd think they were spoiled kids! But they deserved every one.

We were hoping to reach the outskirts of Olympia in five days—then take a day off before embarking on the final two-day stretch run to the finish line, just outside of the city of Aberdeen-Hoquiam. Little did we know, we had one more test to overcome.

On our second day in Gifford Pinchot National Forest, around late afternoon, we were approaching the small mountain town of Packwood. Chet and I had spotted Dave in the rig waiting for us on the side of the road, just as we planned. Riding up, I noticed the Preacher had cleaned out the horse trailer and shoveled manure out onto the grassy berm on the side of the road.

"You even spread the remains just like I said. You're a good hand!" I crowed.

"I shovel shit with the best of em," Dave said.

"You sure do. Or was that Andrew?" Chet joked.

Chet and I dismounted and had a cup of his famous cowboy coffee with Dave (extra strong from the early morning brew) while discussing our next rendezvous point. We figured we'd ride another ten miles until late afternoon then call it a day.

As Chet and I were saddling up, I noticed something out of the corner of my eye: it was a local police cruiser quietly creeping up on us from the East. Uh oh! The officer was less stealth when he flipped on his sirens, and the whole team froze.

"Well, shit, they finally caught us," Chet said. "We had a good run."

Was it the fruit thievery?

Or the Yellowstone Federales?

It was a real mystery.

The officer came to a stop about twenty yards behind us. I couldn't imagine why he was pulling us over, but surmised it must be for the same reason so many others had stopped us—from Pennsylvania to Indiana to Illinois—to see what the hell we were up to! I naïvely said, "No reason to be paranoid, men. It's always fun to make friends with the Boys in Blue." So, I tied Thunder off to the trailer and walked over to greet him.

"Howdy officer," I said, "How's it going?"

"What are you gentlemen up to? Can I see some I.D.?"

I could tell by his tone, this was no social call. After explaining the nature of our trip, I could see he was checking the rig's registration.

"Is there a problem, officer?"

I showed him my driver's license and registration. "Yeah, someone reported manure being spread on the grass from your horse trailer. This true?"

"Well." I showed him the manure spread evenly over the grass beside us, "From time-to-time, we have to clean the trailer out to keep the horse's feet as clean and dry as possible. As their feet goes, so goes our trip—ya know?" The officer said nothing. "So, I figured we'd help grow some new grass and flowers in the process."

I thought a bit of humor might cut the tension. It didn't.

"You know, in Washington State, that's against the law?"

"You don't say? We didn't. We're from Connecticut."

"Connecticut, huh?"

"Two Connecticut Yankees—that's us."

"Uh-huh." I could tell the officer wasn't buying it even though our ratty-looking rig looked like we had traveled across the surface of Mars to get here.

"Afraid I'm gonna have to cite you, and take y'all down to the station."

"Come again?"

The officer was in no mood to talk. Clearly not a horse lover, his arrogance was palpable, at least to me. This was the third time some bullheaded officer had threatened to arrest us for doing nothing. Back in Indiana, after the 7-11 incident—Chet and I vowed no one was going to arrest us on this trip. The absurdity of it didn't sit well with us, so you can bet my dander was up.

I had to say something.

"Ya know, I don't think that's necessary, officer; we need to keep moving. I will make sure this doesn't happen again."

"Afraid that's not possible."

"But we really need to keep moving."

"Don't move. Stop talking."

At this point, Chet was standing beside me. We had agreed (after previous run-ins) that the best approach would be for one of us to do the talking unless the situation got out of hand. By the tone of my voice, Chet could tell I needed backup. I was steaming, so I had to walk away and pretend to check Thunder's hooves to calm down, a routine procedure to make sure he hadn't picked up any rocks along the road.

I whispered to Chet, "I'll stay calm. Try to get us out of this."

"Let me handle this," Chet said.

After muttering to myself while checking Thunder's hooves, which were clean, I glanced up to check in on the action. It didn't look like Chet was having much success laying on the charm either! He kept taking his Stetson on and off, and stroking his hair—a Tomasiewicz tradition when flustered. Trouble was officially brewing. Would this officer really arrest two cowboys on horseback for fertilizing a few flowers?

Composed again, I walked back to the cruiser to plead our case.

But now Chet was the one steaming, leaning against the driver side door of the cruiser with his arms crossed, while the Officer sat in his car writing us a ticket. It didn't take a rocket scientist to realize the officer would not be able to get out of his vehicle with Chet leaned up against his closed door.

"Get off his door, so he can get out," I said.

Then I saw "that look" in Chet's eye. He was about to go rogue.

So, I grabbed his arm and walked him to the front of the cruiser to calm him down.

"I made it worse. My mojo works better on female officers," Chet said.

"Just keep your cool, and let me handle this now," I said.

We were tag-teaming the guy now. And it was doing no good.

I walked back and tried to defuse the rapidly deteriorating situation.

"Look, officer, can we try to work this out? We have an appointment with the governor of your fine state in about four days to rendezvous at Ocean Shores. You know the place? We've ridden all the way across the country on horseback the past five months to get here, and are on a tight schedule. We really need to get moving."

"You have a meeting with the governor?"

"We do, sir."

"Right."

"I'm not making it up," I said.

"How about if I call it in then?"

"I think that might be a good idea, officer."

What happened next was unforgettable.

The officer got back in his cruiser and grabbed his CB receiver, "This is unit 425 in Packwood, calling state police headquarters, come in."

"This is Washington state police headquarters, over."

"This is Officer 443 from the Packwood Police Department. I have two guys who claim they are riding their horses cross-country who say they have a meeting with the governor's office in four days in Ocean Shores. I'm about to write them a citation for dumping horse manure on the side of the road. Can you verify their story, if possible?"

There was a long silence.

Chet and I thought we were about to be arrested for dumping horse manure, of all things. But then the officer's radio came to life.

"This is state police officer 808. We advise you to let the gentlemen pass. We have confirmed their meeting with the governor's office in Ocean Shores. Repeat—let the gentlemen be on their way. Please copy."

Chet and I locked eyes. I knew what he was thinking. We all heard those words! I could see a little smile peeking out from under his heavy mustache. Our mutual gaze slowly shifted back to the officer who was staring straight ahead, trying to determine his next words. After a long pause, he said, "Yes sir, copy that."

Somewhere icebergs were melting in the North Pole, wedding bells were chiming, babies were being born, and the sun was shining bright. But here in Packwood, the only thing dawning was a phony smile rising on this officer's face.

"Hey guys, sorry about that. You really started on the East Coast?"

Chet, complete with his Catholic school upbringing, replied, "Yes sir."

We told him our story again, but this time he believed every word. "I'll be on my way then. Can I drive you into town and buy you a case for holding you up?"

This shocked us. What surprised us more was when the officer pulled out a ten-dollar bill and said, "Next case is on me. Sorry for all the trouble. Good luck, and congratulations on your trip." I bet Butch and Sundance never got an apology case of beer from their pursuers. Naturally, the polite thing to do was take him up on his offer.

"Well, that's mighty nice of you, thank ye," I said.

"Thank ya kindly for supporting the cause," Chet said.

I asked Dave to stay with the horses while Chet and I went for a short drive in the officer's police cruiser to pick up a case of Olympia, the local brew, and bring it back to the trailer—nothing like a police escort to pick up cold case of beer!

Afterward, the officer dropped us back with Dave.

Chet and I shook his hand and watched him pull away. We tipped our hats as the officer waved. When he disappeared out of sight, Chet and I looked at each other and broke into uncontrollable laughter. I reckon the boys were snickering too. I could see four heads with eight giant years pointed forward, and bobbing up and down, as they gazed wide-eyed at our silly human antics. We had dodged another bullet from the local P.D.

F.M. forever, I say!

Chet and I began saving our "days off" a few states ago. Days off?

Shoot, you might not know this, but I wasn't a taskmaster the entire trip. I didn't include many of our off days in the book since they were routine and fairly uneventful—but we had taken days off in Indiana, Illinois, Iowa, and Nebraska—but not many. So by this point, we had saved quite a few "vacation hours," that I figured, now that we're getting close to the Pacific, we might want to use them.

"Soak in the moment, a bit—know what I mean? Use it or lose it."

"Don't have to convince me," Chet chuckled. "I'm the lazy one. Remember?"

"This moment won't come around again so, may as well enjoy it," I said.

"I guess you are softening in your old age, boss," Chet said. "Sue will like that."

I had been the fiery catalyst that had kept our wagon train moving west at a pretty demanding pace for the past five months. But after we voted Andrew off the team back in Wyoming—Dave, Chet, and I hadn't had any trouble keeping a steady clip—so we used our furlough time. About ten miles south of Olympia, we found a small local fairground where the rodeo came through and performed twice a year. It had suitable corrals and some real nice folks working there, who were quite happy to leave the boys with them for a day or two. Once we had settled in to the fairgrounds and unhitching the horse trailer, Chet and I decided we would take the rig into Olympia and see what we could get up to. We hadn't showered in days, but that didn't stop us.

"Map says the Olympia Brewery ain't far," Chet said. "Whaddaya say, boss?"

"A brewery? With a little bit of luck, might be able to catch the free tour."

"And a few complimentary cold ones," Chet said.

I asked Dave to keep an eye on the horses while we're gone.

"We'll smuggle out a few for ya," Chet said to Dave. "Don't you worry."

"Careful. We already got the local fuzz on our tail," Dave kidded.

It had been several weeks since Chet and I had enjoyed a cold draft with Ford's Angels back in Virginia City. I reckon the siren's song coming from the Olympia Brewery was beckoning us lonely cowboys like sailors to the rocky shores.

Would this turn into another draft-related misadventure?

Chet and I drove the rig up a few miles and found the visitor parking lot at the Olympia Brewery. It was 3 P.M. You can bet we turned a few heads and noses as we signed up for the last brewery tour of the day. We had put on our cleanest dirty shirts—but we still stank to high heaven! Our Stetson's were covered with thick road dust, our jeans were ripped, and our boots were grimy as all get out. And I haven't mentioned our craggy mugs, which were sporting grizzled beards with a few tics jumping around, just for good measure. "You two look like you should be on the Marlboro factory tour," our guide said.

"No, ma'am, we don't smoke," Chet joked with Amanda, our tour guide.

"What Chet's tryin' to say is we were born to take this tour," I smiled.

"Well, excellent, let's get going then," Amanda replied, leading us (and twenty other tourists) on a tour of the brewery and the factory. On the way in, I checked my armpits and recoiled in horror, as my stink mixed with all the aromas you'd find in modern civilization—deodorant, hair spray, perfume, cologne, disinfectant—smells that neither Chet nor I had encountered in months. Thankfully for everyone else on the tour, a strong hoppy aroma began to dominate our senses and fill our fun deprived nostrils with the smell of Olympia beer. The hops did a pretty good job masking the ripe odor coming from the two mangy horsemen who had infiltrated the tour.

Amanda, our friendly tour guide, made just one mistake.

She asked, "Where are the two cowboys from?"

Which led to Chet and I explaining ourselves to everyone on our tour.

This led to many questions and comments and a few pictures.

When the tour was over, Chet and I didn't forget to pick up our complimentary beers (which was the whole point of the trip). When you've consumed nothing but water and cowboy coffee for weeks—I tell you, an ice-cold Olympia draft straight from the brewery, slides down your dusty gullet real easy—too easy, in fact! It went down like manna from heaven, like pure spring water from the Fire Hole River.

As you might imagine, Chet and I were satisfied as hell being around all these nice people—but what happened next was a continuation of the F.M. we had been blessed with from the footsteps of the Hartford State Capitol building, all the way to Olympia Brewery here in Washington State. While sipping our complimentary beers—Amanda said, "Why don't you guys come see our employee lounge? The team would enjoy meeting two real cowboys."

Never one to turn down an invitation (or a free draft) on our days off—we heartily accepted her offer. She led us up to the employee lounge, which was the best employee lounge I had ever seen. It had three live taps of beer, all pouring more complimentary ice-cold brew. Maybe we were in heaven, after all?

Forget all the questions about our trip. "Lager, pilsner, or ale?" was the only pressing question we had to answer for the next few hours.

"Hot damn, it doesn't get any better than this," I said to Chet, who was wide-eyed with excitement. With two fresh beers in hand, Chet and I were introduced to the entire Olympia Brewing team. We learned they liked to get together after work to discuss the day over a few cold ones. "I want to work here when I grow up," Chet said.

"You'd fit in like a pea in a fermented pod," I replied.

"Wait. Don't tell me. We have to leave after this one," Chet said.

"Nah.reckon, today is the day we let our hair down," I said.

"You're a gentleman and a scholar. The cowboys are still in the building!"

Which led to some cheers from the Olympia team.

As you might imagine—many follicles were let down as day turned to night, and the crowd around us grew larger with each story told. After a couple of hours with these fine folks, Chet and I were about to cross over into the proverbial danger zone, beer-wise, but it felt so good to relax, laugh, and be around the locals, I gave Chet the green light to blast past our caution flag. "You only live once," I said as another round was poured.

Before we knew it, Chet and I were drunker than Cooter Brown, and being taken on a behind-the-scenes VIP tour of the brewery, shuttled around in the flatbed of one of the manager's pickup trucks (with cold drafts in hand). It's probably good that so many years have passed since this day, as my recollection of our tour certainly included some pratfalls. But, after five months of choking on fleas, dust, and tics for dessert—this was like being let loose in Willy Wonka's Chocolate Factory.

Except this factory had adult candy.

Chet and I couldn't tell you how the rest of our night went. But I vaguely remember Dave waking us the next morning to let us know "Coffee's on." As for the rest of the night. I left it up to the horse gods, and they didn't let us down. I would be remiss if I didn't thank the two Olympia employees who drove us (and our rig) back to camp. I have no real memory of those two amazing folks, or of how our night ended—but I reckon some things are better left unremembered in this life. And that is one of them!

We spent the next day recovering from our Olympia brewery hangover and soaking in this moment in time that we knew would never come again.

"Who drove us home?" I asked.

"Mr. Olympia, I think?" Chet said.

"I do recall a flat-bed pickup truck."

"Too much temptation for two thirsty cowboys," Chet said. "Too much."

"You boys drink your weight in beer last night?" Dave asked. "Where's mine?"

"We probably drank yours, sorry, Preach."

"Thanks for remembering me," Dave joked.

"Uh, *remembering* is not something I'm doing much of today," Chet said.

"Can y'all believe we only got two days, maybe, one night left?" I asked.

"I can't. In 70 miles, we'll hit Ocean Shores," Dave said.

"It all went by so damn fast," Chet said.

"It did, didn't it?" I said.

Dave laughed, "Not in Nebraska, it didn't. Or in the Red Desert."

"Oh yeah," Chet said.

"Guess y'all don't want to ride with me back to Connecticut then," I said.

Dave hooted, "You'd have to be crazy."

"You've lost your mind. The vat of beer finally did it," Chet said.

"Is a doubleheader too much to ask?" I was messing with them.

"Way too much! You're makin' my head hurt," Chet tried to laugh.

Behind all my kidding, was a real sense of loss I was dealing with—as you probably figured out by now—I'm a bit of a soft-hearted cowboy who never likes to say goodbye when I don't have to. So I was having a hard time dealing with this chapter closing on our lives. I kept fighting it because it just didn't seem real.

"Shit, we have to be 'normal' again in a few days," I said to no one in particular, "What does that even mean, anymore?"

"I sure got a kick out of being a cowboy," Chet said, "Reality sucks!"

I sighed, "Wonder how Sue's comin' along? It's been almost six months."

"Jesus," Chet exclaimed, "Where did 1986 go?"

"Went the way of the troubadour," I said, "Gone forever, but the tune will linger."

As reality set in for all of us, a hungover panic washed over me. The conceptual stage was over. Shit, now I have to go home and learn to be a good dad? How do you do that, exactly? I needed to call Jack.

The uncertainty I felt was an indescribable mix of unbridled joy and impending terror. Part of me was so dang thrilled to be reunited with Sue and be a new Poppa—yet, at the same time—the cowboy in me was filled with melancholy that this dream was about to come to an end. Looking back all these years later, I would still gladly trade in my Stetson for our two amazing sons, any day.

But don't tell Thunder that.

He might get jealous.

That's not to say there isn't a lingering sadness (inside me) and sense of regret for how this story ended in real life. Part of the reason why I wrote this book is to attempt to honor every member of the outfit and exorcise some of the so-called demons that have haunted me ever since I lost my two best friends in the world.

But let's not get ahead of ourselves.

The last two days were what I call surreal riding.

The hours flew by faster than I thought possible.

With every mile we rode and every pine, hickory, and oak tree we passed, we tried slowing down the clock as much we could, but it was a futile gesture. *No one beats Father Time.* The excruciating miles we clocked across Nebraska in the dead of summer—now flew by us like a lightning flash. "How do we perceive time so differently?" I wondered, "Do the horses feel their time bend, too?"

"Nah, bet they just know they're going straight ahead," Chet said.

"Reality's creepin' in Hoss and I don't like it," I said.

"Me either. Block it out. Click your heels! There's no place like home."

"The horse is out of the barn on that un," I said. "Reckon we've ridden this yellow brick road as far as it'll take us. We have finally arrived in Oz."

"Hope the Great and Powerful one rewards me with a heart, brains, and courage."

"You're the most courageous, heartfelt guy I know," I said.

"Really? Uh, what about my brains?"

"Well, you took this trip. You can't be too smart!" I joked.

The last night of our adventure, we camped in a heavy forest somewhere along Route 12, which has been our yellow brick road throughout Washington. We were now like a platoon of soldiers who were set to return home after the war. We had bonded in wartime and survived so much—we didn't want the hell to end. It seemed unbelievable that it even could. How could it after setting a modern world record? How could it after crossing America together on horseback? "What could ever break up a crew like this?" I asked over our last campfire.

"I guess reality does. Life does. Family does," Chet said profoundly.

The big boy was full of wisdom tonight.

"Shit Slim. Looks like that fruit cleanse worked, you lose weight," I said.

"You too. How did we not notice till now? Preacher, you look exactly the same."

Dave said, "I'm still young."

"Guess we were getting a workout while sitting on our ass," I said.

"Or you got our food budget from Jenny Craig," Chet said, going into his commercial voice, "Take the Jenny Craig cowboy diet, and lose weight on only forty bucks a week."

"Maybe they'll ask you to be their spokesman after this trip?" I laughed.

"Keep dreamin'," Chet said, "I plan on gaining it all back, and then some!"

Chet and I would later discover we both lost over forty pounds on the trip. But strangely, this last night on the trail was the first time we allowed ourselves to relax enough even to notice. "No offense, but I may not eat spaghetti, ever again."

"Hell, I won't be guzzling any more pints of rotten chocolate milk ever again," Chet said, "I'm sticking to rotten beer from now on!" True to his word, I never saw Chet drink another chocolate milk for the rest of his life.

Our final day of playing Butch and Sundance had finally arrived.

It was emotional for all of us. I won't pretend it wasn't. Old Chet and I took our time packing up and getting on the road since we were so close to Ocean Shores. We picked up Route 109 (our last gray road) outside of Aberdeen Hoquiam and rode it west as it hugged Grey's Harbor, and ended at this narrow jetty of beach that would lead us to Ocean Shores. "Kinda ironic, we're riding a gray road along Grey's Harbor here on the last stretch of our gray road adventure."

"What's ironic mean again?" Chet said.

"This road is the perfect illustration of our main goal of the trip," I replied.

"What? Huh?" Chet was messing with me now. "I only speak horse now."

Riding our last gray road along Grey's Harbor was damn appropriate if I do say so myself. Mostly tree-lined with occasional breaks where construction crews were working on widening the road, the gray road gave us plenty of room to stay in the trees, away from cars and people. I can't remember Chet or I speaking much that final ride; I reckon he was as deep in thought as I was.

Chet was in a serious relationship with Diane and pondering marriage (to the point of getting engaged) before our departure. Not sure where he stood on that now. My mind was in another place. Sue's arrival had consumed my thoughts all morning, but I was able to compartmentalize her for a few more minutes as we approached the finish line. I kept telling myself—Just enjoy this. Stay in the moment. Be here now, for just a little while longer. Our adventure wasn't over yet.

Chet and I still had our meeting with the governor. I wasn't bluffing about that. We really did organize a meeting. My dear friend back home, Kathy Wyler did all the work—so I want to give her all the credit. Kathy was instrumental in us raising the $100,000 for charity. She was a popular Hartford radio personality and publicist back in 1986. She volunteered to help me arrange the publicity for our ride.

Behind the scenes of this trip, Kathy, Sue, and I had been plotting this "big splash finale" for months. So I called Kathy a few days back from a payphone in orchard country to confirm we would be meeting the Governor's people somewhere on the beach today. Kathy confirmed a representative from the governor's office would be there.

"I didn't want to meet the Governor anyway," I said. "They're never interesting."

"You need to buck up Jeff before you arrive. You've been out in the wilderness for months; don't forget your manners. Act gracious—you know the routine." Kathy then informed me that *The New York Times* and CBS radio had contacted her.

"Every dog has its day, and this is yours. CBS wants to interview you and Chet on one of their national shows after the beach. And *The Times* wants to interview you when you get home."

"Wow, OK. Great job generating interest in us, Kath," I said.

"This is real news, be proud of your accomplishment, and try to enjoy it."

Kathy knew me too well.

She knew how I'd be taking this ending—hard!

Besides that, I always had mixed feelings about speaking with the press. I was happy that people cared so much about our charity work (and the plight of the Connecticut homeless back home) since we had almost reached our goal of raising a hundred thousand dollars. But after the past five months on the trail where I used my words less than I had since I was a toddler (most of our days were spent riding in silence)—I honestly wasn't sure what would come out of my mouth, or how I would handle speaking to the national media after all we had been through.

Would I break down in tears of joy? Would Sue and I kiss in front of the cameras until they packed up and went home? Would the *Monty Python* routine be enacted? Would Chet spray beer all over the governor's emissary? Or would I just ride away on Thunder and never be heard from again?

A part of me just wanted to be left alone with Chet, Dave and the boys, but I knew after all this hullaballoo to get here, that wasn't going to happen. In fact, if all was working to plan, sweet Sue was going to be here in a matter of hours. Sigh.

This cowboy's heart was all aflutter.

I decided I had to gussy up for her, if not the cameras. "Now where's that deodorant I brought for special occasions?" I fished around my saddlebag and pulled out my comb and a stick of Old Spice.

"You had that the whole time?" Chet laughed, "Give it here!"

"I was saving it for a special occasion!" I laughed and tossed it to him.

"This should keep them from fleeing immediately," he said, applying Old Spice.

We both gazed out at the Pacific Ocean ahead of us.

"Well, this is it, partner. What a beautiful sight, huh?"

"Yep. Always felt like the Atlantic was a rough-and-tumble ocean while the Pacific was the more feminine of the two. She's a real beaut."

"Makes you feel pretty small, don't it?" Chet replied.

"You're an ocean unto yourself," I said. "A force of nature."

"I'll be an unemployed force of nature when we get back," Chet said, patting Rebel on his nape. "You old turd, you've earned an apple the size of Connecticut for getting us here."

I patted Thunder, "You know how many cars would've broken down driving across the country? You never did once, did you? What a hero you are."

The boys hopped around in place on the sand like they knew it was time for something important to happen. After taking in the view for a spell, I looked at my watch.

"It's time," I said.

"Lead the way, boss."

We found our way to the outskirts of Ocean Shores and looked for the Main Access sign to the beach that we found on a wide sandy road. When we turned onto the final grey road of our trip, we were suddenly facing due west. We could see the Pacific Ocean in all its glory. "Elvis has entered the building," Chet said.

That moment with Chet is still burned in my memory. With the breaking waves 200 yards off, it felt like reaching out and touching a dream. Thunder and Rebel trod lightly on the sandy road like it might turn to quicksand and swallow us whole. Caught up in the moment, I almost forgot about the Preacher. So, I turned and signaled for Dave, who had been following us in the rig, to park and join us.

"You waited the whole trip to comb your hair, I see," Dave said.

"Yep. Well, we made it, Preacher Man," I said.

"We sure did. now what?"

"Will you take Sonny out of the trailer and saddle him up?"

"You wanna ride him now?" Dave asked.

"No, I want you to," I said. "You've earned it."

"Come meet the Gov and ride into the Pacific with us," Chet said.

Dave stood there, processing the news. He was a man of few words but had a great deal of calm and inner strength. He took this time to speak his feelings.

"Shoot. Thank ye, Jeff," Dave replied. "I'm touched."

"You can ride, right?" I had to make sure.

"Hell yeah!" Dave said. I saw a faint smile spread across his face. That's all I needed to know how grateful he was. Dave was a big part of our outfit and deserved to share the feeling of charging into the Pacific with Chet and I. He'd earned it, and then some. We waited for Dave to saddle up. Meanwhile, behind us, our dream of riding into the Pacific crept closer with every sound of a crashing wave.

With our team in full regalia on horseback looking as sharp as we had the entire trip (which was *not very*)—Chet, Dave, and me riding on Thunder, Rebel, and the Wizard—rode up to the beach and our destiny.

"Cinch it up, boys. Time to do a wave dance!" I shouted.

We moseyed onto the beach.

"From the Connecticut shores to here, "Maaaan, what a feeling," I said.

I could smell the salt air and burgers cooking on a grill somewhere in the distance. "Where's the BBQ?" Chet asked, "I'm starved!"

"We're back in the land of the living, pard, that's for sure."

Just then, I spotted a small group huddled on the north side of the sandy road.

I spied a short Latino man in an expensive suit who was staring at us.

"Hadn't seen a suit in months," I said.

"Damn, that one looks official," Chet said. "Is that the Gov?"

Next thing I knew, the sharp-dressed man was calling my name.

"Jeff, are you Jeff Pappas?"

Since I didn't know anyone 'round these parts, I figured it was the governor's representative—so I swung down from Thunder, tucked his reins into my chaps as I'd done so often, and made my way over to him.

"Howdy, I'm Jeff," I said, and we shook hands.

"I'm Jose, nice to meet you two. Welcome to Ocean Shores."

Dave and Chet dismounted and ambled over to the fifteen or so folks who turned out to be the "media throng" we were expecting. The questions and flashbulbs came fast and furious: "You two really ride across the country?"

"How long did it take you? "

"Did you do it to set a modern world record?"

"Would you do it again?"

"Did you ride the same horses?"

"Did you really leave your pregnant wife back in Connecticut?"

We got all the same questions we had answered countless times before. But this would be the last time—Hallelujah! I say. The cordial answers flowed naturally. I didn't throw up on camera or curse a blue streak after all. While we got our pictures taken, I was mesmerized by the sound of crashing surf. As I answered question after question, it occurred to me that we were all *dust in the wind*, as the song goes. After all this was over, the repetitive beat of the surf would be the only thing that remained of this clambake.

It was a humbling feeling. But I kept that to myself.

On the outside, I was beaming from ear to ear. Jose offered some kind words from Governor Booth Gardner—who commended us for our trip and our efforts to raise money for the homeless. "As of this Governor's proclamation—September 12th, 1986 will now be 'Chet Tomasiwiecz and Jeff Pappas Day' in Washington. Let's all thank Jeff and Chet for their amazing accomplishment." After Jose's speech, we got a round of applause on the beach from the media and the Governor's people, plus a few bystanders who happened to be there. I felt a little sheepish about it all, I admit.

"Well, I'll be damned," I blurted while examining the certificate. "Never had a day co-named after me. But Chet and I know who the real heroes of the trip are," I said, pointing to the boys, who also got a round of applause. Chet and I thanked Jose and shook hands with everyone in his group. "Now it's time for the fun part," I said, looking at Chet. "Get the Gatorade ready. It's time for our touchdown dance!" Chet, Dave, and I remounted to take the ride that Chet and I had dreamt about for two years.

I looked at Chet and Dave—"Ready?"

No reply was necessary—the two smiles were all I needed.

"Yeee-ha!" I hooted, and off we went, galloping into the Pacific. Thunder burst into third gear, galloping toward the crashing waves—Rebel and Wizzer followed. The sensation of cold saltwater splashing over my body was heavenly.

I almost got soaked—but Thunder made a quick turn right once we were in two feet of water, and began running parallel with the tide, hitting a 6th gear I didn't know he had. He raised his legs to clear the surf, charging to the edge of the tide for about 100 yards at full gallop. Over my shoulder, I saw Chet and Dave fifty yards behind me, hootin' in a cloud of surf and mist. Once Thunder showed off his wheels, he slowed to a walk and splashed around a little bit in the surf. I wasn't sure how he would react—but the many times we crossed rivers, streams, and lakes on the trip, Thunder would often linger in the knee-deep water, thrashing around with his front legs, alternating splashes to cool himself off.

Not sure where he learned that.

I swung down into the cold surf—water up to my knees—soaked, but ecstatic. I dropped Thunder's reins and put both my arms around my best four-legged friend. "Thank you, big guy," I said into that long Belgian Cross ear. Thunder had a relaxed, calm look in his eye with a little glint (I think) acknowledging what we had just accomplished. I looked up to the heavens with moist eyes and thanked the Great Spirit and Old Ones for looking out for us. I'm not a religious man, but on that day, I knew there was a greater power than us humans in the universe. With Chet, Dave, and me jumping around in celebration, the media walked over to ask us more questions.

"How does it feel to ride into the Pacific?"

"It's impossible to describe!" I said. "Relief, joy, sadness, exhaustion. Love!" I trailed off. I saw a woman in the crowd that almost reminded me of Sue—almost.

"What about your pregnant wife, did she make the trip?" A female reporter asked.

I sighed, "I wish—Sue is seven months pregnant so she can't fly. I really should have planned this better," which made some of the reporters laugh. As much as I wanted Sue to appear magically—it was not meant to be—her surprise pregnancy a month before leaving for the trip made sure of that. Looking back, it was fitting; I had to finish the trip without her. At the time, I thought it was a proper punishment for all the hell I put her through. I still think that.

Once the commotion died down, the bystanders scattered, and the reporters left to write their stories. I looked around, and it was suddenly just us and the Pacific.

"Well, I guess that's it," I said.

"Let's party! Why the hangdog face? You miss your lady or something?"

"Something like that, Hoss."

"Were you hoping she'd surprise us, like in Illinois? C'mon. Admit it!"

"Yeah, guess I kinda was—but she's too pregnant to fly, so it was just wishful thinking. But still."

"Now that you put it like that, what's Diane's excuse?" Chet looked around.

"It's been so long, may as well wait a few more days," I said, "Where's the bar?"

"That's the spirit!" Chet shouted, spraying cheap beer that he'd saved for this day.

"Manna from heaven! What you gonna open with yours?" Chet asked, admiring his own key to the city, "Sue's heart? After leaving her barefoot and pregnant?"

"Shoot, her heart has no key; it's open as the day is long—that's why I love her."

"No, that's why she loves you," Dave replied with wisdom beyond his years.

"You got an excellent point there, Preacher. I stand corrected."

"Should we hurl them into the sea?" Chet pretended to chuck his like a football.

"Nah, but I'd trade this thing for a church-key, and a cold one right about now. This beer's warm and flat."

"Just one?" Chet laughed and put his arm around my shoulder. "How about ten?"

"Think I saw a hotel down the beach," Dave said, still scouting campsites.

"You're still a good scout, Preacher," I said, "Let's go see."

The three Connecticut cowboys who never quite fit into the hustle and bustle of the crazy modern world moseyed down the beach with the boys trailing behind us and talked about our futures. A few beachcombers asked us for pictures. We obliged with a smile, "Who knows when another person's gonna want our autographs? Maybe never," Chet pointed out accurately. I don't recall anyone asking me for an autograph since.

Once we'd signed autographs, Chet noticed I was still not right, "Boss, you look like you need a hug!" Before I could talk my way out of it, Chet bearhugged me like a true grizzly, cracking my back in the process, which felt nice.

Out of adrenalin and sandy terrain to cross, we found that hotel Dave had spied down the beach. It was nothing fancy—but it was nice enough—so we checked in. Must say, we were quite the bedraggled outfit when we strolled into the lobby. "You look like you just walked out of the Sahara Desert," the sassy receptionist said. "Can I help you?"

"Close, we'd like one room, please," I said.

The receptionist took one look at us and asked the eternal question—so we told her about our trip, which she enjoyed, I thin—because she got on her computer, pushed a few buttons, and was pleased to announce, "We suddenly have a penthouse suite available with an outdoor patio overlooking the beach." Funny that.

The receptionist offered to upgrade our regular room to the penthouse for free, so we thanked her kindly, and accepted the upgrade.

"Reckon F.M. pays off one more time," I said.

"Think we can keep it going in real life?" Chet asked.

"Gonna have to live that question, I suppose," I replied.

"What does F.M. stand for again? I missed the memo," Dave asked.

"You're too young for those words," Chet said and laughed.

"Nah, c'mon—it's fucking magic," I said. "Get it?"

You should have seen the look on Dave's face as he processed that bit of information. "Now, it makes sense," Dave replied.

This final act of magic was cause for a mighty celebration—so Chet and I got young Dave to rustle us up some beer, whiskey, and snacks while we checked in. I had grown so dang used to sleeping with my saddle by now—often using them as headboards and protection from the weather—I dragged mine up to the penthouse without even thinking. "Would you like us to check your, uh, saddles?" the receptionist asked, half-joking. "We also have a safe if you're expecting a midnight raid."

"Nah, thanks, but just old habit," I said with a smile.

Inside, our penthouse digs were remarkably spacious and nice—too nice, almost. Can you believe no one volunteered to sleep on the king-sized bed? We were all so used to the ground by now—we had to shoot for it (rock, paper, scissors)—and the loser got the bed! Dave won! Guess you can take the cowboy off the range, but can't take the range out of the cowboy—at least not yet. After living outdoors for six months, it sure was a surreal feeling to be in that penthouse surrounded by modern amenities. Even though it was several thousand square feet, I felt confined by the four walls and felt (somewhat) rudderless by our sudden lack of structure. Our daily routine of feeding the horses, saddling up, and riding all day, only to rinse and repeat indefinitely—was finito for good!

I couldn't help but wonder: What do I do with my life now?

Once I had taken the longest shower in recorded history, shaved, and de-loused as best I could (I still had a few of those pesky ticks in my beard and other places)—I finally began to decompress. I felt this huge weight lift off my shoulders, while a part of me didn't want to trip to end, even though much of it was arduous as hell.

At the time, I likened it to coming home from war.

"Here's something to relax you, Sarge," Dave handed me a cold Olympia beer. "Thanks, pal, you know me well by now." The three of us sat back with a cooler full of beer and just talked about life.

Later, Bruce, one of the WDRC radio executives from Hartford (the radio station that promoted our charity trip), surprised us that afternoon by flying out to meet us. We were too tired to leave the penthouse, so Bruce came up and updated us on our charity. The great news was we had reached our goal of $100,000, which felt truly amazing. Kathy Wyler, my second in command on the charity end, called and told me, "I've got CBS radio on the phone, Jeff, this is a national show, so you need to talk to them before you and Chet start celebrating too much."

I listened to Kathy's instructions, and went into the bedroom and called CBS to record our phone interview (Chet wasn't interested). While the CBS reporter interviewed me, I stared out at the ocean and tried to process the magnitude of the moment—what had we just accomplished? I still wasn't sure.

After the CBS interview ended, I closed the door and called Sue.

Finally. In those days, there were no cell phones—so I had to call home collect. "Cowboy rehabilitation clinic" was how Sue answered the phone to give you an idea of her sense of humor.

"Oh, hi, I got a cowboy I'd like to check-in for the full treatment."

"Well-well-well, look what we have here. I was hoping to hire someone to help me birth this baby. Can you rope yourself a Lamaze class and get your ass home, P.D.Q?"

"Damn straight, I can. Where do I sign?" There was a long pause.

"Is that really you?"

"Yep. Think so."

"So—you really did it, huh?"

"Reckon we did."

"No one died?"

"Not yet. Though we're gonna feel like death tomorrow, I bet."

"Well, I wish I were there to hug your neck, my love. I bet you're tired of sleeping with that smelly old dirty saddle." I looked over at my saddle on the ground and smiled.

"You don't even know," I chuckled.

I hadn't spoken to Sue in four days, which felt like an eternity. I told her I'd call her when we reached the Pacific (whenever that would be), so she wasn't expecting my call right now. She said she'd been painting the baby's room blue, "I needed some bigger support shoes, so I borrowed your Nikes and your shorts. Hope you don't mind."

"OK, but fair warning: I may need a new wardrobe. Just weighed myself. I lost forty pounds."

"You're skin and bones. Well, you're not getting any compassion from me—I've gained forty! We're gonna look like Laurel & Hardy when you get back. We'll freak out the neighbors."

"They'll get used to it," I laughed.

"I'm so proud of you for really doing it," she said.

"I was about to say the same thing about you. Proud isn't the word," I replied.

I'm not a big tears guy, but you can bet the tears flowed at this point.

Mine were tears of relief, joy, love, and lots of guilt. Sue's were tears of happiness that I was finally coming home in one piece. I do recall some romantic words were exchanged (by me mostly)—but if you've ever been a parent, you know a woman in her seventh month of pregnancy doesn't exactly have romance on her mind. There was an element of, "What have you done to me, and when can I have this kid!" to our conversation, and rightly so. I will always be grateful to Sue for giving me her blessing—she was the true unsung hero of this trip. There aren't many women in this world that would be as supportive of my cockamamie dream, and there may only be one that would let me run off and leave her pregnant for the first time, and in the summer, no less.

She'll never let me forget that part.

I sure got a keeper. And I'm never letting her go.

Once Chet, Dave and I drank our weight in beer, and then slept for two days—I took a flight out of Seattle, back home to Connecticut. It was strangely poignant saying goodbye to Chet, Dave (and the boys) as they dropped me at the airport in my rig. The plan was for Chet and Dave to sell Big Red and Whizzer to local ranchers who would give them good homes. Then they would trailer Thunder and Rebel back home across the country—using the money we got for the horses to pay for gas and food.

Feeling pretty raw at the time, I got a little choked up saying goodbye to Red and Wizard for the last time. Then Dave unveiled his inner jokester to lighten the mood. Who knew he had it in him?

"Thanks for taking six months of my youth that I'll never get back," Dave joked.

"No problem. Appreciate your steady work, Preacher. You get top marks."

Chet got out of the rig and helped with my gear, "Well, this is it, boss. It's been real. Very very real. See you back home if Dave doesn't drive us to Canada instead."

"I bet his steady hand will steer you home. Just sit back and relax."

"Screw that, Chet's driving half of the way!" Dave yelled out the window.

"OK, OK—where did he get that smart mouth?" Chet asked me.

"He's off the clock now, guess he's been saving it," I said, "Have fun!"

"I'll be hearing it all the way back home. It was a good trip, though, huh, boss?"

"Better than we could have dreamt, I reckon."

"If you ever need another wingman."

"You're my Sundance for life, Hoss."

"Aw hell, you're my Butch. Cassidy, that is."

"Right," I said, "Well. Guess that 'bout does it."

"Guess so. No one I'd rather take a bullet for, boss. Thanks for believing in me."

"I should be thanking you for believing in this crazy trip."

"Aw hell, come here!" Chet grabbed me for a hug.

"Don't break my back this time," I joked.

"Enough with the hug-fest. Let's get on the road!" Dave yelled out the window.

"It's not a bear hug if I don't hear that. Crack! There it goes."

Chet put me down.

"That actually worked," I said, rubbing my back.

I gathered my gear and tipped my cap his way one final time.

So long, old friends. See you on the Ponderosa back home.

The Hartford Airport was (and still is) located out in the country, only fifteen minutes from my house. In those days, you could walk right up to the gate to meet your party, which was a feature I looked forward to the entire flight home. The flight was horrible (though I slept through most of it)—it didn't matter. Knowing I was going to see Sue at the gate, gave me the chills like I had the first day we met. I will never forget walking off that 747 and seeing Sue, as pretty as the Montana sunrise, with her sweet smile, running towards me as you see in the movies. It's a crying shame modern couples don't get to have that romantic scene at the airport anymore, but we took full advantage of our chance.

Sue planted an amazing kiss on my weathered face that just about knocked my Stetson off. We embraced for several minutes. Not many words were spoken—they weren't needed; we could feel it all.

Then she took a good look at me, "Hey, slim. What a fine pair we make, eh?"

"You're beautiful. We're gonna be great parents."

"Never leave me again. Promise?"

"Promise. I won't. I won't."

And I never did.

Sue is not one to speak of personal woes, so I had to learn (in increments) via payphones across the United States that it had been a tough pregnancy for her. I felt so guilty she had to go through her first pregnancy without me. Being a man, little did I know that being pregnant in the summer heat while living alone and working two jobs (without any help) would be unpleasant as hell. Who would have thought that? Everybody, that's who! Even 32 years later, I still owe her a debt of gratitude for letting me take the amazing adventure I recounted on these pages. Hopefully, reading this book has helped her understand some of the feelings and events I kept inside all these years. Us cowboys aren't big talkers, so maybe this book did some of the talking for me. If I hadn't been clear before, thank you again, sweet Sue, for making me a better man and for being a wonderful person, businesswoman, mother, and now grandmother.

You're the true leader of our modern-day outfit.

All these years later, Suzie likes to say she kept me around to "allow me" to prove that I could be a good husband and father, and not just some hard riding cowboy, always looking for the next adventure. I got to work on that challenge the moment I landed, and I haven't stopped since. You'll have to ask Sue, but I've done my best to show her my appreciation all these years (for all she did and does). We may not be in the *Guinness Book of World Records*, but Sue and I have done some amazing things together. One of our masterworks was (future Sergeant) Mike Pappas, the first of our two boys—who, in case you're curious, made his grand entrance into our world a few months later, on Thanksgiving Day in 1986. F.M., I still say.

Even to this day.

Good ol' Thunder would live another ten happy years and was the best pal I ever had with four legs. When I moved to Las Vegas three years later, ol' Thunder retired to Montana to live on Mark White's ranch. I'd ride him every time I came up to visit Mark, but his mighty Belgian Cross frame could only ride so far. I stopped riding Thunder after his knees got arthritic and would visit with him in the field and comb his mane and feed him oversized Washington apples. He always loved those.

I still remember the early morning call I got from Mark one October morning in 1996, telling me that Thunder had passed away of natural causes on his favorite hill out on Mark's back acreage. Thunder was the only horse I ever cried like a baby over losing. I kicked myself a little because I never got to say one last goodbye.

So now I am saying it. Thank you, old pal. I miss you every day.

The same goes for Rebel, Big Red, and Wizard. They've all moved on to the Big Ranch in the Sky, and all are missed terribly, even today. I never had a four-some like those boys ever again. They were a legendary outfit that accomplished something not many have ever even attempted. The boys have my love and respect always.

See you on the back acreage up in Horse Heaven boys.

Save me a ride, will ya?

Nearly 25 years after our trip ended—long after old Thunder, Rebel, Red, and Wizzer had moved on to the big ranch in the sky—I planned a little CA86 reunion trip for December 9, 2012, to rendezvous with my long-lost friend and riding partner, Chet. We had drifted apart over the years, for no good reason, really. Funny how we humans can just let a friendship wither on the vine for no good reason. Egos, hurt feelings, and lots of petty stuff can get in the way, which is, unfortunately, what happened to us. I can't even remember why we drifted apart, but ol' Chet decided to stay back the East to raise a family, and I moved to Las Vegas with Sue and my two boys and painfully sold my ranch in Montana. We had grown apart over the years, but you can bet I was excited to see him again. Chet had fallen on harder times than myself in the ensuing years, and looking back, maybe I wasn't there for him as much as I could have been, when he really could've used a friend. For all these reasons, I wanted to tell him how much I loved him and how sorry I was for allowing outside forces to come between us.

Sadly, I never got the chance.

Two weeks before our reunion (on November 29th), Chet fell ill and passed away suddenly at the age of 57, long before he should have left us. His shocking death left a hole in my heart that I have frankly never properly patched. Not to take anything away from Sue—who I'm proud to report is still the light of my life after 37 years of marriage—but having been so close to seeing Chet again, only to have our reunion fall through my fingers was devastating.

He left behind three wonderful children, a lifetime of amazing memories (than I could ever put in one book), and a lot of unfinished business, including many more trails he was going to ride with me. His larger-than-life personality and zest for life is unmatched and still is, to this day. The memory of his enduring spirit has been an inspiration (and the driving force) to helping me complete this book. After the trip, Chet struggled with some of life's challenges, a few failed marriages, and some excessive drinking at times. I always wondered if they ever saw all the amazing aspects of Chet as I did. The trip brought out the very best in him every day. He was so funny, smart, courageous, full of passion for life, and one tough mother scratcher. Everywhere we went, people gravitated to him—some even fell in love with him. There was a magic about Chet that drew people into him. It was amazing to witness. I wish his ex-wives and kids knew the Chet I knew. My dream is for his kids to believe their Daddy was a good man, and a good horseman, because he sure was—I was there!

My bigger wish is this book will give his children, Sadie, Augusta, and Donovan, a better glimpse into the soul of the man I trusted with my life—the man they called "Dad." I'm telling you, your Dad was much more than the man you knew. He was a true American hero, a throwback to the Old West, and a great best friend. The Chet I knew was the funniest, bravest, strongest, and most brilliant man (and chef) I ever met. I'm saying all this because there are many "unsung" heroes in this crazy world, just like Chet, who touch people's lives every day—but they never get the headlines. Well, this is your closeup, old pal. Chet truly had a heart the size of Montana, which became his most beloved place to visit after our trip.

Chet, if you can hear me, I hope your spirit is riding free across the Montana plains on Rebel—with Butch and Sundance, and all the old ones who came before us. We all come from the same wellspring of energy in this world and are all destined to return to the Great Spirit in the sky someday. You just beat me in a foot race, for once! But I'll see you again, old friend. Know that you are missed more than you will ever know. Rest in peace, Chester. Keep the ponies movin' west. One day, we'll see each other again in horse heaven, my friend—I just know it. F.M. I say.

ABOUT JOEL DAVID HUNTINGTON

DAVE was a former Air Force mechanic in his early 20s, a very quiet guy but very handy and willing to learn. He turned out to be a top hand. I learned to trust him with the horses and scouting open fields/places for us to camp at night.

He was an extremely quiet and introverted person, and after the trip I lost touch with him and have been looking for him for years unsuccessfully.

On the trip I bought him a black hat that looks like something Doc Holiday would've worn in the movie *Wyatt Earp*.

It was a black hat with no roll in it; looked like a preacher's brim so I nicknamed him "Preacher." The name stuck pretty well. He had a young daughter at the time but never married the mother of his daughter.

I have been googling him periodically with no success and googled him the week before Christmas of 2019 on a whim.

His obituary came up, stating he had passed away on November 19, 2019.

Apparently after the trip, Dave canvassed door to door in Connecticut for environmental groups. He crisscrossed the country driving an 18-wheeler for a period of time as well. He was cast as an extra in the movie based on Jon Krakouer's book, *Into the Wild*. He was a self-taught herbalist, and an eager student of the natural world which I could see from spending 4½ months with him. He transcribed love poems written in script by his great-great-great grandfather, a nineteenth century steamboat captain on the Ohio River; then produced not only a book, but also a recording of the poems. Theology, apologetics, and other seminary subjects occupied many of his hours in serious study. For the last eleven years he was known as Pastor Dave, a title given to him by his church in Slab City, California. He lived simply and was known for his compassionate counseling and selfless giving.

Rest in Peace "Preacher" Dave. Chet and I couldn't have done the journey without you!

—Jeff

ABOUT THE AUTHORS

JEFF PAPPAS has more than thirty years of entrepreneurial experience with a strong focus on the restaurant and service industries. He has held executive positions with multiple growth brands with responsibility for recruiting, training, unit expansion, franchising, and all facets of operations. Jeff has particular skill in start-up and turn-around scenarios.

In 1994, Jeff was nominated "Entrepreneur of the Year" in a nationwide contest sponsored by *Inc.* magazine, Merrill Lynch, and Ernst & Young. Jeff finished in the top five qualifiers. He has developed, coordinated, and promoted both local and national events including fundraisers and seminars. Jeff created seminar curriculum, oversaw marketing campaigns, and managed relationships with both sponsors and staff.

In the past, Jeff has served as president of a fifteen unit regional gourmet pizza/pasta chain, Mackenzie River Pizza (winner of 1998 Hot Concept award given by *Nations Restaurant News.*)

Jeff has also launched an international service company with his brother Brian in the 1980s through the 1990s and grew the start-up to system-wide sales of $50 million annually over a twelve-year period before leaving to move to Montana in 1993.

Jeff Pappas has been involved for over 26 years in national/international franchising sales, management, and ownership, and has 22 years of food and beverage experience.

Jeff was also one of the co-founders of Heroes and Horses (www.heroesandhorses.org) in 2013. Jeff left the organization in 2014 due to time constraints but still supports the organization.

Jeff currently works with Spirit Therapies in Las Vegas, a local non-profit focusing on combat veterans interactions with horses, providing instruction and advice on care and riding lessons/advice with horses and veterans suffering from PTSD.

Jeff earned his Bachelor of Arts degree from Denison University in 1976 (Granville, Ohio) and holds his 1st degree Black Belt (Cho Dan) in Tang Soo Do Mi Guk Kwan (www.tsdmgk.com) under Grand Master and founder of TSDMGK, Charles Ferraro.

Jeff currently resides in Las Vegas with his wife of 40 years, Suzanne, and sons: former Corporal Michael Pappas and Brazilian jiu-jitsu student (Sergio Penha school) and Metro police officer, Julien Pappas.

MURPHY HOOKER is an award-winning screenwriter, author, and ghostwriter of fifteen published books, including two books for *New York Times* bestselling authors and a book that was named the Best Entrepreneurial Book of 2017 by Forbes. Driven by a passion to lay bare the shared absurdities of the human condition, he brings stories to life through crackling dialogue, soulful characterizations, and irreverent humor. Murphy lives in Austin, Texas with his daughter.

Made in the USA
Las Vegas, NV
18 November 2024

12024062R10198